Professor John F. Richards

Expanding Frontiers in South Asian and World History

Essays in Honour of John F. Richards

Edited by
Richard M. Eaton
Munis D. Faruqui
David Gilmartin
Sunil Kumar

CAMBRIDGE UNIVERSITY PRESS
Cambridge, New York, Melbourne, Madrid, Cape Town,
Singapore, São Paulo, Delhi, Mexico City

Cambridge University Press
4381/4, Ansari Road, Daryaganj, Delhi 110002, India

Published in the United States of America by Cambridge University Press, New York
www.cambridge.org
Information on this title: www.cambridge.org/9781107034280

First published 2013

Printed in India by Sanat Printers, Kundli

A catalogue record for this publication is available from the British Library
Library of Congress Cataloging-in-Publication data

Expanding frontiers in South Asian and world history: essays in honour of John F.
Richards/edited by Richard M. Eaton, Munis D. Faruqui, David Gilmartin, Sunil Kumar.

pages cm

Summary: "The essays focus on 'frontiers' in multiple contexts, all relating to John F.
Richards's work: frontiers and state building, frontiers and environmental change, cultural
frontiers, frontiers and trade and drugs, and frontiers and world history"--Provided by
publisher.

Includes bibliographical references and index.
ISBN: 978-1-107-03428-0 (hardback)
1. South Asia--Boundaries--History. 2. South Asia--Politics and government. 3. South
Asia--Relations. 4. Human ecology--South Asia--History. 5. South Asia--Commerce-
-History. 6. Imperialism--History. 7. World History. I. Eaton, Richard Maxwell. II.
Faruqui, Munis Daniyal, 1967- III. Gilmartin, David. IV. Kumar, Sunil, 1956- V.
Richards, John F.

DS336.E95 2012
954--dc23   2012029787

ISBN 978-1-107-03428-0 Hardback

Contents

———— • ✦ • ————

List of Contributors
———— • ✦ • ————

Muzaffar Alam is George V. Bobrinskoy Professor in South Asian Languages and Civilizations at the University of Chicago, USA. Prior to this, he was Professor of Medieval Indian History at Jawaharlal Nehru University, Delhi. He has published extensively on history of Indo-Islamic culture, Mughal history, religious and literary cultures in pre-colonial northern India and comparative history of the Islamic world. His publications include *The Crisis of Empire in Mughal North India* (1986); *The Mughal State 1526–1750* (co-edited with Sanjay Subrahmanyam, 1998); *A European Experience of the Mughal Orient* (co-edited with Seema Alavi, 2001); *The Languages of Political Islam in India: c. 1200–1800* (2004); *Indo-Persian Travels in the Age of Discovery: 1400–1800* (co-authored with Sanjay Subrahmanyam, 2007) and *Writing the Mughal World: Studies in Political Culture* (co-authored with Sanjay Subrahmanyam, 2011).

Stephen F. Dale is a Professor Emeritus of South Asian and Islamic History at the Ohio State University, USA. He specializes in Indo-Muslim history and the Islamic history of Afghanistan, Iran and Central Asia. He has studied and published on the history of Malabar Muslims of Kerala in Southwest India, the diaspora of Indian merchants in Iran, Central Asia and Russia in the seventeenth and eighteenth centuries and early modern Muslim Empires of the Ottomans, Safavids and Mughals. His recent publications include *The Garden of the Eight Paradises: Babur and the Culture of Empire in Central Asia, Afghanistan and India* (1483–1530) (2004) and *The Muslim Empires of the Ottomans, Safavids and Mughals* (2009).

Richard M. Eaton is Professor of History at the University of Arizona, USA. He is the author of several monographs and edited volumes pertaining to the history of medieval and early modern South Asia, including *Sufis of Bijapur, 1300–1700: Social Roles of Sufis in Medieval India* (1978); *The Rise of Islam and the Bengal Frontier, 1204–1760* (1993); *Essays on Islam and Indian History* (2000); *India's Islamic Traditions, 711–1750* (edited, 2002); *A Social History of the Deccan, 1300–1761: Eight Indian Lives* (2005); *Slavery and South Asian History* (co-edited with Indrani Chatterjee, 2006) and *Power, Memory, Architecture: Contested Sites in India's Deccan Plateau, 1300–1600* (co-authored with Phillip B. Wagoner, forthcoming).

Munis D. Faruqui is a historian and Associate Professor in the Department of South and Southeast Asian Studies, University of California, Berkeley, USA. He focuses on the Muslim experience in South Asia, especially Mughal India. His books include *Princes of the Mughal Empire, 1504–1719* (2012) and an edited volume, *Religious Interactions in Mughal India* (co-edited with Vasudha Dalmia, 2013). His various journal articles have interrogated the creation of the Mughal Empire under Emperor Akbar (r. 1556–1605), the founding decades (c. 1720–40) of the princely state of Hyderabad, and the relationship between religion and politics in the life and work of the Mughal prince, Dara Shukoh (1615–59). He is currently working on a book reevaluating the Mughal Emperor Aurangzeb (r. 1658–1707).

David Gilmartin is Professor of History at North Carolina State University, USA. His current research focuses on the history of election law in colonial and postcolonial India. His publications include *Empire and Islam: Punjab and the Making of Pakistan* (1988) and an edited volume, *Beyond Turk and Hindu: Rethinking Religious Identities in Islamicate South Asia* (co-edited with Bruce B. Lawrence, 2001).

Sumit Guha is Professor of History at Rutgers University, USA. Prior to this, he has taught at University of Delhi, India. His current research interests centre on the political, cultural and linguistic processes by which identities take historical shape in western and central India. He has published extensively on the economic and social history of medieval and modern South Asia. His publications include *Environment and Ethnicity in India, 1200–1991* (1999) and *Health and Population in South Asia from Earliest Times to the Present* (2001). He is a member of the editorial and advisory board of the journals, *India Review* and *Medieval History Journal*. He is the Review Editor of H-Asia.

Gordon Johnson was President of Wolfson College, University of Cambridge from 1993 to 2010. He has served as a Deputy Vice-Chancellor of Cambridge and was the first Provost of the Gates Cambridge Trust. He was President of the Royal Asiatic Society from 2009 to 2012. Dr Johnson was Director of the Centre of South Asian Studies at Cambridge for eighteen years, and edited *Modern Asian Studies* from 1971 to 2008. His publications include *Provincial Politics and Indian Nationalism: Bombay and the Indian National Congress 1880–1915* (1973), *University Politics: F. M. Cornford's Cambridge and His Advice of the Young Academic Politician* (1994) and *A Cultural Atlas of India* (1995). He was a Syndic of Cambridge University Press for thirty years and Chairman from 1993 to 2009. He continues as a Fellow of Wolfson College and as the General Editor of *The New Cambridge History of India*. He is currently writing about Cambridge University and its Press in the twentieth century, and researching the relationship between India and Britain in the late eighteenth and early nineteenth centuries.

Sunil Kumar is Professor of Medieval History in the Department of History, University of Delhi, India. He has also taught, most recently (2008–10) at the School of Oriental and African Studies, London University, and earlier at the University of California at Berkeley (2008), the EPHE (2006) and EHESS (2001) in Paris. Other than several articles, his book publications include *The Emergence of the Delhi Sultanate* (2007, 2010); *The Present in Delhi's Pasts* (2002, 2nd ed., 2010) and *Demolishing Myths or Mosques and Temples?* (edited, 2008). He was a member of the editorial collective that produced the current editions of class 7 and class 11 NCERT history textbooks. Prof. Kumar is the joint managing editor of the journal, the *Indian Economic and Social History Review* and editorial advisor to the journal, *South Asia Research*.

Patrick Manning is Andrew W. Mellon Professor of World History and Director of the World History Center at the University of Pittsburgh, USA. His research has focused on demographic history (African slave trade), global migration, the African Diaspora as a dimension of world history, and social and cultural history of francophone Africa. His publications include *The African Diaspora: A History through Culture* (2009); *World History: Global and Local Interactions* (2005); *Migration in World History* (2005); *Slavery, Colonialism and Economic Growth in Dahomey, 1640–1960* (2004) and *Navigating World History: Historians*

Create a Global Past (2003). Prof. Manning also directs the Center for Historical Information and Analysis, a collaborative project to build a world-historical dataset.

Claude Markovits is Emeritus Directeur de Recherche (Senior Research Fellow) at the Centre National de la Recherche Scientifique (CNRS), Ecole des Hautes Etudes en Sciences Sociales, Paris. He specializes in the history of colonial India, particularly the Indian mercantile community, and has authored books such as *Indian Business and Nationalist Politics* (1985); *The Global World of Indian Merchants* (2000); *The Un-Gandhian Gandhi: The Life and Afterlife of the Mahatma* (2004); *A History of Modern India 1480–1950* (2002) and *Merchants, Traders, Entrepreneurs: Indian Business in the Colonial Period* (2008).

Peter C. Perdue is Professor of History at Yale University, USA. Prior to this, he has taught for more than two decades at School of Humanities and Social Science, Massachusetts Institute of Technology, USA. His research interests centre on modern Chinese and Japanese social and economic history, agricultural development and environmental history, history of frontiers and world history. He is the author of *Exhausting the Earth: State and Peasant in Hunan 1500–1850 AD* (1987) and *China Marches West: The Qing Conquest of Central Eurasia* (2005).

Velcheru Narayana Rao is Visiting Distinguished Professor of South Asian Studies at Emory University, USA. He has taught Telugu and Indian literature for nearly four decades at University of Wisconsin–Madison, USA. He has been a Visiting Professor at University of Chicago. Professor Rao has written more than fifteen books and some of his recent works include *Symbols of Substance: Court and State in Nāyaka Period Tamilnadu* (co-authored with David Shulman and Sanjay Subrahmanyam, 1992); *Textures of Time: Writing History in South India* (co-authored with David Shulman and Sanjay Subrahmanyam, 2003), *Girls for Sale, Kanyasulkam: A Play from Colonial India* (2007) and *How Urvasi Was Won*, a translation of Kalidasa's *Vikramorvasiyam* (co-authored with David Shulman, 2009).

George Bryan Souza is Adjunct Associate Professor in the Department of History, University of Texas, San Antonio, USA. His research focuses on global maritime economic history (cross-cultural contacts, European relations with Asia, America and Africa) and early modern European history and its expansion from about 1600 to 1800. His publications include *The Survival of Empire: Portuguese Trade and Society in China and the South China Sea, 1630–1754* (1986) and numerous articles and essays. He is the General Editor of the Brill EURO series. He was recently appointed a Mercator Guest Professor at Tübingen University, Germany.

Sanjay Subrahmanyam is Professor and Doshi Chair of Indian History at the University of California, Los Angeles, USA and has taught at Delhi, Paris and Oxford. He is the joint Managing Editor of the *Indian Economic and Social History Review*. Prof. Subrahmanyam has authored and edited more than twenty books; some of his recent publications include *The Portuguese Empire in Asia, 1500–1700: A Political and Economic History* (2nd edn, 2012); *Textures of Time: Writing History in South India, 1600–1800* (co-authored with Velcheru Narayana Rao and David Shulman, 2001); *Explorations in Connected History*, 2 Vols (2004); *Writing the Mughal World* (co-authored with Muzaffar Alam, 2011) and *Three Ways to be Alien: Travails and Encounters in the Early Modern World* (2011).

Cynthia Talbot is Associate Professor of History and Asian Studies at the University of Texas at Austin, USA. Her publications include *Precolonial India in Practice: Society, Region and Identity in Medieval Andhra* (2001); *India before Europe* (co-authored with Catherine B. Asher, 2006) and *Knowing India: Colonial and Modern Constructions of the Past* (edited, 2011). Her current research project explores historical traditions and memories relating to King Prithviraj Chauhan from the twelfth century to the present day, and asks how he came to be a national hero.

Carl A. Trocki is an independent scholar based in Queensland. He was formerly the Professor of Asian Studies at the Queensland University of Technology in Brisbane, Australia. He specializes in the history of the Chinese migration to Southeast Asia and Australia and the history and politics of Asia in the nineteenth and twentieth centuries. His publications include *Opium and Empire: Chinese Society in Colonial Singapore, 1800–1910* (1990); *Opium, Empire and the Global Political Economy: A History of the Asian Opium Trade, 1750–1950* (1999) and *Singapore: Wealth, Power and the Culture of Control* (2006).

Foreword

Gordon Johnson

——————— • ✦ • ———————

The essays published here celebrate the work of Professor John F. Richards, a historian who significantly changed our understanding of Mughal history, and who, long before it became fashionable, argued the case for tackling certain historical problems from a global perspective. A list of his publications appears at the end of this volume and it is, by any measure, an impressive contribution to knowledge and understanding.

He was born on 3 November 1938 in Exeter, New Hampshire, USA and was the first of his family to go into higher education. They were happy to support him in this venture, since, whatever his undoubted intellectual prowess, he demonstrated from an early age an amazing lack of practical ability when it came to tasks like changing light bulbs or mowing grass. (Later in life he would, with a twinkle in the eye, rather trade on these shortcomings, despite the fact that they sat rather uneasily against his mastery of difficult languages and complex financial spread-sheets.) In 1961, he graduated Valedictorian of his class at the University of New Hampshire, marrying his childhood sweetheart, Ann Berry, on the same day. After Ann had completed her own Bachelor's degree, the couple moved to the West coast where John pursued a doctorate at the University of California, Berkeley.

Working under the supervision of Professor Tom Metcalf, John took as his subject Mughal rule in south India in the first part of the eighteenth century—a topic of considerable importance and one that required exceptional linguistic and technical skills to pursue successfully. The resulting book, *Mughal Administration in Golconda*, published by Oxford

University Press in 1975, is an outstanding monograph. Firmly based on original archival material, it broke new ground in its clear analysis of institutional and financial structures, and of the political policies that were deployed by the intruding Mughal state as it attempted to assert control over a large part of the Deccan. The study showed how deeper knowledge of the component parts of the Mughal empire—particularly the constitutional arrangements and finding where wealth and power actually lay—contributed to a better understanding of both the successes and limitations of imperial systems. This would lead in future to an assessment of the Mughal enterprise, and of the challenges it faced as the eighteenth century progressed, as being not dissimilar to state-building efforts in other parts of the world. India was not, therefore, to be seen as somehow exotic or 'medieval', but a participant in some more general move of the time to create coherent, centralizing and financially robust states that were in every sense of the word 'modern'.

From Berkeley John moved in 1968 to the University of Wisconsin in Madison, where he proved an effective and stimulating teacher of undergraduates and graduate students alike, a reputation that was to follow him when he was lured to a senior Professorship at Duke University, Durham, North Carolina in 1977, and was undiminished at his untimely death on 23 August 2007. Moreover, he never shirked administrative or other collegial responsibilities and displayed a remarkable degree of academic entrepreneurialism. John was an inveterate arranger of meetings and conferences, and an increasingly effective promoter of his subject within a history establishment dominated by American and European topics.

In 1971 he spent a sabbatical term in Cambridge and was co-opted as a founding editor of the *New Cambridge History of India*, a project then newly approved for development by Cambridge University Press. Out of the thirty-odd volumes planned for that series, nearly half owe their inspiration to him and more than half of those published at the time of his death bear his editorial imprint. His own volume in the *New Cambridge History of India* is a masterly synthesis of contemporary historical knowledge about Mughal India. It steered its way brilliantly between different interpretations of the nature of the Mughal Empire, and did so without offending unduly any of the competing schools of thought. The book has been reissued in paperback, continues to sell well, and deservedly remains the first port of call for anyone with a serious interest in the history of India from Babur's invasion to the end of the eighteenth century.

John had a wide range of intellectual interests and as he matured as a historian he contributed not just to the study of the Mughal Empire but to economic history and comparative world history. John perceived very early that a critical understanding of the impact of the movement of bullion, or of the effect of deforestation, climate change, and other things affecting the relationship between people and the environment, could often be understood only within the broadest international setting. To some this may now seem obvious, but John pioneered a more comprehensive approach to this type of study. From the late 1990s, he sought to understand the financial underpinnings of the British Empire in its Asian context. He gave a preliminary report of his findings in his 2001 Cambridge Kingsley Martin Memorial lecture (revised and expanded in *Modern Asian Studies*, Vol. 36, 2002, pp. 375–420) and in the *Indian Economic and Social History Review*, (Dharma Kumar Special Issue, 2002, pp. 149–80). His major contribution to environmental history was the ground-breaking *The Unending Frontier: Environmental History of the Early Modern World*, published by California University Press in 2003.

After the turn of the century much of John's managerial energies went into arguing for and then establishing the American Institute of Afghanistan Studies—an attempt (still much needed) to support research in the history and culture of Afghanistan, and to promote scholarly ties between the United States and that country. He was a trenchant critic, but a valiant advocate of new work that was soundly based on archival research and made good use of demanding techniques (such as foreign languages or financial expertise). He was particularly supportive of younger scholars in fields of global significance that universities in the West have persistently ignored or undervalued. John also maintained an impressive network of colleagues and friends, was good at keeping in touch with them, exchanging news and gossip, or prodding them to get on with some project or other, promised but long overdue.

Sanjay Subrahmanyam, in a tribute in the *Economic and Political Weekly* (15 September 2007), wrote appreciatively of John's many and varied scholarly achievements. He also captures well John's essential character:

> But behind all that organization and productivity, there was both a mischievous and a tempestuous side. I have seen John lose his temper

rarely, but it was quite a sight. Rather like one of those British summer storms, there would be a thunderclap, a sharp shower (of words), and then all of a sudden the clouds would clear and all would be forgiven. As for the mischief, I can remember him shocking a leading historian … by holding forth at great length on the need to legalise drugs. Was he serious, the historian asked me in puzzlement? Well, at least half-serious. The other half was done for effect, for John certainly liked to provoke at times. It is that provocation and humour, as much as the energy and productivity, and the capacity to keep track of everybody with a singular personal touch that we will all miss.

The essays in this book, which were first presented at a conference in John's honour at Duke University in September 2006, and originally published in a special issue of *Modern Asian Studies* (Vol. 43, no.1, 2009), are testimony to John's far-reaching intellectual interests and to the affection in which he was held by students, colleagues and friends. It is also fitting that the American Historical Association has established an annual prize named in his honour. The publication of this volume brings to new readers a reminder of the important histories that continue, and need, to be written; and serve in turn as homage to an outstanding historian who led the field.

Introduction

David Gilmartin

———— • ✦ • ————

These essays were originally presented at the retirement conference for Professor John F. Richards, which was held at Duke University on 29–30 September 2006. The conference, entitled 'Expanding Frontiers in South Asian and World History', brought together students, colleagues and associates of Prof. Richards to discuss themes that have marked Richards' work as a historian in an academic career of almost 40 years. These themes focused on 'frontiers' in multiple contexts, all relating to Richards' work: frontiers and state building; frontiers and environmental change; cultural frontiers; frontiers, trade and drugs; and frontiers and world history.

Richards' academic work began with his study of Mughal administration on the Deccan frontier in Golconda in the late seventeenth and early eighteenth centuries. His first book, *Mughal Administration in Golconda* (1975), which grew out of his doctoral dissertation, introduced two themes that were to run through much of his later work. The first was a focus on the frontier as a key arena for understanding the processes of state building. Relations between state bureaucracy and local actors, including regional warrior elites, were central to Richards' story. Second, and perhaps even more important for the long-term trajectory of his interests, Richards emphasized the importance of state institutions and finance to the Mughal system. State institutions were something that Richards took very seriously, and if these ultimately failed to cement Mughal rule in Golconda, he attributed the fault to various failed policies pursued by individual Mughal rulers.

Richards later developed this view of the Mughal Empire more fully in numerous essays, and perhaps most importantly, in his synthesis of Mughal history written for the New Cambridge History of India series, of which he was an editor (*The Mughal Empire*, 1993). In debates between those who have emphasized the negotiated patrimonial form of the Mughal empire and those who have stressed its relatively centralized bureaucratic and fiscal institutions, Richards has tended to be a strong advocate of the latter position. Although recognizing the older roots of Mughal forms of cultural authority and loyalty—and the empire's decentralized and patrimonial elements—Richards has been a leader in emphasizing the importance of new forms of state institutions as the defining feature of the Mughal polity. A concern with state finance and administration during the Mughal era (and most recently during the British colonial period as well) has thus been an ongoing preoccupation of his scholarly work.

Perhaps most importantly, however, Richards has seen these new forms as not simply South Asian, but as evidence of South Asia's participation in the broader, worldwide processes of transformation marking the early modern period. He has been forceful in rejecting the common Indian periodization that consigns Mughal history to a 'medieval' past contrasted with the 'modern' colonial period. As Richards argued most persuasively in a 1997 article in the *Journal of World History*, the early modern period was one marked by rapid changes on a worldwide scale, and in these changes, Mughal India fully shared. Many of these changes were products of an expanding global economy. But as Richards emphasized, these were not a product simply of expanding global interconnections (or of European-based capitalism), but of the deployments of new forms of state power on a worldwide scale, producing new forms of exploitation of land and nature in this period. Richards' emphasis in his earlier work on the importance of Mughal state institutions thus led in his later work to a broader emphasis on the importance of new forms of state authority in defining more generally the worldwide transformations of the early modern era.

These emphases were most evident in Richards' massive study of the environmental transformations of the early modern world, *The Unending Frontier* (2003). Here we can see most clearly Richards' concern for placing the development of the state in a world historical context. The expansion of early modern capitalist societies in Europe is a critical element in Richards' story, an expansion that led to unprecedented levels of demand for commodities and pressures on the natural environment. But central to Richards' argument is his connecting this to new forms of state power that had emerged from a 'shared evolutionary progress in human organization' and had pushed state capacities in multiple areas of the world to new thresholds of growth. Critical institutions in Richards' story, such as the triumph of new forms of property rights, were thus a product not only of new economic pressures, but also of new technologies of state power.

The effects of these early modern transformations were, of course, nowhere more visible than on multiple frontiers—frontiers of state power, frontiers of expanding settlement, frontiers of cultural and ethnic interaction, and frontiers of trade. As in much of Richards' work, whether on bandits or drugs, the frontier was a critical arena in which the transformations marking new forms of economic organization, commodity trade, land settlement and state authority intersected. Central to these processes, of course, were the specificities of the varying milieus in which they occurred. Richards' work has, from the beginning, been marked by a combination of concern for large-scale global processes, and for the detailed specificities of each historical case. The essays that follow have attempted to capture the range of interests and approaches that have marked John Richards' career.

1

At Empire's End:

The Nizam, Hyderabad and Eighteenth-century India

MUNIS D. FARUQUI*

——— • ✦ • ———

INTRODUCTION

In May 1748, Nizam-ul-Mulk Asaf Jah arrived in the central Indian city of Burhanpur. He was seventy seven years old and exhausted after undertaking an extensive tour of his dominion. While in Burhanpur, the Nizam caught a cold that caused his health to swiftly deteriorate. Sensing death upon him, the Nizam called a gathering of close confidants and family. The atmosphere was intimate and sad. Among other matters, the Nizam dictated his last testament (*wasiyyatnama*). Spanning seventeen clauses, this testament was intended to provide insights into a lifetime of almost unparalleled success in statecraft and a template of how to govern Hyderabad, the nascent state founded by him in the early 1720s in south-central India. Although the tone and content of the will suggest

* Research for this essay was made possible by a COR Junior Faculty Research Grant from the University of California, Berkeley. I would like to warmly thank Clare Talwalker, Farina Mir, Kavita Datla, the late John Richards, Richard Eaton as well as the participants in two conferences, 'New Elites, Old Regimes' (held at Yale University in April 2006) and 'Expanding Frontiers in South Asian and World History' (held at Duke University in September 2006), for their comments and encouragement. Thanks also go out to V. K. Bawa, Omar Khalidi, and the staff of the British Library for their help in tracking down archival materials. I am especially grateful to Ben Cohen for generously sharing an invaluable copy of *Ma'asir-i Nizami* that he acquired from the Andhra Pradesh State Archives (Hyderabad). Any mistakes are mine alone.

the Nizam is worried about the future of Hyderabad, he also seems concerned to shape his own historical legacy. There is little doubt that the Nizam wished to be remembered as the most successful politician, general and administrator among the post-Mughal rulers. The will is occasionally pontificatory and self-aggrandizing, yet there can be no disagreeing with the Nizam's own conclusion that he had lived a blessed life.[1] Here, after all, was a man who had not only survived, but also thrived amidst the uncertainty accompanying the collapse of the Mughal Empire during the first decades of the eighteenth century.

Using the career of Nizam-ul-Mulk Asaf Jah I as its backdrop, this essay will explore three broad questions. First, what can a revisiting of a 300-year-old corpus of literature on the Nizam tell us about changing and contested portrayals of the man and the state he helped found? Second, how does an understanding of Mughal court politics from the 1680s onwards help explain Nizam-ul-Mulk's transition from being a loyal Mughal in the late 1600s to the founder of a Mughal 'successor' state in 1724? Third, why did Hyderabad survive as an independent state despite a hostile post-1724 environment in which various external and internal enemies confronted it? In exploring these questions, this essay offers preliminary and tentative insights into a period that, following the withering of the Mughal 'imperial banyan tree',[2] offered tremendous possibilities and also perils for elites formerly linked with the Mughal Empire.

This essay marks a preliminary attempt to engage some of the problems and lacunae surrounding studies on the Nizam's career and also the first few decades of Hyderabad's history. Thus, even as Section I seeks to ground Nizam-ul-Mulk's post-Mughal career in critical political developments *prior* to the Emperor Aurangzeb's death in 1707, it more specifically contests the widely held view that political strength (rather than weakness) dictated the Nizam's decision to embark on a new career in the Deccan. Section II focuses on the creation of the Hyderabadi state itself. Specifically, it argues that Hyderabad's establishment and survival depended on its ability to reconcile previously hostile ethnic groups to its existence, to move beyond Mughal frameworks of governance

---

[1] See clauses 4, 5 and 6. Tajalli Ali Shah, *Tuzuk-i Asafiya* (Hyderabad: Matba'-i Asafi, 1892), p. 40. See also *Wasiyyatnama-i Asaf Jah*, Salar Jung Museum and Library, Ms. Hist. 454, fols. 1a–5a; Lala Mansaram, *Ma'asir-i Nizami*, Andhra Pradesh State Archives, Ms. Or. 1749, fols. 51a–54a.

[2] Richard B. Barnett ed., *Rethinking Early Modern India* (Delhi: Manohar, 2002), p.22.

even as it maintained the fiction that it was a Mughal dependency, and to position itself as a tolerant and inclusive but nonetheless Muslim-ruled state. In the end, Hyderabad was neither a poor imitation nor a miniature version of the Mughal Empire. Furthermore, even if it did ultimately devolve into a ramshackle state with weak political, social and military institutions by the nineteenth century, this later history *must* be distinguished from that of its founding years. For Hyderabad's early history highlights a state that was dynamic, innovative and strong enough to hold off a range of regional enemies—a far cry from its later counterpart.

I. THE MAKING OF A POST-IMPERIAL MUGHAL NOBLEMAN

Familial Background and Early Connections to Aurangzeb

Mir Qamar-ud-Din (hereafter referred to by his imperial title, Nizam-ul-Mulk, given to him in 1713) was born in 1671 in Delhi—the Mughal imperial capital—to Ghazi-ud-Din Khan and Safiya Khanum. The Mughal Empire was at its height with the Emperor Aurangzeb (r. 1658–1707) at its helm. Despite minor military setbacks in northeastern India in the early 1660s, the dynasty's political and military authority in the late-seventeenth century was largely unchallenged. At its heart lay a small and elite group of nobles whose unswerving loyalty to the empire was richly rewarded in the form of pecuniary and political benefits. The Nizam was the scion of two such elite noble families. On his mother's side, he was the grandson of Sa'dullah Khan—the illustrious and long-serving prime minister of the preceding emperor, Shah Jahan (r. 1628–58). Although Sa'dullah Khan passed away in 1656, his family continued to enjoy great imperial favour. Thus, the women in the family continued to contract excellent marriages. Safiya Khanum was one of them. At the behest of the Emperor Aurangzeb himself, Safiya Khanum was married (in 1670) to Ghazi-ud-Din Khan—the eldest son of 'Abid Khan, one of the emperor's favourite noblemen. This marriage undoubtedly represented a powerful match-up connecting as it did an impeccably credentialed noble family (that of the Nizam's mother) with a fast-rising family of recent immigrants from Central Asia.

'Abid Khan first came to Mughal India in the early 1650s; he was skirting Safavid and Shiite Iran on his way from his Central Asian hometown of Samarkand to Mecca to perform the *hajj*. While in India, he met the recently appointed governor of the Deccan, Prince Aurangzeb, who promised him great rewards if, on completing his religious obligations, he returned to Mughal India and joined the prince's service. Although the reason for Aurangzeb's interest in 'Abid Khan is unclear, it may have been related to the Khan's lineal descent from the honoured Central Asian sufi saint, Shaykh Shihab-ud-Din Suhrawardi (d. 1234). More likely, however, Aurangzeb's efforts to cultivate 'Abid Khan were part of a much larger attempt to recruit individuals in anticipation of an impending war of succession between the Emperor Shah Jahan's four adult sons. Regardless of Aurangzeb's motives, 'Abid Khan did return to South Asia in late 1656—just in time to fight in the 1657–58 war of succession in which Aurangzeb was victorious. Following Aurangzeb's enthronement as emperor, 'Abid Khan was richly rewarded for having fought with distinction during the conflict. Thus, began an enduring fifty-year long association between Aurangzeb and 'Abid Khan's family that lasted until the emperor's death in 1707.

Over the next few decades, and until his death during the siege of Bijapur in 1686, 'Abid Khan was one of Aurangzeb's favourite noblemen. Appreciated for his candor and loyalty, 'Abid Khan was especially liked because he shared many of the emperor's views regarding Islamic religious practice. Ultimately, he was appointed the imperial *sadr-us-sudur* (head of religious endowments). Other members of 'Abid Khan's family similarly enjoyed imperial favour. This was especially true for 'Abid Khan's son, Ghazi-ud-Din Khan. Besides the honour of marriage to Safiya Begum, Ghazi-ud-Din Khan received steady increments in his noble rank alongside such affectionate sobriquets as *farzand-i arjomand* (noble/distinguished son) from Aurangzeb. Throughout his long political career, Ghazi-ud-Din Khan remained a committed Aurangzeb loyalist.

Although there are many examples of Ghazi-ud-Din Khan's devotion to Aurangzeb,[3] two instances stand out. In the early 1680s, he played

---

[3] Following the Khan's success in bringing grain to a starving and beleaguered Mughal army commanded by Aurangzeb's son, Prince A'zam, a deeply appreciative emperor went so far as to pray: 'As God Almighty has saved the honour of the house of Timur (*sharm-i aulad-i Timuriyya*) through the efforts of Feroz Jang (i.e. Ghazi-ud-Din Khan), so may he guard the honour of his descendants until the Day of Resurrection (*ta daur-i qiyamat*)'. Khafi Khan, *Muntakhab-ul-Lubab*, ed. Khairuddin Ahmad and Ghulam Ahmad, Vol. II, Part I (Calcutta: Asiatic Society of Bengal, 1860–74), p. 319. For a slightly different rendition of the same, see Mir Abu Turab 'Ali, *Hadiqat-ul-'Alam*, Vol. II (Hyderabad: Matba'-i Saiyidi, 1892), p. 37.

a central role in thwarting an almost successful rebellion by one of Aurangzeb's son's, Prince Akbar (who ultimately fled Mughal India for a life of exile in Safavid Iran). Later, in 1686–87, Ghazi-ud-Din Khan accused another son—Prince Mu'azzam—of engaging in secret negotiations with the Kingdom of Golkonda in order to thwart his father's attempts to conquer the Deccan sultanate. How did the emperor respond? He turned aside Prince Mu'azzam's protestations of innocence and placed him under house arrest for almost a decade!

Needless to say, Ghazi-ud-Din Khan's relations with Aurangzeb's sons were strained. Ghazi-ud-Din Khan's antipathies would be passed on to his eldest son, Nizam-ul-Mulk. Can an understanding of the complex relations between Aurangzeb, his royal sons and high-ranking Mughal nobles provide us with any insights into the Nizam's transformation from an ultra-loyal Mughal nobleman in the late 1600s to someone who deserted the Mughal system in the 1720s? This essay will argue in the affirmative. In so doing, it suggests a different emphasis from the accounts of Yusuf H. Khan, Satish Chandra, M. A. Nayeem and Muhammad Umar among others, all of who focus on the post-Aurangzeb period to explain the Nizam's later career trajectory.[4] Any understanding of the Nizam's role in the political jockeying between Aurangzeb and his sons, however, does demand some insight into Mughal succession practices.

Aurangzeb, Mughal Succession Practices and Imperial Nobles

Unlike their Ottoman and Safavid counterparts after the 1590s, the Mughals never instituted ordered rules of dynastic succession. Operating within an open-ended and highly competitive system of succession that encouraged rebellion against the emperor and conflict amongst contending siblings, Mughal princes spent decades cultivating groups and forging alliances across a wide geographical terrain. The rules of this deadly contest were simple and are best summed up by the terse Persian phrase: *Ya takht, ya tabut* (either the throne or the tomb). Ultimately, however, inasmuch as a prince's competitive impulses directly benefited his own dynastic ambitions

---

[4] Yusuf H. Khan, *The First Nizam* (Bombay: Asia Publishing House, 1963 reprint); Satish Chandra, *Parties and Politics at the Mughal Court, 1707–1740* (Delhi: Oxford University Press, 2002 reprint); M. A. Nayeem, *Mughal Administration of Deccan under Nizamul Mulk Asaf Jah, 1720–48 AD* (Bombay: Jaico Publishing House, 1985); Muhammad Umar, *Muslim Society in Northern India during the Eighteenth Century* (Delhi: Munshiram Manoharlal, 1998).

they also—more crucially—drew disparate social groups beyond the Mughal court into partnership with the imperial dynasty.

Rather than threatening the strength of the Mughal Empire, princely activities of retinue and alliance building and competition were crucial cornerstones of Mughal state formation in the dynamic economic, political and social climate of sixteenth- and seventeenth-century South Asia. Even as successive generations of princes scrambled for the throne for fear of death, they built and nurtured relationships with all manner of potential allies. These efforts would not only unfold in the opulence of the imperial court but, more importantly, in the arid mountains of Afghanistan, the steamy riverine areas of Bengal, the coastal plains of the Konkan, the cotton-weaving areas of the Coromandel and also the high plateau of the Deccan. In fact, it was to recruit support that individual princes often travelled to the geographical peripheries of the Mughal Empire and in so doing both expanded these peripheries and also incorporated potential opponents into an imperial Mughal framework.

Crucially, service within princely establishments became one of the primary mechanisms through which the Mughal Empire accommodated groups that were distant from and unfamiliar with Indo-Mughal norms of statecraft and sovereignty. Put differently, princely retinues were the outstations where Indo-Islamic and Mughal political and social norms were learnt and loyalty to the dynasty cultivated and tested. The institution of the Mughal Prince arguably played a central role in extending and sustaining Mughal state formation until Aurangzeb's reign.[5]

The position of the Mughal princes, however, declined dramatically during Aurangzeb's reign. Although it is impossible to definitively explain Aurangzeb's motives for undermining his sons' critical role within the Mughal system, this much is clear: he, unlike his imperial predecessors, increasingly deprived his sons of opportunities to build independent bases of authority. He also made it difficult for them to cultivate and sustain ties to powerful political, social and economic networks. The emperor used a panoply of tools to achieve these ends, including frequently rotating his sons through provincial assignments and independent military commands, weakening princely establishments by

---

[5] These arguments are laid out in my book: *Princes of the Mughal Empire, 1504–1719* (Cambridge: Cambridge University Press, 2012).

transferring princely loyalists out of them and, more generally, crushing any signs of opposition to the emperor.

Most significantly, however, Aurangzeb fostered a powerful and ultra-loyal core of high-ranking nobles—among whom were Ghazi-ud-Din Khan and Nizam-ul-Mulk—to serve as a counterweight to his sons. Although these nobles continued to pay lip service to the authority of the emperor's sons and grandsons, Aurangzeb implicitly encouraged them to view princes as potential competitors rather than overlords. Indeed, the success of Aurangzeb's political strategy is manifest in Ghazi-ud-Din Khan's direct challenge of Prince Akbar and Prince Mu'azzam when they opposed their imperial father.[6]

As long as Aurangzeb was alive, men like Nizam-ul-Mulk and his father never wavered in their loyalty to the ageing but relentless emperor. This was true even when large swathes of the Mughal nobility had clearly lost all confidence in achieving the emperor's goal of conquering and pacifying the Deccan.[7] In the face of widespread demoralization and defeatism, Nizam-ul-Mulk remained a standout general; contemporary sources describe him as showing a casual disregard for his own personal safety when on imperial duty.[8] How can we explain the Nizam's determination to stay the course until Aurangzeb commanded otherwise? The Nizam's personal letters and anecdotes provide us with some initial insights.

The Nizam and Aurangzeb

On one level, the relationship between the Nizam and Aurangzeb was one of deep personal regard. Reading the Nizam's materials, one is

---

[6] Other high-ranking noblemen would similarly challenge Aurangzeb's sons. In 1693, for example, Zulfiqar Khan and Asad Khan temporarily imprisoned Prince Kam Bakhsh (Aurangzeb's youngest son) following bitter disagreements over military strategy during a campaign in the Deccan. Although Aurangzeb subsequently ordered his son released and even reprimanded Zulfiqar Khan for over-reaching, the Khan's reputation was not affected in any significant way. See Saqi Musta'id Khan, *Ma'asir-i 'Alamgiri*, ed. Maulavi Agha Ahmad Ali (Calcutta: Asiatic Society of Bengal, 1870–73), pp. 354–59.

[7] Beginning in 1683, Aurangzeb shifted his attention towards a long-standing imperial goal: the conquest of the Deccan. The emperor seemed assured of success especially following the conquest of the independent sultanates of Bijapur (1686) and Golkonda (1687), and the capture and execution of Shambhaji, the leader of the Maratha opposition (1689). Through the 1690s, however, the initiative slowly slipped away from the Mughals. By 1700, the Mughals were trapped in a quagmire of their own making. Unable to crush the Marathas militarily, political prestige dictated that they stay an increasingly hopeless course as long as Aurangzeb was still alive.

[8] During the 1705 siege of Wakhinkheda, for example, the horse he was riding was blown apart by a cannon shot. How did he react? He called for a fresh horse and continued his inspection of the Mughal frontlines.

struck by the depth of his reverence for Aurangzeb, even decades after his death in 1707. Nizam-ul-Mulk clearly felt that he had learned much of what he knew about people, politics, loyalty, leadership and religion through his association with Aurangzeb.[9] The two men, despite a fifty three-year age gap, by the Nizam's account, enjoyed a strong relationship that went all the way back to the Nizam's infancy when Aurangzeb himself personally chose the Nizam's non-noble and birth name—'Mir Qamar-ud-Din'. Other examples of intimate relations abound: when the Nizam was a very young boy, the emperor requested that Ghazi-ud-Din Khan (his father) leave him under Aurangzeb's personal charge for one day a week so that the emperor might train him;[10] when the Nizam was only six years old Aurangzeb granted him his first noble rank;[11] and the emperor took it upon himself on at least two occasions (in 1698 and 1705) to mediate breaches in relations between the Nizam and his estranged father.[12] Such favours—not to mention unusually close contact with the emperor—bred loyalty over and above that of an ordinary *khanazad* (house-born) Mughal nobleman who spent most of his youth imbibing Mughal political and social values while in residence at the imperial court.[13]

Two additional factors, however, may explain the Nizam's unquestioned loyalty to Aurangzeb. First, even as Aurangzeb promoted the Nizam and his father to the highest rungs within the Mughal nobility, he extended his generosity to other members of their extended family as well. Muhammad Amin Khan—who was Ghazi-ud-Din Khan's first cousin and the Nizam's uncle—is a case in point. Within nine years of his arrival in India from Central Asia in 1687, Muhammad Amin Khan was promoted to the much-coveted position of *sadr-us-sudur*— the position once held by the Nizam's grandfather. Later, just prior to Aurangzeb's death, Muhammad Amin Khan was further honoured with the imperial title of 'Chin Muhammad Khan' and another rise in his

---

[9]   Lala Mansaram, *Ma'asir-i Nizami*, fol. 73b.

[10] Murad Ali Taali, *Nizam-ul-Mulk Asaf Jah Awwal* (Hyderabad: Idarah-i Adabiyat-i Urdu, 1944), p. 11.

[11] For this and other marks of imperial favour, see Mir Abu Turab 'Ali, *Hadiqat-ul-'Alam*, Vol. II, p. 49.

[12] *Ibid.*, Vol. II, pp. 49–50.

[13] See generally John F. Richards, 'Norms of Comportment among Mughal Imperial Officers', in *Moral Conduct and Authority*, ed. Barbara Metcalf (Berkeley: University of California Press; 1984), pp. 255–89.

imperial rank.[14] Such examples of imperial favour towards the Nizam's extended circle, including uncles, cousins, nephews and family retainers, abound. Having received seemingly boundless imperial patronage and generosity, could there be any question that the Nizam would not, to use a favourite Mughal expression, be true to his salt?

Second, Aurangzeb's success in drawing the Nizam and his extended family into an ever-closer political relationship led the emperor's sons to foreclose any possibility of a political alliance with them. This further reinforced the Nizam's loyalty to Aurangzeb.

Survival and Isolation in the Post-Aurangzeb Era

Everyone knew that the emperor would not live forever. By the early 1700s Aurangzeb was already in his mid-eighties (an astounding fact given that the average life expectancy at the time was likely not more than thirty years). Having mostly burnt their bridges with Aurangzeb's three surviving sons (Mu'azzam, A'zam and Kam Bakhsh), the Nizam, his father, and their supporters were thus faced with the real possibility that the next emperor would destroy their collective power. Rather than resigning themselves to this fate, or turning belatedly (and most likely futilely) to the task of allying with one of the princes and thus betraying Aurangzeb's trust, the Nizam and Ghazi-ud-Din Khan chose a risky strategy, one for which there was no precedent. They were going to sit out the much-anticipated war of succession, maintaining strict neutrality towards the rival contenders.

At the same time, they prepared themselves for the possibility of princely aggression. Towards this end, the Nizam and his family began stockpiling weapons—especially artillery—in the early 1700s. The buildup did not go unnoticed. In a 1703 letter from Aurangzeb to his grandson, Bidar Bakht, the emperor states:

> . . .Khan Firuz Jang's (i.e. Ghazi-ud-Din Khan) expenses for his followers are greater than the requirements for his rank and salary (*ziyadah az zabit-i mansab wa tankhwah*). I noticed all manner of guns... horsemen with weapons... and many other things, some of which are necessary and others not. As a result I confiscated many of those things.[15]

---

[14] See generally, Shahnawaz Khan, *Ma'asir-ul-Umara*, ed. Maulavi Mirza Ashraf Ali, Vol. I (Calcutta: Asiatic Society of Bengal, 1888–91), pp. 346–50.

[15] Aurangzeb, *Ruq'at-i 'Alamgiri*, ed. Sayyid Muhammad Abdul Majeed (Kanpur: Matba'-i Qayyumi, 1916), pp. 31–32.

If Aurangzeb's decision to confiscate some weapons proved a set back, it nonetheless was only a temporary one. For, by the time the emperor passed away in February 1707, the Nizam, his father, their extended family and their supporters were ready to implement their plan of armed neutrality.

Upon learning of the emperor's death, the Nizam and Muhammad Amin Khan undertook a series of difficult manoeuvres as they simultaneously negotiated their noble duties and their desire for neutrality. First, they deserted their commander Prince Kam Bakhsh (then governor of Bijapur). They then journeyed to the imperial encampment near Daulatabad where they paid their last respects to Aurangzeb and also congratulated Prince A'zam—who was in the camp at the time—on declaring himself emperor. Under some duress they agreed to accompany Prince A'zam's army northwards to fight against Prince Mu'azzam who, meanwhile, was marching southwards from his stronghold in Kabul. During the journey, however, the Nizam and Muhammad Amin Khan deserted Prince A'zam's army, plundered its supply train, and made off towards the city of Burhanpur where they quietly awaited the outcome of the conflict. Their actions matched those of Ghazi-ud-Din Khan who refused to leave his armed encampment in Daulatabad despite many invitations to also join Prince A'zam's army.

After three months, Prince A'zam was defeated and killed by Prince Mu'azzam at the Battle of Jajau (June 1707). With military momentum and almost all the personnel and financial resources of the Mughal Empire under his control, Prince Mu'azzam now moved towards the Deccan to confront Prince Kam Bakhsh. The outcome of the conflict between the princes was never in doubt (Prince Kam Bakhsh died following a brief battle near the city of Hyderabad). What was uncertain, however, was Prince Mu'azzam's response to Ghazi-ud-Din Khan, the Nizam, and their supporters. Would he order their elimination? Their disgrace and banishment? Or, would he favour forgiveness and magnanimity? In the end, and likely following calculations concerning their military strength, Prince Mu'azzam (now crowned as Emperor Bahadur Shah) chose the third option. It would soon become clear, however, that the rewards and high-ranking assignments granted by Bahadur Shah were nothing more than sops. The Nizam, his family, and their supporters were not going to be trusted in any significant way and they certainly were not going to be admitted into the emperor's inner circle. This was the price for having been so closely associated with Aurangzeb against his sons and grandsons.

Between 1707 and 1720, over the course of the short reigns of several Mughal emperors, the Nizam was largely isolated at the imperial court. In 1710, for example, the Nizam took the unusual step of resigning all his imperial positions; he groused that Bahadur Shah was unfairly favouring 'low-born' individuals (that is, those without lineage) over those with deep roots in the Mughal nobility (himself and, by extension, his own supporters).[16] Bahadur Shah paid little heed to the nobleman's complaints. The bad blood lasted until the emperor's death in 1712 and the subsequent war of succession. As in 1707, the Nizam again took the extraordinary step of sitting out the conflict. Naturally, this did not endear him to the next emperor—Jahandar Shah (r. 1712–13).

What likely irritated Jahandar Shah even further, however, was the Nizam's threat to again resign all imperial commissions (including the recently acquired governorship of Malwa) if the new emperor continued to favour individuals whom the Nizam deemed unworthy.[17] All indications suggest that the Nizam would have been militarily crushed by Jahandar Shah had the latter not been dethroned in 1713 by his nephew, Farrukh Siyar (r. 1713–19).[18]

The Nizam played no part in Farrukh Siyar's accession. As a result he continued to remain fairly marginal to the imperial court's inner workings. This is attested by the fact that although the Nizam received the much-coveted governorship of the Deccan in 1713, he was summarily dismissed from that post in 1715. Through the early years of Farrukh Siyar's reign, the Nizam's political and military strength vis-à-vis the imperial court declined as his diverse and often-fractious coalition of family members, political allies and clients fell apart. Muhammad Amin Khan, in particular, proved a weak link for he had never accepted the Nizam as the head of the extended family following the death of Ghazi-ud-Din Khan in 1710. The two men also seem to have disagreed over the direction of the empire. Where the Nizam felt the empire was

---

[16] Mir Abu Turab 'Ali, *Hadiqat-ul-'Alam*, Vol. II, p. 54. For a fuller discussion of the larger political context informing the Nizam's resignation, see Muzaffar Alam, *The Crisis of Empire in Mughal North India: Awadh and the Punjab 1707–1748* (Delhi: Oxford University Press, 1986), pp. 20–23, 58–63.

[17] See generally, Muhammad Qasim Lahori, 'Ibratnama, ed. Zahuruddin Ahmad (Lahore: Intisharat Adabiyat-i Pakistan, 1977), p.162; Mubarakullah Wazih, *Ta'rikh-i Iradat Khan*, ed. Ghulam Rasul Mehr (Lahore: Idarah-i Tahqiqat-i Pakistan, 1971), p. 129; Khafi Khan, *Muntakhab-ul-Lubab*, Vol. II, Part II, p. 689.

[18] Ghulam Husain Tabatabai, *Siyar-ul-Mutakherin* (Lucknow: Nawal Kishore, 1859–1860), Vol. II, p. 386. See also Iradut Khan, 'Memoirs of the Mogul Empire', trans. Jonathan Scott in *History of Dekkan*, Vol. II, Part IV (Shrewsbury: J. and W. Eddowes, 1794), fn. 2, 81.

increasingly adrift (and reacted by withdrawing to his estates in the Moradabad region between 1715 and 1719), Muhammad Amin Khan was committed to accruing power at the imperial court. Initially the Khan sought to do so through the patronage of the Sayyid brothers— the primary backers of Farrukh Siyar's 1712–13 campaign to ascend the Mughal throne. After 1716, however, the Khan worked to supplant the brothers as the main powerbroker at the Mughal court.

Although Nizam-ul-Mulk would reassert his importance in Mughal politics by helping Muhammad Amin Khan engineer the downfall of the Sayyid brothers in 1719–20,[19] he would be shortchanged in the political jockeying that followed. Despite widespread expectations that he would be rewarded with the position of *wazir* (prime minister) of the Mughal Empire by the new emperor—Muhammad Shah (r. 1720–48)—the Nizam found himself thwarted by none other than Muhammad Amin Khan who grabbed the position for himself. In so doing, according to a very bitter Nizam, Muhammad Amin Khan had betrayed him.[20] In order to avoid a conflict with his uncle, however, the Nizam accepted the governorship of the Deccan for the second time in his career.

While the Nizam made the most of the opportunity (as detailed in the next section), the Deccan clearly remained a second-choice assignment. If the Nizam was privately contemplating a post-Mughal future, then his public actions certainly give us no hint of that possibility. In fact, following the premature death of Muhammad Amin Khan in 1722, the Nizam lost no time in pressing for and ultimately getting the post he had coveted for so long: that of *wazir*.[21]

A Pyrrhic Victory

Nizam-ul-Mulk's tenure as *wazir* lasted less than two years. During this time, he proposed various reform-minded administrative measures

---

[19] The Nizam crushed multiple attempts by the Sayyid brothers to assert their control over the Deccan. The Sayyids' power rapidly disintegrated thereafter. See generally, Muhammad Qasim Aurangabadi, *Ahwal-ul-Khawaqin*, British Library Add. Ms 26244, fols. 152a–78a. See also William Irvine, *Later Mughals* (Delhi: Munshiram Manoharlal, 1996 reprint), 16–93. For a pro-Sayyid perspective, see Ghazanfar Husain's 1720 versified account, *Jangnama-i Sayyid 'Alam 'Ali Khan*, ed. Abdulhaq (Aurangabad: Anjuman Taraqqi-yi Urdu, 1932).

[20] Muhammad Qasim Aurangabadi, *Ahwal-ul-Khawaqin*, fols. 178b–79a.

[21] In a surviving letter to Emperor Muhammad Shah, he speaks about Muhammad Amin Khan's earlier betrayal and claims he has earned the right to the *wazir*ship. Just in case the emperor missed the urgency of the Nizam's demand, he concludes by saying that giving it to anyone else will cause 'heart-burning... [and] we shall have to resign from the imperial service'. Cited in Yusuf H. Khan, *The First Nizam*, p.117.

(especially in fiscal matters), sought greater control over the imperial bureaucracy and attempted to tame some of the powerful factions at the imperial court. Each of these initiatives ended in spectacular failure. Undermined at every turn by powerful opponents, the Nizam was finally driven out of the Mughal court after a rebellion was engineered against him in the Deccan.[22] Forced to protect the foundation of his power—namely his control over the Deccan—the Nizam journeyed southwards in 1724. In so doing, he completed a decades-long transition from loyal Mughal *khanazad* to semi-independent ruler.

Ultimately, it was the Nizam's marginality and weakness—not his strength, as much of the historiography on Hyderabad suggests[23]— that forced him to countenance the possibility of a life beyond the imperial court in 1724. Similarly, studies that suggest that the Nizam deliberately abandoned or even wrecked the Mughal system in order to consolidate his own power in the Deccan misread the Nizam's intentions.[24] Although there is no denying his poor relations with and lack of regard for the rulers who followed Aurangzeb, the Nizam was undoubtedly invested in reviving the empire's glory, albeit on his own terms. This fact does not, however, render him a renegade or traitor to the system that spawned him. If anything, the Nizam's desperation to achieve the rank of *wazir* in 1722 suggests a deep desire to fulfil his political ambitions within the purview of Mughal politics; it is not hard to imagine the Nizam picturing himself as a latter-day Sa'dullah Khan (his maternal grandfather who was Emperor Shah Jahan's renowned prime minister).

---

[22]   Among the key players seeking the Nizam's removal from the ambit of Mughal politics were Emperor Muhammad Shah, the emperor's foster-sister (Koki Jiu), Samsam-ud-Daula (whose death at the Battle of Karnal in 1739 would be blamed on the Nizam), Raushan-ud-Daula (a favourite of the emperor), and Qamar-ud-Din Khan—the son of Muhammad Amin Khan and therefore a cousin of the Nizam—who secretly desired (and ultimately received) the position of wazir. For more details, see generally, Muhammad Mahbub Junaidi, *Hayat-i Asaf* (Hyderabad: Ahed Afrin Barqi Press, 1946), pp.187–209.

[23]   See generally, William Irvine, *Later Mughals*; Satish Chandra, *Parties and Politics at the Mughal Court, 1707–1740*, and a long line of Hyderabad-based historians from Yusuf H. Khan, *The First Nizam*, to those of the eighteenth century, including Muhammad Qasim Aurangabadi (*Ahwal-ul-Khawaqin*, 1739), Vir Rai (*Tazkira-i Asafiya*, 1752–1753), Abul Faiz Ma'ani (*Ta'rikh Futuhat-i Asafiya*, 1750s), Yusuf Khan Turani (*Ta'rikh-i Fathiya*, 1754), Lala Mansaram (*Ma'asir-i Nizami*, 1785), and Munshi Ram Singh (*Gulshan-i 'Ajaib*, 1783).

[24]   See generally, Satish Chandra, *Parties and Politics at the Mughal Court, 1707–1740*, as well as earlier eighteenth-century historians like Rustam 'Ali (*Ta'rikh-i Hindi*, 1741–1742), Muhammad Mohsin Siddiqui, (*Jauhar-i Samsam*, 1740–1741), and the anonymous authors of *Tawarikh-i Nadir Shahi* (1740s?) and *Risala-i Muhammad Shah wa Khan-i Dauran* (1740s).

In retaining a commitment to the Mughal enterprise into the 1720s, the Nizam's egress from the imperial system was crucially different from that of other Mughal noblemen who founded Mughal 'successor states'—like Murshid Quli Khan (d. 1727) in Bengal, 'Abdus Samad Khan (d. 1738) in the Punjab or Burhan-ul-Mulk (d. 1739) in Awadh. Unlike the latter three who parlayed increasingly lengthy stints in their respective regions towards quietly asserting their independence, the Nizam had to fight to establish himself in the Deccan. He, after all, had spent less than five years in the region between 1707 and 1724. Ultimately, understanding what distinguishes the Nizam from the rulers of the other so-called 'successor states' is important for at least two reasons.

First, it is crucial towards advancing the larger historiography of the eighteenth century. Without a nuanced understanding of differences between the different 'successor states', there will be a continued tendency to elide their unique histories.[25] This would be especially unfortunate in the case of Hyderabad given its status as the only 'successor state' outside of the former Mughal heartlands in northern India. There is no doubt that Hyderabad faced unique sets of challenges in asserting its statehood and identity compared to the other (northern) 'successor states'. Second, any significant efforts to engage comparative approaches to eighteenth-century political history or even complicate long-standing debates about eighteenth-century economic 'crises' and Mughal 'decline', will continue to be stymied if we are unable to make more finely graded judgments about the various 'successor states'.[26]

---

[25]   The best evidence of this can be seen in a recent slue of concise histories including: Ayesha Jalal and Sugata Bose, *Modern South Asia* (New York: Oxford University Press, 2004), and Barbara and Thomas Metcalf, *A Concise History of India* (Cambridge: Cambridge University Press, 2002). See also Barbara Ramusack, *The Indian Princes and their States* (Cambridge: Cambridge University Press, 2004), pp. 25–26.

[26]   For a rare comparative approach, see Muzaffar Alam, *The Crisis of Empire in Mughal North India: Awadh and the Punjab 1707–1748*. Otherwise, for studies on Awadh, see Michael Fisher, *A Clash of Cultures: Awadh, the British and the Mughals* (Delhi: Manohar, 1987) and Richard Barnett, *North India between Empires: Awadh, the Mughals, and the British, 1720–1801* (Berkeley: University of California Press, 1980). For the Punjab: see Chetan Singh, *Region and Empire: Punjab in the Seventeenth Century* (Delhi: Oxford University Press, 1991) and Muzaffar Alam, *The Crisis of Empire in Mughal North India: Awadh and the Punjab 1707–1748*. For Bengal: see Sushil Chaudhury, *The Prelude to Empire* (Delhi: Manohar, 2000) and *From Prosperity to Decline: Eighteenth Century Bengal* (Delhi: Manohar, 1995), Kumkum Chatterjee, *Merchants, Politics and Society in Early Modern India, Bihar: 1733–1820* (Leiden: E. J. Brill, 1996), John McLane, *Land and Local Kingship in 18th Century Bengal* (Cambridge: Cambridge University Press, 1993), P. J. Marshall, *Bengal: The British Bridgehead, Eastern India 1740–1828* (Cambridge: Cambridge University Press, 1987), and Shirin Akhtar, *The Role of the Zamindars in Bengal, 1707–1772* (Dacca: Asiatic Society of Bengal, 1982).

The next section will explore Hyderabad's distinctive founding history while also explaining the state's survival. As will be clear, Hyderabad was neither fully formed in 1724 nor did it survive the next few decades without continuous and innovative work under the most challenging circumstances. Unfortunately, contemporary understanding of the socio-political processes that went into the creation of Hyderabad remains, at best, vague.[27] Furthermore, there is a marked tendency to view pre-1748 Hyderabad through the same prism as its slothful and hopelessly mismanaged late eighteenth- and nineteenth-century avatar. Such views beg revision.

II. THE ESTABLISHMENT AND CONSOLIDATION OF HYDERABAD, 1724–48

The Challenges Confronting Hyderabad

Upon his arrival in the Deccan in 1724, the Nizam faced a number of problems. The most threatening was the political and military strength of the Marathas. Having first ground down Aurangzeb's armies in the Deccan and then forced subsequent Mughal rulers to acknowledge their right to tax the inhabitants of the Deccan, the Marathas were bent on preventing the Nizam from establishing an independent state. The Marathas had good reason to be wary of the Nizam; he had built a reputation since the early 1710s as an opponent to any tax concessions to the Marathas. Thus, although the Marathas initially helped the Nizam establish himself in the Deccan in 1724 by lending him support against a rival Mughal general (Mubariz Khan), they quickly rued their assistance.

---

[27] This is reflected in, for example, P. J. Marshall's introduction to *The Eighteenth Century in Indian History*. Although he is absolutely correct in highlighting the importance Mughal successor states attached to gaining the support of intermediate gentry and merchantile groups, he is (not surprisingly) forced to confine his comments to Awadh, Bengal and the Marathas. Hyderabad does not even make a cameo appearance. This lack can be attributed to the almost complete absence of scholarship on the early nizamate's evolving relations with almost all intermediate groups. See P. J. Marshall, *The Eighteenth Century in Indian History* (Delhi: Oxford University Press, 2003), pp.7–8. By contrast, even the statelet of Arcot, a subsidiary of Hyderabad along the eastern coast of south India, has received more attention. The best contemporary work is: Muzaffar Alam and Sanjay Subrahmanyam, 'Exploring the Hinterland: Trade and Politics in the Arcot Nizamate (1700–1732),' in *Politics and Trade in the Indian Ocean World. Essays in Honor of Ashin Das Gupta*, eds Rudrangshu Mukherjee and Lakshmi Subramanian (Delhi: Oxford University Press, 1998), pp.113–64.

The Marathas were only one of many threats facing the Nizam. Other groups in the Deccan—including Afghans, Berads and Telugus—similarly saw the Nizam and his supporters as political interlopers. Having previously evaded or opposed encroaching Mughal rule in south India, they were not about to give up their relative political or economic autonomy to the Nizam without a fight. On top of these challenges, Nizam-ul-Mulk was confronted by three additional and arguably more profound challenges.

First, he could not entirely rely on the institutional structures of Mughal imperial rule to boost his authority. This was because Mughal rule in the region was both a relatively recent imposition (dating from the late 1680s at the earliest) and shallow in its application because of conditions of almost non-stop warfare across the region. The Nizam's difficult circumstances contrasted greatly from those of the post-Mughal rulers of Awadh, the Punjab and Bengal where a century or more of Mughal imperial experience provided more solid foundations upon which to build new states. So, how was the Nizam to build institutions that simultaneously drew on Mughal expertise but also were sensitive to the local applicability of Mughal models?

Second, the Nizam had to overcome a series of profound cultural chasms between Hyderabad's new ruling elites and many of their subjects—especially those living in the extreme south. Nowhere was this more apparent than in the relationship to Persian. Whereas, the Nizam and most of his closest associates grew up in and operated in a world where Persian was central to the articulation of power, authority and legitimacy,[28] Persian's importance faded to insignificance in the southern reaches of peninsular India. In areas such as Mysore, Kerala and Tamil Nadu local languages were the language of statecraft. How was the Nizam to cement his rule in these areas if he did not have the cultural tools to back his military strengths?

Third, while establishing his rule over the six Mughal *subas* (provinces) that comprised the Deccan, the Nizam was painfully aware of their different historical, political and cultural trajectories. The Nizam knew that a one-size-fits-all approach to governance was bound to imperil his authority.[29] So, how was he to balance this difficulty without fatally

---

[28] See generally, Muzaffar Alam, 'The Pursuit of Persian: Language in Mughal Politics', *Modern Asian Studies* 32 (1998), pp. 317–49.

[29] Tajalli Ali Shah, *Tuzuk-i Asafiya*, 40–41. See also Munshi Ram Singh, *Gulshan-i 'Ajaib*, British Library Add. Ms. 26236, fols. 107a–b.

undermining the administrative and political unity that he hoped to establish over the entire region?

Building Blocks of the New State

For all the challenges he faced, Nizam-ul-Mulk did enjoy a number of powerful advantages in his quest to establish the state of Hyderabad. Among the more important was his deep personal knowledge of the region's political, social and economic networks. These insights came from time spent in the Deccan—first as a commander through the last twenty five years of Aurangzeb's reign, and then as governor between 1713–15 and 1720–22. Ultimately, the Nizam had a clear sense of which groups had to be conciliated and which threatened with violence, which trusted and which sidelined as he went about building Hyderabad. His complex and carefully calibrated relations in the post-1724 period with such varied groups as the Marathas, Afghans, Dakhinis, Gond and Bhil tribals, and Telugus underscore the Nizam's sensitivity to the minutiae of Deccani politics. The success of Nizam-ul-Mulk's enterprise in the final analysis, however, depended on yet another fundamental strength: the ability to threaten, and if needed, use violence against recalcitrant opponents. In this regard, the Nizam wielded two powerful tools—first, a disciplined, experienced and well-equipped core of loyalists, and, second, strong support from the imperial military and bureaucratic apparatus, such as it was, in the regions that had come under Mughal control over the previous decades.

As detailed in Section I, the armed strength of the Nizam and his family was a key factor protecting them against retribution from Aurangzeb's successors. This strength would also be crucial in establishing the Nizam's political and military fortunes in the Deccan. Who were the Nizam's supporters, and what made them such a potent force? Contrary to the view of many historians,[30] this essay finds little merit in the argument that the Nizam commanded a 'Turani' faction (comprising mostly familial and clan members, recent unrelated immigrants from Central Asia and various Barlas, Chaghatay, Kazakh, Qalmaq and Mughal Turks who were

---

[30] See generally William Irvine, *Later Mughals*; Yusuf H. Khan, *The First Nizam*; Satish Chandra, *Parties and Politics at the Mughal Court, 1707–1740*; Zahiruddin Malik, *The Reign of Muhammad Shah* (Bombay: Asia Publishing House, 1977); M.A. Nayeem, *Mughal Administration of Deccan under Nizamul Mulk Asaf Jah, 1720–48 AD*; and Muhammad Umar, *Muslim Society in Northern India during the Eighteenth Century*. For a more recent example, see Nile Green, 'Geography, Empire and Sainthood in the Eighteenth-century Muslim Deccan', *Bulletin of SOAS* 67 (2004), pp. 207–25.

long settled in India).[31] Although 'Turanis' were important supporters of the Nizam, his household forces also included many Afghans (including Deccan-based Khweshgis and Ansaris), Indian Muslims (including many members of the Nizam's maternal family—who were originally from the Punjab), Khatris, Kayasths, Bundelas, Rajputs and Dakhinis. Indeed, one of the Nizam's closest advisors was a north Indian Muslim from the town of Shikohabad—Abu'l Khair Khan, the founder of the famous Paigah lineage that would dominate Hyderabad's nobility until the destruction of the state in 1948.

Despite great ethnic and religious diversity, the Nizam's supporters repeatedly proved their cohesiveness and loyalty. Cementing the bonds among the Nizam's loyalists were conditions of long-standing service to the Nizam (and in some cases his father and grandfather). The Nizam also benefited from perceptions that he was a generous, kind and principled patron,[32] spiritually blessed,[33] and Aurangzeb's last living political legatee.[34] After the Nizam abandoned the Mughal court in 1724, there was also a sense among the Nizam's supporters that they were fighting both for their patron's political future as well as their own right to begin new lives in the Deccan. Their élan and bravery during the 1724 campaign contrasted sharply with that of their fractious opponents under the command of Mubariz Khan (who was ordered by the Mughal court to destroy the Nizam's base in the Deccan). The Nizam's military strength, however, depended on a second crucial source: strong support within the Deccan-based imperial administration itself. It had been cultivated well before the first volley was fired in the battle against Mubariz Khan.

---

[31] 'Turan' was a commonly used generic name to describe the regions north of the River Amu in Central Asia. See generally, V. Minorsky, 'Turan', *Encyclopaedia of Islam*, Vol. IV: II (Leiden: E. J. Brill, 1934), pp. 878–84.

[32] In this regard, the Nizam was following an old family tradition. Aurangzeb once noted that 'Abid Khan (the Nizam's grandfather) was among a small group of noblemen who when mounting guard duties, would offer coffee, breakfast and dinner to their soldiers. At times of departure (*waqt-i rukhsat*), they would gift perfumes and betelnut. They would also send all manner of food to their soldiers' homes to alleviate complaints by the soldiers' dependents that the men alone were receiving generosity. *Ruq'at-i 'Alamgiri*, p. 23. See also Yusuf. H. Khan, *The First Nizam*, p. 8.

[33] Yusuf H. Khan, *The First Nizam*, p.125.

[34] Muhammad Qasim Aurangabadi, *Ahwal-ul-Khawaqin*, fol. 178b. The Nizam played a crucial role in enhancing this image by, for example, suggesting that his military conquests in South India were intended to complete Emperor Aurangzeb's goals. See Munshi Ram Singh, *Gulshan-i 'Ajaib*, fol. 92a, fol. 99b.

During his second stint as governor of the Deccan (1720–22), the Nizam made an important decision. Unsure of his political future in the imperial capital, the Nizam began to build a base for himself in the Deccan.[35] It is unlikely that the Nizam was working towards a declaration of independence, as suggested by some scholars.[36] Rather, it seems that he hoped to use his control over the Deccan to leverage the position of *wazir* at the imperial court. Whatever his motives, the impact of the Nizam's actions are clear; he installed family members and imperial loyalists in many of the most important positions across the Deccan. These appointments were complemented by enhanced imperial positions (*mansabs*) and land assignments (*jagirs*) for supporters, the assertion of direct control over departments (such as revenue and intelligence) previously outside the governor's control, the transfer of individuals who were deemed politically unreliable,[37] and tribute-extracting expeditions against various groups—especially Afghans—aimed at garnering financial resources.[38] By 1722—when the Nizam left the Deccan to become *wazir* of the Mughal Empire—he had largely stamped his authority over the imperial administration across the region. Mubariz Khan would only belatedly learn this lesson when the expected support from fellow Deccan-based imperial officials did not materialize.[39]

After 1724, the Nizam would use his personal retainers and supporters alongside members of the (former) imperial establishment to assert his political and military authority across the entire Deccan.[40] The state of

---

[35] This followed upon earlier, if slightly half-hearted, efforts—in 1713 to 1715—to strengthen his position in the Deccan. See Murad Ali Taali, *Nizam-ul-Mulk Asaf Jah Awwal*, pp. 19–20; Muhammad Mahbub Junaidi, *Hayat-i Asaf*, pp.184–86; John F. Richards, *Mughal Administration in Golconda* (Oxford: Oxford University Press, 1975), pp. 269–71.

[36] For an example, see Satish Chandra, *Parties and Politics at the Mughal Court, 1707–1740*.

[37] For details, see generally M. A. Nayeem, *Mughal Administration of Deccan under Nizamul Mulk Asaf Jah*, pp. 35–36. Having failed to transfer Mubariz Khan out of his governorship of Hyderabad between 1722 and 1724 (despite his best efforts), the Nizam sought to weaken Mubariz Khan by instituting inquiries into financial malfeasance (income from imperial crown lands, *khalisa*, were supposedly misappropriated). Shahnawaz Khan, *Ma'asir-ul-Umara*, Vol. III, p. 736.

[38] John F. Richards, *Mughal Administration in Golconda*, p. 294.

[39] Mir Abu Turab 'Ali, *Hadiqat-ul-'Alam*, Vol. II, pp. 128–30.

[40] The Nizam's unwillingness to alienate any part of the former Mughal imperial apparatus in the Deccan is, perhaps, best attested by the kind treatment accorded to the defeated supporters of Mubariz Khan as well as the dead Khan's surviving sons. Most were reaccommodated into the emerging administrative institutions of Hyderabad. Muhammad Qasim Aurangabadi, *Ahwal-ul-Khawaqin*, fol. 198a; Lala Mansaram, *Ma'asir-i Nizami*, fol. 57b, fols. 61a-b. See also Akhtar Yar Jang Bahadur, *Ta'rikh-i Dakkan* (Hyderabad: Dar al-Matba'-i Sarhar-i Ali, 1929), pp. 316–18;

Hyderabad was born out of these efforts. Hyderabad's long-term survival, however, ultimately depended on other processes as well. None was more important than finding a way to contain the nascent state's many regional and ethnic opponents.

There is an interesting anecdote in Lala Mansaram's contemporaneous text, *Ma'asir-i Nizami*. He quotes the Nizam stating: 'For the efficient administration of the province of the Deccan it is absolutely imperative that three communities should be avoided. . . first Afghans, second Deccanis, and third Marathas'. According to the Nizam each believed that they had a claim to ruling the Deccan.[41] Contrast this statement with another one—namely the very first clause of the Nizam's 1748 final testament. Here he advises his successors differently: 'It is necessary for the ruler of the Deccan who desires his own safety, peace from war, and the prosperity of his country to have peace with the Marathas who are the landholders (*zamindaran*) of this region'.[42] These quotes get at the heart of Hyderabad's dilemma: even as it needed collaborators among the major ethnic groups in the region, most of the latter viewed the newly emergent state as a threat to their own political aspirations and claims on the land. Put differently, the Nizam was widely seen as an interloper in the region. How did he resolve this conundrum? In brief, he used political compromise, financial inducements and the application of military force. Relations with the Marathas richly illustrate use of all these tactics.

Hyderabad and the Marathas

In 1724, there were two major Maratha factions in the Deccan; each acknowledged different grandsons of the great Maratha commander, Shivaji (d. 1681), as their leader—Shahu of Satara or Shambhaji of Kolhapur. Although deeply divided, the two factions temporarily united to help the Nizam defeat Mubariz Khan at the Battle of Shakarkheda. They supported the Nizam for a mixture of reasons: important individuals in both factions had personal relations with the Nizam going back to

Syed Hossain Bilgrami, *A Memoir of Sir Salar Jung* (Bombay: Times of India Press, 1883), p. 5; Maulvi Abdul Rahim Khan, *Tarikh-i Nizam-i Urdu* (Charlestown, Mass: Acme Bookbinding, Reprint, 2002), pp.43–44; John F. Richards, *Mughal Administration in Golconda*, p. 299; Muhammad Mahbub Junaidi, *Hayat-i Asaf*, pp. 239–40. One of Mubariz Khan's sons—Hamidullah Khan—eventually even married into the Nizam's family. Maulvi Abdul Rahim Khan, *Ta'rikh-i Nizam-i Urdu*, p. 43.

[41] Lala Mansaram, *Ma'asir-i Nizami*, fol. 65a.

[42] Tajalli Ali Shah, *Tuzuk-i Asafiya*, p. 38.

his previous stints in the Deccan;[43] the Marathas hoped to reap large political and economic rewards for their support of the former Mughal strongman; and both Maratha factions wanted to prevent an exclusive alliance between the Nizam and the other faction. On the Nizam's side, he felt he could use the Marathas to his advantage as long as he offered them some direct political and economic benefit. Thus, shortly after defeating Mubariz Khan, the Nizam confidently predicted that 'this entire army (that is, the Marathas) is my own. I will get work done through them... I will entrust the governance on that side of the (River) Narmada to them... Their armies will not enter my dominions (*taluqa-i man*)'.[44]

Unfortunately, Shahu of Satara had grander expectations of recompense. Foremost among them was the right to collect certain taxes (*chauth* and *sardeshmukhi*, amounting to 35 per cent of total revenue) across the entire Deccan—including the Nizam's territories. After trying in vain to negotiate with Shahu, the Nizam resolved to fight. He did so by invading areas under Shahu's control and also sealing a controversial military alliance with Sambhaji.[45]

The struggle between Shahu and the Nizam (who was supported by Sambhaji) lasted three years. By 1728, however, Shahu was victorious. Seeing the writing on the wall, the Nizam agreed to recognize Shahu as Shivaji's sole successor; support for Sambhaji was dropped. The Nizam also agreed to all of Shahu's taxation demands except one: the creation of a Maratha-operated bureaucracy to collect the tributary taxes. Instead, he insisted on creating his own tax collection administration, led either by a Nizam-appointed *jagirdar* (military assignee) or *tahsildar-i chauth* (a revenue farmer or *ijaradar*).[46] Although the Nizam's pride was severely

---

[43] Yusuf H. Khan, *The First Nizam*, p. 67; A.G. Pawar, 'Some Documents Bearing on Imperial Mughal Grants to Raja Shahu (1717–1724)', *Indian Historical Records Commission*, Vol. XVII, (1940), pp. 210–13.

[44] Lala Mansaram, *Ma'asir-i Nizami*, fol. 85b. For more on the Nizam's delicate balancing act, see the correspondence detailing his 1726 campaign in Karnataka. Although reliant on Maratha military support, he remained deeply mistrustful of their support—*beh anha i'timad-i dilli nabud*. Munshi Ram Singh, *Gulshan-i 'Ajaib*, fol. 138b.

[45] Two of the Nizam's foremost commanders, Muhammad Ghiyas Khan and 'Iwaz Khan, warned that support for Sambhaji was inadvisable. After all, 'To replace one tyrant (*zalim*) with another makes no sense; after all the wolf cub will grow to be a wolf'. Muhammad Qasim Aurangabadi, *Ahwal-ul-Khawaqin*, fol. 199b. For more on the political manoeuvres to entice Shambhaji to the Nizam's side, see Munshi Ram Singh, *Gulshan-i 'Ajaib*, fol. 122b.

[46] M.A. Nayeem, *Mughal Administration of Deccan under Nizamul Mulk Asaf Jah*, p. 219; Zahirud-din Malik, 'Chauth-Collection in the Subah of Hyderabad in 1726–1748', *Indian Economic and Social History Review* 8 (1972), pp. 395–96.

dented by this capitulation, he remained committed to meeting Maratha tax demands over the next two decades (even if he continued to fight them outside the Deccan for control over the former Mughal province of Malwa or the southern region of Arcot).[47]

His determination to maintain good working relations is suggested in an angry exchange with his uncle 'Iwaz Khan (d. 1731). Upon learning that the nobleman had shown great disrespect towards visiting Maratha representatives, the Nizam rebuked him for being uncomprehending (nafahm), lacking in wisdom (nadan) and shortsighted (kamandesh). The Nizam explained that the Marathas 'are the landholders of this country' who could not even be defeated by Emperor Aurangzeb, 'despite his immense army and expenditure of the entire treasure of Hindustan (that is, northern India)'. Due to the Khan's lack of courtesy (ta'azzum), all of the Nizam's efforts to make them 'obedient and loyal to me through diplomacy' are now threatened. Such behaviour is 'inexcusable'.[48]

The Nizam's words suggest an understanding that if the Marathas really focused their energies they could destroy Hyderabad,[49] and that as long as relations with the Maratha state were poor, he could not hope to win the support of Marathas living in regions under his control.[50] Often, the Nizam sought justification for his conciliatory policies by invoking the memory of Emperor Aurangzeb's failure to militarily crush the Marathas despite being supported by the vast resources of the Mughal Empire.[51]

---

[47] Muhammad Qasim Aurangabadi, Ahwal-ul-Khawaqin, fol. 200a.

[48] Lala Mansaram, Ma'asir-i Nizami, fols. 68b–69b.

[49] This sentiment is echoed in a letter from 1736 where he asserts: 'The operations against the Marathas cannot succeed; although Hazrat Khuld Makan (that is, Aurangzeb) spent a great part of his precious life, poured immeasurable treasure and used his large forces against them (he failed)... If I had the necessary strength to destroy them (that is, the Marathas) and their home-lands, I would not have asked for meetings, mutual consultations, and united action'. Selections of Musavi Jur'at's correspondence on behalf of the Nizam—'Insha'-i Musavi Jur'at'—have been translated by P. S. M. Rao. See 18th Century Deccan (Bombay, 1963), p.140.

[50] Tajalli Ali Shah, Tuzuk-i Asafiya, p. 38. For the historic importance of Marathi as the language of local administration across parts of western India, see generally Sumit Guha, 'Transitions and Translations: Regional Power and Vernacular Identity in the Dakhan, 1500–1800', Comparative Studies of South Asia, Africa and the Middle East 24 (2004), pp. 24–25. The Marathi Modi script continued to be used alongside Persian in some revenue assessment documents from the early nizamate period. M. A. Nayeem, 'Some Aspects of Land Revenue System in the Deccan during the Eighteenth Century', in Studies in History of the Deccan: Professor A. R. Kulkarni Felicitation Volume, eds, M. A. Nayeem, Aniruddha Ray and K. S. Mathew (Delhi: Pragati Publication, 2002), p.194.

[51] See Munshi Ram Singh, Gulshan-i 'Ajaib, fols. 18b-19a, fol. 83b, fol. 117a, fol. 123b.

By the late 1730s, the Nizam's policy of seeking relatively stable relations with the Marathas began to bear both financial and political fruits. The former is borne out by the revival of agriculture (and taxation) across much of the Deccan—even regions like Khandesh that had been devastated by decades of incessant warfare began to recover.[52] On the political front, no longer fearful that the Marathas would take advantage of his absence to crush the state of Hyderabad, the Nizam left the Deccan in order to contest Maratha attempts to control the province of Malwa. The province lay on the northern flank of the nascent Hyderabadi state. More importantly, however, steady relations with Shahu enabled the Nizam increasingly to draw previously hostile Maratha *zamindars* into serving his administration as low-level revenue officials (*deshmukhs*, *amils*, *deshpandias* and *desais*) and revenue contractors (*ijaradars*)— especially in the provinces of Khandesh, Aurangabad and Bijapur (all adjoined the Maratha dominion). Other Marathi-speaking groups were similarly drawn into service in the Hyderabadi state. Among them were various Brahmin groups (but especially Karhades and Deshasthas) who brought highly valued scribal and administrative skills, and crucial political, economic and social networks that reached back into the Maratha state. These links played a key role in fostering ties between Hyderabad and the Marathas. Many Marathi-Brahmans would rise over the coming decades to positions of power and authority within the nizamate.[53]

Of greatest significance, however, was the steady influx of Maratha military men—like Rao Rambha Nimbalkar—who decided that rich

---

[52] Stewart Gordon, 'Burhanpur: Entrepot and Hinterland, 1650–1750', in *Maratha, Marauders, and State Formation in Eighteenth-century India,* ed. Stewart Gordon (Delhi: Oxford University Press, 1994), p. 173.

[53] Prime examples being the brothers Dhodaji Shankar (d. 1783) and Nanaji Shankar (d. 1785) who reached positions of great honour during the reign of the Nizam's fourth son, Nizam Ali Khan (r. 1762–1803). Syed Siraj ul Hassan, *The Castes & Tribes of HE.H. The Nizam's Dominions* (Bombay: Times of India Steam Press, 1920), p. 115. See also 'Risala-i Darbar-i Asafi' which states: 'There are no objections to the Brahmin practicing the profession of wakil'. Cited in Muhammad Mahbub Junaidi, *Hayat-i Asaf,* p. 442. The growing presence and importance of Marathi-speaking Brahmins in the state's administration marked a significant comeback following a loss of influence in the aftermath of the Mughal invasions and the collapse of the sultanates of Bijapur and Golkonda in the 1680s. See generally Stewart Gordon, 'Kinship and Pargana in Eighteenth-century Khandesh', in *Maratha, Marauders, and State Formation in Eighteenth-Century India,* ed. Stewart Gordon, pp. 143–44. For the growing economic and, later, political importance of Marathi-speaking Brahmins at the end of the seventeenth and the beginning of the eighteenth century, see generally Richard M. Eaton, *A Social History of the Deccan, 1300–1761: Eight Indian Lives* (Cambridge: Cambridge University Press, 2005), pp. 191–92.

opportunities for career advancement and wealth now lay in employment with the Nizam.[54] Besides bringing large contingents of Maratha troops with them (supposedly 20,000 in the case of Rao Rambha), they brought badly needed fighting skills (such as the Maratha mastery over fast-moving, horse-based guerilla tactics). The Nizam would use various Maratha commanders, including Rao Rambha, to good effect against not only the Afghans and Berads of southern India, but also fellow Marathas.[55] Warfare nevertheless always remained a second option for the Nizam; whenever possible, he preferred to achieve his goals through diplomacy, compromise and financial incentives.[56] His relations with ethnic groups like the Afghans, Telugus and Berads highlight this policy.

Hyderabad's Relations with Afghans, Telugus and Berads

In the years immediately following the establishment of Hyderabad, Nizam-ul-Mulk faced bitter military resistance from various Afghan, Berad and Telugu groups. This was despite efforts at reconciling high-ranking individuals in each group. Summing up the failure of his conciliatory policies vis-à-vis the Afghans, for example, the Nizam stated:

> Izd-ud-Daula (i.e. 'Iwaz Khan, the Nizam's uncle) wrote to me that I should win over and ally myself with the Afghans... His advice was reasonable. I did my best to give them proper advice. In spite of my efforts, however, the Afghans did not listen to me... it is then that I realized the danger in waiting for this duplicitous group (that is, Afghans) since the Marathas have already entered into an unholy alliance with them.[57]

Between 1725 and 1730, the Nizam launched military campaigns against not only the Afghans, but also the Telugus and Berads as well; all were defeated. The Nizam, however, generally eschewed calls to destroy their power.[58] Instead, he settled on a policy of deliberately including

---

[54] As of the 1970s, Nimbalkar's sumptuous mansion 'Rao Rambha ki Deorhi' was still standing in Hyderabad. H. K. Sherwani, 'Deccan, the Region of Co-existence and Integration', *Medieval India—A Miscellany*, Vol. IV (Bombay: Asia Publishing House, 1977), p. 148.

[55] Muhammad Qasim Aurangabadi, *Ahwal-ul-Khawaqin*, fol. 215b; Munshi Ram Singh, *Gulshan-i 'Ajaib*, fol. 17b., fol. 99a, fol. 125a, fol. 128a.

[56] The 10th clause of the Nizam's will is explicit in its condemnation of war as the primary means towards settling disputes. It states: '. . . as far as possible, it is better to not take the initiative in war... save yourself and your men as best as you can'. Tajalli Ali Shah, *Tuzuk-i Asafiya*, p. 42.

[57] Munshi Ram Singh, *Gulshan-i Ajaib*, fols. 135b–36b.

[58] Only those individuals who proved particularly recalcitrant—like Subbana Rao, the Valama Reddy chief of Gundugolanu—were defeated and killed. The Nizam's patience undoubtedly

them within the apparatus of the Hyderabadi state. Thus, Afghans were confirmed as military intendants (*faujdars*) and fort commandants (*qiladars*) in areas where they had previously dominated (such as Cuddapah, Savanur and Kurnool).[59] In similar fashion, more than a dozen Telugu 'little kingdoms' (*samasthans*) were allowed to retain their autonomy within the Hyderabadi state as long as they paid an annual tribute, contributed a certain number of troops for military campaigns, and occasionally sent representatives to attend the Nizam's *darbar* (court).[60] The Nizam's generous treatment of the Telugu *nayaks* (chiefs) marked a clear departure from the policies pursued by his predecessor, Mubariz Khan, in the early 1720s.[61] The Nizam, however, handled the Berads slightly differently. Arguably because they proved the toughest group to subjugate (alongside ever present fears that they were colluding with the Marathas), the Nizam refused to leave former strongholds— like the fortresses of Wakhinkheda, Sagar, Devadurg—in the possession

was affected by Subbana Rao's long-standing willingness to fight any assertion of authority by non-local, Hyderabad-based rulers. For Subbana Rao's poor prior relations with Mubariz Khan, see generally John F. Richards, *Mughal Administration in Golconda*, pp. 280–83. The Nizam likely was also irritated by the strong support extended by Subbana Rao and his brother Appa Rao of Nuzvid to a 1725 rebellion by Kazim 'Ali Khan, faujdar of Bhongir, who remained an unapologetic loyalist of the now-deceased Mubariz Khan. Akhtar Yar Jang Bahadur, *Ta'rikh-i Dakkan*, p. 318; Yusuf H. Khan, *The First Nizam*, p.137; Muhammad Mahbub Junaidi, *Hayat-i Asaf*, pp. 237–38.

[59] The level of mistrust vis-à-vis the Afghans nevertheless remained high. This is indicated by an incident in 1735 when an Afghan chief was warned off by the Nizam's bodyguards when, during an interview, he drew his elephant too close to that of the Nizam. Muhammad Qasim Aurangabadi, *Ahwal-ul-Khawaqin*, fols. 234b–35a. For other examples of the Nizam's suspicions regarding the Afghans, see Munshi Ram Singh, *Gulshan-i 'Ajaib*, fol. 105b, fol. 106b, fol. 136b.

[60] Ben Cohen, *Hindu Rulers in a Muslim State, 1850–1949* (Ph.D., University of Wisconsin, 2002), pp. 70–71, 79. See also Makhan Lal Shahjahanpuri, *Ta'rikh-i Yadgar-i Makhan Lal*, ed. Maulvi Sayyid Burhanuddin Ahmad (Hyderabad: Matba'-i Burhaniya, 1883), pp. 78–82; Ram Raj Saxsena, *Tazkira-i Darbar-i Hyderabad* (New Delhi: Taraqqi-yi Urdu Buro, 1988), p. 39. For a contemporary Hyderabadi perspective on the subjugation campaigns of the Nizam, see Muhammad Qasim Aurangabadi, *Ahwal-ul-Khawaqin*, fols. 202b–14b. For a contemporary Telugu perspective, see A. G. Pawar, 'Nizam-ul-Mulk Asaf Jah I: From a Telugu Chronology', *Transactions of the Indian History Congress, 5th Session* (1941), pp. 618–21.

[61] 'Mubariz Khan made no attempt to use the services and thus gain the loyalties of the Telugu nayaks... Instead he relied on fear to keep zamindars docile and caution to cause them to disgorge long-unpaid tribute and tax payments'. John F. Richards, *Mughal Administration in Golconda*, p. 301. According to Muhammad Qasim Aurangabadi, however, such policies proved a complete failure. *Ahwal-ul-Khawaqin*, fol. 215a. The Nizam did not remove all safeguards against possible future rebellion. Thus, for example, even as he maintained hostages from various Telugu clans at his court, he also strengthened his control over strategically important fortresses across the region. Akhtar Yar Jang Bahadur, *Ta'rikh i Dakkan*, p. 310. See generally M. A. Nayeem, *Mughal Administration of Deccan under Nizamul Mulk Asaf Jah*, pp. 57–62.

of their *nayaks*.[62] He did, however, allow large numbers of Berad chiefs to become *peshkashi zamindars* (tribute-paying landholders) and *mal-wajib zamindars* (landholders who paid land revenue).[63] He also heavily recruited Berads into the Hyderabadi army and accommodated them within the lower ranks of the nascent Hyderabadi land-revenue administration in southern India.[64] Judging from the lists of *deshmukhs* and *deshpandias* for the region of Hyderabad, large numbers of Telugus were similarly accommodated within the lower ranks of the state's bureaucracy.[65]

The Results of Accommodation

The slow absorption of groups like the Afghans, Telugus, Berads and Marathas within the newly created state structures of Hyderabad was absolutely crucial for its survival. On the most fundamental level, social, political and economic linkages were now forged between different arenas of power. This was important for a number of reasons. First, it began a process whereby the cultural chasm between an almost exclusively Persian-speaking (and often north Indian immigrant) elite and non–Persian-speaking majority was slowly bridged through the use of locally based but state-approved intermediaries. In the decades after 1724 these individuals slowly but surely began to learn at least a modicum of Persian in order to qualify or retain administrative jobs in the emerging Hyderabadi bureaucracy.[66] Second, with the cooptation of local elites

---

[62] Makhan Lal Shahjahanpuri, *Ta'rikh-i Yadgar-i Makhan Lal*, 78; Syed Hossain Bilgrami and C. Willmott, *Historical and Descriptive Sketch of His Highness the Nizam's Dominions*, Vol. II (Bombay: Times of India Steam Press, 1884), p. 438.

[63] See Munshi Ram Singh, *Gulshan-i 'Ajaib*, fol. 99b; M. A. Nayeem, *Mughal Administration of Deccan under Nizamul Mulk Asaf Jah*, pp. 203, 205; Syed Hossain Bilgrami and C. Willmott, *Historical and Descriptive Sketch of His Highness the Nizam's Dominions*, Vol. II, pp. 674, 727.

[64] In the late 1740s, the Nizam warned Anwar-ud-Din Khan—his local representative in Arcot—to avoid land confiscations as they spawn resentment and opposition. Lala Mansaram, 'Risala-i Darbar-i Asafi', cited in M. A. Nayeem, *Mughal Administration of Deccan under Nizamul Mulk Asaf Jah*, p. 93. A few years earlier (in 1743), he had similarly warned Khwaja 'Abdullah Khan (who had been appointed as governor of the Karnatak and Arcot) to continue patronizing people who had been formerly favoured by Sa'datullah Khan (a previous strongman in the region who had actively cultivated Telugus, Tamils and Berads). Lala Mansaram, *Ma'asir-i Nizami*, fol. 77b.

[65] See generally, M. A. Nayeem, *Mughal Administration of Deccan under Nizamul Mulk Asaf Jah*, pp. 198–202. The Telugu Kalpirata script continued to be used alongside Persian in some revenue assessment documents from the early nizamate period. See M. A. Nayeem, 'Some Aspects of Land Revenue System in the Deccan during the Eighteenth Century', pp. 194, 196–97.

[66] Hyderabad's decision to eschew adopting Dakhani—the southern linguistic cousin of northern Hindavi—as its main administrative language highlights a determination to prevent tying the

into potentially lucrative administrative jobs, we see the first signs of political and military investments in the survival of Hyderabad. These are in evidence in the early 1740s when Hyderabad waged a difficult (and successful) military campaign against the Marathas in the southern region of Arcot. Hyderabad's victory was in no small part linked to strong Afghan, Telugu and Berad support. Why did they side with Hyderabad? Unlike the Marathas who sought to implant Maratha and Marathi-speaking land-revenue administrators (*kamaishdars* and *gumashtas*) across the region, Hyderabad had already indicated its willingness to work with/through local power structures and their representatives. Third, although Hyderabad's share of the all-important land-revenue taxes was somewhat compromised by its bargain with powerful local groups, it nonetheless gained access to a regular flow of income that helped it maintain critical financial solvency through the 1740s.[67] Ultimately, nothing mattered more to the state's administrators.

There is a second over-arching reason, however, as to why the absorption of large numbers of Afghans, Telugus, Berads and Marathas (and other groups as well, including Tamils, Bhils and Gonds[68]) ensured Hyderabad's survival: it forced the state to build administrative structures that were flexible, locally adapted and cognizant of limits on its power. Nowhere is this more apparent than in Hyderabad's relationship to Mughal models

new state too closely with former (but now displaced) regional elites or state structures. It also enabled the state to maintain a critical connection to the Mughal imperial legacy. For the significance and also limits of Dakhani as a regional vernacular, see generally Sumit Guha, 'Transitions and Translations: Regional Power and Vernacular Identity in the Dakhan, 1500–1800', pp. 23–31. For Persian's importance as a language of administrative authority in the Deccan, see p. 26.

[67] Hyderabad's desire to maintain positive relations with its *zamindars* is attested by its unwillingness to issue *in'am* (rent and service-free) grants to state-backed outsiders. As the Nizam stated on more than one occasion, giving such grants often causes *zamindars* to revolt. Lala Mansaram, *Ma'asir-i Nizami*, fol. 65b. Such generally prudent policies would enable the state to slowly extend its tentative efforts in 1726–1727 at surveying the tax potential of the territories under its control. For similar accommodations in another 'successor' state, namely Awadh, see Muzaffar Alam, *The Crisis of Empire in Mughal North India: Awadh and the Punjab 1707–1748*, pp. 212–19.

[68] Interestingly, unlike the Marathas who consistently sought to disarm and settle the Bhils of western and central India, the early nizamate barely interfered in Bhil affairs following a successful subjugation campaign in 1726–1727. This enabled generally good relations to evolve. Indeed, the Bhils of the Sahyadri and Satpura mountains were to prove one of the critical bulwarks against Maratha incursions into the northwestern region of Aurangabad from the late 1720s onwards. See generally Syed Siraj ul Hassan, *The Castes & Tribes of HE.H. The Nizam's Dominions*, pp. 66–67, 71. For contrasting Maratha-Bhil/Gond relations in the same period, see Sumit Guha, *Environment and Ethnicity in India 1200–1999* (Cambridge: Cambridge University Press, 1999), pp. 108–30; Stewart Gordon, 'Bhils and the Idea of a Criminal Tribe', in *Maratha, Marauders, and State Formation in Eighteenth-century India*, ed. Stewart Gordon, p. 152.

of administrative control. Even as Hyderabad proclaimed its continuity with Mughal administrative regulations,[69] the reality was quite different; the state consistently broke basic Mughal administrative rules. Thus, for example, officials were not transferred as frequently as required; multiple administrative posts were often combined within a single person; complex processes of bargaining rather than cadastral surveys (although one was taken in 1726–27) tended to determine revenue payments by *zamindars*; many lower-level revenue offices were allowed to become hereditary; and revenue farming (*ijaradari*) was tolerated, albeit reluctantly.[70] These are just some of the many examples of Hyderabad's administrative pragmatism in an environment where a wholesale and rigid application of Mughal imperial models would have been futile at best or provoked massive resistance at worst. Such flexibility was one of Hyderabad's defining early traits and it would be apparent in other areas of the state's identity as well—among them its political relationship to the Mughal court.

Hyderabad and the Mughal Court

Following the Mughal court's abortive 1724 attempt to assert its control over the Deccan, the Nizam did the unexpected. Rather than detach himself from the authority of the empire, he insisted on maintaining the fiction that Hyderabad was a Mughal dependency. This state of affairs would continue until the Nizam's death in 1748. As a result, the Nizam never crowned himself king; he refrained from using marks of imperial authority—such as the colour red or the *chattri* (royal umbrella); he continued to issue coins and have the *khutba* (Islamic Friday sermon) read in the name of Emperor Muhammad Shah (r. 1720–48); official documents continued to use the emperor's regnal year for dating purposes; and the Nizam's own seal—where he called himself a *fidvi* (servant) of Muhammad Shah—attested to his public submission.[71]

---

[69] Hyderabad was not unusual in this regard; even the Marathas, avowed enemies of the Mughals, maintained administrative mechanisms and practices that were 'suspiciously Mughal'. See Stewart Gordon, 'The Slow Conquest: Administrative Integration of Malwa into the Maratha Empire, 1720–1760', in *Maratha, Marauders, and State Formation in Eighteenth-century India*, ed. Stewart Gordon, p. 60.

[70] Most of this information is drawn from M. A. Nayeem's *Mughal Administration of Deccan under Nizamul Mulk Asaf Jah*.

[71] *Ibid.*, p. 19. The Nizam's correspondence with Muhammad Shah also inevitably refers to himself as a servant of the court (*fidvi-i dargah*) or the emperor (*fidvi-i padshah*). For some examples, see Munshi Ram Singh, *Gulshan-i 'Ajaib*, fol. 17b, fol. 101a.

Other actions were similarly intended to highlight the lack of any ill will towards the emperor.[72] Indeed, on his deathbed, the Nizam would importune his heirs to:

> Under all circumstances remember that the governance (*riyasat*) of the Deccan is dependent on our constant service and fidelity to the emperor. It is necessary that you should under no circumstances be remiss in showing the proper respect (*adab*) to the emperor ... You should under no circumstances be cursed (*mat'un*) for violating the bonds of respect.[73]

Why did the Nizam pursue this political course? Why did Hyderabad not conclusively break with the Mughals after 1724?

Scholars have tended to emphasize two reasons for the Nizam's decision. The first claims that the Nizam felt a deep residual loyalty to the Mughal royal family. Pride in his own past as an imperial nobleman led him to maintain his loyalty.[74] The second asserts that since the nizamate was the outcome of Central Asian, Persian and north Indian 'colonization', its political, religious and social traditions remained firmly anchored in a north Indian ecumene. Ultimately, Hyderabad did not break with the empire because its elites were invested in maintaining their cultural roots in the north.[75] Neither of these arguments is entirely satisfying, however. A more convincing explanation stems from asking what Hyderabad stood to lose by maintaining its association with the imperial court.

---

[72] According to the 'Risala-i Darbar-i Asafi' 'the Emperor's royal orders were never disobeyed'." Cited in Muhammad Mahbub Junaidi, *Hayat-i Asaf*, p. 444. Furthermore, the Nizam continued to receive all royal *farmans* (imperial order) with decorum and ceremony; he never failed to congratulate the emperor on birthdays, coronation anniversaries, and 'Id; and he even kept the emperor informed of unfolding political and financial developments in the Deccan. See generally Zahiruddin Malik, *The Reign of Muhammad Shah*, pp. 229, 233. For the Nizam's respectful tone and willingness to keep the Emperor informed about political and military developments in the Deccan, see examples of his correspondence in Munshi Ram Singh, *Gulshan-i Ajaib*, fols. 17b–19a, fols. 83a–84a, fols. 91a–b, fols. 91b–93b, fols. 98b–99b, fols. 111b–12a, fols. 116a–17a, fols. 121b–24a, fols. 135a–39a.

[73] Tajalli Ali Shah, *Tuzuk-i Asafiya*, p. 42.

[74] By far the most common position, best articulated by M. A. Nayeem. See generally, M. A. Nayeem, *Mughal Administration of Deccan under Nizamul Mulk Asaf Jah*, pp. 15–23. Yusuf H. Khan's biography on the Nizam offers an earlier echo of this view. In it he claims that for all his difficulties with the Mughal court, 'his loyalty to the Emperor remained unshaken'. *The First Nizam*, p. 132. See also Muhammad Mahbub Junaidi, *Hayat-i Asaf*, pp. 234–35.

[75] Nile Green states that 'Mughal conquests and the continuance of their imperial claim to the Deccan through the presentation of the Asaf Jahs as their viceroys, redefined the Deccan in ways that are easily blurred from a distance of centuries'. Nile Green, 'Geography, Empire and Sainthood in the Eighteenth-century Muslim Deccan', p. 216. See also pp. 207–08, 225.

The answer appears to be very little. With the imperial court at a safe geographical distance and the Maratha state acting as a political barrier, the emperor could not intervene in Hyderabad's local affairs.[76] The attempt to pit Mubariz Khan against the Nizam in fact marked Emperor Muhammad Shah's final hand. After 1724, the Nizam ensured that all imperial officials remaining in the Deccan swore loyalty to him alone or else forfeited rank and position.

It may be argued that, by maintaining its ties to the imperial centre, Hyderabad was sacrificing its ability to forge a new non-Mughal and non-imperial identity, one that was in greater synch with the regional politics of peninsular India. While there may have been some truth to this assertion at the level of elite politics, Hyderabad's extra-imperial links actually seem to have had little to no impact on its stature at the local level—the level at which taxes were levied, foot soldiers recruited and social connections forged. Here the state was being judged purely on its ability to provide financial and political accommodations for various regional and local ethnic groups.

What, then, did Hyderabad gain through its fictive allegiance to the emperor in distant Delhi? Muzaffar Alam has highlighted the important role the Mughal court played in bestowing 'institutional validation' on 'successor' states that desperately needed to 'legitimize their acquisitions'. According to Alam, recognition by the Mughal court was crucial to negotiate relations between 'successor' states as well as to reinforce the new elites' dominance over local groups in their respective regions.[77] While Hyderabad certainly was interested in maintaining stable relations with other post-Mughal states,[78] Mughal validation itself arguably offered few advantages to the Nizam in his attempts to dominate such Deccan-based groups as the Marathas, Telugus, Berads or Afghans. But it did play a significant role in Hyderabad's desire to entice southward immigration from the old heartlands of the Mughal Empire, a task that appears to have been somewhat difficult.

[76] Contrast this situation with that of the Punjab (and to a lesser degree Awadh) where imperial interference was an important destabilizing factor. See Muzaffar Alam, *The Crisis of Empire in Mughal North India: Awadh and the Punjab 1707–1748*, pp. 15–16.

[77] *Ibid.*, pp. 16–17.

[78] The Nizam's continued interest in maintaining a hand on the pulse of the Mughal court is evidenced in his willingness to marry his son, Nasir Jang, to the daughter of one of Emperor Muhammad Shah's favourite noblemen, Zafar Khan Roshan-ud-Daula, in 1730–31; his acceptance of the post of *mir bakhshi* (imperial paymaster-general) in the aftermath of Nadir Shah's invasion; and his appointment of Ghazi-ud-Din Khan, his eldest son, as his *na'ib* (deputy) at the Mughal court between 1740 and 1748.

In an essay on Sufism in eighteenth-century Deccan, Nile Green writes 'prior to as well as during the eighteenth century the Deccan was very much felt to be a different country from Hindustan (that is, northern India)'.[79] Besides physical distances being great and journeys between the two regions arduous, Hyderabad had to contend with widespread perceptions among northerners that the south was a completely alien political and cultural zone. One way in which Hyderabad hoped to parry such negative views was by reassuringly emphasizing both its lineage and continuing links to the Mughal Empire. All of this ultimately mattered only because Hyderabad was desperate to draw upon the remaining administrative, military and cultural resources of the now increasingly defunct Mughal Empire in order to build itself up. Raising the stakes for Hyderabad, however, was intense competition for the same resources from all manner of northern 'successor states'.

Despite this competition, Hyderabad was very successful in its recruitment efforts. This was due in large part to its continuing connection with the Mughals. Indeed many north Indians viewed the state as a robust imperial dependency.[80] The Nizam, however, also proved a master recruiter. When he marched back to the Deccan after a two-year stint in Delhi between 1738 and 1740, for example, he returned with thousands of administrators, religious scholars, intellectuals, military men and master craftsmen in tow. He seems to have personally recruited many of them. Equally significant to Hyderabad's success in recruitment was the fact that it benefited from diminishing competition from major post-Mughal states in the late 1730s and 1740s: the Punjab was increasingly consumed by Sikh rebellions, Awadh was moving towards a narrower definition of itself as a Shiite state, and Bengal was weakened by Maratha invasions and political instability. Ultimately, Hyderabad's success in attracting the talented and the adventurous can be seen in the arrival of large numbers of often highly skilled and educated Punjabi Khatris, north Indian Kayasths, Shaikhzadas and Awadhis, and ethnic Iranians and Central Asians. Others who joined this influx included trading, cultivating and warrior groups as the Banjaras, Bundelas, Afghans, Kurmis, Kumbis and Kachhis. Although the sources are extremely sketchy, it is also clear that

---

[79] Nile Green, 'Geography, Empire and Sainthood in the Eighteenth-century Muslim Deccan', p. 216.

[80] Even today some historians consider 'restoring the Mughal conquests in the Deccan' as among the Nizam's greatest achievements. See M. A. Nayeem, *Mughal Administration of Deccan under Nizamul Mulk Asaf Jah*, p. 230.

many north Indian moneylenders and small-scale bankers (*sahukars*) took advantage of recently created familial networks (particularly true for Punjabi Khatris) and conditions of greater security offered by Hyderabad to move to the Deccan in the 1730s and 1740s.[81] Indeed, massive waves of migration from north India to the Deccan comprise one of the great-untold stories of the early-to-mid eighteenth century.

Hyderabad's relations towards Deccan-based ethnic groups as well as the Mughal Empire provide important illustrations of its keen instinct for survival. This story, however, would not be complete without examining one final area—namely Hyderabad's relationship to Islam and Hinduism.

Of Islam and Hinduism

There is a line of scholars extending back to such contemporaries of the Nizam as Khafi Khan and Ghulam Ali Azad Bilgrami who have claimed that Hyderabad was an Islamic bastion in the Deccan.[82] The historical evidence is far more ambiguous, however. The Nizam's political correspondence exemplifies this.

When corresponding about the Marathas with the Mughal emperor, Muhammad Shah, the Nizam often describes his forces as 'holy warriors' (*ghaziyan* or *mujahidan*),[83] or an 'army of Islam' (*lashkar-i Islam* or *fauj-i Islam*)[84] who were engaged in a '*jihad*'[85] aimed at upholding the 'prestige of Islam' (*ghairat-i Islam*)[86] against the '*kafirs*'.[87] This overblown rhetoric

---

[81] For references to the presence and importance of bankers (*sahukars*) or merchants at the Nizam's court, see Lala Mansaram, 'Risala-i Darbar-i Asafi', cited in Muhammad Mahbub Junaidi, *Hayat-i Asaf*, pp. 438, 440, 442. See also M. A. Nayeem, *Mughal Administration of Deccan under Nizamul Mulk Asaf Jah*, pp. 89, 90; Omar Khalidi, 'Business Rajas: The Gujaratis, Gosains, and Marwaris of Hyderabad', *Deccan Studies* 4 (2006), p. 54. The significance of maintaining good relations with *sahukars* even comes up in the 13th clause of the Nizam's last will. In it he states that the presence of both treasure and *sahukars* on one's side will cause extreme distress (*parishan wa mutalashi*) to an enemy and his army. Tajalli Ali Shah, *Tuzuk-i Asafiya*, p. 42. For a comparative discussion of Khatris in the Punjab, see Muzaffar Alam, *The Crisis of Empire in Mughal North India: Awadh and the Punjab 1707–1748*, pp. 169–75.

[82] Khafi Khan, *Muntakhab-ul-Lubab*, Vol. II, Part II, p. 972; Ghulam 'Ali Azad Bilgrami, *Rauzat-ul-Auliya'*, ed. Nisar Ahmad Faruqi (Delhi, 1996), p. 113.

[83] Munshi Ram Singh, *Gulshan-i 'Ajaib*, fol. 83b, fol. 94a, fol. 97b, fol. 104b, fol. 119b, fol. 130a.

[84] *Ibid.*, fol. 80b, fol. 97a, fol. 98a, fol. 98b, fol. 99b, fol. 110b, fol. 117b, fol. 118a, fol. 199b, fol. 124a, fol. 125b.

[85] *Ibid.*, fol. 112a, fol. 116b, fol. 117b, fol. 122b, fol. 124a, fol. 130a.

[86] *Ibid.*, fol. 92b, fol. 93b, fol. 95b.

[87] *Ibid.*, fol. 17b, fol. 18a, fol. 84a, fol. 116a, fol. 122a, fol. 122b, fol. 125b.

is not surprising given that the Marathas were the Mughals' sworn enemies and played a key role in the Empire's collapse. At the same time, the Nizam's language followed standard conventions and forms that dated back to the reign of Aurangzeb and were used by Muslim and non-Muslim employees of the Mughal state alike.[88]

When corresponding with others, however, the Nizam's language rarely drew on this normative Islamo-Mughal vocabulary. The Nizam's correspondence with Sawai Jai Singh II, a non-Muslim, non-Mughal ruler, provides an example of this. Here the Marathas are only referred to as 'misguided people', 'Marathas', the 'enemy', or 'partisans of Shahu'.[89] Reading these two sets of correspondence without reference to the other it is easy to reach diametrically opposing judgments about the Nizam— committed *jihadi* or droll politician. More likely, the Nizam was a pragmatic ruler who understood the importance of contingency—tailoring different languages for different actors/audiences and situations. The same judgment seems applicable to Hyderabad's relationship to Muslims and Hindus.

Hyderabad undoubtedly placed great store in cultivating Islamic religious groups. Valued for their widespread social contacts, their political connections, their literacy, their judicial skills and (more than occasionally) their military competence, these groups were an invaluable component in Hyderabad's larger efforts at state formation. The task of honouring and cultivating Muslim religious figures therefore was taken seriously. This is attested by both the Nizam's words and actions. Thus, on his deathbed, the Nizam enjoined his successors to remember that:

> . . . the respect and esteem in which I hold the community of supplicants (*firqa-i duagu*) has been constant. Without them no army will be of any use. I respect them above all other affairs of the state. I receive strength and courage from the mendicants (*ghurba*) and the *faqirs*. I consider them as the gateway to God. They are the followers of the Prophet. I consider it my primary duty to treat them with respect. You should also favour this practice.[90]

Such statements were complemented by direct efforts at cultivating all manner of Muslim religious figures. Thus, for example, the Nizam

[88] See generally, Ishwardas Nagar, *Futuhat-i Alamgiri*, trans. M. F. Lokhandwala and Jadunath Sarkar (Baroda: Oriental Institute, 1995), Bhimsen Saxsena, *Ta'rikh-i Dilkusha*, trans. V. G. Khobrekar (Bombay: Dept. of Archives, Maharashtra, 1972), and Bakhtawar Khan, *Mirat-ul-'Alam*, ed. Sajida Alvi (Lahore: Idarah-i Tahqiqat-i Pakistan, 1979).

[89] 'Two historical letters of the Great Asaf Jah I', trans. Jadunath Sarkar, *Islamic Culture* 15 (1941), pp. 341–42.

[90] Tajalli Ali Shah, *Tuzuk-i Asafiya*, p. 40.

forged close personal relations with a large number of distinguished Sufis across a number of different *tariqas* (orders).[91] Significantly, he also chose to be buried in the shrine complex of Shaikh Burhan-ud-Din Gharib (in Khuldabad). In so doing, the Nizam directly connected the political legitimacy of his family with the spiritual legitimacy of not only the powerful Deccan-based branch of the Chishti *tariqa* and the Chishti *tariqa* across India, but even the Mughal dynasty itself (which had a long and storied history of patronage towards the Chishtis).[92]

The Nizam accorded great importance to honouring non-Sufi Islamic religious scholars and clerics (*'ulama*) as well.[93] In fact, Hyderabad's reputation for generosity supposedly spread so rapidly and widely that, according to one contemporary source, *'ulama* arrived from Arabia (Hejaz), Central Asia (Mawara-al-nahr), Iran ('Ajam), Iraq and northern-eastern Iran (Khurasan) to benefit from the promise of honour and financial security.[94] Among those arriving from closer afield were large numbers of religious scholars from northern India. Many, having lost their stipends and imperial patronage, were looking for fresh beginnings in Hyderabad. The region of Awadh was particularly well represented in this migration.[95]

Despite clear indications of Hyderabad's munificence and respect for Muslim religious figures, its generosity had real practical limits. Nowhere is this more apparent than the state's unwillingness to grant *in'am* (rent-

---

[91] Among them were such Deccan-based luminaries as Shaykh Nizam-ud-Din Aurangabadi (d. 1731)—who, it has been suggested, initiated the Nizam into the Chishti order—Saiyid Inayat Mujtaba, Saiyid Ahmad Gosfandalah (d. 1719–20), Shah Janullah (d. 1727–28.), Shah Daud, Saiyid Shah 'Abdul Qadiri (d. 1746), Shah Ghulam Muhammad, and Pirzada Saiyid Husain. For an instance of his patronage of the tomb of Shah Abdul Qadir (in Aurangabad), see Lala Mansaram, *Ma'asir-i Nizami*, fols. 59a-b.

[92] See generally Nile Green, 'Geography, Empire and Sainthood in the Eighteenth-century Muslim Deccan', p. 215.

[93] According to the 'Risala-i Darbar-i Asafi', the first order of business at the Nizam's court entailed a daily review of charity grants. Depending on a person's need, cash grants were given for a daughter's marriage, for undertaking the hajj, or gaining an education. Rare was the occasion when thirty to forty thousand rupees were not granted in a single session. Cited in Muhammad Mahbub Junaidi, *Hayat-i Asaf*, p. 439. See also instructions for regular calls to prayer to ensure full attendance in mosques and orders demanding that all *qazis* and (Muslim) district officials attend Eid prayers. *Ibid.*, p. 444.

[94] Ghulam 'Ali Azad Bilgrami, *Khizana-i 'Amra* (Lucknow, 1871), p. 38. See also Muhammad Mahbub Junaidi, *Hayat-i Asaf*, p. 395.

[95] This is indicated by the arrival of many imminent scholars from Bilgram—including Ghulam 'Ali Azad Bilgrami, Wasiti Bilgrami Hanifi Chishti and Azad bin Saiyid Muhammad Nuh Husaini—and Lucknow—particularly Maulvi Haidar Lakhnavi Farangi Mahali.

free) grants to religious figures (*a'imma*) in areas where such grants might provoke *zamindari* hostility. This policy effectively restricted the *a'imma*—and especially recent migrants to the Deccan—from settling outside most urban centres or even in large swathes of southern India. The attempt essentially to quarantine the Muslim religious class in urban areas was a powerful departure from earlier Mughal policy that especially encouraged settlement in areas that were deemed seditious or rebellious (*zortalab*).[96] Hyderabad departed from post-1691 Mughal policy in other significant ways as well: it essentially entrusted *zamindars* with the authority to report any illicit attempts by the *a'imma* to transfer or exchange land specifically granted for religious purposes.[97] It also refused to allow *madad-i ma'ash* grants (assignments of rent-free lands to support religious families) to become automatically inheritable.[98] This is an especially interesting position given that Hyderabad actually loosened previously strict Mughal regulations governing the inheritability of offices within the land-revenue administration. We might conclude, then, that Hyderabad had no real interest in cultivating the entrenchment of Islamic religious classes, but did wish to encourage the emergence of a locally based, ethnically diverse and mostly non-Muslim revenue-collecting intermediary class. If limits on the inheritability of *madad* grants marked an important curb on the Islamic religious establishment, continuous efforts to reform the system of daily allowances and cash stipends (*wazifa*)—ostensibly to root out corruption and mismanagement—effectively undermined any possibility of entrenched Islamic privilege.[99]

The ambiguities that are apparent in Hyderabad's dealings with the Islamic religious establishment are on similar display in its relations with non-Muslims. Taking the Nizam's own words as a case in point, it is impossible to ignore the fifteenth clause in his final testament:

> The Dakhini Brahmins are all fit to be killed and their heads severed. Special mention should be made of two leaders (*sar-i guruh*) of this com-

---

[96] Muzaffar Alam, *The Crisis of Empire in Mughal North India: Awadh and the Punjab 1707–1748*, pp. 116–17, 121–22.

[97] Lala Mansaram, 'Risala-i Darbar-i Asafi', cited in Muhammad Mahbub Junaidi, *Hayat-i Asaf*, p. 443. Following a different trajectory vis-à-vis the *a'imma* class, the state of Awadh used loyalist zamindars to crush them militarily. See generally Muzaffar Alam, *The Crisis of Empire in Mughal North India: Awadh and the Punjab 1707–1748*, pp. 117–33, 219–24, 241.

[98] M. A. Nayeem, *Mughal Administration of Deccan under Nizamul Mulk Asaf Jah*, p 197

[99] Lala Mansaram, *Ma'asir-i Nizami*, fol. 60a-b.

munity: one is Moru and the other is Ramdas. These two have been undermining the state (*daulat*) for a hundred years. I have imprisoned them...
They should never be released! The word *Pandit Khana* is well known in
the world. It means the house of imprisonment of this community.[100]

The vituperative and anger is apparent. Yet how are we to make sense
of this statement if we juxtapose it with the seventh clause in his will?

. . . After me it would be fitting if every family is taken care of and
employed by the government according to their merits—regardless of
whether they belong to the Muslim or Hindu community (*che az firqa-i
ahl-i Islam wa che az firqa-i Hunud*).[101]

Or, the 9th clause of his will in which he pointedly praises Puran
Chand, his Hindu *diwan* (revenue and finance minister), for being a
'good man' who deserves security of tenure following the Nizam's
demise?[102]

Indeed, the Nizam's actions and Hyderabadi state policies largely point
to a non-sectarian attitude towards non-Muslims. Most importantly, the
Nizam unequivocally rejected calls for the imposition of the *jizya* (poll
tax on non-Muslims);[103] he allowed Hindus to continue to have civil and,
in certain instances, criminal cases be tried by local councils (*panchayats*)
where Islamic law was not *de rigueur*;[104] he extended the state's patronage to
Marathi-speaking Brahmans as well as Khatris, Kayasthas and other Hindu
groups;[105] and he occasionally took personal charge of the upbringing of
non- Muslim boys—like Raja Sagar Mal—whose families had served him
with devotion.[106] Finally, in a case of no gesture being too small, the Nizam

---

[100] Tajalli 'Ali Shah, *Tuzuk-i Asafiya*, p. 43.

[101] *Ibid.*, p. 41.

[102] *Ibid.*, p. 41–42.

[103] M.A. Muttalib, *Administration of Justice under the Nizams, 1724–1948* (Hyderabad, 1988), p. 66.

[104] *Ibid.*, p. 32.

[105] For Hindu participation in the early history of Hyderabad's formation, see generally, Makhan
Lal Shahjahanpuri, *Ta'rikh-i Yadgar-i Makhan Lal*, pp. 66–76. For a snapshot view from the
1820s, see Makhan Lal Shahjahanpuri, *Ta'rikh-i Yadgar-i Makhan Lal*, pp. 149–64; for the
1830s and early 1840s, see Ghulam Husain Khan, *Ta'rikh-i Asaf Jahiyan*, ed. Muhammad Me-
hdi Tavassoli (Islamabad: Marhaz-i Tahqiqat-i Farsi-i Iran va Pakistan, 1999), pp. 233–67. For
short biographical notices of important Hindu-Hyderabadi figures between the eighteenth and
the twentieth centuries, see Sayyid Iltifat Khan, *Nigaristan-i Asafi* (Hyderabad: Aziz al-Matba',
1910), pp. 90–106. For a post-eighteenth-century case study of a single caste group—the
Kayasths—see Karen Leonard, *Social History of an Indian Caste: The Kayasths of Hyderabad*
(Berkeley: University of California Press, 1978).

[106] Muhammad Mahbub Junaidi, *Hayat-i Asaf*, pp. 428–29.

also ordered that special food and grain arrangements be made for Hindus during military or administrative tours.[107] Whether these and other gestures were informed by a true lack of animus towards non-Muslims or whether they were based on the practical reality that Hyderabad needed qualified people to serve it, regardless of their religious affiliations, is impossible to answer. This much, however, can be said: Hyderabad's religious policies were undoubtedly tempered by the knowledge that the vast majority of the Nizam's subjects were not Muslim. Having watched Aurangzeb stir up a hornet's nest with religious actions that may have seemed principled, but were clearly not politic, may the Nizam have been hoping to avoid the same fate two decades later and in the same region?

III. CONCLUSION

Two shortcomings commonly appear in histories of both the Hyderabadi state and the Deccan. On the one hand, we witness a widespread failure to distinguish the dynamic early career of Hyderabad from its often lethargic and later counterpart. Even individuals familiar with the charged ethnic and religious politics of post-1930s Hyderabad project (incorrectly) the same history to the first decades of Hyderabad's existence. On the other hand, important characteristics of nineteenth- and twentieth-century Hyderabad are often seen as being anomalous and idiosyncratic, in other words disconnected from an earlier history. Thus, important points of continuity are often overlooked. For example, the state's continuing dependence (well into the nineteenth and twentieth centuries) on a steady stream of immigrants from north India—both Hindu and Muslim—to enable administrative expansion was a pattern first set up by Nizam-ul-Mulk. Also, many of the political and economic compromises reached by the Nizam remained in place through the rest of Hyderabad's history. This is attested by the survival of a number of Telugu 'little kingdoms' (*samasthans*) into the twentieth century and administrative patterns that relied heavily on *zamindars* for the collection of revenue and the maintenance of law and order. An essentially non-sectarian approach to relations between different religious communities would similarly survive for much of the state's history.

---

[107] Lala Mansaram, 'Risala-i Darbar-i Asafi', cited in M. A. Nayeem, *Mughal Administration of Deccan under Nizamul Mulk Asaf Jah*, p. 89.

Through the years of its existence Hyderabad faced many political, military and financial crises. In every instance it was able to overcome its challenges through a combination of luck, pluck and commonsense. These qualities, however, proved to be in increasingly short supply through the reign of the seventh and final Nizam, Osman Ali Khan Asaf Jah VII (r. 1911–48). Unlike his ancestor, Nizam-ul-Mulk, who successfully weathered the transition from an imperial to post-imperial order, Osman Ali Khan proved unable to master the shift from a colonial to post-colonial order. Buffeted by the winds of anti-British secular, Hindu, Telugu and Islamic nationalisms, the last Nizam proved unable to steer a course that would have protected some vestige of the old Hyderabadi order. How might the Nizam have acted in the same situation? Although historians need to be careful with counterfactuals, in this case it is well to speculate that the first Nizam would have likely avoided staking his career on upholding an older and dying political order. Instead, he would have probably negotiated, bargained and received an honoured space for himself within the newly emerging order. After all, flexibility and opportunism were hallmarks of his career. Nothing attests to this more than the remarkable story of his transition from a loyal Mughal *khanazad* to a post-Mughal ruler in the Deccan and Hyderabad's early survival against all odds.

2

The Ignored Elites:
Turks, Mongols and a Persian Secretarial Class in the Early Delhi Sultanate

SUNIL KUMAR[*]

———— • ✦ • ————

INTRODUCING THE SULTANATE FRONTIER MILITARY COMMANDERS

Social and political formations in the Indus and Gangetic plains were not unduly troubled by political developments in the mountainous Hindu Kush or Karakorum regions in the north-west. These lands were too poor and fragmented to support large state systems and the pastoral inhabitants of the area indulged in relatively localized plundering expeditions into the plains. Although trade routes into Iran and Central

[*] This essay is a part of a larger study on Tughluqabad, which will be incorporated in my forthcoming book provisionally titled *Sites of Power and Resistance: A Study of Sultanate Monumental Architecture*. An earlier version of 'Tughluqabad' and this essay was drafted years ago under the supervision of John F. Richards. I am extremely grateful to him for his comments, for all his kindness and support while I was at Duke. Earlier incarnations of the essay profited from the comments of David Gilmartin, Sanjay Subrahmanyam, Kristen Neuschel, Charles Young, Steven Wilkinson, Judith Dillon, Joe Arlinghaus, Michael McFarland and Ann Farnsworth. The comments of audiences at Delhi University, Jawaharlal Nehru University, Delhi School of Sociology, Columbia University and the Ecole Pratique des Hautes Etudes, Paris were extremely useful during revisions. This version of the essay was presented at the conference on 'Expanding Frontiers in South Asian and World History' held at Duke University in 29–30 September 2006. I would like to thank participants at the conference for their comments, the anonymous referee for the careful reading of the essay, and Anjali Kumar for patient discussions on the subject.

Asia were more easily disturbed by the turbulent politics of the region, Afghanistan seized the attention of political regimes in north India only when the area became a part of larger geopolitical developments. In the tenth through the twelfth centuries this happened when the Ghaznavid and Ghurid regimes attempted to sustain their control over eastern Iran by the revenues extracted from north India. The challenges posed by these developments were completely dwarfed by the Chinggisid invasions of the thirteenth centuries. The Mongols seized much of western Punjab and periodically threatened the Gangetic plains, destroying agriculture, displacing pastoralists and pillaging cities. Beyond the very real threat of Mongol depredations was the 'great fear' that gripped the land in the 1220s and after, when it seemed as if a holocaust of proportions already witnessed in eastern Iran, Transoxiana, and Afghanistan was awaiting north India.[1]

The need to secure the Sultanate regime from Mongol marauders led to the delineation of a 'frontier' that needed to be defended. At least during the early thirteenth century this was carried out through garrisoned cantonments in the Punjab. These cantonments were placed under trusted slave-commanders, the *bandagan-i khass*, of the monarch. They were of Turkish origin, but the patronage of their master, together with systematic efforts to bond and incorporate them in the household of the monarch, oriented their allegiance away from their ethnic roots and towards the realm of Delhi. Judging by their military records, Turkish slaves did not hesitate in opposing the invading Mongol hordes, which carried in their train a large number of Turks. In other words, shared ethnicities notwithstanding, Sultanate commanders on the frontier were acculturated to serve a regime that oriented them in ways quite distinct from their original steppe habitats.[2] The frontier between the Mongols and the Sultanate was therefore marked by different cultural and political orientations, even if the social groups who inhabited the region were not always dissimilar.

This essay is concerned with developments of a slightly later period—the decades after the 1250s—when political fragmentation

---

[1] For a useful account of Mongol invasions into north India during the thirteenth and fourteenth centuries see Peter Jackson, 'The Mongols in India', Cambridge University, Department of History, Ph.D. dissertation, 1976.

[2] See Sunil Kumar, 'When Slaves were Nobles: The Shamsi *Bandagan* in the Early Delhi Sultanate', *Studies in History* 10 (1994), pp. 23–52 and idem, 'Service, Status, and Military Slavery in the Delhi Sultanate: Thirteenth and Fourteenth Centuries', in *Slavery and South Asian History*, eds Richard Eaton and Indrani Chatterjee (Bloomington: Indiana University Press, 2006), pp. 83–114.

within the Delhi Sultanate and the Mongol confederacies complicated relationships across the Punjab frontier. In the years after Shams al-Din Iltutmish's death (1236) increasing competition amongst Sultanate slave commanders drove discontented *amirs* into alliances with the Mongols.[3] Concurrently, the old concordance amongst the Chinggisid descendants was ending and the lands of eastern Iran, Afghanistan and Transoxiana were populated by rival political dispensations. Internal conflict and the search for alternative opportunities pushed many Mongol commanders and their subordinates into Hindustan and the service of the Delhi Sultans.[4] Although Mongol raids into north India continued through the second half of the thirteenth century, there was considerable migration of Mongol and Turkic groups searching for Sultanate patronage and instances of disaffected Sultanate *amirs* looking for allies in Mongol camps.

In focusing upon the second half of the thirteenth and the early fourteenth century, the first part of the essay draws attention to the recruitment of frontiersmen by successive Sultanate regimes to guard the Punjab marches from Mongol depredations. The old traditions of policing the frontier by slave commanders slowly shifted to include new bodies of immigrants who had intruded into the region. These developments were first noticeable in the reign of Balban (1266–87) and Kaiqubad (1287–90) and then more apparent during the succeeding Khalaji regime (1290–1320). Political fortunes in the marches of the Punjab, areas that lay in the interstices between the Mongol and Sultanate dominions, fluctuated constantly and military successes (and failures) were often transient. Service here, remote, as it was, from the cohering and disciplinary structures of Delhi, also allowed for great opportunities. Ambitious Sultanate commanders adroitly used frontier manpower resources to accumulate large war bands and construct local reputations as warriors and patrons even as they remained marginal, distant groups in the courtly intrigues of the capital. And yet, when the opportunity

---

[3] Note the examples of the Shamsi slaves Qutlugh Khan and Kushlu Khan, competitors at different times with Ulugh Khan for influence over the Delhi Sultan, both of whom sought sanctuary with the Mongols. Slightly earlier, Ulugh Khan had supported the Shamsi prince Jalal al-Din Mas'ud who had fled to the Mongols for sanctuary in 1248. Ulugh Khan's cousin, Shir Khan, had also sought sanctuary for a brief time with the Mongols. See Peter Jackson, *The Delhi Sultanate: A Political and Military History* (Cambridge: Cambridge University Press, 1999), pp. 73, 88–89, 111–14.

[4] Peter Jackson, 'The Dissolution of the Mongol Empire', *Central Asiatic Journal* 22 (1978), pp. 186–244, idem, *The Delhi Sultanate*, pp. 80–82, 115–16.

presented itself, these frontier commanders possessed sufficient assets and initiative to march into Delhi, seize power and establish their own dynasties. Nor were these exceptional moments in the history of the Sultanate. Although in this essay I study the Khalajis peripherally and give greater attention to the early Tughluq regime, it is important to note that every Sultanate dynasty from 1290 through 1526—the Khalaji, Tughluq, Sayyid and the Lodis—had frontier origins.

The following sections of the essay unravel the social and cultural backgrounds of the frontier commanders and study the ways in which these might have complicated their relationship with Delhi. During the Khalaji regime many of the frontier commanders and their contingents were of Turkish or Mongol background and had a record of past service with Chinggisid subordinates active in the Afghanistan region. Hence the curious paradox in the deployment of these commanders: many of the frontiersmen patronized by the Delhi Sultans shared a history of past service and cultural affinities with the very people who periodically threatened the Sultanate.[5] Although their loyalties and investments in the cause of the Delhi Sultans must have been adequately ascertained to justify their deployment, these frontier commanders had not undergone the processes of training and acculturation characteristic of the *bandagan-i khass*. They were not a deracinated group but had arrived in the Sultanate with intact lineage networks and were linked to significant parts of their retinues by shared natal, ethnic and/or past service associations. Although they had accepted service with the Delhi Sultans and went on to become monarchs themselves, we are indifferently informed about the extent to which these military commanders and their retinues had made the transition from their old steppe-descended, frontier milieus to the urbane world of Delhi. Certainly, prior to their arrival as Sultans, Delhi's literati had looked askance at people of similar social and cultural profiles. What was their reaction when groups of frontiersmen arrived in the capital as lords and masters?

As I argue in this essay, not only is the evidence on this subject extremely scanty, it is also deliberately evasive. The discourse of the fourteenth-century Persian historical narratives (*tawarikh*) carried their author's vision of an ideal public order tempered by their class, cultural and ethnic prejudices. This was transcribed into an idealized history of the court of

---

[5] For a valuable comparison from China see, Owen Lattimore, 'Frontier Feudalism', in *Studies in Frontier History, Collected Papers, 1928–1958* (London: Oxford Univeristy Press, 1962), pp. 514–41.

Sultan Mahmud Ghaznavi and held as a touchstone of good governance to be followed by future generations. These social and intellectual precommitments meant that the lords and masters of Delhi could not be reported as frontiersmen or ex-servants of the loathed Chinggisids. To have done so would have conveyed the sense of a Sultanate in crisis and decline.[6] To communicate the sense of stability and order, on the other hand, frontier commanders like Ghiyas al-Din Tughluq had to be creatively reinvented as paradigms of virtue, a veritable 'saviour of Islam'.

Although the narratives of Sultanate histories were selective in their inclusion of information, there were other more episodic records that provided incidental information on the backgrounds of the Delhi Sultans. I use these not just to detail the frontier origins of the monarchs of Delhi, or study the impact of their arrival as Sultans on a world that had only recently treated them as 'rustics'. As I argue in the concluding sections of the essay, it is crucial for historians today to draw attention to the ways in which the chronicles and eulogies of the Delhi Sultans ignored crucial aspects about their protagonists, how their silences and elisions (and sometimes their ignorance) misrepresented the character of their patrons. It is absolutely vital that we foreground the discursive intervention of the Persian chronicles in their representations of Sultanate history because without a sensitivity to their objectives and their prejudices we will never be able to disengage and texture their representations of a monolithic Islam, a hegemonic state and a timeless Persianate culture. Retrieving the history of the frontier military commanders allows us to recall the role of a vital, if marginalised, group of people involved in the framing of Sultanate history. That these marginalised groups happened to be the political elites and Sultans of Delhi is in itself a telling commentary on the state of the evidence and the dire need to renarrativise the history of the Sultanate. To that end this essay starts with an analysis of the reportage on the Khalajis and the Tughluqs during their deployment as frontier commanders.

THE ORIGIN OF THE KHALAJIS AND TUGHLUQS AS FRONTIER COMMANDERS

Trying to follow the early history of the founders of the Khalaji and Tughluq regimes is easier said than done. Despite the importance of Jalal

---

[6] For a discussion of these kinds of narratives see Sunil Kumar, 'Service, Status and Military Slavery', pp. 97–102.

al-Din Khalaji (1290–96) and Ghiyas al-Din Tughluq (1320–24) in the history of the Sultanate, Persian chronicles are remarkably silent about their frontier backgrounds. It is from a fifteenth-century chronicle that we know the name of Jalal al-Din Khalaji's father, Yughrush.[7] We have to turn to Il-Khanid chronicles to learn that Jalal al-Din was the Mongol commander (*shahna*) of Binban, just west of the Indus.[8] Amir Khusrau quotes him on his exploits against refractory Mongol and Afghan tribes in the Salt range. He does not provide any context to these events which, if not hyperbole, might have occurred before he joined service with the Delhi Sultans.[9] An incidental reference in Juzjani informs us that the son of Yughrush (Jalal al-Din?) visited Delhi with a Mongol embassy in 1260.[10] It is not clear when Jalal al-Din started serving the Delhi Sultans but it must have been a few years later, sometime during Balban's reign. 'Isami mentions that he was in the service of Balban's younger son, Prince Bughra Khan.[11] The account is chronologically unclear but this must have occurred before 1280 while the Prince was still located in Samana, a town which would later become Jalal al-Din's headquarters. Jalal al-Din's political influence increased as commander of the north-west marches until Sultan Kaiqubad invited him to the capital as a counterweight to the old Balbani elites and the new parvenu commanders entrenched in Delhi. Although given the exalted title of Shaista Khan and the military assignment of Baran, Jalal al-Din found it difficult to integrate himself in the politics of the court especially with the murder of the young Sultan. Faced with political marginalization, he acted against the clique who controlled the capital and seized the throne in 1290. Even after his accession, insurrection led by members of the old regime continued and it was not until 1292 that his reign approximated some degree of stability.[12]

---

[7] Yahya Sirhindi, *Ta'rikh-i Mubarak Shahi*, ed. M. Hidayat Husain (Calcutta: Asiatic Society of Bengal, 1931), p. 61. The text has Bughrush, which must be a mistake for Yughrush the form found in Minhaj-i Siraj Juzjani, *Tabaqat-i Nasiri*, ed. Abd al-Hayy Habibi (Kabul: Anjuman-i Ta'rikh-i Afghanistan, 1963–64, 2 vols.), Vol. 2, p. 88.

[8] Cited in Peter Jackson, *The Delhi Sultanate*, p. 80.

[9] Amir Khusrau, *Miftah al-Futuh*, ed. Shaikh Abdur Rashid (Aligarh: Publication of the Department of History, Aligarh Muslim University, 1954), p. 8. Peter Jackson, *The Delhi Sultanate*, p. 118 suggests a later date for these campaigns. The evidence is ambiguous on this point.

[10] Juzjani, *Tabaqat-i Nasiri*, Vol. 2, p. 88.

[11] 'Abd al-Malik 'Isami, *Futuh al-Salatin*, ed. A. S. Usha (Madras: University of Madras, 1940), p. 195.

[12] For an account of these years see Ziya' al-Din Barani, *Ta'rikh-i Firuz Shahi*, ed. Sayyid Ahmad Khan (Calcutta: Bibliotheca Indica, 1860–62), pp. 170–84 and Peter Jackson, *The Delhi Sultanate*, pp. 81–85.

As obscure as Jalal al-Din's early history is the past of Ghiyas al-Din Tughluq, the other military commander on the north-west frontier who went on to become Sultan. Although Amir Khusrau provided a eulogy of Ghiyas al-Din's campaign against the usurper Khusrau Khan Barwari (1320), we are informed by the Moroccan traveller, Ibn Battuta, and not a chronicler of the Delhi court, that Ghiyas al-Din was a Qara'una Turk.[13] Aubin had clarified years ago that the Qara'una epithet was used to describe the followers of the Mongol commander Negüder who belonged to the Jochid-Golden Horde dispensation. Negüder and his followers were marooned in the Afghanistan-Khurasan region as the territories under the sons of Chinggis Khan hardened into antagonistic regimes.[14] In the 1260s the Qara'unas found themselves sandwiched between the Il-Khanid and the Chaghatayid realms on the one hand and the territory of the Delhi Sultans on the other. They were eventually scattered amongst the other Mongol groups but their identities were not completely erased. In his description of the areas near Ghazni in the early sixteenth century, the Mughal Emperor, Babur, noted, 'in the mountains of Ghazni are Hazaras and Negüderis, amongst some of whom Mongolian is spoken'.[15]

Ghiyas al-Din was not a great Negüderid amir when he migrated to India. According to Ibn Battuta he worked for a merchant as a humble keeper of the horses, perhaps a cattle driver (*gulwaniya* > *guala*), and received patronage first from Ulugh Khan, the brother of Sultan 'Ala al-Din Khalaji.[16] Amir Khusrau was less explicit. He recalled Ghiyas al-Din's statement about his early years as a nomad (*awara mardi*) when the patronage received from Sultan Jalal al-Din Khalaji (not Ulugh Khan in this version) raised him to high status.[17] The discrepancies amongst his early patrons notwithstanding, there is no dispute about how Ghiyas al-Din's military activities on the frontier improved his fortune until by the second decade of the fourteenth century he was commander of Dipalpur,

---

[13] Ibn Battuta, *Rehla*, trans. Mahdi Husain (Baroda: Gaekwad's Oriental Series, no, 122, Oriental Institute, 1976 reprint), p. 47. See also the alternative translation of H. A. R. Gibb, (Cambridge: Hakluyt Society, 2nd series, no. 141, Cambridge University Press, 1971), Vol. 3, p. 649.

[14] Jean Aubin, 'L'ethnogenése des Qaraunas', *Turcica* 1 (1969), pp. 65–94. See also Beatrice Forbes Manz, *The Rise and Fall of Tamerlane* (Cambridge: Cambridge University Press, 1990 reprint), pp. 159–61, Peter Jackson, *The Delhi Sultanate*, pp. 119–22, 217–27, 328.

[15] Zahir al-Din Babur, *The Babur Nama, Memoirs of Babur, Prince and Emperor*, trans. Wheeler M. Thackston (New York: The Modern Library Classics, 2002 reprint), p. 156.

[16] Ibn Battuta, *Rehla*, trans. Mahdi Husain, p. 47; trans. Gibb, Vol. 3, p. 649.

[17] Amir Khusrau, *Tughluq Nama*, ed. Sayyid Hashmi Faridabadi (Aurangabad: Urdu Publishing House, 1933), p. 136.

with some respect as a successful general against the Mongols.[18] His frontier background and his successes did not endear him with the Khalaji military commanders and Amir Khusrau details their refusal to join him in his effort to remove Sultan Khusrau Khan Barwari from power.[19] Like Jalal al-Din Khalaji, Ghiyas al-Din was also outside the charmed circle of military confreres in the capital and, as an outsider, not regarded worthy enough to be a potential candidate to the throne of Delhi.

The progenitors of both, the Khalaji and the Tughluqid regimes shared many features. Both had served the Mongols in the early part of their careers and both had risen to power as 'wardens of the marches'. In trading their old Mongol associations for opportunities present in the service of the Delhi regime, the two protagonists were representative of the larger social and political milieu on the north-west frontier of the Sultanate that we have already described. Unlike many other migrant Mongol commanders who had made their way to Delhi, both Jalal al-Din and Ghiyas al-Din stayed on the frontier. They had greater success here than their compatriots in Delhi many of whom were indicted in conspiracies and purged in 'Ala' al-Din Khalaji's reign. And yet, when they tried to capitalize on their achievements on the frontier and seize power in the capital, they were opposed by the military elite. Their indifferent networks of political support in Delhi certainly weakened their cause in the capital. But as I will show in the following sections, the arrival of frontiersmen in the capital was also the cause of considerable unease, an awkwardness that the seizure of political authority was not quite able to erase from the narratives of the court chroniclers.

FRONTIERSMEN, THE TUGHLUQS AND DELHI'S PERSIAN LITERATI

Although all the records relating to Jalal al-Din Khalaji and Ghiyas al-Din Tughluq underline the distance of the two frontier commanders from the Delhi-based elites, the narratives of the Persian chronicles remained

---

[18] For a useful account of Ghiyas al-Din Tughluq's early career on the frontier see, Ibn Battuta, *Rehla*, trans. Mahdi Husain, pp. 47–49; trans. Gibb, Vol. 3, pp. 648–52.

[19] For a useful collation of Ghiyas al-Din's allies and opponents see Peter Jackson, *The Delhi Sultanate*, pp. 178–79. I am in agreement with Jackson's conclusion: '[Ghiyas al-Din] Tughluq's affinity. . . was markedly regional; his lieutenants were commanders who had fought alongside him on the Mongol frontier, sometimes themselves Mongol renegades, or Hindu warlords who were his close neighbours in the western Punjab.' For further details see below.

quite neutral, if not eulogistic, about their personal qualities. Their early histories were quite ignored and, as we noticed, only Ibn Battuta recalled Ghiyas al-Din Tughluq's origins as a keeper of horses, perhaps a cattle driver (*gulwaniya*). But the future Sultans also brought to Delhi their contingents and associates recruited from the frontier tracts. And their qualities were sometimes expatiated without as much reservation. To place some of these sentiments in context it might be useful to reflect upon some of the early instances that we have of Sultanate recruitment of frontier groups.

In 1260, six years before his accession, the future Sultan Balban had deployed Afghans in areas just south of the capital. These were a new group of people not mentioned as a part of any Sultanate military contingent prior to this date. The impact of these warriors on the Delhi literati was evident in Juzjani's awe-struck description of their fearful, strange presence:

> . . . each one of them, one could say, is like an elephant with two braided manes (*du ghazhgha*) on [their] broad shoulders, or is like a bastion (*burji*) ... and each one of them would seize a hundred Hindus, [whether] in the mountain or the jungle, and on a dark night would reduce a demon to helplessness.[20]

In marked distinction to Turkish slaves brought to the Sultanate from the Eurasian steppes, whose fighting qualities and abilities to adapt in their host societies were applauded by early thirteenth century chroniclers, Juzjani underlined how the Afghans were a strange, unfamiliar body of soldiers.[21] Although Balban went on to deploy the Afghans in armed camps around Delhi, they remained socially and culturally distanced from the world of the urbane literati. Sometime around 1280, a decade before Sultan Jalal al-Din Khalaji's arrival in Delhi, Amir Khusrau penned a letter to Ikhtiyar al-Din Begtars complaining about his plight at being forced to reside near Afghans. Amir Khusrau noted:

> In this (?) fortress live the Afghans—nay man-slaying demons, for even the demons groan in fright at their shouts. Their heads are like big sacks of straw, their beards like the combs of the weaver, long-legged as the stork but more ferocious than the eagle, their heads lowered like that of the owl of the wilderness. Their voices hoarse and shrill like that of a jack-daw, their

mouths open like a shark. Their tongue is blunt like a home-made arrow, and flings stones like the sling of a battering ram. Well has a wise man said that when speech was sent to men from the sky, the Afghans got the last and least share of it.[22]

Amir Khusrau was more ambiguous when it came to a description of Ghiyas al-Din Tughluq's armed forces as they marched to the capital. In the *Tughluq Nama*, Amir Khusrau's eulogy to the monarch, the author noted 'his troopers were mainly from the upper lands (*iqlim-i bala*, a euphemism for Khurasan and Transoxiana) and not Hindustanis or local chieftains. They included Ghuzz, Turks and Mongols of Rum and Rus and some Khurasani Persians (*tazik*) of pure stock (*pak asl*)'.[23] To this motley crowd, 'Isami detailed the presence of Khokars, a body of frontier pastoralists, forever in conflict with Sultanate armies and at least one Afghan commander.[24]

The Turks and Mongols mentioned by Amir Khusrau are of some interest. If we take the latter first, the reference to Mongols of Rum and Rus referred to the Mongols who occupied the Eurasian steppes in pre-modern Russia, the *dasht-i Qipchaq*, at this time under the hegemony of the Golden Horde. The Negüderids/Qara'unas (of which Ghiyas al-Din Tughluq was a part) belonged to this larger body of people. Amir Khusrau was actually quite familiar with them; he was briefly captured by a Negüderid in 1285. In his elegy written at the death of Balban's son, Amir Khusrau had described his captor as a Qara'una, a coarse detestable being:

He sat on his horse like a leopard on a hill. His open mouth smelt like an arm-pit, whiskers fell from his chin like pubic-hair.[25]

Harsh sentiments, perhaps, and brought about by the experience of captivity no doubt; Amir Khusrau certainly never repeated these sentiments in the *Tughluq Nama* dedicated to his Qara'una patron.

Amir Khusrau had mentioned Turks as well. The first were the Ghuzz, Turkoman nomads, present in the Afghanistan region. These

---

[22] Amir Khusrau, *Tuhfat al-Sighar*, IOL Persian Ms 412, fol. 50 seq., cited by Wahid Mirza, *The Life and Works of Amir Khusrau*, pp. 51–52.

[23] Amir Khusrau, *Tughluq Nama*, p. 84.

[24] 'Isami, *Futuh al-Salatin*, pp. 382–83. Although Amir Khusrau ignored the Khokars in this list he gives them a prominent role in the battle with Khusrau Khan. See *Tughluq Nama*, p. 128.

[25] Amir Khusrau, *Wasat al-Hayat*, cited in 'Abd al-Qadir Bada'uni, *Muntakhab al-Tawarikh*, ed. Maulavi Ahmad Shah (Calcutta: Asiatic Society of Bengal, 1868), Vol. 1, p. 153.

were fragmented, pastoral groups who nomadized in the Khurasan, Transoxiana, Afghanistan belt and had a long history of conflict with regimes as diverse as the Seljuqs, the Ghaznavids and the Ghurids. Sultan Mu'izz al-Din Ghuri had managed to secure Ghazni only after clearing the Ghuzz out of the region in the 1170s.[26] So far as I know there is no prior reference to their movements in the subcontinent beyond the Punjab.

In his other reference to Turks in Ghiyas al-Din's retinue, Amir Khusrau conflated them with the Mongols of Rum and Rus presumably because they belonged to the same *dasht-i Qipchaq* region. This would be the large, loosely organized confederacy of the Qipchaq Turks lately feeling the impact of Chinggisid invasions. Many Qipchaq tribes came under the dominance of the Jochids and were absorbed in their military retinues. Some of them had already made their way into Hungary where they were known as the Cumans.[27] Others were enslaved and sold in Egypt and India. In Egypt they formed the ruling elite of the Mamluk (Bahri) Sultanate and in India they were the dominant Turkish group in the political dispensation of Sultan Iltutmish. Their presence in the Kabul region into the sixteenth century—or certainly the memory of their presence—is suggested by Babur who mentioned a Qipchaq road, a Qipchaq pass on the Andarab River in the vicinity of Kabul, even a Qipchaq gate in the city of Herat.[28] Like the Ghuzz, the Qipchaqs were a fragmented body of people seeking sanctuary from Mongol incursions in enclaves of sanctuary between large state formations. They congealed into war bands and, when not predators themselves, were an accessible body of recruits for military commanders like Ghiyas al-Din Tughluq on the north-west marches of India.

How did Delhi's Persian literati respond to the arrival of these people in Delhi? The level of discretion displayed by the Persian chroniclers in their accounts of frontiersmen-turned-Sultans and their retinues does not mean that they knew very little about the Turk and Mongol tribes or their dispersal in Central Asia. Indeed, they often used the ethnic term 'Turk' in a very generic sense to signify a military slave or a military commander.[29] And yet the occasional usage of very precise markers

---

[26] Juzjani, *Tabaqat-i Nasiri*, Vol. 1, pp. 357–58, 396.
[27] For further details and references see below.
[28] Babur, *Babur Nama*, trans. Thackston, pp. 150, 155, 231.
[29] See Sunil Kumar, *The Emergence of the Delhi Sultanate* (Delhi: Permanent Black, 2007), pp. 196–202.

clarified that Persian chroniclers possessed a relatively clear knowledge of Turko-Mongol ethnicities, tribal affiliations and dispersal in the lands adjacent to the Sultanate.

In his *Tabaqat-i Nasiri* (completed ca 1260) Minhaj-i Siraj Juzjani provided the provenance of the Turkish slaves purchased by the Delhi Sultan. These range from fairly precise identification of clans and tribes like the Ilbari/Ölperli and Qipchaq to vaguer references to a 'Turk from Rum' or '[Qara] Khita'i'. There is nothing particularly exceptional about this information. It is when Juzjani enlarged on Sultan Balban's background that he displayed the extent of his knowledge regarding the eastern Qipchaqs. He mentioned that Balban was an Ilbari/Ölperli Turk, a tribe associated with the Qipchaq, Qanqali and Yimak.[30] In the concluding verse to his chronicle he eulogized Balban as 'Khan of the Ilbari/Ölperli and Shah of the Yimak [*Khan-i Ilbari ast wa Shah-yi Yimak*]'.[31] That they were all associated tribes in close proximity to each other is clarified in his account of the campaigns of Batu, Khan of the Golden Horde, in the region of the *dasht-i Qipchaq*. Juzjani listed Batu's victories against (amongst others) the tribes of the Qipchaq, Qanqali, Yimak, Ölperli and Rus.[32]

Details mentioned by Juzjani echo in Amir Khusrau's incidental remarks concerning the spread of the Turkish language in north India. In the *Nuh Sipihr* (completed 1318), the author observed that there were three pearl-like languages in the world: Arabic, Persian and Turkish. While Arabic was used by those in the religious sciences for scholastic purposes ['*ilmwari*], Turkish possessed a grammar and dictionary [*ahl-i hunar sarfeh-yi surf wa lughat-i zir o zabarwan*] but was used (only) by the administrators and the military personnel [*sahib-i 'amilan; saran-i sipah*].[33] Amir Khusrau further noted that the Turkish language came from the Qanqali, Uyghur, Irti (? = Irtyush?) and Ghuzz tribes, from the lands of the Qipchaq and Yimak. It then spread through the world.[34]

Although in the *Nuh Sipihr* Amir Khusrau never clarified whether Turkish was spoken in India, suggesting instead that Persian or the

---

[30] Juzjani, *Tabaqat-i Nasiri*, Vol. 2, pp. 175–76.

[31] *Ibid.*, Vol. 2, pp. 220–21.

[32] *Ibid.*, Vol. 2, pp. 175–76.

[33] Amir Khusrau, *Nuh Sipihr*, ed. M. Wahid Mirza (London: Oxford University Press, 1950), p. 173.

[34] *Ibid.*, p. 176.

vernacular subcontinental languages were more popular, in the *Dibacha-i Diwan Ghurrat al-Kamal* (compiled 1286–93) he made some other interesting observations. Here he exclaimed at the unique linguistic abilities possessed by Persian scholars of Hindustan in mastering foreign languages. 'I have seen many Persians, not Turks [*chandin tazik na Turk*]', commented the Persian poet, 'who have learnt Turkish studiously and industriously [*ba-ta'allum wa kasab*], in Hindustan. And they speak [Turkish thus] that (when) the eloquent speakers of that language, (*fusaha'yi an ta'ifa*), come from Turkistan/'upper lands', they are astonished [*furu mandand*].[35]

According to Amir Khusrau, Persian litterateurs in India—individuals like himself—had mastered Turkish because it was the language of governance, and they had learnt these languages without ever visiting the 'upper lands'. The possibility that this was no idle pastime but a consequence of the need for patronage was incidental to his fulsome remarks about the superlative intellectual capacities of the Persian secretaries to learn foreign languages. At any rate, an aspiring courtier such as Amir Khusrau, searching for patronage amongst frontiersmen of Turko-Mongol background, displayed a remarkably cogent knowledge of Turkish tribes and their relationships with each other. This was obvious from the confident connections he made between the Qipchaq and Yimak/Kimak tribes.

In the tenth century the Qipchaqs were dependent but distinct from the northern Yimak/Kimak people from whom they had already separated. By the twelfth century the two groups were in association again, but the Yimak/Kimaks were the dependent, depleted group who had migrated south to settle near the Qipchaqs in the Khwarazm region. Both Juzjani and Amir Khusrau remained sensitive to these associations. This is further clarified by the connections they made between the Qanqali, the Irtyush and the Ölperli tribes located on the eastern belt of the *dasht-i Qipchaq*, all of whom, as P. Golden has shown, were a part of the Qipchaq confederacy.[36] Chinggisid invasions had devastated these

---

[35] Amir Khusrau, *Dibacha-yi Diwan Ghurrat al-Kamal*, ed. Sayyid Ali Haidar (Patna: Institute of Postgraduate Studies and Research in Arabic and Persian Learning, 1988), p. 40. These sentiments were very similar to Fakhr-i Mudabbir's in the first decade of the thirteenth century. For details see Sunil Kumar, *Emergence of the Delhi Sultanate*, pp. 196–97.

[36] On the background and dispersal of the Turkish tribes, see: Anonymous, *Hudud al-'Alam*, trans. V. Minorsky (Karachi: Indus Publications, 1980 reprint), pp. 99–101, 304–12, 315–17. See also *The Encyclopaedia of Islam*, 2nd edition, s.v. 'Kankli'; 'Kipchak'; 'Kimak'; 'Ghuzz'; P.

tribes, pushing survivors westwards. Nor were they secure here: Juzjani described how in the western lands of the *dasht-i Qipchaq*, the Golden Horde under Batu, conquered, enslaved and dispersed these groups. While the information on the Turkish tribes is extremely fragmented in Sultanate chronicles it is also unexpectedly accurate; the Persian literati based in Delhi were remarkably well informed of geopolitical developments in the steppe 'upper lands'. This information may have reached them from a variety of intermediaries: geographical texts and travelogues perhaps, as also travellers and merchants, and most definitely their kin—Amir Khusrau himself was of Turkish descent. Their sources notwithstanding, it was certainly germane information to carry as the literati searched for patrons amongst immigrants from the 'upper lands'.

And yet this was a knowledge that the Persian secretaries chose, as it were, not to wear on their sleeves. As we have already noticed, their scanty remarks concerning the Turko-Mongol provenance of the Tughluqs and their frontier retinues were quite remarkable for their silences. Equally noteworthy was their actual cognizance of the background and languages of these new migrants. The silences and elisions were deliberate, a difficult task because frontier commanders who went on to become Sultans were also the subjects of their elaborate eulogies. These eulogies had to reinvent their protagonists in ways that displaced their troublesome ethnicities. Ghiyas al-Din Tughluq is a good example of this phenomenon.

The Qara'una military commander who arrived to sedentary habits only as an adolescent is remembered in Persian historiography primarily as a warrior in the cause of Islam. According to the mid-fourteenth-century historian, Ziya' al-Din Barani, Ghiyas al-Din stood as an impenetrable wall against the onslaught of the Mongols. This service on

B. Golden, 'The Migration of the Oghuz', *Archivum Ottamanicum* 4 (1972), pp. 45–84; idem, 'The Peoples of the South Russian Steppe', in *The Cambridge History of Early Inner Asia*, ed. Denis Sinor (Cambridge: Cambridge University Press, 1990), pp. 277–84; idem, 'Cumanica IV: The Tribes of the Cuman-Qipcaqs', *Archivum Eurasiae Medii Aevi* 9 (1995–97), pp. 99–122; idem, 'Cumanica II: The Ölberli (Ölperli): The Fortunes and Misfortunes of an Inner Asian Nomadic Clan', *Archivum Eurasiae Medii Aevii* 8 (1986), pp. 5–29; idem, 'Nomads in the Sedentary World: The Case of Pre-Chinggisid Rus and Georgia', *Nomads in the Sedentary World*, eds Anatoly M. Khazanov and André Wink (Cornwall: Curzon Press, 2001), pp. 24–75; Charles J. Halperin, 'The Kipchak Connection: The Ilkhans, the Mamluks and Ayn Jalut', *Bulletin of the School of Oriental and African Studies* 63 (2000), pp. 229–45; and O. Pritsak, 'The Decline of the Empire of the Oghuz Yabghu', *The Annals of the Ukrainian-American Academy of Arts and Sciences in the U.S.*, Vol. 2 (1952), pp. 279–92.

the frontier was further embellished by his actions against the reigning usurper, Sultan Khusrau Khan Barwari. Persian chronicles were not only depreciative of Khusrau Khan's slave origins, his recent conversion to Islam and his apostasy after becoming Sultan, they also condemned him for murdering and despoiling the harem of his master, Mubarak Shah Khalaji (1316–20). If Islam was threatened by the Mongols across the frontier, it was challenged in the capital by the usurper-Sultan under whose malevolent influence all appropriate norms governing service and loyalty were forsaken and idol worship had commenced in the palace. In these circumstances, Barani narrated, Ghiyas al-Din fulfilled the promise carried in his title: by thwarting Mongol invasions and overthrowing Khusrau Khan Barwari, he was indeed the 'saviour of religion'.[37]

Amir Khusrau's text complicated Barani's narrative by recollecting sufficient details about the frontier commander's retinue and the degree of animosity he faced in Delhi.[38] But this also served a useful purpose. Despite the odds faced by the frontier commander, and at the brink of disaster, Ghiyas al-Din's fortune changed because of divine benediction. Even though rectitude was by his side he was almost bested in battle until a God-sent opportunity turned fortune in his favour.[39] As the account of his reign unfolded in these histories, Ghiyas al-Din proceeded to rule according to the norms of governance of his more worthy predecessors. The Qara'una frontier commander together with his retinue of Ghuzz, Turks and Mongols of Rum and Rus, and a smattering of Khokars vanished as if they had never existed.

PERSIAN HISTORIOGRAPHY AND THE TURKS AND MONGOLS

Imbedded in the narrative of Ghiyas al-Din's rise to power and accession to the throne were all tensions faced by the Persian literati as they wrote their histories of the Delhi Sultanate. The literati were a fairly composite body of people with some training in Islamic theology and jurisprudence and considerable facility in Persian prosody and poetry. Their juridical training, their skills in diplomatics, accountancy, as

---

[37]   Barani, *Ta'rikh-i Firuz Shahi*, pp. 409–13, 422–23.
[38]   Amir Khusrau, *Tughluq Nama*, pp. 55–70 for details on military commanders in opposition to Ghiyas al-Din.
[39]   *Ibid.*, pp. 128–30.

scribes and raconteurs made them a very valuable body of people in the administration of the Sultanate. Their intellectual training, acquired skills and professional preferences are an important reason why I use the euphemism a 'Persian Secretarial Class' to describe them. Although a small number of these individuals had appeared in north India at the end of the twelfth century, their large-scale immigration into north India occurred during the 1220s following the invasions of the eastern Iranian lands by Chinggis Khan and his commanders. By training and disposition, by their shared aristocratic backgrounds and, not least of all, through their shared traumatic experiences of displacement and immigration, the literati were an extremely class conscious, conservative body of people. They linked their interests with the state and produced histories (*tawarikh*) that valorized the stable and safe universe that *hazrat-i Dehli*, the sacred city of Delhi, provided to Muslims while the rest of the Islamic world was in ruins.[40]

These literati presented a synthetic image of an ideal Muslim-Persianate civilization whose finest protocols were present in the court of the Delhi Sultan. And yet, it is important to note they did not all speak with one voice. We need to distinguish the early thirteenth century authors from the mid-fourteenth, two ends of a continuum which was bisected, so to speak, by the maverick Amir Khusrau.

Thirteenth-century chronicles were produced during the rule of the Turkish Slave regime, a time when the rulers and dispensers of patronage were of unfree origin. As I have detailed elsewhere, Turkish military commanders were rich, powerful and could be generous patrons but, in the context of the aristocratic pretensions of the litterateurs and their violent experience of the Turks and Mongols, writing a panegyric for Turkish slaves demanded considerable ingenuity. But these Turks, Fakhr-i Mudabbir and Juzjani argued, were quite different from their marauding compatriots in the steppe. Turkish slaves did not carry any lingering affection for their 'hearth and homes' in the steppes.[41] Instead, once they were reborn as servants of Islam they brought glory to their master. Juzjani sometimes ruminated on how the protagonists in his work were not ordinary Turks. They were of aristocratic families in the steppes (thus, Iltutmish and Balban), removed from the steppes and their

---

[40] For a full discussion see Sunil Kumar, *Emergence of the Delhi Sultanate*, chapters 2 and 4.

[41] Fakhr-i Mudabbir, *Ta'rikh-i Fakhr al-Din Mubarak Shah*, ed. E. Denison Ross, (London: Royal Asiatic Society, 1927), p. 36.

families to serve a greater destiny.[42] Their passage into slavery was God's way of rescuing them from the Mongol holocaust and casting them on a path where they were fated to be rulers and protectors of Islam in India. The quality of being a Turk, *per se*, was not a problem in these texts; it was their slave origin that posed the conundrum. Elaborate attempts were therefore made to discuss one without the other and when the two could not be resolved it was left to the mystery of divine providence where their positive contributions as Sultans in the service of Islam remained as proof of supernatural intervention.[43]

We need to keep in mind that these records were produced in the early years of the Sultanate and its chroniclers struggled to place the history of the regime within a constellation of Muslim Sultanates. This was a Herculean enterprise because it seemed at that time that the Mongol holocaust marked the end of history itself. While Juzjani's chronicle mimed the traditions of 'universal' history it carried no grand theorization regarding the arrival of Islam in India or of the nature of the political regime. Juzjani's narrative, and those of his contemporaries, rarely shifted beyond the annals of events, battles and literary tropes recording the victory of Muslim arms against infidels.[44]

By contrast, mid-fourteenth-century histories were far more complicated. They were produced by authors of subcontinental provenance, descendents of émigrés who had prospered in their new homes. By the middle of the fourteenth century they had family histories that boasted of aristocratic, urbane accomplishments. These authors were also distant from many of the events that they described and the hindsight allowed them the perspective to contextualize their world within a larger political experience of Muslim governance on Islam's eastern frontier. In the 1350s, scholars such as 'Isami and Barani were the first to suggest that the prehistory of the Delhi Sultanate lay in the Ghaznavid state and that its ruler, Mahmud Ghaznavi, provided the foundation and inspiration integral in the making of the Delhi

---

[42] For Iltutmish see Juzjani, *Tabaqat-i Nasiri*, Vol. 1, p. 441, and for Balban, Vol. 2, pp. 47–48.

[43] For a fuller discussion see Sunil Kumar, 'Service, Status and Military Slavery'.

[44] Juzjani's history was exceptional in its internal organization where he adroitly used the *tabaqat* genre to detail events in eastern Iran, Afghanistan and India. And yet his chronicle remained devoid of more general introspection into the discipline of history, the chronicling tradition or kingship, the fundamental subject of his narrative. In this Juzjani was quite different from the Ghaznavid chronicler Baihaqi (on whom see Marilyn R. Waldman, *Towards a Theory of Historical Narrative* (Columbus: Ohio State University Press, 1980) and Barani on whom see Sunil Kumar, *Emergence of the Delhi Sultanate*, pp. 370–73.

regime. The Mongols and infidel Hindus were the great 'Others' in these narratives and the Persianate and class conscious, aristocratic virtues of the ideal state were creatively memorialized in the Ghaznavid state, now the templates for the Delhi Sultanate.[45] Cast within a historical narrative it allowed for a more self-reflective, linear rooting of the Sultanate in the great traditions of Muslim statecraft. But it also left little space in these narratives for frontier commanders and their retinues— with 'breath that smelt like an arm-pit' with 'voices hoarse and shrill as a jackdaw'—whose origins lay amongst the Mongol hordes or frontier tribesmen who were the great threat to the Sultanate. These people were reinvented like Ghiyas al-Din Tughluq as the 'saviour of religion', and their more problematic qualities were blithely ignored.

Bisecting the two worlds was the maverick figure of Amir Khusrau: the son of a Turkish slave, born and brought up in Patiali and Delhi, whose personal experience never went beyond the subcontinent. He was a court eulogist and a poet, comfortable and proud of his background and of his skill as a litterateur, able to reproduce the most difficult literary styles *and* innovate with great ease. His grand paeans extolled the virtues of respective patron-Sultans setting new standards in form, style and rhetoric. And yet it was when he wrote about his domicile, his craft and his friends that a rare sensitivity and eloquence crept into his work. He received patronage from different Sultans but rendered homage only to his *pir* Shaykh Nizam al-Din Auliya, near whom he was eventually buried. His historical works were constructed around specific themes and episodes: the victories of 'Ala al-Din Khalaji, the seizure of power by Jalal al-Din Khalaji and Ghiyas al-Din Tughluq, the meeting between father and son, the rulers of Lakhnauti and Delhi.[46] These were not large texts and the constant shifts in themes, styles and patrons also meant that the author never theorized on the role and character of the Delhi Sultanate. If there was an overarching, comprehensive ideology regarding its political manifestation, it was to suggest that

---

[45] See 'Isami, *Futuh al-Salatin*, ed. A. S. Usha (Madras: University of Madras, 1940), and Ziya' al-Din Barani, *Fatawa-yi Jahandari*, ed. A. Salim Khan (Lahore: Idarah-i Tahqiqat-i Pakistan, no. 25, 1972). The normative text, *Fatawa-yi Jahandari* and the didactic history of Barani, *Ta'rikh-i Firuz Shahi* share the same rhetorical frame. This is well brought out by Peter Hardy, *Historians of Medieval India: Studies in Indo-Muslim Historical Writing* (London: Luzac and Company Ltd., 1966 reprint), pp. 20–39.

[46] See respectively, Amir Khusrau, *Khazain al-Futuh*, *Miftah al-Futuh*, *Tughluq Nama* and *Qiran al-Sa'dain*.

the subcontinent—more so than the Sultanate—housed a vibrant and unique Persian culture.[47] This allowed the incredibly successful court poet the freedom to discourse and insert random insights regarding the conditions of his age. These were fleeting remarks and observations but, as we have already noticed, they covered subjects that were often erased in the master narratives of the fourteenth-century grand histories.

Through this essay, it is the information provided by Amir Khusrau that often led to a further interrogation of other literary materials. But it has also left us with a host of unanswered questions. It is clear from the information already discussed that the Sultanate was not a cultural monolith, that its rulers came from social and cultural backgrounds quite distinct from that of its Persianate secretarial class who provided the histories and eulogies of the state. These differences generated some discomfort especially when these 'frontiersmen'—a useful term to capture their marginal status in the representations of urbane, Persianate Sultanate society—emerged as the lords and masters of the realm.[48] In the next section, I interrogate the Persian materials further to see how some of these tensions were manifest in their records.

TURKO-MONGOL PRACTICES AND A PERSIANATE MUSLIM ORDER

Delhi was the 'Sanctuary of Islam' for a large number of immigrants of different social backgrounds, ethnicities and regions. A poet such as 'Isami writing in the mid-fourteenth century dutifully recorded the diverse backgrounds of these people but also went on to suggest that the common denomination of being 'Muslim' bonded immigrants as they sought asylum from the Mongols.[49] Penetrating this discourse is extremely difficult; it was certainly a subject that the Sultanate chroniclers did not want to accommodate in their narratives. Once the frontier commanders became Sultans, however, 'difference' was harder to ignore and their new patrons tested the creativity of their eulogists in

---

[47] This was most clearly developed in his *Nuh Sipihr*. For a useful recent assessment of the poet see Sunil Sharma, *Amir Khusrau: The Poet of Sultans and Sufis* (Oxford: Oneworld, 2005).

[48] For a valuable interpretation of some of the intellectual roots of this urbane Sultanate society, see Muzaffar Alam, *The Languages of Political Islam in India, c. 1200–1800* (Delhi: Permanent Black, 2004), pp. 26–46, 81–91.

[49] Isami, *Futuh al-Salatin*, pp. 114–15.

interesting ways. They introduced traditions that were clearly outside the experience of the Persian literati and yet many of their novel practices were seamlessly assimilated in the records of the chroniclers without a comment. There were other Turko-Mongol traditions of the émigrés that were far harder for the Persian literati to gloss. In their efforts to work out resolutions—not always very effective ones—literary materials of the time left spaces that can be usefully enlarged for an insight into the dialectical processes through which a Persianate Muslim order was rather uneasily fashioned. The evidence on the subject is quite dispersed and rather than pursuing random and decontextualized instances I have selected three examples through which I can develop the range of cultural interaction more precisely in my discussion. .

The first example concerns an administrative system used by 'Ala' al-Din Khalaji and Ghiyas al-Din Tughluq. Concerning the vital communication system established by Ghiyas al-Din to knit his expanding empire, Barani refers to *ulagh/ulaq* on several occasions as a 'horse-post' without any need for further elaboration.[50] The same institution was described by the Morrocan traveller Ibn Battuta, who found the system novel enough to merit a description. He distinguished *ulagh/ulaq*, a horse-post, from *dawa*, a courier who travels on foot.[51] Clearly the system was new; but it did not have a long life. At the end of the sixteenth century the Mughal historian Nizam al-Din was not at all confident that his audience would know the meaning of the term. When he narrated the events of Ghiyas al-Din's reign and mentioned the *ulagh/ulaq* system he explained the term with a synonym: 'During this time, the *dak chowki*, which in the language of those people was called *ulagh/ulaq*, arrived from Delhi and brought orders'.[52]

Barani did not need to explain the meaning of *ulagh/ulaq* because his audience was familiar with it. There is no evidence to suggest, however, that they knew of its history and that it was an administrative innovation authored by Chinggis Khan, a universally hated figure in Sultanate historiography. The Mongol historian, Juwaini, clarified that *ulagh/ulaq* was a courier system that connected the vast Mongol domains of the Great Khan. His history had explained how it was originally one of the

---

[50] Ziya' al-Din Barani, *Ta'rikh-i Firuz Shahi*, p. 447, and for a reference from the reign of 'Ala' al-Din Khalaji see also p. 245.

[51] Ibn Battuta, *Rehla*, trans. Mahdi Husain, pp. 3–4; trans. H. A. R. Gibb, vol. 3, p. 594–95.

[52] Nizam al-Din, *Tabaqat-i Akbari*, ed. B. De (Calcutta: Bibliotheca Indica, 1927), Vol. 1, p. 195.

qubchur taxes, a contribution levied upon the Mongols for providing mounts and other sustenance for the couriers. This changed through the thirteenth century until *ulagh/ulaq* came to be a tax levied on the peasantry. Certainly by Ghazan Khan's reign (1295–1304) it was a part of the *qalan* taxes levied on non-Mongols.[53]

It was clearly in its late thirteenth century form that Barani used the term *ulagh/ulaq* when he was describing the postal relay system in 'Ala' al-Din Khalaji and Ghiyas al-Din's reign. Under Ghiyas al-Din *ulagh/ ulaq* was a courier system maintained through local provisions/taxation, connecting Delhi with its frontier regions. The mutations in the *ulagh/ ulaq* system could have occurred independently in the Sultanate and Il Khanid territories; otherwise its transmission into Khalaji and Tughluq administration was very quick—'Ala' al-Din Khalaji and Ghazan Khan were contemporaries. In Ghiyas al-Din's reign this courier system had broken down while Ulugh Khan, the future Sultan Muhammad, was besieging Arangal in the Deccan.[54] It is unlikely that *ulagh* is of an earlier Oghuz inheritance: the Seljuqs (of Qiniq, Oghuz background) much to the wazir Nizam al-Mulk's dismay, paid scant attention to the *barid* (postal, spy system) network within their dominion and much of the *Siyasat Nama* was spent marketing its virtues.[55] Certainly, by the time that the Qara'una military commander Ghiyas al-Din used the system, it had reached a stage of development roughly coterminous with the Chaghatayid and the Il-Khanid political dispensations (post-1227 and post-1256, respectively).

Although the usage of the *ulagh* system by Ghiyas al-Din Tughluq does show Sultanate administrative proximity to a Mongol source, it did not carry with it any implication of large-scale social and political reorganization as it had for the Mongols under Chinggis Khan. In other words, *ulagh/ulaq* did not challenge the structures of early

---

[53] On the *ulagh/ulaq*, see 'Ata' al-Mulk Juwaini, *Ta'rikh-i Jahan Gusha*, trans. J. A. Boyle, *The History of the World Conqueror* (Manchester: University Press, 1958), Vol. 1, p. 30, Vol. 2, pp. 524, 599; John M. Smith Jr., 'Mongol and Nomadic Taxation', *Harvard Journal of Asiatic Studies* 30 (1970), pp. 48–85; I. P. Petrushevsky, 'The Socio-economic Condition of Iran under the Il-Khans', in *Cambridge History of Iran*, ed. J. A. Boyle, (Cambridge: Cambridge University Press, 1968), Vol. 5, pp. 483–537; Gerhard Doerfer, *Turkische und Mongolische Elemente im Neupersischen* (Wiesbaden: Franz Steiner Verlag, 1965), Vol. 2, pp. 102–107, s.v. 'ulag'.

[54] Ziya' al-Din Barani, *Ta'rikh-i Firuz Shahi*, pp. 446–47.

[55] Nizam al-Mulk, *Siyasat Nama*, trans. Hubert Darke (London: Routledge and Kegan Paul, 1978). See also Ann K. S. Lambton, 'The Internal Structure of the Saljuq Empire', in *Cambridge History of Iran*, Vol. 5, pp. 203–82.

fourteenth-century Sultanate society. For a narrator such as Barani it was an efficient administrative system and, since its provenance was without any apparent consequence, it provoked little interest. For all that it seemingly mattered, *ulagh/ulaq* was a new name grafted on to old administrative procedures that were revamped and made more efficient during dynastic change.

On the other hand, the response of the Persian chroniclers to the titles used by the Delhi Sultans and their important military commanders indicates a more complex response to steppe traditions. The Khalajis and early Tughluq Sultans used fairly conventional titles couched in Arabic and Persian. But they also defined membership in the imperial kin-group by the Turko-Mongol honorific *khan*, designating brother, son, or honoured kinsman of the monarch. This was in contrast to the usage of *malik* and *amir*, a title used by military commanders. While *khan* designated kinship within the imperial lineage, it was also deployed by the Khalajis and Tughluqs as a title of privilege through which some fictive kinsmen were honoured while others clearly excluded. The nuances in status become evident from the following example narrated by Barani at the time of Ghiyas al-Din Tughluq's accession when he honoured his kinsmen and collaborators. Barani reported:

> Bahram Ai-aba was honoured like a brother [*baradari mashruf gardanidah bud*], was addressed as Kishlu *Khan* and granted the areas of Multan and Sindh. (Ghiyas al-Din's) son-in-law, *Malik* Shadi was entrusted with the *diwan-i wazirat* (register of finance), and his (Ghiyas al-Din's) adopted son Tatar *Khan* was addressed as Tatar *Malik* and given the *iqta'* of Zafarabad.[56]

In other words, the son-in-law, and the adopted son were not honoured by the title of Khan, but the non-kinsman and honoured associate, Bahram Ai-aba, was treated like a brother and hence given that title. Furthermore, seniority between the sons of Ghiyas al-Din, all Khans, was further clarified by the grant of the title Ulugh Khan to Malik Fakhr al-Din Juna, the future Sultan Muhammad Shah (1324–51), and his public acknowledgement as *wali ahd* (heir-apparent). Ulugh which literally means 'great' in Turkish distinguished the future Sultan from his peers.

Turkish titles were also used by the Khalajis. The father of Sultan Jalal al-Din Khalaji (1290–96) was Yughrush and Mahmud Kashgari explained

---

[56] Ziya' al-Din Barani, *Ta'rikh-i Firuz Shahi*, p. 428.

that the title Yughrush meant *wazir*;[57] his nephew 'Ali Garshasb was the future Sultan 'Ala al-Din (Garshasb was an ancestor of Afrasiyab). On seizing power in 1296, 'Ala al-Din's lineage became the imperial one and the monarch could appropriately dispense the honorific Khan upon his kinsmen. This appellation was absent in their earlier titles and he now proceeded to distinguish his brother Almas Beg with the title Ulugh Khan (Great Khan); another brother was entitled Qutlugh Tegin (Qutlugh = auspicious, and Tegin = prince, hence an auspicious prince); his brother-in-law Malik Sanjar received the title Alp Khan (Alp = powerful).

Turkish titles were not a novelty for the Tughluqs or the Khalajis; they were systematically given by Iltutmish to his *bandagan-i khass*, Turks and non-Turks, alike. Iltutmish's actions were, however, quite innovative; the title of Khan was never used by his predecessors. Perso-Arabic titles were in currency under the Ghaznavids, the Ghurid Sultans and in the usage of his own master, Qutb al-Din Ai-beg. The use of the royal honorific *khan*—far be it for slaves—was unprecedented and the Persian secretaries were aware of its novelty. This is apparent from Juzjani's long anecdote of an embassy sent by Ulugh Khan (the future Sultan Balban) to the court of the Il-Khanid monarch Hulegu. The letter to the Mongol monarch was in Persian and when it was translated into Mongolian the emissary replaced Khan in Balban's title with Malik. Juzjani clarified: 'the custom of Turkistan [*qa'ida-i Turkistan*] is this that there is but one Khan, no more, and all the others have the title of *Malik*.' In Juzjani's narration, Hulegu Khan knew of Balban's usage of the Khan title and honoured him sufficiently to protest its omission when his letter was read out with the honorific missing. He asked for the title of Khan to be restored. Juzjani concluded his report:

> all of the Khans from the lands of Hind and Sindh who went to the presence of the Khans, their titles were altered [*tabdil kard*] in all of the documents proffered to the Mughal and they were referred to as *Malik*. But they confirmed the title of the great Ulugh Khan without change [as in] the original.[58]

The assumption of titles of steppe provenance served as effective communicators of status for a local as well as a distant audience. It is

---

[57] Robert Dankoff, 'Kasgari on the Tribal and Kinship Organization of the Turks', *Archivum Ottomanicum* 4 (1972), pp. 23–43.
[58] Juzjani, *Tabaqat-i Nasiri*, Vol. 2, p. 87.

therefore interesting to note the emergence of specific protocols relating to the kind of titles that monarchs and their subordinates could carry. Some of the early Sultans—Qutb al-Din Ai-Beg, Shams al-Din Iltutmish and Ghiyas al-Din Balban—carried 'compound' titles, with both Turkish and Perso-Arabic elements.[59] Barring these three examples no Sultan after 1286 ever took on a Turkish title, not even Khan. As princes they had either taken Turkish titles or 'compound' ones, but these were given up for formal Perso-Arabic ones when they ascended the throne. From the individuals already cited note the examples of 'Ali Garshasb who became 'Ala' al-Din Khalaji and Ulugh Khan who later took the title of Sultan Muhammad Shah Tughluq.

It would appear from the evidence cited thus far that administrative practices of steppe provenance that promoted efficient governance were not a subject of concern to the Persian literati. They were as candid in reporting the usage of Mongol and Turkish titles and comprehended their manipulation at the time of dispersal of new honours. As Juzjani's report suggests, the Persian secretaries understood the cultural value attached to these titles and were sometimes involved in adjusting them according to the demands of the situation.

At least as far as the Persian literati were concerned the ethnic backgrounds of the ruling elites were not a problem as long as they abided by the larger templates of a Persianate Muslim order. The Turkish slaves of Iltutmish, all of whom were given Turkish titles by their master, were applauded for their abilities to forsake their homes and families for their new world. This fiction allowed for the acceptance of the military slave as a loyal servant of his master and the realm. In the long duration the logic of this discourse was useful enough in persuading frontier commanders to abandon their old titles that carried significant Turkish elements and aspire to high status in their new world as 'Ala' al-Din (Glory of Religion) Khalaji or Ghiyas al-Din (Saviour of Religion) Tughluq.

Transitions from one world to another, however, were never quite as definitive, especially when moving from a frontier environment to the core territories embraced a large entourage and not just the individual military commander. The Persian secretaries were familiar with many details of the inhabitants of the Eurasian steppes but there were other

---

[59] For example, Qutb al-Din Ai-Beg/'The Axis of Religion—*Moon Prince*'; Shams al-Din Iltutmish/'The Light of Religion—*Grasper of the Realm*'; Ghiyas al-Din Balban/'Rescuer of Religion—*the Powerful*'.

specifics about the lives and traditions of the steppe peoples that were completely unfamiliar to them. On their part, frontier commanders like Jalal al-Din Khalaji and Ghiyas al- Din Tughluq must have retained Persian secretaries to help them keep accounts and manage their diplomatic life. Our ignorance of their service notwithstanding, it would not be presuming too much to assume that these secretaries were important members of the governor's household. Their influence—and through them, the influence of urbane Persianate traditions—were always tempered in the frontier camps by the large-scale recruitment of mobile warriors that constituted the retinue of the commanders. Bonds of ethnicity, common natal origins and the contingencies of marginalization on the frontier created forces of social and cultural cohesion that Persian secretaries could not always penetrate.

At Ghiyas al-Din Tughluq's accession, the Ghuzz, the Turks and Mongols of Rum and Rus were the new political elites of the Sultanate and the monarch was as reliant on their continuing support as he was on the Persian Secretarial class. The new monarch had to remain sensitive to the contrasting bodies of people and lexicon of associations that he had knitted together in the making of his war band. Acculturation into the Persianate world of the secretarial classes, even if such transitions could be accomplished quickly by commanders who were only recently *awara mardi*, would have meant distancing himself from the very fraternity that had made his rise into political prominence possible. Since this was not a feasible alternative, when Ghiyas al-Din Tughluq marched into the capital, he actually brought the frontier with him to Delhi.

The hegemonic narratives of mid-fourteenth-century Persian chroniclers are quite impoverished on subjects concerning cultural plurality within the Muslim community. On the other hand, the amateur ethnography of the Moroccan traveller Ibn Battuta, a travelling jurist, is far more direct in recording the unfamiliar rituals and traditions of his Muslim coreligionists. He arrived in north India during the reign of Muhammad Shah Tughluq and described the ritual procession of the king in ways that was very different from the Persian chronicles.

This was the ritual procession of the king where his ornately decorated saddle cover, *ghashiya*, was carried before him. Ibn Battuta provided descriptions of the ritual from the reign of Muhammad Shah Tughluq, which was apparently celebrated on the occasion of major festivals and whenever the Sultan returned to the city. Concerning feast days ('Id) the traveller noted:

On the morning of the feast all the elephants are adorned with silk, gold and precious stones. There are sixteen of these elephants which no one rides, but they are reserved to be ridden by the Sultan himself, and over them are carried sixteen parasols of silk embroidered with jewels, each one with a shaft of pure gold... .The Sultan himself rides on one of these elephants and in front of him there is carried aloft the *ghashiya*, that is his saddle-cover, which is adorned with the most precious jewels. In front of him walk his slaves and his mamluks.[60]

Ibn Battuta added further details regarding the ritual at the time of the Sultan's entry into the capital:

. . . On some of the (sixteen) elephants there were mounted small military catapults and when the Sultan came near the city, parcels of gold and silver coins mixed together were thrown from these machines. The men on foot in front of the Sultan and the other persons present scrambled for the money, and they kept on scattering it until the procession reached the palace....[61]

While *ghashiya* has an Arabic etymology, meaning to cover, veil,[62] the origin of the ceremony lies in the accession and ceremonial rituals of the early Turks where the 'Lord of the Horse' would be identified with the newly enthroned leader, and the procession would celebrate the conquest of the four quarters by the Universal Emperor.[63] Although the paths of its transmission into the central Islamic lands are unclear the tradition was followed in some of the major steppe-descended polities: by the Seljuqs, the Zangids and the Bahri Mamluks of Egypt (with a military elite of Qipchaq origin).[64] At least in Syria and Egypt it was accepted as a ritual associated with royalty and performed by the Kurdish Ayyubids, who learnt of it from their Turkish patrons the Zangids. With the Ayyubids it was integrated as a part of their accession

---

[60] Ibn Battuta, *Rehla*, trans. H. A. R. Gibb, Vol. 3, pp. 663–64, trans. Mahdi Husain, p. 60. The translation is Gibb's.

[61] *Ibid.*, trans. H. A. R. Gibb, p. 668, trans. Mahdi Husain, p. 64. The translation is Gibb's.

[62] See also the Qur'an, chapter 88, *al-Ghashiya*.

[63] For a review of Turko-Mongol ideals of universal dominion see Osman Turan, 'The Ideal of World Domination among the Medieval Turks', *Studia Islamica* 4 (1955), pp. 77–90, and for a discussion of iconographic representations from the Seljuq period of the monarch, 'the equerry and the honorific spare horse with saddle- cover' see, Emel Esin, 'Ay-Bitigi, the Court Attendants in Turkish Iconography', *Central Asiatic Journal* 14 (1970), pp. 108–09.

[64] H. A. R. Gibb, et al. eds, *Encyclopaedia of Islam* (Leiden: E. J. Brill, 2nd edition, 1956), Vol. 2, s.v. 'ghashiyya', and P. M. Holt, 'The Position and Power of the Mamluk Sultan', *Bulletin of the School of Oriental and African Studies* 38 (1975), p. 245.

ceremony together with the ritual pledge of allegiance, *bay'a*, and the investiture from the Caliph.[65]

Detailed descriptions of the *ghashiya* ritual exist from the Mamluk Sultanate of Egypt where Ibn Taghribirdi clarified that it was a part of the accession ceremonies of the monarch and repeated on major festivals. Its performance in Egypt mirrors Ibn Battuta's description of the ceremony from Muhammad Shah Tughluq's court and al-Qalqashandi gives us the following description:

> (The *ghashiya*) is a saddle cover of leather, decorated with gold so that the observer would take it to be made entirely of gold. It is borne before him (the Mamluk Sultan) when riding in state processions for parades, festivals, etc. The Rikabdariyya (grooms, i.e., *ghulams*) carry it, the one who holds it up in his hands turning it right and left. It is one of the particular insignia of this kingdom.[66]

An important common feature between the Mamluk state in Egypt and the Delhi Sultanate were the common reliance upon Turko-Mongol personnel from the *dasht-i Qipchaq* for their respective armies. The Sultanate's link with the Eurasian steppe already present in Iltutmish's reign continued into the reign of Ghiyas al-Din Tughluq who was of Negüderid background, and his retinue of 'Turks and Mongols of Rum and Rus'.

Just as most of the Persian chronicles ignored the composition of Ghiyas al-Din's retinue they paid no attention to his royal procession ceremony. Since Ibn Battuta's observations remained largely 'unsubstantiated' in the accounts of the Persian literati they did not draw the attention of modern scholars. Yet, Barani's description of 'Ala al-Din's triumphant march to Delhi after Jalal al-Din's murder (1296) does possess some of the elements present in Battuta's description although completely different motives to the discharge of gold coins (*panj-man akhtar*, five mans of gold stars) amongst the crowds observing the Sultan's march are ascribed by the author.[67] Equally selective was Yahya Sirhindi's early fifteenth century

---

[65] See references above and P. M. Holt, 'The Structure of Government in the Mamluk Sultanate', in *The Eastern Mediterranean Lands in the Period of the Crusades*, ed. P. M. Holt (Warminster: Aris and Phillips Ltd., 1977), p. 47.

[66] al-Qalqashandi, *Subhal-a'sha* (Cairo), Vol.4, p.7, cited in P. M. Holt, 'The Position and Power of the Mamluk Sultan', p. 243.

[67] Ziya' al-Din Barani, *Ta'rikh-i Firuz Shahi*, p. 243. Edward Thomas, *The Chronicles of the Pathan Kings of Delhi* (Delhi: Munshiram Manoharlal, 1967), pp. 157, 169–70, explains that the *panj-man akhtar* referred to the gold coinage, *fanam/panam*, i.e. fractions of the *hun*, seized as plunder by 'Ala al-Din in his Deccan campaigns.

account of Muhammad Shah Tughluq's celebratory procession after his accession. The narrative is close enough to Ibn Battuta's description of the *ghashiya* ritual for us to follow its main features but the elisions are important as well. Sirhindi noted:

> ... the lanes were decorated with coloured and embroidered cloth. From the time that the Sultan set his foot in the city till he entered the imperial palace, gold and silver coins were rained from the back of the elephants among the populace, and gold was scattered in every street, lane, and house.[68]

In Sirhindi's account, as in Barani's, the Sultan's triumphal processions receive due recognition but there is no reference to the *ghashiya*. Was the omission deliberate or was it an aspect of Turko-Mongol practice quite unfamiliar to Persian secretaries? Were they, in other words, just inadequate historians reifying the practice of their subjects either through ignorance or because of their own class and cultural prejudices?

This is a difficult question to answer and it might help if we disaggregated the two reports of Barani and Sirhindi; different factors influenced the production of the two texts. Barani was a contemporary of Ibn Battuta and both authors were in Delhi during Muhammad Shah Tughluq's reign. If the Moroccan visitor could notice and learn about the *ghashiya* during the brief period of his visit, so, theoretically speaking, could Barani. He noticed the *ulagh* and the manipulation of the Khan title to enunciate hierarchy within Ghiyas al-Din's new political dispensation without any problem. But these details did not disturb the larger point that the author wanted to make about the monarch in his history. In Barani's narrative Ghiyas al-Din was a 'Saviour of Islam', a morally righteous Muslim, renowned for his combat with the infidel Mongols. Now he was waging a war against a different heathen menace located in Delhi, a neo-convert slave, an apostate, who had killed his master and his heirs. The conflict between Ghiyas al-Din Tughluq and Khusrau Khan Barwari was over the future well being of the Muslim community. Incorporating details about the Turko-Mongol composition of Ghiyas al-Din and his retinue, or the practice of steppe rituals by the frontier commander would have complicated the binaries on which Barani had framed the qualities of his protagonist—the Muslim versus the non-Muslim—and his narration of the triumph of rectitude over evil. The author preferred not to tread these waters.

---

[68] Yahya b. Ahmad b. 'Abd Allah Sirhindi, *Ta'rikh-i Mubarak Shahi*, ed. M. Hidayat Hosain (Calcutta: Bibliotheca Indica, no.254, 1931), p. 97, trans., K. K. Basu (Baroda: Oriental Institute, 1932), p. 99. I have followed Basu's translation.

Writing a century later Yahya Sirhindi, a litterateur himself, was familiar with the writings of his predecessors. His history of the Sultanate, from the late twelfth into the early fifteenth century, is an interesting piece of synthesis. For the better part the narrative is reliant upon the histories of Juzjani and Barani but there are significant additions and omissions.[69] Sirhindi followed 'Isami in suggesting personal proximity between Yaqut and Sultan Raziyya and, while otherwise staying close to Barani's text, omitted any mention of 'Ala' al-Din Khalaji's price regulations. While Barani's rhetorical statements were deleted, the author inserted contemplative passages in verse and prose regarding destiny's stranglehold on humans. And yet none of these insertions and deletions shifted the larger narrative framework of Sirhindi, which remained entirely dependent on Juzjani and Barani. Sirhindi ignored alternative narratives, such as 'Isami's, or details from Amir Khusrau that disturbed Barani's conclusions. This independent line of investigation would have complicated the author's work considerably and, in forcing him to question and depart from Barani's reportage, required the author to write the history of the Delhi Sultans afresh. Instead Sirhindi was satisfied with paraphrasing, pruning and collating material, shifting details about individuals without actually rewriting the history of the Delhi Sultans. As he excavated Juzjani and Barani for their information, he also treated them as artefacts that needed to be dusted off and preserved. The elisions and silences regarding frontier commanders, Turko-Mongol traditions and customs present in the earlier master narratives were then transported into the history of the other.

CONCLUSION: FRONTIER COMMANDERS IN A PERSIANATE MILIEU

In the beginning of this essay, I had clarified my intent to study the 'ignored elites' in the early Delhi Sultanate. This was an unusual project given that modern historiography on the Sultanate has ignored many subjects, but alas, not elites. Elites, of course, are never ignored; they get to be reinvented by their narrators in various ideological hues. Frontier

---

[69] Sirhindi apparently used Barani's first recension of the *Ta'rikh-Firuz Shahi* where the Mongol invasion of Tarmashirin was mentioned in Muhammad Shah Tughluq's reign. Other than 'Isami, whose text seems to have been ignored by Sirhindi (note the contrasting accounts of Sultan Nasir al-Din Mahmud's death), only Barani's first recension mentioned this event.

commanders who seized power in the Sultanate in 1290 and later, were grandiloquently panegyrized by the Persian literati. The extent to which these patrons challenged the skills of their eulogists, however, should not be minimized. As the case of Ghiyas al-Din Tughluq clarifies, for a variety of reasons relating to his background, the geopolitics of his age, and the social and ideological precommitments of his eulogists, it was necessary for the Qara'una military commander to receive a brand new profile. There was a lot else about these frontiersmen which it was safer to simply ignore. Once ignored, the salient characteristics of these military commanders and the politics that made them important participants in the events of the Delhi Sultanate simply passed out of the realm of history. It is hardly surprising then, that many historians mark 1290 as the termination of Turkish dominance in the history of the Sultanate and the arrival of new 'plebeian' forces.[70] As Barani explained, these plebeians were the new Indian converts to Islam that Sultans like 'Ala al-Din Khalaji and Muhammad Shah Tughluq started patronizing. In modern historiography this started the process of 'rooting' the Sultanate in the subcontinent, processes through which Islam came to have the unique features so admired today in the practice of its sufis and bhakta sants.

Much of this essay was occupied in recovering the pasts of frontier commanders and discussing the ways in which their presence was elided in the records of the Persian literati. Reintegrating them in the histories of the Sultanate implies charting new genealogies for the state, its ruling elites and the processes that shaped the pasts of the Muslim community in the subcontinent. This would imply that rather than focusing only upon processes of indigenization and vernacularization of Islam in the regions of the subcontinent, historians need to be sensitive to the processes through which Muslim society in Delhi and its adjoining regions were constantly reconstituted through the infusion of immigrants from the Afghanistan-Punjab frontier. Barani, for example, gestured to the presence of these migrants in his chronicle. He referred to them quite derisively as *nau-Musulman*, or new Muslims. Although these Mongols were apparently Muslims, Barani used the epithet of *nau-Musulman* to communicate their alien, novel character since their

---

[70] For the most influential exposition of this argument see Irfan Habib, 'Barani's Theory of the History of the Delhi Sultanate', *Indian Historical Review* 7 (1980–81), pp. 104–10 and for an alternative assessment, Sunil Kumar, 'Service, Status and Military Slavery', pp. 97–102.

politics and social and cultural practices were so abhorrently different from people of his upbringing. Some of these Mongol migrants gained patronage in the short duration but, if we follow Barani most of these people remained segregated in Sultanate society and were executed. And yet, despite Amir Khusrau's information on the composition of Ghiyas al-Din's retinue and the resistance that they faced from the elites of Delhi, the military commander and his contingent were never ascribed the epithet *nau-Musulman*. One of the reasons why this did not happen, of course, is because Ghiyas al-Din and his retinue were rulers and patrons and it would not be politic to refer to them as new Muslims.

Another reason for the hesitation to refer to these frontiersmen-turned-Sultans as *nau-Musulman* arose from the fact that the new rulers were themselves sucked into the structures of power and social hierarchies present in Delhi. All the information that we have on Ghiyas al-Din suggests that he moved very quickly to install conventional modes of governance once he became Sultan. This included collaborating with the Persian literati in the preservation of the social and moral order familiar to them. Ibn Battuta communicated the extent to which Ghiyas al-Din Tughluq's son, Muhammad Shah Tughluq (1324–51) was invested in this project. Muhammad Shah Tughluq issued orders that 'all were required to show a knowledge of the obligations of ablution, prayers and the binding articles of Islam. They used to be questioned on these matters; if anyone failed to give correct answers he was punished and they made a practice of studying them with one another in the audience hall and the bazaars and setting them down in writing'.[71]

Records of this nature suggest ways in which an Islam that abided by a rigorous interpretation of its rituals was reproduced in the core territories of the Sultanate. It consolidates the dominant historiographical image where creative ferment in Islam came through sectarian and doctrinal controversies amongst Muslims in the core territories of the Sultanate in contrast to the more heterogeneous populations on the frontier where there was interaction between Muslim and non-Muslims.[72] And yet the 'creative encounter' that occurred in Ghiyas al-Din Tughluq's capital was not just between Muslims and non-Muslims, it was between old and new Muslims, between the urbane elites of the capital and the frontier

---

[71] Ibn Battuta, *Rehla*, trans. Gibb, Vol. 3, p. 693.

[72] Note the argument in Richard Eaton, 'Introduction', in *India's Islamic Traditions, 711–1750*, ed. Richard M. Eaton (Delhi: Oxford University Press, 2003), p. 25.

commanders, the Sultan and his entourage. In this interaction, however, hierarchies were reversed. It was the new, rustic Muslim, recently arrived from the frontier who was the Sultan. The 'saviour of Islam' may have patronized the Persian literati and the learned jurists, but he also continued to practice his steppe rituals in Delhi.

It is in this context that we need to remember the *ghashiya* ritual performed by Muhammad Shah Tughluq, a ritual that Sultanate chroniclers ignored, but a public ceremony that was performed during *'id*. In the retinue that followed the procession to the festival ground were the great *qazis* of the city. Should it happen to be *bakr-i 'id*, Ibn Battuta noted, the Sultan himself did the honours of sacrificing the camel. Commingled in the rituals of the *ghashiya* and *'id* were strands from multiple backgrounds but the elements that reminded observers of the frontier origins of their masters were not the ones that were transmitted to posterity.

It is hard to determine how long royal rituals like the *ghashiya* were practiced in Delhi because no Persian chronicler wished to record its performance in the first place. We know of it only by accident through Ibn Battuta's travelogue. But we can gauge the slow loss of comprehension of some steppe traditions if we recall the example of the *ulagh/ulaq*. By the end of the sixteenth century the term was equated with an alternative system and its specificity was erased. Alternatively, while Mongol titles like Khan were seamlessly incorporated within a Persianate tradition and persisted over the long duration, there were other Turkish titles like Iltutmish whose meaning, as Simon Digby's research has brought out, was already confused by the end of the sixteenth century. Digby also points out that the manuscripts copied in the 1700s altered the name of the Sultan according to a false identification with a word (*altamish*) current at that time.[73] Copyists thereafter were less sure how to spell the more exotic Turkish titles and errors crept in. As Peter Jackson's efforts have shown, restoring Turkish titulature to their correct form is now an incredibly laborious task.[74]

It may appear commonsensical to note that what is understood today as a part of 'Muslim' tradition is quite removed from the ways in which

[73] Simon Digby, 'Iletmish or Iltutmish? A Reconsideration of the Name of the Delhi Sultan', *Iran* 8 (1970), pp. 57–64.
[74] Ironically, the diligent restoration of Turkish titles by Peter Jackson, *The Delhi Sultanate*, passim, did not lead the author to ask why these titles came to be corrupted to such a large extent.

it was understood in 1700 or 1324. But having said that, researching the contours of Muslim society in 1324 means that we have to step out of teleological modes of analysis and remain sensitive to the ways in which the culture and politics of that moment constructed or elided their complex aspects. The study of Jalal al-Din Khalaji, Ghiyas al-Din Tughluq, or the much later Bahlul Lodi—all frontier commanders who became Sultans—stands as a salutary reminder that the great traditions of Islam were not just the product of interaction amongst social groups in the Gangetic plains or the Deccan; a variety of frontier traditions brought by periodic migrations of military commanders also impacted on this world. What kind of responses did these intrusions raise? Is it possible to locate the contexts in which they were produced? It is through a study of this dialectic—sometimes only fleetingly visible in our historical narratives—that we can understand the construction of the social and cultural lineages of Muslim society and structures of authority in the history of the Sultanate. Otherwise the complexities introduced by the presence of frontier traditions and their importance in the formation of Muslim societies and politics will remain where the Persian literati of the age sought to consign them: on the periphery of our narratives, on the frontier. That would be an ironic location to place many of the Sultans of Delhi.

3

'Silk Road, Cotton Road or ... Indo-Chinese Trade in Pre-European Times'

Stephen F. Dale

———— • ✦ • ————

INTRODUCTION

In his discussion of Southeast Asia's commerce with India and China, Anthony Reid remarks, 'Situated between the world's two major sources of fine cloth—India for cottons and China for silks—Southeast Asia became internationally known as a consumer rather than as a producer of textiles.'[1] Reid's allusion to Southeast Asian consumption of Chinese silk and Indian cotton cloth implicitly raises questions about the nature of commercial relations between these two great Asian civilizations. While it is well known that India and China supplied much of the Southeast Asia and West Asia with cotton and silk cloth respectively, much less is recorded about the degree to which these 'countries' or regions sold their apparently complementary textile products to each other, and whether or not other additional natural or manufactured goods comprised an important segment of Indo-Chinese trade. While

---

[1] Anthony Reid, *Southeast Asia in the Age of Commerce 1450–1680* (New Haven: Yale University Press, 1988), p. 90. For Southeast Asian trade, see also G. R. Tibbetts, *A Study of the Arabic Texts Containing Material on South-East Asia* (Leiden and London: E. J. Brill, 1979). Hans Bielenstein, *Diplomacy and Trade in the Chinese World 589–1276* (Leiden: Brill, 2005), pp. 72–77 summarizes Indo-Chinese diplomatic/trade missions between the seventh and tenth centuries CE.

the available sources to study the commerce between South Asia and China in pre-European times are predictably fragmentary, they suggest a pattern of complementary trade relations in textile manufactures as well as a broader range of commercial exchanges.

In broad outline, Indian and Chinese sources suggest two things about Indo-Chinese commerce in textiles prior to the sixteenth century. These are, first, that China sold silk textiles to India throughout nearly two millennia from the early years of the Han dynasty (206 BCE to 220 CE) to the period of the Ming dynasty (1368–1644 CE), and did so even though Indians began producing the cloth in the early Gupta period and vastly expanded silk cloth production from the thirteenth century onwards. Second, it is equally likely, although much harder to document, that India or its cultural surrogates—the Indianized states of Southeast Asia—sold cotton cloth to China at an early but undetermined date in the Christian Era, and that certain kinds of Indian cotton cloth continued to be sold in China well after the Chinese cultivation of cotton and production of cotton cloth blossomed in the late thirteenth and early fourteenth centuries. Put another way, silk cloth production originated in China and the Chinese always produced certain varieties of silk cloth or thread not matched in India or other silk-producing regions, while cotton cloth was first manufactured in South Asia, where Indians continued to produce certain varieties that always found a market in China. And the knowledge of silk and cotton cultivation was transmitted to India and China, respectively, both via the so-called 'Silk Road' routes of Central Asia as well as the southeast overland route that linked Szechwuan and the Chinese heartland with Burma, Assam, Bengal and the Ganges valley.

Chinese silk, Sanskrit *cinapatta* or 'Chinese cloth' was imported into India during Mauryan (322–183 BCE) or early Han times. It may first have arrived via Burma, but undoubtedly came in larger amounts via Xinjiang to Kashmir, or through Bactria and Kabul. Later, especially from the eighth century CE onwards, the maritime route steadily grew in importance for Sino-Indian commerce of all kinds.[2] Chinese silk cloth is referred to in early Indian Buddhist texts and, more specifically, identified in the *Arthashastra* (c. second century CE).[3] It is not known when Indians first began weaving silk cloth themselves, but silk weavers' guilds are known to have existed

[2] Tansen Sen, *Buddhism, Diplomacy and Trade* (Honolulu: University of Hawaii Press, 2003), p 176

[3] A. L. Basham, *The Wonder that was India* (New York: Grove Press, repr. 1959), p. 197.

by the fourth and fifth century CE. However, until the Sultanate era, that is, between the thirteenth and fifteenth centuries CE, Indians used only silk from wild cocoons, not knowing, evidently, how to use mulberry silk cocoons or how to unravel thread from boiled cocoons.[4] The Chinese Buddhist pilgrim Hsüan-tsang describes this Indian silk by its indigenous name, *kauseya*. Therefore, it is not surprising that substantial amounts of Chinese silk continued to be highly prized and were sold in India during the next millennium. Various Sanskrit texts attest to its use by the Indian royalty from the first through the seventh century CE; it was valued by the Indian elite, male and female, who in the plays of Kalidasa (c. first century BCE to fifth century CE) wear it for weddings. Embassies from T'ang rulers (618–907 CE) visiting India in the seventh century are known to have brought large amounts of silk to Indian courts.[5] The ample Sanskrit vocabulary and literary references to silk give an idea of the prevalence of silk cloth among the Indian elite of this period, although some of this cloth also came from Iran.[6] Even though the warm, humid Indian climate has left no identifiable Chinese silk artefacts from the pre-European age, substantial amounts of Chinese silk continued to arrive in India in the thirteenth and fourteenth centuries. The Chinese chronicler Ma Huan discusses this trade in his account of the 1433 Ming voyage to the Indian Ocean, although he also mentions Indian silk production both in Bengal and Kerala.[7]

Although Indian use of Chinese silk is generally known, the Chinese consumption of cotton cloth is rarely discussed in the surveys of Asian trade. However, what was the 'Silk Road' for Chinese silk was, in the reverse direction, a 'Cotton Road'. Cotton and cotton cloth, known by its Sanskrit-derived name as *pai-tieh*, first reached territories where China periodically exercised suzerainty in the present-day Xinjiang.[8]

---

[4] Xinru Liu, *Silk and Religion: An Exploration of Material Life and the Thought of People*, AD 600–1200 (Delhi: Oxford University Press, 1996), p. 50.

[5] Sen, *Buddhism, Diplomacy and Trade*, p.185 and Bielenstein, *Diplomacy and Trade in the Chinese World*, p. 72.

[6] Xinru Liu, *Silk and Religion*, p. 52. For the varieties of Chinese silk, see Shelagh Vainker, *Chinese Silk, A Cultural History* (New Brunswick, N. J.: Rutgers University Press, 2004).

[7] Ma Huan, *Ying-yai Sheng-lan The Overall Survey of the Ocean's Shores* [1433], trans. and ed. J. V. G. Mills (Cambridge: Cambridge University Press for the Hakluyt Society, 1970), pp. 143, 163.

[8] *Pai-tie* from the Sanskrit, *patta*. Cotton cloth may have been produced in South Asia as early as 2300 BCE, in the Indus Valley cities of Harappa and Mohenjo Daro. Joseph Needham, *Science and Civilization in China*, Vol. 5 'Chemistry and Chemical Technology,' Part IX 'Textile Technology: Spinning and Reeling,' by Dieter Kuhn (Cambridge: Cambridge University Press, 1968), p. 58.

Fragments of cotton cloth with an Indian Buddhist design dating to the eastern or later Han have been found in the ruins of a site near Niya, east of Khotan, on the southern and most Indianized section of the 'Silk Road'.[9] Whether or not this cloth was actually produced in Niya or imported from India, cotton cultivation and cotton cloth production seems to have developed in Xinjiang at roughly the same time as Indians began producing their own silk cloth. By the sixth century CE, the administrative and military city of Gaoch'ang, near the present-day Turfan, was known to produce *pai-tieh* or, in Chinese, *mien-hua* cloth, and in tribute lists from the T'ang era, Gansu is identified as a source of cotton, as well as hides and other exotica from the wilds of Central Asia.[10] Cotton cloth production is described in *The History of the Liang Dynasty* (502–556 CE).

> The State of Kaoch'ang was abundant in a special kind of herb which had fruit resembling cocoons.... The fruits of this herb were called *pai-tieh* seeds. People in this state used this fibre material for weaving cloth, which appeared very soft and white. Such cloth used to be exchanged for other commodities.[11]

The other route for the transfer of cotton cultivation to China was from east Bengal, Assam and Burma to western Yunnan, and this may also have occurred during the Han dynasty.[12]

However, just as it took several more centuries for Indians to develop silk industry on a large scale, so too the production of cotton cloth in China proper, that is beyond the border territories of Xinjiang and Yunnan, did not develop into a major industry until the late thirteenth and early fourteenth centuries. Scholars offer different reasons for this relatively slow development. One is that hemp had long been successfully cultivated and used for cloth in China.[13] A second is that the prevalence and popularity of silk cloth, especially in major production centres such

---

[9] Gau Hanyu, *Chinese Textile Designs*, trans. Rosemary Scott and Susan Whitfield (Hong Kong: Viking, 1992), 26 and plate 25.

[10] Edward Schaefer, *The Golden Peaches of Samarkand* (Berkeley: University of California Press, 1985), p. 106.

[11] Quoted by Kang Chao, *The Development of Cotton Textile Production in China* (Cambridge, Ma.: East Asian Center, 1977), p. 5.

[12] Sen, *Buddhism, Diplomacy and Trade*, p. 10.

[13] Xiaozhai Lu and Robert C. Clarke, 'The Cultivation and Use of Hemp (*Cannabis sativa* L.) in Ancient China,' www.hempfood.com/IHA/iha02111.html, pp. 1–7, and Needham, *Science and Civilization in China*, 5, Part IX, pp. 18–22.

as Xian, made it difficult for this foreign cloth to penetrate the Chinese market.[14] A third and related reason is that the variety of cotton grown in Xianjian, *Gossypium herbaceum,* a short-stem variety, was inferior both to that grown in India, as well as to the variety that entered China through the south. This variety, *Gossypium arboreum,* which originated in East Bengal, became the basis for the Chinese cotton industry. As for the reason(s) why cotton production expanded so quickly in the thirteenth century, this has been attributed to the development of a new ginning frame sometime in the late twelfth and early thirteenth century and, second, to the virtually simultaneous Mongol, Yuan dynasty (1271–1368 CE) stimulus of cotton cultivation, in which the Mongols demanded cotton to clothe their troops, not the first or last time in world history that warfare stimulated a major industrial development.[15] Under the Mongols, five provinces paid a cotton tax in kind, and later during the Ming era, peasants with certain sized holdings were required to use part of their land to produce cotton.[16]

Yet, as in the case of Indian use of Chinese silk, even as China's cotton cloth industry developed, China continued to import cotton cloth throughout the pre-European centuries. It is impossible to estimate the volume of these imports, or always to identify the original source, whether India or Southeast Asia. It seems likely from the extant fragmentary evidence that it was aristocratic Chinese consumers who sought out certain especially fine varieties of cotton cloth. While the tribute of inferior Gansu cotton took place, T'ang sources indicate that cotton was an expensive foreign product and that most Chinese monks who wished to follow strict *vinaya* texts requiring them to wear cotton found it too expensive.[17] T'ang era texts also extol the 'sunrise clouds of morning' or 'rosy cotton' or 'morning sunrise clouds', beautifully printed fine cloth that came from the Indianized states of Southeast Asia and Burma. Burmese Buddhists, like Chinese Buddhist monks, were said to wear cotton cloth because of their Buddhist non-violent beliefs, which forbade them to use silkworms and thus injure living things.[18] At least some of the cotton cloth that T'ang writers praised

---

[14] Chao, *The Development of Cotton Textile Production in China,* p. 7.

[15] Chao, *The Development of Cotton Textile Production in China,* p. 18 and Needham, *Science and Civilization in China,* 5, Part IX, pp. 58–59.

[16] Chao, *The Development of Cotton Textile Production in China,* p. 19.

[17] Liu, *Silk and Religion,* pp. 51–52.

[18] Schaeffer, *The Golden Peaches of Samarkand,* p. 206.

probably came from India, for Indian musicians who played in Xian (Ch'ang-an) are described in at least one source as being clothed in 'dawn-flushed cotton'.[19] Hsüan-tsang also records giving fine silks in China to 'foreign Brahman guests' while coveting fine Indian cottons presented to him by visiting Indian Buddhist monks. It is during the early Ming era, when Chinese cotton production was widespread, that Ma Huan offers specific information about Chinese knowledge of and interest in Indian cotton. He is particularly informative about Bengali fabrics, and after remarking, 'The land [of Bengal] produces five or six kinds of fine cloth,' he enumerates six types of cotton cloth, followed by several types of silk. One of these cotton fabrics, a 'cloth as fine as starched paper,' known as *pi cloth,* perhaps the fine muslin cloth for which Bengal was famous, is a type often mentioned in Chinese sources.[20] Ma Huan's careful description of Bengali cotton cloth—and one South Indian, probably Coimbatore variety sold in the Kerala port of Calicut (Kozhikode)—indicates that the Chinese continued to purchase fine varieties of Indian cotton cloth in the pre-European era.

While there appears to be a reciprocal symmetry to Indo-Chinese cloth production and sales, it is impossible to estimate the overall 'balance of payments' relationship of these great continental economies. Apart from the political differences of the two regions—a centralized Chinese state that could dictate production and commerce, as opposed to a decentralized South Asia with regional Indian economies—there is not even the kind of substantial anecdotal information available for Indo-Chinese commerce that is extant for Indo-Roman trade, in which Roman currency paid for Indian cloth and spices. However, one thing is certain, and that is the connection suggested above, between Buddhism and Indo-Chinese commerce in textiles. Thus, during the T'ang era, when rulers enthusiastically patronized Buddhism, T'ang embassies and Buddhist monks exchanged silk in India for Buddhist artefacts. Buddhist religious artefacts seem to have been the Indian equivalent of Chinese export porcelain. Even in the earlier 'Six Dynasties' era, the demand for such artefacts was 'enormous'. It is difficult to overestimate their popularity in China and equally difficult, of course, to estimate their value relative to Chinese silk in India, as they represent quite distinct types of commodities. Nonetheless, during the T'ang,

[19] *Ibid.*, p. 207.
[20] Note by J. V. G. Mills in Ma Huan, *Ying-yai Sheng-lan*, p. 162, n. 1.

Along the familiar trade routes through the deserts of Central Asia, or through the Southern Seas, a great traffic in holy and venerable objects passed from India and its cultural dependencies into T'ang [China] .... The reverence shown to relics of the saints and masters of Buddhism, and even the Buddhas themselves, was phenomenal, and what is more these objects fetched a great price in the public markets.[21]

Bodhi trees, while not exactly artefacts, were one of the commodities the Chinese coveted; they arrived in China with a mission from the north Indian ruler, Harsha of Kanauj, in 641 CE and again from the Gangetic kingdom of Magadha in 647 CE.[22]

Apart from these cotton and Buddhist artefacts, India exported a number of other commodities to China. In the late Han, when Indo-Chinese trade was stimulated by the Kushanas' (first–third centuries CE) control of Indian and Central Asian territory, Indians sent coral, pearls and glass to China.[23] Incense also appears in sources as Buddhism spread into China in the early centuries of the Christian Era, yet another example of the connection between Buddhism and Indo-Chinese trade. The T'ang era also saw the Chinese import Indian drugs and medical texts, many of them also associated with flourishing Chinese Buddhist culture of the period.[24] Indian scientists also arrived in China. Astronomy, one of the most respected Indian sciences in the T'ang, is not necessarily directly linked to Buddhism, although one of the most eminent Indian astronomers residing in China in the eighth century was named Gautama Siddhartha. However, two other Indian families, who along with Gautama Siddhartha monopolized the science of calendrical calculations at the Chinese court, bore the names Kasyapa and Kumara.[25]

The presence of Indian scientists in China is only one indication of the relative frequency with which Indian merchants, pilgrims, medical crackpots and others visited China. The idea of the *kala panni*, the belief that Indian caste restrictions inhibited Indians from travelling overland or overseas, may have been true for certain Indians at certain times, but it did not prevent Brahmins from taking up residence in Xian—or from

---

[21]   Schaeffer, *The Golden Peaches of Samarkand*, pp. 265–66.

[22]   *Ibid.*, p. 122.

[23]   Liu, *Ancient India and Ancient China*, pp. 53–63.

[24]   Schaefer, *The Golden Peaches of Samarkand*, p. 182.

[25]   *Ibid.*, p. 275.

offering their magical, legitimizing services to monarchies in Southeast Asia—much less prevent the northern and southern Indian merchants from travelling to Chinese territories to trade. Iranian or Iranized merchants, principally Parthians and Sogdians, apparently dominated the Indo-Chinese trade in the pre-Buddhist and Buddhist era. Parthians, who controlled Iran and parts of Central Asia for several centuries from the second century BCE to the early Christian Era, competed with Roman merchants to supply Indian and Chinese goods to the Red Sea region, but in the second century CE during the Kushana era, Sogdian and to some degree Indian merchants became increasingly influential. Sogdians controlled much of the trade along both the Central Asian land and Southeast Asia sea routes from the fourth century CE to the end of the T'ang, and their letters reveal the presence of sophisticated Sogdian merchant guilds operating in Xinjiang, northwestern India and Southeast Asia.[26]

Yet, even though Sogdian merchants dominated both Central Asian and Southeast Asian Indo-Chinese commerce during these centuries, Indian merchants are still known to have been active in Xinjiang. The Sogdian letters cited above also contain hints that in Loulan, in the northeast Taklamakan desert region, Indian merchants cooperated with Sogdians. A document dated to the seventh century CE found near Turfan records that three merchants surnamed Zhu, a probable Chinese designation for Indian merchants (*tianzhu*), received silver payment for some unnamed goods.[27] At a much later date, Indian merchant guilds from the South Indian Chola kingdom are known to have played an undefined role in the Indo-China trade, although it is difficult to determine how many may have traded in Southeast Asian or even Chinese ports. However, it is certainly well established that the Chola kingdom welcomed merchants as enthusiastically as the Zamorins of Calicut, whose entrepôt Ma Huan describes in his account of the 1433 voyage as 'The great country of the Western Ocean.'[28]

The picture of Indo-Chinese trade that emerges from the fragmentary sources of the pre-European era suggests a kind of economic symmetry

---

[26] Sen, *Buddhism, Diplomacy and Trade*, p. 161 and Frantz Grenet, 'Les marchands sogdiens dans le mers du Sud à l'époque préislamique' in *Inde-Asie Centrale, Routes du commerce et des idées* ed. Pierre Chuvin (Tashkent and Aix –en-Provence, 1996), pp. 65–84.

[27] *Ibid.*, pp. 140–63.

[28] Ma Huan, *Ying-yai Sheng-lan*, p. 137.

where the export of cloth and Buddhist artefacts may possibly have balanced off the Indian imports of silk and, during the Sultanate era, the occasional shipment of porcelain. The latter was sought after by Muslim monarchs but not usually by their Hindu predecessors or contemporaries, except those, perhaps, who had been influenced by Muslim tastes.[29] Given the enormous time period of this survey and the knowledge that even in discussing Indo-Chinese trade, one is often citing regional peculiarities, it is difficult to make many categorical judgements about the economic relations of the two great Asian civilizations. Thus, while Chinese merchants may have been willing to pay an Indian merchant in seventh-century Turfan with silver and, on other occasions, to purchase Indian products with gold and copper, Ma Huan mentions the Chinese purchasing 'precious stones, pearls and corals' in Calicut with 'hemp-silk or other such articles which must be given in exchange for it' in 1433.[30] And the value of Chinese silk must usually have been sufficient as an exchange commodity, even for overpriced Buddhist artefacts.

Apart from this apparent symmetry of trade, the other obvious fact of Indo-Chinese commerce was the central importance of Buddhism in stimulating commerce of all kinds. This cultural dictate also caused the Chinese to value Indian commodities such as incense and to regard Indians as a people skilled not only in spiritual matters but in professions such as medicine. Records from the Sung dynasty indicate, for example, that during the course of the eleventh century Indian Buddhist monks, who were by then making pilgrimages to Wu Tai Shan in Shanxi province, brought vast quantities of aromatics and medicine coveted by the Chinese. This aspect of Indo-Chinese relations seems to have been largely one sided, no doubt reflecting China's enormous wealth, particularly the wealth of its centralizing dynasties—and also perhaps, during the T'ang era, the 'Occidentalism' of a confident empire—for whom Indians as well as Central Asian Turks were an intriguing curiosity.

---

[29] Chinese porcelain fragments have been found in the ruins of buildings at Vijayanagar. I am indebted to Sanjay Subrahmanyam and Cathy Asher for suggesting that 'Hindu' rulers in times of Muslim dominance may also have valued the Chinese export porcelain. For a reference to porcelain fragments, see John M. Fritz and George Michell, *City of Victory, Vijayanagara* (New York, N.Y.: Aperture, 1991), p. 100.

[30] Ma Huan, *Ying-yai Sheng-lan*, p. 141.

4

The Political Economy of Opium Smuggling in Early Nineteenth Century India:

Leakage or Resistance?

Claude Markovits

———— • ✦ • ————

INTRODUCTION

The link between narcotics, imperialism and capitalism has long attracted the attention of scholars. Recently, Carl Trocki has reiterated the classical Marxist position, dating back to Karl Marx himself, on the incestuous relationship between drugs and empire, while recognizing that the opium trade also nurtured certain forms of indigenous capitalism in Asia.[1] While he has focused on the global Asian opium scene, including India, China and Southeast Asia, other scholars have given more attention to the Indian context of the trade. Amar Farooqi, in a book which is probably the most detailed history of the opium trade as seen from India, has stressed the contribution of the 'illegal' trade in Malwa opium to capital accumulation in Western India in the first three decades of the nineteenth century.[2] John Richards, more than twenty

---

[1] Carl Trocki, *Opium, Empire and the Global Political Economy: A Study of the Asian Opium Trade 1750–1950* (London, New York: Routledge, 1999).

[2] Amar Farooqi, *Smuggling as Subversion: Colonialism, Indian Merchants and the Politics of Opium* (New Delhi: New Age International, 1998).

years after his pathbreaking essay on peasant production of opium[3] has returned to the topic with a wide-ranging survey of the contribution of the drug to the finances of British India.[4] In this essay, I propose to revisit the history of the Malwa opium trade with a view to discussing both its general impact on capital accumulation in early nineteenth century western India and its link with imperial expansion. I shall focus more specifically on the case of Sindh, a largely neglected region of the subcontinent, whose transformation into the main smuggling route for the drug after 1819 was one of the factors that led to its integration into the British Indian Empire.

SMUGGLING MALWA OPIUM TO CHINA THROUGH THE PORTS OF PORTUGUESE INDIA: A BRIEF SUMMARY OF THE FACTS

Cultivation of poppy in that region of Central India, traditionally known as Malwa, went back far in time: the crop of poppy in *subha* Malwa is mentioned in the *Ain-i-Akbari*,[5] and the first Portuguese visitors to India remarked on the existence of an active export trade in 'Cambay opium' from the west coast of India, which was destined mostly for the Indonesian archipelago. In the seventeenth century, Surat became the main hub of this trade, in which the Dutch East India Company was actively involved[6] before it shifted to Bombay, from where it seems that, starting in the 1770s, small quantities were shipped to China. But this did not affect the official trade of the English East India Company (EIC) in 'Bengal' or 'Patna' opium, mostly shipped from Calcutta, over which the Company had established a monopoly between 1773 and 1797. The drug, smuggled into China by private traders because of the official interdiction of the trade by the Chinese authorities, but grown in Bihar under strict Company supervision, became the main item in the Indo-Chinese trade, basically allowing the British to import Chinese

---

[3] John F. Richards, 'The Indian Empire and Peasant Production of Opium in the Nineteenth Century', *Modern Asian Studies* 15 (1981), pp. 59–82.

[4] John F. Richards, 'The Opium Industry in British India', in *Land, Politics and Trade in South Asia*, ed. Sanjay Subrahmanyam (Delhi: Oxford University Press, 2004), pp. 44–81.

[5] Farooqi, *Smuggling as Subversion*, p. 60.

[6] See the contribution by George Bryan Souza in this book.

tea without sending too much specie to China.[7] It was only in 1803 that the Supreme Government in Calcutta, worried about the breach of its monopoly, started enquiring about the so-called 'clandestine' Malwa opium trade from officials in Bombay who reported on its antiquity and provided some information as to the producing areas and the trading circuits. They mentioned the role played by the ancient city of Ujjain as the major market for the drug: there it was brought in a semi-manufactured state from all over Malwa and further refined before being sent towards the coast for export. The purchasers were 'native merchants' who bought the opium either on their own account or as agents for firms located in port cities.

On receipt of this information about the trade, Governor-General Lord Wellesley instructed the Bombay Government to take immediate steps for its 'complete annihilation'.[8] In 1804, the authorities were further informed that 100 piculs (a Chinese measure of weight equivalent to 133 1/3 lb or 60.453 kg) of Malwa opium had been brought to Macao on board the ship *Lowjee family*, apparently from Goa,[9] which added to their determination to put an end to that trade. It was however easier said than done, and, when in 1805, the Bombay Government forbade to ship the drug through Bombay, the trade shifted largely to the Portuguese ports of Diu, Damao and Goa, which had regular maritime links with Macao. That Portuguese enclave on the South China coast had become after 1799, following the strict measures taken by the Chinese authorities against the contraband trade at Canton, the main point of entry of the drug into China.[10] The British turned then to the Portuguese authorities, and, under British pressure, the viceroy of Portuguese India agreed to forbid shipments from Goa and to instruct his subordinates at Damao and Diu to take similar action. During the British occupation of Portuguese India, in 1805–10, the trade appears to have decreased significantly but did not disappear altogether, as ports in Saurashtra or even in British Bombay were used as alternatives. With the return of

[7] M. Greenberg, *British Trade and the Opening of China, 1800–42* (Cambridge: Cambridge University Press, 1951).

[8] Trocki, *Opium*, p. 78.

[9] D. E. Owen, *British Opium Policy in China and India* (New Haven, CT: Yale University Press, 1934), pp. 69–70.

[10] On the emergence of Macao as the major hub of the opium trade around 1800, see P. Y. Manguin, *Les Nguyen, Macau et le Portugal: Aspects politiques et commerciaux d'une relation privilégiée en Mer de Chine, 1773–1802* (Paris: Ecole Française d' Extreme-orient, 1984), pp. 135–38. I am grateful to Sanjay Subrahmanyam for bringing this source to my attention.

Goa, Damao and Diu to Portuguese control in 1810, there was a new spurt in the trade, unnoticed by the British authorities till, in 1815, the supercargoes of the EIC at Macao heard that 300 chests of Malwa opium had been brought to Macao and more than 200 to neighbouring Whampoa.[11] They tried to persuade the Portuguese authorities to intervene against the trade, but, as a result of their interference, were themselves barred from dealing in opium at Macao till 1823.

Prevented from blocking the sea route by the attitude of its Portuguese ally, which understandably did not want to be excluded from the benefits to be gained from participating in such a lucrative activity, the EIC focused on trying to block the land routes between the producing areas, which were situated far inland and the exporting ports in Portuguese India. To that effect, it sought to conclude treaties with its other allies, the native states of Gujarat, through which the drug had to transit. Although the Gaekwar of Baroda, the Kathiawar chiefs and the rulers of Palanpur, Chhota Udaipur, Rajpipla and Porbandar duly signed agreements by which they promised to take measures against the transit of opium through their territories, the latter were not always actually enforced by their officials, some of whom were most probably in cahoots with the drug smugglers. To satisfy the growing demand in China (itself, let us recall, a result of British policies, ineffectively resisted by the Chinese authorities), the 'Malwa sowcars' (*sahukars*), the mostly Marwari and Gujarati merchants-financiers who financed the cultivators, multiplied their advances to the producers. As a result, the output grew from an annual average of 300 to 600 chests of one picul each in the early 1800s to 900 chests in 1817. In 1818, a chest of Malwa opium sold in Canton for (Spanish) $680 as against $840 for a chest of 'Patna' opium.[12] It is not that the peasant in Bihar got more for his poppy than the one in Malwa: on the contrary, one estimate is that peasants in Malwa were paid three times as much for their crop as the cultivators in Bihar.[13] The price differential[14] reflected mostly the overcharging of the Chinese consumer

---

[11] Owen, *British Opium Policy*, p. 70.

[12] Trocki, *Opium*, pp. 79–87.

[13] B. B. Chaudhuri, *Growth of Commercial Agriculture in Bengal (1757–1900)*, Vol. I (Calcutta: Indian Studio Past and Present, 1964), p. 11. This estimate, however, appears exaggerated. On the conditions of the opium-growing peasantry in Malwa, see Farooqi, *Smuggling as Subversion*, pp. 66–71.

[14] Which tended to increase, as data from early 1823 reveal that the price of Bihar opium had climbed to (Spanish)$2,350 per chest, while that of Malwa opium had only increased to $1,380.

by a greedy monopolistic organization. Although it was sometimes stated by Company officials that the Patna product was of better quality than the Malwa sort, the Chinese consumer reacted mostly to price and sales of Malwa opium in China boomed.

In 1819, the Company decided to adopt a new strategy vis-à-vis that trade, which it was obviously not able to stop; it decided to take control of it, in the same way as it controlled the Bengal opium trade. It proceeded to buy the entire Malwa opium crop and to auction it, both at Bombay and Calcutta, from where it could be shipped by the same merchants who shipped 'legally' (from the British point of view, the Chinese view being of course different) the Bengal opium. The new plan however failed, as it proved impossible to control the entire supply, one of the reasons being that the Malwa sowcars responded to the new conjuncture by raising production considerably. The more the Company bought, the more money they advanced to the producers, while continuing to smuggle through various outlets the part of the crop which they did not sell to the Company. In 1821–22, sales of Malwa opium in China reached 1,715 chests, and the following year they shot up to 4,000 chests, a level at which they remained during most of the 1820s.[15] At the same time, to compensate for the closure of the route through Gujarat, a new route was found through Sindh, an independent polity which had delicate relations with British India.

The new route appears to have been in use from 1819, but it was only in 1821 that Company officials took notice of it. As it is described in various official reports,[16] it started in Pahli, in the territories of the maharaja of Jodhpur, a small locality to which the drug was conveyed by caravans from the various marts in the producing areas of Malwa, of which the most important was Mundissore, near Ujjain. From Pahli, it was carried on camelback to Jaisalmer and then crossed the Thar Desert via Umarkot on the Sindh side (Akbar's birthplace) to Hyderabad in the Indus valley from where it reached Karachi. From there, small boats

---

Consultation 7A, 17 April 1823, Bengal Board of Revenue (Miscelleaneous) Proceedings (Opium), 7 January to 27 June 1823, Oriental and India Office Collections of the British Library, London.

[15] Trocki, *Opium*, pp. 79–87.

[16] See in particular, Bengal Board of Revenue (Miscelleaneous) Proceedings, Opium, Consultation 8A, 9 March 1824, enclosing letter from opium agent in Malwa to Board of Revenue, dated 17 February 1824, enclosing 'Memorandum respecting the export of opium to Pahlie and Demaun', and Consultation 18, dated 22 April 1824, *Ibid.*, enclosing information collected at Pahli by a native informant.

took it to Damao in Portuguese territory from where it was shipped to Macao, to be smuggled into Canton (via the island of Lintin, which had become after 1815 the main hub of the contraband trade) and sold on the Chinese market. From Mundissore, it took approximately two months for the drug to reach Damao: fifteen days by mulepacks from Mundissore to Pahli, twelve days on camelback from Pahli to Jaisalmer, thirty days for the crossing of the Thar desert and the Indus valley to Karachi, and a five day boat journey between Karachi and Damao.[17]

In February 1822, in a letter to the Supreme Government in Fort William, the Bombay Revenue Department expressed confidence that the restrictive measures taken to counteract the clandestine transit of the drug through the territories of British India and the allied native states had so forced up the cost of transit through what it called the 'circuitous' Sindh route as to render the operation unprofitable.[18] In a cautious aside, however, tending to show that the officials in the Department had only limited faith in their own reasoning, they added that these difficulties 'would be considerably enhanced if the route through Jeysalmer and Pallie (sic) be closed, and above all if the Ameers of Scinde could be induced to prohibit the transit of opium through the Scinde territories, and the port of Currachee in particular'. But they made it clear that the Company Government had 'not ventured to solicit such a favour from a government whose policy and suspicion of our views are of so averse a character'. Even if it had been solicited, one must add, it is most unlikely that the government of Sindh would have deferred to British wishes, as opium transit duties were increasingly providing it with the bulk of its revenues, a point to which we shall return. Unable to block the route to the sea, the EIC tried to impose treaties on the producing states so as to regulate the output and the prices, and most of them entered into agreements by 1826. But Gwalior held out, and this considerably limited the effectiveness of the EIC policy.[19]

In 1830, faced with its continued failure at preventing the 'illegal' trade, the Company government officially abandoned its policy of restrictions and tried to at least benefit from it by taxing it heavily. It

---

[17] Enclosure no 8B in *Ibid*.

[18] Bombay Revenue Department to Secretary to the Supreme Government in the Territorial Department at Fort William, 27 February 1822, enclosed in Bengal Board of Revenue (Miscellaneous) Proceedings, Opium, 4 January to 28 June 1822, consultation no 16.

[19] Farooqi, *Smuggling as Subversion*, pp. 94–106.

levied a duty of Rs 175 per chest on all Malwa opium transiting through Bombay, but, since the smuggling through Damao continued unabated, it reduced it to Rs 125 in 1835.[20] Epistolary exchanges between the authorities in Bombay and the opium agent in Malwa, the man on the spot in charge of implementing government opium policy in the producing areas, led to the airing of some detailed information about costs, which is worth mentioning here. The agent, in a letter to the Bombay Revenue Department, explained that, when the pass had first been introduced, the differential in the cost of transport of one chest from Malwa to the coast between the Bombay route and the Damao route had amounted to Rs 85 in favour of the former (which was not enough to cover the price of the pass, fixed at Rs 175), and that it had since been reduced to only Rs 66. He estimated the cost of transport of one chest of opium from Malwa to Damao to be about Rs 100, as against Rs 34 for transport from Malwa to Bombay,[21] an estimate which, by the way, does not tally exactly with the evidence he appended to his letter, based on information provided by native opium trading firms. The latter indicates a cost of only Rs 88 for the Damao route, as against Rs 42 for the Bombay route, that is a differential of only Rs 46, which seems more plausible.

Whatever the true figures were for the cost of land transport (and the agent might well have 'doctored' figures to exaggerate the differential, a way of defending his own record), given that the cost of maritime freight on the India-China run was only marginally lower on Portuguese than on British vessels (Rs 19-7-0 as against Rs 20-0-0, for one chest of opium), it was clear that the big difference in the total cost of transit of one chest of opium between Malwa and Lintin was entirely due to the price of the pass. According to the calculations presented by the agent, the transit cost of that chest amounted to approximately Rs 100 less via Damao than via Bombay. The price of the pass amounted to much more than the total of the duties levied at different stages by various non-British authorities on the route. Curiously, duties levied in Sindh do not figure in the calculations, which may be an oversight, but may also be due to a lack of detailed information. But another source estimates them

---

[20] Trocki, *Opium*, p. 86.

[21] Opium Agent in Malwa to Bombay Revenue Department, 29 May 1835, Bombay Revenue Proceedings for 1835, 17 June 1835, no 2740, Oriental and India Office Collections of the British Library.

to have been Rs 100 by chest[22] in 1838, which would have tended to equalize costs. In spite of his own (not too reliable) evidence pointing to the fact that the high price of the passes was the main parameter enhancing the Damao route over the Bombay route, the opium agent did not plead for a drastic reduction. He advised the authorities at Bombay to reduce the price by a minimum of Rs 25. Although the government eventually settled for a reduction of Rs 50, from Rs 175 to 125, even this concession did not stop the trade through Damao, which continued unabated till at least 1839. It is clear that, in their dealings with the 'illegal' Malwa opium trade, the Company authorities were hampered by their fiscal policies, especially after they had ceased, in 1833, to deal directly in opium. Only a drastic reduction in the price of passes could have brought about an end to the trade through Sindh by making the attractions of the Bombay route irresistible. But it would have meant accepting a fall in revenue for which the authorities were not ready. One can therefore surmise that the stopping of that illegal trade was not really a top priority for the Company.

It was only when the Company occupied Karachi in 1839, as a preliminary step to its ultimately disastrous Afghanistan campaign, that it could actually close the Sindh route. After the annexation of Sindh in 1843, some residual smuggling probably continued through other routes, but basically the Company was thence able to channel the trade through Bombay and to raise transit duties to Rs 200 per chest in 1843, to 300 in 1845 and to 400 in 1847.[23] By the 1850s, the Malwa opium trade was yielding to the Government of India an annual revenue of over Rs 30 million, that is approximately 60 per cent of total Indian opium revenue,[24] having thus superseded 'Bengal' opium.

The 'illegal' trade in Malwa opium, which occurred on a significant scale between 1803 and 1839, was certainly a thorn in the flesh of the EIC and prevented it, prior to 1833, from enjoying the fruits of a complete monopoly of this most lucrative of trades. As to its economic effects, they are difficult to estimate. The Bombay government lost revenue,

---

[22] In 1838, duties amounted to 234 kora or kashani rupees (local currencies of Sindh), equivalent to 200 Company rupees per camel load of two chests, that is Rs 100 per chest. See Alexander Burnes, 'On the Commerce of Hyderabad and Lower Sind' in *Reports and Papers, Political, Geographical and Commercial, Submitted to Government by Sir Alexander Burnes, Lieutenant Leech, Dr Lord and Lieutenant Wood Employed on Missions in the years 1835–36-37 in Scinde, Afghanistan and Adjacent Countries*, Calcutta, 1839, p. 21.

[23] Trocki, *Opium*, p. 87.

[24] Richards, 'The Opium Industry', Tables 1, 2, pp. 54–58, and Table 5, pp. 74–77.

mostly after 1819, but on the other hand, Bombay's loss was a gain to the governments of several native states, including Sindh. Whether they put this increased revenue to good or ill use is of course a different question, to which no answer can be given here. It seems to me that the story of the Malwa opium trade, which I have here briefly recounted, raises two different kinds of question: the role of Indian merchants in the trade and the latter's contribution to capital accumulation in India, as well as the role the opium trade had in integrating certain areas of the subcontinent, in particular Sindh, which is the special focus of my attention, into the global colonial economy.

SUBVERSION OR OPPORTUNISM?: THE ROLE OF INDIAN MERCHANTS AND OFFICIALS IN THE MALWA OPIUM TRADE

The Malwa opium trade mobilized different types of operators, whose identities varied overtime. Hence, the difficulty of presenting a clear picture and the temptation to exaggerate the degree of coherence of the operation. Four different locations were involved: the native states in Malwa, mostly Gwalior and Indore, where the poppy cultivation and the preparation of the drug took place; the transit areas, that is the territories through which the drug had to be carried to reach the coast; the ports, from where the drug was shipped to China; and lastly, the cities where the capital was raised to finance the trade, and where also the official auctions took place, which had a direct impact on the 'illegal' trade. In each type of location, there were different kinds of operators involved, which is why they have to be considered separately.

In Malwa, the producing area, apart from the peasants who cultivated the poppy, three different groups of agents were involved. The first group consisted of the 'Malwa sowcars' (*sahukars*), a generic term for a whole range of operators, from local moneylenders to city bankers, often Marwari, who controlled the money market in Malwa. Amongst them were village banias who made advances to the cultivators and purchased the raw produce as well as big opium dealers in the cities of Malwa who centralized the produce.[25] The former often borrowed from the latter funds, which they lent to the cultivators. The second group consisted of the *gomasthas*, both Marwari and Gujarati, who were the local agents

---

[25] For a good description of the trading circuit, see Farooqi, *Smuggling as Subversion*, pp. 71–73.

of big Indian firms from Bombay or Ahmedabad. They bought the semi-refined produce from the *sahukars* and had it further refined so as to transform it into chests of opium ready for transportation. The third group was made of officials from the native states, who, apart from 'protecting' the merchants, were often themselves directly involved in the trade. Thus, it is mentioned in one British source of 1824 that Ganga Appa, or Appa Gangadhar, who is described as 'the manager of Scindia's territories', is 'under hand' a partner with a big local merchant in all opium transactions.[26] In another document, mention is made of a particular trading house 'belonging to Tantiah Joog,[27] Holkar's (the ruler of Indore) Minister' having sent to Damao 2,000 chests of opium.[28] These three different kinds of agents were closely interlinked: the big *sahukars* had particularly close relations with state officials, to the point that the two groups could be difficult to distinguish one from another.

The transit areas presented a particularly complex picture. They were a patchwork of native states of various sizes, at first mostly situated in Gujarat, but after the area had fallen in 1803 under British direct or indirect domination, mostly in Rajputana, to which, from 1819 onwards, was added Sindh, an area I shall consider separately. In the states of Rajputana, the main agents involved in the opium trade were, on the one hand, Marwari merchants, who organized and financed the caravans crossing the Thar Desert; and on the other hand, state officials whose actions did not however attract much attention from the British and remain largely anonymous to us. Under British pressure, they seem to have acted sometimes to interrupt the caravans, but without much success,[29] which tends to suggest that some of them had been bribed.

---

[26] Enclosure no 8B, in Consultation no 8A, Bengal Board of Revenue (Miscellaneous) Proceedings, Opium, 9 March to 22 June 1824. On Appa Gangadhar, the main revenue farmer of Sindhia in northern Malwa, see Farooqi, *Smuggling as Subversion*, pp. 113–14.

[27] Tantiah Jog, or, as he is more frequently called, Tatya Jog, was a Maharashtrian Brahmin, the head of the firm of Ganesdas Kisnaji, which belonged to the Kibe family. He played a major role at Holkar's court. See *Ibid.*, pp. 46–47.

[28] Swinton, Opium Agent in Malwa, to Trotter, Secretary to the Board of Customs, Salt and Opium, Fort William, 2 January 1827, enclosure no 12 in Extract Bengal Salt and Opium Consultations, 8 February 1827, Board's Collections, 1784–1858, no 29139, Oriental and India Office Collections of the British Library.

[29] It is thus reported by the Political Agent at Udaipur in December 1827 that 'a party of smugglers have found their way in spite of opposition of Maharajah's troops', although a further report appended describes an 'affray' with 200 Megnahs (tribals?), in which 149 bags of opium were seized by the army of the Rana of Mewar. Political Agent at Udaipur to Captain Dangerfield, 5 December 1827, enclosed in consultation no 11, 5 January 1828, Board's Collections, no 29139.

The ports of shipment of the drug to China were many, but there was an increasing concentration of the trade in Damao. Prior to 1819, Mandvi in Kutch, Diu and Goa in Portuguese India, and other places are also mentioned, but at a later stage, they tend to disappear from the records. Portuguese trade returns recently published by Rudi Bauss show that, in the years 1816–19, the share of Goa in Macao imports of opium (which came entirely from the ports of Portuguese India) varied between 4 per cent and 23 per cent, meaning that Goa accounted for a significant share of the trade.[30] But after 1819, Damao seems to have practically monopolized the opium trade between Portuguese India and Macao. The main advantage of Damao seems to have been that it was less easily accessible by land than Goa (or Diu), and therefore, better adapted to the clandestine nature of the trade. British officials rarely ventured there,[31] and the smugglers who entirely dominated the trade of the port (there was apparently no other trading activity) could operate quite freely. They just had to bribe the few local Portuguese officials (in Goa, where Portuguese officials were much thicker on the ground, many more would have had to be bribed). The 'Damao merchants' mentioned in British documents seem to have been mostly Gujaratis, judging from their names. In one document dated 1824, it is reported from Ujjain by the opium agent in Malwa that 'the heads of all the Gujarat Houses (i.e. firms) residing there. . . have sent and established a House at Damao both for the purpose of present and future sales'.[32] It is clear that the Damao merchants were thus directly linked to the Malwa *gomasthas*. As to the boats doing the run between Karachi and Damao, they seem to have belonged either to native or to Portuguese merchants. Shipping

---

[30] R. Bauss, 'Textiles, Bullion and Other Trades of Goa: Commerce with Surat, Other Areas of India, Luso-Brazilian Ports, Macau and Mozambique, 1816–1819', *Indian Economic and Social History Review* 24 (1997), pp. 275–87. See also C. Pinto, *Trade and Finance in Portuguese India: A Study of the Portuguese Country Trade 1770–1840* (Delhi: Oxford University Press, 1994).

[31] A visit by two Englishmen, probably government spies, who requested that the Customs house be shown to them, is described in an intelligence report written by an official, the 'Native Superintendent of transit customs'. When alerted to the presence of the Englishmen, the Bombay merchants who were there 'writing out contracts for 4000 maunds of opium', 'concealed themselves in a room', so that the English gentlemen-spies 'did not see the merchants'. Enclosed in Collector of Surat to Secretary to the Government, Bombay, 2 May 1823, Bengal Board of Revenue (Miscellaneous) Proceedings, Opium, 7 January to 27 June 1823.

[32] Swinton to Secretary, Board of Customs, Salt and Opium, 4 March 1824, consulation no 18, 23 March 1824, Bengal Board of Revenue (Miscellaneous) Proceedings, Opium, 9 March to 22 June 1824.

from Damao to Macao was on Portuguese ships, often hailing from Bombay.[33]

The fourth tier in the system was represented by the big capitalists and speculators operating from a few cities, mostly Ahmedabad, Bombay and Calcutta. At different moments in time, European merchants and speculators were heavily involved in the illegal Malwa opium trade. In a minute dated April 1823, an official of the Bombay Opium Department, Warden, offered a brief history of that trade. He stressed that the trade in Malwa opium had been 'founded and increased by the enterprise of British Merchants, carried on by British capital, in position not of national but of foreign interests, as nearly the whole has found protection and encouragement under the Portuguese flag from Damao and Goa, ostensibly for Portuguese merchants'.[34] This was a familiar pattern in the history of British private capital in India: when it found itself hampered by the regulations of the East India Company, it assumed the guise of non-British European interests. Although European capital was present in the initial stages, the major role seems to have been increasingly played by Indian capitalists,[35] mostly Parsis and Gujarati Hindus based in Ahmedabad and Bombay, who had their agents both in Malwa and in Damao. They shipped the opium to Macao on Portuguese-owned vessels, and had Portuguese agents in Macao who despatched the opium to Lintin. They were the ones who invested the largest amounts in the trade and probably reaped most of the benefits, although many operators at different stages also took their cut.

Having thus described the different kinds of participants in the Malwa opium trade, and shown that they were interlinked in many

---

[33] In the above-quoted intelligence report, the British intelligence agent in Damao reports that '3500 maunds of opium have arrived, and two ships belonging to Sir Roger de Faria, Portuguese, are expected soon from Bombay to take it to Macao'. See note 31 above.

[34] Minute dated 30 April 1823 by Warden, enclosed in Territorial Department, Revenue Opium, Bombay, to Secretary to the Supreme Government, 5 May 1823, Bengal Board of Revenue (Miscellaneous) Proceedings Opium, 7 January to 27 June 1823.

[35] In a report to the Governor General by three officials in the Opium Department in 1823, it is mentioned that 'During the first three years, it was Macao and Calcutta capital, mostly the latter, which financed the purchases of smuggled opium. However, Calcutta capital in present year withdrew and Bombay merchants have become the principal if not the only purchasers'. The officials added that 'the principal speculators resident in Bengal and China' had turned to the purchase of the Company's Malwa opium in the Bombay auction with Calcutta and Macao capital. Larkin, Lindsay, Sargent, of the Opium Department, to Governor General in Council, 4 August 1823, Bengal Board of Revenue (Miscellaneous) Proceedings, Opium, 11 July to 30 December 1823, consultation no 12, 8 August.

ways, forming a whole supply chain which linked central India with western India and southern China, we are faced with the question of whether they formed a real combine, or represented an aggregate of operators pursuing diverse aims and brought together artificially by the opportunities for profit represented by the opium trade. The British at times saw them as a combine. Thus, the opium agent at Indore, James Taylor, wrote in July 1822 that the Government faced 'combined, active and persevering competition on the part of the merchants of Malwa, Kota and Mewar in conjunction with the Chief Native Merchants of Bombay and Damao'.[36] But this kind of statement was rare, and no big conspiracy theory surfaces through the mountains of official documents available on the Malwa opium trade. Company officials saw their adversaries as a circumstantial alliance of wily speculators and corrupt state officials out to deprive the Company government of legitimate revenue. But they did not see in that smuggling operation a major challenge to British rule. Amar Farooqi makes much of the presence of fairly large armed contingents to escort the smugglers' caravans, which did not hesitate to engage in skirmishes with the troops of the Company and its allies.[37] Although such breaches of Company Bahadur's monopoly on violence at times worried its officials, they were not of such magnitude as to represent a real threat to British law and order. The British were after all used to fighting armed smugglers at home: in Britain, the last encounter between the forces of the law and a gang of smugglers took place in 1833.

It is difficult to pinpoint the motivations of this range of very diverse operators. But the idea advanced by Farooqi of a conscious political defiance of the East India Company by indigenous capitalists[38] does appear far-fetched, considering that in 1817–18, the last indigenous power standing up to the Company, the Marathas, had been soundly defeated and that, after that date, nothing stood in the way of Company Bahadur's domination over the whole of India. It would have been

---

[36] James Taylor to Opium Agent, Bombay, 13 July 1821, enclosed in Revenue Department, Bombay, to Secretary to the Supreme Government in the Territorial Department, 27 February 1822, consultation no 16, Bengal Board of Revenue (Miscellaneous) Proceedings Opium, 4 January to 28 June 1822.

[37] Farooqi, *Smuggling as Subversion*, pp. 145–51.

[38] He writes: 'What we encounter here is not just "resilience of the bazaar economy". . . but a serious conflict between colonialism and Indian capitalists, wherein indigenous merchants were able to engage in a contest at various levels including that crucial arena-the market', *Ibid.*, p. 8.

extremely unlike Indian merchants—on the whole stark realists (at least it is my reading of them)—not to accept the new realities and to harbour any hope of some return to the past. The key to their behaviour more likely resided in opportunism rather than in any 'subversion'. This is not meant to deny them agency, but 'subversion' is a strong term when applied to capitalists: it cannot be equated with the everyday forms of resistance by poor and illiterate peasants. Unless we have some kind of proof of subversive intent on the part of Indian capitalists, we cannot simply ascribe to them that kind of intentionality. Their interests largely coincided with those of the rulers of the native states of Central India, and one of the keys to the success of the whole operation was undoubtedly the close relationship established between the merchants-financiers and the authorities of the native states of Central India where the poppy cultivation took place. To sustain the thesis about 'subversion', one would have to be able to prove that the rulers of the native states of Central India were also engaged in trying to subvert British rule. Given the fact that they had just been defeated by British armies, it seems more plausible to assume that they were only trying to survive in the new conjuncture of unalloyed British domination.[39] Opium, which carried a higher rate of land tax than other crops,[40] was a big potential money earner for them, and they had no reason to spurn its benefits. By encouraging poppy cultivation in their dominions, they were just imitating what the British were doing in Bihar, and there was no moral or legal ground on which the Company could prevent them from doing so. While the disbanding of their large armies had undoubtedly reduced the expenditure of the surviving Marathas states of Gwalior and Indore, it had also dried up large sources of revenue, and these states were in a dire financial condition. Opium revenue was the remedy at hand to avoid financial collapse, and there is nothing intrinsically subversive in the fact that the native states of Central India seized on it.

As far as the merchants were concerned, they were reacting to a certain shrinking of opportunities linked to the advent of British domination in western and central India. Lakshmi Subramaniam has shown how the end of the 'Anglo-Bania' partnership led to a diminishing role for the merchants-bankers of western India in the first decade of the

---

[39] Farooqi distinguishes between the attitude of Holkar's regime, which he finds more amenable to British pressures, and that of Sindhia's which appears to have been more intransigent. *Ibid.*, p. 49.

[40] *Ibid.*, p. 70.

nineteenth century.[41] Trading in Malwa opium, for which there was a constantly growing demand in China, was an opportunity not to be missed. The Government was aware that restrictions on the trade might provoke 'discontent among the trading classes', but 'the fact that the development of the Malwa trade in the drug. . . was of very recent origin and was the result of the pacification of central India by British arms and treasure, was considered to be a sufficient justification of an artificial restriction of their commercial dealings'.[42] Ironically, the ineffectiveness of official attempts at restricting the trade between 1819 and 1829 saved the Government from facing the discontent of the trading classes, the prospect of which it appeared to take so lightly.

It is difficult to measure the specific contribution this branch of the opium trade made to indigenous capital accumulation in western India. While there is no doubt that overall the profits of the opium trade were a major source of capital to the Bombay trading classes and largely account for the initial investment in cotton mills in Bombay from 1854 onwards, there is no way one can disentangle the profits gained in the 'illegal' Malwa trade from those accumulated in the 'legal' trade after 1819, since the same merchants were involved in both. Besides, it is easy, in the absence of reliable figures, to form an inflated idea of the size of the profits gained in the 'illegal' trade. It was a highly speculative venture, in which some undoubtedly earned large profits, but others severely burnt their fingers. A report of a visit to the producing area in 1824 written by the opium agent in Malwa, Swinton,[43] brings out how different outcomes could be for different types of operators. According to Swinton, 'Sowcars lose considerably by their speculation to Damao', and he provided detailed figures to support his point. 'But', he added,

. . . merchants such as Punnah Chand, Hurruck Chand and Lalloo Beyo (?), who purchase for the house of Bhoomanjee Hormusjee of Bombay, their case is widely different; they watched the market and the moment it fell under 60 Rs. . . they purchased largely in every mart...; they are safe receiving a Commission, and their principal the opium at rates that promise profit.

[41] Lakshmi Subramanian, *Indigenous Capital and Imperial Expansion: Bombay, Surat and the West Coast* (Delhi: Oxford University Press, 1996), pp. 336–37.

[42] Letter from Deputy Secretary to Government in attendance upon Governor-General to Resident at Indore quoted in 'Historical Memorandum' by R. M. Dane, Appendix B to *Royal Commission on Opium, 1894–95, Vol. VII, Final Report, Part II, Historical Appendices*, London, 1895, p. 54.

[43] Enclosure, dated 17 February 1824 in Consultation no 8A, 9 March, Bengal Board of Revenue (Miscellaneous) Proceedings, Opium, 9 March to 22 June 1824.

Here we see a clear distinction between on the one hand some Sowcars, probably endowed with limited capital and forced to dispose of their stocks at the lowest point in the price cycle, and on the other hand, the *gomasthas* working for a big Bombay Parsi capitalist firm, supplied with an abundance of funds, and therefore, able to play the market successfully.

The overall contribution of opium to their capital accumulation is likely to be exaggerated in the absence of reliable figures on firms' profits, even in the case of Bombay capitalists, both European[44] and Indian, some of whom undoubtedly made great gains in the Malwa opium trade, both legal and illegal. As to the 'Malwa sowcars', mostly Marwaris, we have seen that at times they lost heavily on the opium market, and it is impossible to evaluate precisely the contribution of opium to their own process of capital accumulation. In his seminal work on the Marwaris, Thomas Timberg focuses mostly on those profits that some Marwari merchants made in speculating on opium futures in the last years of the nineteenth century and the first decade of the twentieth century,[45] which are well documented. But he has little to say on the earlier period, for which understandably (since the Malwa opium trade was then a 'clandestine' operation) no records seem to have survived.

A narrative of Indian capitalism that gives central place to the Malwa opium trade as a source of capital accumulation is therefore an alluring proposition, and different authors have succumbed to the slightly perverse appeal of that tune.[46] But it remains largely speculative, in the absence of precise quantitative data on profits and investment in India in the first half of the nineteenth century. On the other hand, a closer look at one particular region, Sindh, shows that the impact of the trade was considerable.

SINDH AS A DRUG FRONTIER OF BRITISH INDIA

Between 1819 and 1839, most of the 'illegal' Malwa opium reached Damao through Sindh. The reasons why the smugglers turned to that

---

[44] Farooqi mentions the names of several Bombay-based British and Portuguese firms involved in Malwa opium. See *Smuggling as Subversion*, p. 115.

[45] T. A. Timberg, *The Marwaris: From Traders to Industrialists* (Delhi: Vikas, 1978), pp. 162–63.

[46] Apart from Farooqi, they include J. F. Richards, 'The Opium Industry in British India' and C. Markovits, 'Bombay as a Business Centre: A Comparison with Calcutta', in *Bombay, Metaphor for Modern India*, eds A. Thorner and S. Patel (Delhi: Oxford University Press, 1995), pp. 26–46.

state were that it was the only coastal state in the subcontinent which was not in a treaty relationship with the Company, and that it was considered rather hostile to the British. Besides, it had in Karachi a port that offered a fairly safe maritime route to Damao. Even if the British resident at Kutch seems to have kept a close watch on the movements of ships between those two ports,[47] there was nothing much the British could do legally to interdict ships plying between the two sovereign states of Sindh and Portuguese India. Their only hope was to cut the land route that passed through some of the Rajputana states, mostly Marwar and Jaisalmer, which were in a treaty relationship with the Company. But even there they failed. One suspects that the Company was not ready to invest too much political capital on a venture that in any case, given the nature of the terrain, had little chance of success. Even nowadays, most of the smuggling between India and Pakistan passes through the Thar Desert between Rajasthan and Sindh! It is not known whether the Sindh authorities did anything to attract smugglers to the route through their territories. It is most probable that the latter saw its advantages on their own and did not need any incentive, but a fruitful relationship appears to have been gradually established involving merchants and capitalists in British India as well as in the native states of Malwa and Rajputana, Sindh merchants, the Sindh authorities, and Portuguese merchants and shipowners who seem to have had their own connections with Sindh. Such was the attraction of the Sindh route in the early 1820s that it was even reported that some 'Patna' opium had been despatched to Damao through Karachi, a very circuitous route indeed.[48]

The Malwa opium trade became a crucial source of revenue for the Sindh darbar in the 1820s and 1830s as well as an important source of income for the Sindh merchants in the three major trading centres of the province, Karachi, Hyderabad and Shikarpur. The notion of 'drug frontier' seems applicable to that region during the 1819–39 period, although it would certainly need further elaboration. It seems to me that 'frontier' connotes both a contact zone, and a certain absence of state regulation, but not necessarily a space ruled by the market. A

---

[47] See the detailed report on ship movements between Karachi and Damao in 1821–22 sent on 19 March 1822 by Charles Norris, the resident at Kutch to the Bombay Revenue Department. Enclosed in Bombay Revenue Proceedings for 1822, 10 April 1822.

[48] In a letter, the Governor of Bombay observed that opium had come 'from Hindoostan' through Sindh. Secretary to Government of Bombay to Secretary Supreme Government at Fort William, 29 July 1822, Bombay Proceedings 1822, 31 July.

'drug frontier' additionally involves the domination of transactions in a commodity, which is at least partly illegal. In as much as its role was that of a transit route between the producing zones in Central India, the ports in western India, and the consumer market in China, and since the trade implied flouting British regulations, Sindh appears to fit the definition. The same notion could be applied to Portuguese India during these years, but my focus here will be on Sindh. The business of the Sindh merchants was not so much in trading in opium itself, in which they were at best junior partners of the big Parsi and Gujarati capitalists based in Bombay and Ahmedabad, as in organizing the caravans throughout the Sindh part of the route and in getting the duties levied on the caravans remitted to the Sindh authorities through their *hundis*,[49] that is, native bills of payment. It is impossible to estimate even roughly the profits the merchants derived from these operations, but they must have been significant, since in the post-annexation period, the loss of that source of profit was often invoked to account at least partially for the overall reorientation in the activities of the merchants.

Although little quantitative evidence is available on the finances of Talpur Sindh, stray British reports underline the importance of opium revenue to that fledgling state. In 1823, the British Resident at Kutch, Gardiner, was informed that, following the restrictions on the opium trade, the value of the revenue farm of Karachi had more than trebbled, while the farms of three small localities in the vicinity had also shot up.[50] In November 1830, Henry Pottinger, then the Resident in the neighbouring state of Kutch, forwarded to the Bombay authorities a letter from the native agent in Sindh, a local official who was the British representative at the Talpur court, asserting that, during the preceding year, a total of Rs 540,000 (Company) had been paid to the Amirs' treasuries in Khairpur, Mirpur and Hyderabad as duties on 2,400 camel loads of opium that had transited through Sindh territory at a rate of Rs 225 per camel load of 8 Surat maunds (a local measure of weight which was roughly equivalent to a quarter of a picul).[51] This probably represented by far the largest single item of revenue for the Sindh

---

[49] See C. Markovits, *The Global World of Indian Merchants 1750–1947: Traders of Sind from Bukhara to Panama* (Cambridge: Cambridge University Press, 2000), pp. 41–43.

[50] Mentioned in Farooqi, *Smuggling as Subversion*, p. 119.

[51] Native Agent in Sind to Colonel H. Pottinger, dated 27 November 1830, translated by A. Burnes, Assistant Resident, 30 November 1830, Bombay Revenue Proceedings, December 1830, no 135.

government, a weak government that could not tax its own population heavily. How important that revenue was to the Sindh darbar is indicated in the same letter by the report of a negotiation into which the Sindh authorities entered with the merchants of Marwar and Jaisalmer. The latter asked for a reduction in the duties levied in Sindh and promised in exchange to bring increased quantities. The report commented, 'The Ameers seeing the loss of revenue which they would suffer by this arrangement. . . immediately sent back word. . . that they would lessen the duty five Rupees on each camel-load and at the same time to tell the merchants to bring the opium quickly'. It is clear also from this piece of evidence that the merchants knew how to play different authorities one against the other so as to bring down their costs. If the Sindhians did not comply, they could threaten to use the Bombay route, which would have brought about an enormous fall in the revenues of Sindh. When the British occupied Karachi in 1839 and imposed a treaty on the rulers of Sindh, no mention was made of opium. In March 1839, Noor Muhammad Khan, the ruler of Hyderabad, applied to the British resident in Sindh, as reported by the latter,[52] to ask him to address a letter to the ruler of Jaisalmer 'to the effect that the drug might come through Sindh as it had done previously to our troops entering that Province'. The Resident declined to comply with the request and asked for instructions from the Government of Bombay, which relayed the demand to Calcutta. The response of the Supreme Government was clear: 'failing the reestablishment of a complete monopoly on the Bombay side like that of Bengal (an outcome which was obviously considered premature), the next best thing for both sides (meaning Bengal and Bombay) is a high rate of duty with limited export'.[53] This was the death warrant of the Sindh route, which de facto ceased to be used.

Looking back on the episode, it becomes clear that, apart from boosting government revenues in the short-term, becoming a drug frontier of British India had other long-term consequences for Sindh. Not only did it tend to focus much more British attention on an unruly neighbour, whom they had previously more or less left to its own devices, it also had the effect of bringing Sindh merchants into the whole structure of

---

[52] Resident in Sinde to Chief Secretary to the Government of Bombay, 26 October 1839, Bombay Revenue Proceedings 1839, no 7477, 31 December 1839.

[53] Secretary to Government of India to Secretary to Government of Bombay, 28 August 1839, ibid., no 6157, 23 October 1839.

colonial trade and finance from which they had remained separated by the fact of the continued political independence of the region. Whether therefore, closing the Sindh route to Malwa opium was or was not the prime motivation for the annexation of Sindh in 1843, as claimed by J. Y. Wong,[54] the fact remains that its participation in the Malwa opium trade at least indirectly contributed to its coming into the British political sphere. The drug trade could be instrumentalized by the British to bring Sindh into their imperial orbit, even if strategic considerations were probably paramount in dictating the decision to annex the province. It had in particular, the effect of integrating the Sindh trading classes, which were mostly Hindu, into a global imperial trading system extending to China. Some of Sindh's biggest merchants, in particular, the great Karachi bania Seth Naomal Hotchand,[55] helped the British conquer Sindh in 1839–43. Although their motivations were complex, and their actions ultimately self-defeating, since they lost the revenues they had derived from the opium trade after the British occupation, it seems nevertheless that their participation in the Malwa opium trade played a role in forging their connection to the British. A different outcome would have been possible only if the Sindh authorities had used the additional income they derived from the opium trade for the purpose of modernizing their army and administration to strengthen their regime in the face of British Indian encroachments. But this they failed to do for reasons of a largely structural nature, as the Baluchi tribal regime of the Talpurs had no cultural propensity or incentive to embark upon far-reaching reforms that would have endangered its own existence. Ultimately, therefore, one is led to emphasizing the link between opium and imperial expansion rather than its role in fostering indigenous capitalism.

In a broader political economy perspective, how to interpret the existence of an 'unofficial' circuit of opium trade to China in breach of

---

[54] J. Y. Wong, 'British Annexation of Sind in 1843: An Economic Perspective', *Modern Asian Studies* 31 (1997), pp. 225–44. The weakness of Wong's argument is that it is purely retrospective and also largely speculative. Because the annexation of Sindh (actually the occupation of Karachi in 1839 four years before the official annexation of Sindh) led to a suspension of the smuggling through Sindh, it is inferred that obtaining it was the real motive for the annexation, a typical ex post facto rationalization. Besides, the emphasis on the role of Ellenborough, who is supposed to have had a particularly good grasp of the financial aspects of the China opium trade, must remain speculative in the absence of policy statements on his part.

[55] See *A Forgotten Chapter of Indian History as Described in the Memoirs of Seth Naomal Hotchand, C.S.I. of Karachi 1804–1878*, Exeter, 1915 (reprint Karachi: Oxford University Press, 1982), a fascinating memoir by this great merchant, translated into English by one of his descendants.

the monopoly of the East India Company and its capacity to survive for almost four decades in a subcontinent which, after 1818, was clearly under British domination? It raises firstly, the general question of the relationship between smuggling and states.[56] Although smuggling tends to deprive states of income, it is also a direct outcome of state policies, and never have states been able to completely prevent smuggling. Smuggling can be said to be structurally linked to the creation of state borders. As the author of a recent history of smuggling in Southeast Asia put it, 'boundary production and boundary transgression' can be shown to be 'two sides of the same coin'.[57] Smuggling has rarely threatened the state and taken on a subversive political dimension, as it did in colonial North America at the time of the Boston Tea Party. There is no compelling reason to view the smuggling of Malwa opium as one of these rare occurrences. Rather than seeing in it a testimony of ongoing resistance to British economic domination by indigenous actors, as Farooqi does, it seems more sensible to characterize it as a phenomenon of residual leakage, due to the fact that the maritime frontiers of India were at the time not entirely controlled by the British. There remained ports that were under the control of non-British rulers, in particular, on the west coast: apart from Dutch Cochin (which was ceded in 1826 to the British), the ports of Sindh, mostly Karachi and the Portuguese ports of Diu, Damao and Goa. The existence of these non-British enclaves offered obvious opportunities to smugglers, especially given that Macao, to which the drug was shipped for entry into China, was also under Portuguese control.

Actually, it was the combination of Portuguese naval enterprise, together with British and Indian speculative capital (in league with the authorities of some of the native states) that made the whole operation possible. Without Portuguese ships to carry the opium from Damao to Macao, it could simply not have reached the Chinese market. The Portuguese input in the Malwa opium trade story is therefore essential, a fact that Farooqi recognizes, but from which he does not derive any qualification of his thesis about indigenous 'resistance'. For their part, Portuguese officials were purely opportunistic and devoid of any

---

[56] Two recent contributions to the topic are: E. Tagliacozzo, *Secret Trades, Porous Borders: Smuggling and States Along a Southeast Asian Frontier, 1865–1915* (New Haven, CT: Yale University Press, 2005), and L.R. Grahn, *The Political Economy of Smuggling: Regional Informal Economies in Early Bourbon New Granada* (Boulder, Col.: Westview, 1997).

[57] Tagliacozzo, *Secret Trades, Porous Borders*, p. 3.

political motives. The Portuguese were too much dependent globally on the British, especially after the loss of Brazil in 1822, to mount any kind of challenge to them in Asia, and Portuguese officials just made use of the opportunities offered by the channelling of the Malwa opium trade through ports that were under their rule to line their pockets. As for the Sindh rulers, they were too weak to do anything more than fill up their depleted coffers while the going was good. No real anti-British alliance between those two minor powers, Sindh and the Estado da India, was in the cards, and Indian capitalists were sufficiently shrewd to know that. They also were content with making the best of a god-sent opportunity, but without harbouring any idea of challenging British economic domination, which would have been a dead end. It is interesting to note that, as soon as China had been 'opened' by British guns in the wake of the First Opium War, the same Bombay Parsis and Gujaratis who had organized the smuggling of Malwa opium became the agents of the big private British firms in Canton. One particular Parsi operator, Sir Jamsetjee Jeejeebhoy is known to have supplied the big firm of Jardine and Matheson with a third of the opium they had in their Canton warehouses in the mid-1840s.[58]

Indigenous capital accumulation was fostered as much if not more by this participation in the 'legal' drug trade after 1842 than by the profits derived from the smuggling of Malwa opium in an earlier period. Even in the post-1842 phase, it is possible to exaggerate the importance of opium's contribution to capital accumulation in Bombay. A quick look at the history of the best-known Bombay firm, the House of Tatas, shows that, while it participated actively in the opium trade with China after 1842, two non-opium ventures contributed even more decisively to the initial fortunes of the firm. One of these was its participation in the financing of the British military expedition to Persia in 1856, and the other was its role in the financing of the military expedition to Abyssinia in 1867, which can be directly traced as the source of J. N. Tata's first venture into the cotton textile industry.[59] Even the fortunes of Bombay's capitalists were more closely intertwined with British-led ventures than admitted by Farooqi, who attempts to make the great western Indian

---

[58] Mentioned in A. Siddiqi, 'The Business World of Jamsetjee Jeejeebhoy', *Indian Economic and Social History Review* 19 (1982), pp. 301–24.

[59] See F. R. Harris, *Jamsetji Nusserwanji Tata. A Chronicle of His Life* (Bombay: Asia Publishing, 1958, 2nd ed.), p. 11.

port-city the stronghold of an 'indigenous' capitalist class relatively independent from the British connection.[60] Actually, Ahmedabad better answers that definition, and its link to Malwa opium, although not insignificant, has been much more tenuous than Bombay's.

---

[60] See in particular, his recent *Opium City: The Making of Early Victorian Bombay* (Gurgaon: Three Essays, 2006).

5

Opium and the Company:

Maritime Trade and Imperial Finances on Java, 1684–1796

GEORGE BRYAN SOUZA[*]

———— • ✦ • ————

INTRODUCTION

The history of Bengal opium and the Dutch East India Company (the *Verenigde Oostindische Compagnie*, the VOC or the Company) over the long eighteenth century (or from 1684–1796) is examined in this essay.[1] From the Company's perspective, it was a period that may be characterized as the end of the age of commerce,[2] metamorphosis from a commercial organization deriving its profits from maritime trade to the exploitation and colonial administration of agricultural production

---

[*] My thanks for the constructive comments on this essay by an anonymous reviewer and Professor Peer Vries on an earlier version presented at the 'Expanding Frontiers in South Asian and World History Conference', Duke University, 29–30 September 2006.

[1] Research on opium has benefited from John F. Richards' contributions, see 'The Indian Empire and Peasant Production of Opium in the Nineteenth Century', *Modern Asian Studies* 15 (1981), pp. 59–82; and 'Opium and the British Indian Empire: The Royal Commission of 1895', *Modern Asian Studies* 36 (2002), pp. 375–420. Research on opium has grown rapidly in recent years, see Amar Farooqui, *Smuggling as Subversion: Colonialism, Indian Merchants and the Politics of Opium* (New Delhi: New Age International Publishers, 1998); Carl A. Trocki, *Opium, Empire and the Global Political Economy: A Study of the Asian Opium Trade 1750–1950* (London and New York: Routledge, 1999); and Zheng Yangwen, *The Social Life of Opium in China* (Cambridge and New York: Cambridge University Press, 2005).

[2] See Anthony Reid, *Southeast Asia in the Age of Commerce*, 2 Vols. (New Haven: Yale University Press, 1988 and 1993).

and mineral resources and revenues from tax farming, and of decline. The Company was not omnipotent. By 1684, the Company may be characterized as being more pragmatic than bellicose in its commercial inter-relationships with other states and Asian and European merchants. By 1796, with its maritime trading activities long surpassed in Asia and Europe by European competitors, especially the English East India Company (EIC), the VOC had to declare bankruptcy.[3]

A series of specific questions are raised and answered in the first and second sections of this essay: how important was Bengal opium in the Company's commercial and imperial activities? What was the relationship of the Company's maritime trade in opium between Bengal and Batavia with the non-Company maritime trade of Asian and other European merchants at Batavia? And, specifically, how important was the revenue from the sale of Bengal opium at Batavia in the Company's local and imperial finances? The Company's prodigious records were examined to find answers to those questions.[4] The empirical data that was found and examined was subjected to a series of traditional quantitative economic—supply or commodity chain, trend and transactional—analyses.

This essay concentrates on the structure, composition and participation of the Company, Asian and other European merchants in maritime trade; and the composition at the micro level of the Company's local *comptoir* accounts at Batavia, its operating expenditures and revenues derived from maritime trade (including opium),[5] tax farming

---

[3] See H. Furber, *Rival Empires of Trade in the Orient 1600–1800* (Minneapolis, MN: University of Minnesota Press, 1976).

[4] The VOC records used in this essay are primarily found: (1) in the General State Archives, [the *Algemeen Rijksarchief* (ARA)] in the *Koloniale Archieven Oost-Indie: Archieven van de Vereenigde Oost-Indische Compagnie,* (VOC) collection and papers in The Hague; and (2) the Indonesian National Archives (ARSIP) in Jakarta. For some of the printed Dutch records used in this essay, see W.P. Coolhaas, et al., eds., *Generale Missiven van Gouverneurs-General en Raden aan Heren XVII der Verenigde Oostindische Compagnie,* 11 vols. (The Hague: Rijks Grote Publicaten, 1960–2005); abbreviated and cited in the text as *GM*; and J. A. van der Chijs, et al., eds., *Daghregisteer gehouden int Casteel Batavia vant passerende daer ter plaetse als over geheel Nederlandts India,* 31 vols. (The Hague and Batavia: Departement van Koloniën, 1887–1931), cited hereafter as *DRB.*

[5] For the useful but dated classic study on this topic, see J. C. Baud, 'Proeve van eene Geschiedenis van het Handel en het Verbruik van Opium in Nederlandsch Indië', *Bijdragen tot de Taal-, Land-, en Volkenkunde van Nederlandsch Indië* 1 (1853), pp. 79–220. F. de Haan, *Priangan: De Preanger Regentschappen onder het Nederlandsch Bestuur tot 1811,* 4 vols. (Batavia: Bataviaasch Genootschap van Kunsten en Weternschappen, 1910–12) is based upon a unique familiarity of the archives in Jakarta and contains helpful observations. For some of the recent work on the Company, which include discussions of opium commercialization, see R. Vos, *Gentle Janus,*

and other sources, and relates them to the finances and functioning of the Company's imperial headquarters in Asia.[6] It is an approach that is in contrast with a relatively recent work by Els Jacobs on the Company, who observed that the role and importance of opium was limited in the history of the Company in the eighteenth century.[7] Since her selected data and criteria focused at the macro level on the relatively smaller volumes and values of opium in comparison with much larger volumes and values of other commodities in the history of the Company's trading patterns and results, Jacobs' view is technically correct. It is suggested, however, that there is an equally acceptable alternative view, which demonstrates at the micro or *comptoir* level an extraordinary, almost dependent relationship by the Company on the trade of Bengal opium to provide significant streams of operating revenues at Batavia.

Prominent differences in the importance of opium in the fortunes of the Company have been found by contrasting the macro versus micro view. This contrast raises additional implications for this research. These broader ramifications, which will be discussed in our conclusions, include questions about the role and nature of commodities and of commerce at this time. What is the spatial importance of locality and the nature and availability of commodities in shaping the early modern global economy? What do these relationships tell us more broadly about the trading capabilities of early modern European commercial institutions—the Dutch and English East India Companies? What implications did the emergence and the proclivity to consume opium by smoking it have on Southeast Asia and China and did this transformation

---

Merchant Prince: The VOC and the Tightrope of Diplomacy in the Malay World, 1740–1800, trans. B. Jackson (Leiden: KITLV Press, 1993); L. Nagtegaal, *Riding the Dutch Tiger: The Dutch East Indies Company and the Northeast Coast of Java, 1680–1743*, trans. B. Jackson (Leiden: KITLV Press, 1996); Gerrit J. Knaap, *Shallow Waters, Rising Tide: Shipping and Trade in Java around 1775* (Leiden: KITLV Press, 1996); Gerrit J. Knaap and Heather Sutherland, *Monsoon Traders: Ships, Skippers, and Commodities in Eighteenth-Century Makassar* (Leiden: KITLV Press, 2004); and Kwee Hui Kian, *The Political Economy of Java's Northeast Coast, c. 1740–1800* (Leiden and Boston: Brill, 2005). For a fascinating recent work on Batavia using the notarial records, see Hendrik E. Niemeijer, *Batavia: Een Koloniale Samenleving in the 17de Eeuw* (Amsterdam: Balans, 2005).

[6]   It is part of a larger research/publishing project, tentatively entitled: 'On Sea, on Land: the Political Economy of Commerce and Commodities in Asia and the Early Modern World'. This recent research on maritime trade and opium at Batavia permits a thorough historical reconstruction and an economic analysis of the maritime trade at Batavia, the major colonial port city within the region and globally, and a supply or commodity chain analysis of Bengal opium from production to consumption in the later half of the seventeenth and the entire eighteenth century.

[7]   Els M. Jacobs, *Koopman in Azië: De handel van de Verenigde Oost-Indische Compagnie tijdens de 18de eeuw* (Zutphen: Walburg Pers, 2000).

make the trade of these areas and in this commodity distinctive from others in the early modern period?

This discussion of opium mentions three centres of cultivation and production in the early modern period that were heavily involved in the regional and global maritime exchanges of the commodity: two in India (in Bihar and via Bengal; and Malwa via Daman and other western Indian ports of extraction) and the other being from the Levant (Turkey or Anatolia via Smyrna), and concentrates upon the production from Bihar that became known as Bengal opium, which the Company claimed as a distribution monopoly in the Indonesian Archipelago.

Opium is viewed in this essay as a transformed, transformational and global commodity. Prior to the long eighteenth century, the use of opium worldwide was limited to a method of ingestion by chewing and/or swallowing that physiologically was handled in the human stomach, which limited and regulated the effect and the amount of the drug that could be consumed. After the introduction and dissemination of American tobacco and the habit of smoking throughout Asia, the practice of including and adding small amounts of opium to be smoked with tobacco developed over this period in particular, in parts of Southeast Asia and South China. The linking of the use of opium to the habit of smoking was a major transformation in the pattern of use of the commodity in social, cultural and commercial terms. While many consumers elsewhere continued to ingest the drug only through chewing and swallowing, ingesting by smoking and inhaling opium meant that the lungs with a different physiological capacity in handling and delivering the drugs narcotic properties produced an enhanced reaction for users and the doses that could be consumed were increased. It was late in this period that the bowl design of pipes developed and incorporated the use of metal bowls that permitted the smoking of pure opium, which excluded altogether the incorporation of tobacco and strengthened the drug's impact on consumers. These shifts in the areas that incorporated these new and transformed patterns of opium use also produced increased demand for the commodity.[8]

Opium was a transformational commodity in several respects. In economic terms, it became one of the primary commodities of exchange

---

[8] For a discussion of these developments in Southeast Asia, see George Bryan Souza, 'Developing Habits: Tobacco and Opium in the Indonesian Archipelago, c. 1650 to 1800', Association for Asian Studies (AAS) Annual Conference, Chicago, Illinois, 31 March–3 April, 2005.

that dominated and transformed local Company finances and, similarly, contributed significantly to the commercial fortunes of individual European, indigenous and overseas Chinese community's merchants in the region. It was also transformational in the lives of the consumer to the degree that its consumption provided medicinal or physical or mental relief and/or recreational pleasure and, of course, to the degree that its use became habitual and/or addictive.

The emergence of opium as a global commodity occurred in the Indonesian Archipelago in the later half of the eighteenth century when the Company faced disruption of the supplies of deliveries of opium from Bengal and deliveries of opium from Anatolia began to arrive at Batavia. Contemporaneously, there was rapid expansion in its cultivation in southeastern China[9] and slightly later, there was an attempt at cultivar diffusion by the Portuguese, when the poppy was transferred, cultivated and produced opium on the island of Madeira in the Atlantic Ocean for sale to China.[10]

Finally, the author intends to place the social biography of opium centre stage in the economic and social history of Southeast Asia. This approach, which will incorporate the findings of this essay and additional recent research in future publication on the topic, raises intriguing supplemental questions that are raised, but will not be discussed. For example, who and how did different commercial groups participate in the purchase of opium from the Company (and later, a sub-company, the Opium Society) and what role did those groups play in the commercial intermediation and distribution of Bengal and Levantine opium on Java and throughout the Indonesian Archipelago? And, what role did opium play in their communal, commercial and political lives? This discussion, however, is confined for the sake of brevity to the maritime trade of the Company and Bengal opium at Batavia.

This essay is organized and presented in three sections: (i) the Company, Maritime Trade and Opium at Batavia; (ii) *Comptoir* Accounts and Imperial Finances; and (iii) Conclusion.

---

[9] David Anthony Bello, *Opium and the Limits of Empire: Drug Prohibition in the Chinese Interior, 1729–1850* (Cambridge, MA: Harvard University Press, 2005).

[10] Jorge Manuel dos Santos Alves, 'O Triângulo Madeira-Achém-Macau: Um Projecto Transoceânico de Comércio de Ópio (1808–1816)', *Archipel* 56 (1998), pp. 43–70.

THE COMPANY, MARITIME TRADE AND OPIUM AT BATAVIA

The VOC was a significant early modern commercial organization with global reach and connections. Recognizing the imperative for the Company to possess and develop a port city independent of Asian interference, the VOC's iron-willed Governor-General, J. P. Coen, ordered the seizure of an appropriate site from the *Pangeran* of Jacatra on the northeast coast of Java in 1619.[11] The Company re-named the site, Batavia, which is present-day Jakarta.[12] Batavia became an archetypical Asian colonial port city, defined as a gateway

> . . . through which European power and influence, economic dominance and technological modernization (to which could be added disease and health care) flowed from overseas to the furthest corners of the continent and as primate cities controlling their hinterlands and acting as vital lynchpins in the development of the world economic system.[13]

Batavia was the primary centre of the Company's imperial and commercial activities in Asia. It was the centre of the Company's naval and military forces and its primary port for preparing and handling the Company's ships. It was the emporium that accumulated and handled deliveries of Asian commodities from near and far and loaded them on the Company's ships for their annual voyages to Europe. It was the emporium from which Asian, European and New World commodities were re-distributed on Java and throughout the Indonesian Archipelago. It also was a commercial and maritime trading centre, where the Company sold the intra-Asian commodities that it controlled or commercialized, (including opium, spices, Indian textiles and other goods), controlled and taxed the local and migrant populations and their commerce[14]

---

[11] For an interesting discussion of the establishment of Batavia from the Chinese (Hokkien) as well as the Company's perspective, see chapters 5 and 6 in the unpublished doctoral dissertation by James K. Chin, 'Merchants and Other Sojourners: the Hokkiens Overseas, 1570–1 760', University of Hong Kong, 1998.

[12] For a useful introduction and summary of Jakarta's early history and geography, especially its spatial characteristics and growth, see James L. Cobban, 'Geographic Notes on the First Two Centuries of Djakarta', *Journal of the Malay Branch of the Royal Asiatic Society* 44 (1971), pp. 108–50.

[13] See F. Broeze, 'Introduction: Brides of the Sea', in *Brides of the Sea: Port Cities of Asia from the Sixteenth to the Twentieth Centuries*, ed. F. Broeze (Honolulu: University of Hawai Press, 1989), p. 4.

[14] See Anthony Reid, 'The Origins of Revenue Farming in Southeast Asia', in *The Rise and Fall of Revenue Farming: Business Elites and the Emergence of the Modern State in Southeast Asia*, eds John Butcher and Howard Dock (London: Macmillan Press, 1993), pp. 67–79.

and controlled and provided incentives or not for the maritime trade of Asian and other Europeans at this port. The Company instigated policies that attracted foreign merchants, Asian (primarily, the Chinese from South China)[15] and other Europeans (primarily, the Portuguese from Macao)[16] to trade at this port. The trade that centred on the port of Batavia on Java was an important nexus for regional, intra-regional and global maritime trade in the seventeenth and eighteenth centuries. Because of the idiosyncrasies in the Company's imperial organization and accounting practices, the local *comptoir* at Batavia was responsible for all of the above expenditures and revenues.[17]

The numbers of shipping and indices of trading activity at Batavia by the Company, foreign and indigenous merchants was prodigious over the period under study. Without including the numbers and movements of arriving and departing smaller inland shipping[18] or limited numbers of Dutch private traders and the regular arrivals and departures of the Company's fleets from Europe,[19] the total number of foreign ships arriving at Batavia from 1684 to 1792 was recorded at 2,606. This number included all of the registered arrivals and departures of foreign ships that called and/or traded at Batavia. Out of that total (2,606), 1,680 ships belonged to the six foreign merchant groups and crowns:

---

[15] See Leonard Blussé, 'Chinese Trade to Batavia during the Days of the VOC', *Archipel* 18 (1979), pp. 195–213; Idem, *Strange Company: Chinese Settlers, Mestizo Women and Dutch in VOC Batavia*, (Dordrecht: Foris Publications, 1986); and Leonard Blussé, Jan Oosterhoff and Ton Vermeulen, 'Chinese Trade with Batavia in the Seventeenth and Eighteenth Centuries: A Preliminary Report', in *Asian Trade Routes: Continental and Maritime*, ed. Karl Reinhold Haellquist (London: Curzon Press, 1991), pp. 231–45.

[16] See George Bryan Souza, *The Survival of Empire: Portuguese Trade and Society in China and the South China Sea, 1630–1754* (Cambridge: Cambridge University Press, 1986).

[17] Many of the historians of the Company have commented on its accounting practices and the difficulties they pose in consolidating its profitability, see Pieter van Dam, F. W. Stapel, C. W. T. van Boetzelaer van Asperen and Herdruk Dubbeldam, eds, *Beschryvinge van de Oostindische Compagnie*, 7 vols. (The Hague: Rijks Grote Publicaten, 1927–1954); Kristof Glamann, *Dutch-Asiatic Trade, 1620–1740* (Copenhagen and The Hague: Danish Science Press and Martinus Nijhoff, 1958); Femme S. Gaastra, *De geschidenis van de VOC* (Zutphen: Walburg Pers, 2002). For an enlightening and detailed explanation of the intricacies of the Company's accounting, see J. P. de Korte, *De Jaarlijkse Financiele Verantwoording in de Verenigde Oostindische Compagnie* (Leiden: Martinus Nijhoff, 1983).

[18] For a discussion of the small vessel/inland shipping reports, which are found in the ARSIP, DRB 1683–1745, see Souza, 'Developing Habits'.

[19] For a description of Company's shipping to and from and within Asia and their organization, personnel and ports of call, see J. R., Bruijn, et al., *Dutch-Asiatic Shipping in the 17th and 18th Centuries*, 3 vols. (The Hague: Rijks Grote Publicaten, 1979–1987), I, pp. 119–42, 195–209, and 223–45.

the Chinese, Portuguese, Spanish, Armenians, Muslim/Moors and the Siamese, who regularly called and traded at Batavia.[20]

The numbers of vessels in general, and the number that actually traded at Batavia is best employed as an indicator of their presence in the market and to a lesser degree, in market trend analysis.[21] The Chinese and the Portuguese from Macao shipping and trading activities predominated.[22] In general, the remaining 914 ships that called at Batavia did not trade and were registered to different European Companies, private traders and powers: English, Portuguese, French, Spanish, Ostend, Danish, Prussian, Swedish and Americans. Around 1755, however, the above characterization has to be modified, since some of the arriving private merchant European (English, French and Danish) owned ships within this number are recorded in the Company's records as being commercially active.[23]

The Company's sales and purchases records or *Samengetrokken Lijsten* are an invaluable summary of the maritime trade by the principal foreign merchant groups, primarily the Chinese, the Portuguese from Macao and the Spanish from Manila, that were commercially active at Batavia for 1684–1796.[24] A thorough examination of fifty one of these annual reports over a slightly shorter period from 1693–1764 reveals the composition, quantities and values of the commodities sold and purchased by the VOC.

The maritime trade by Asian and other European merchants at Batavia, as suggested in these records, was overwhelmingly oriented and structured towards the supply and demand of goods and commodities from and for the China market, with one important exception, that of Manila. The overall composition of the individual goods and

---

[20] See the separate Chinese and foreign shipping lists plus individual cargo details from 1684 onwards for Batavia, ARA, VOC 1382 to 3971. For some of the Asian participants in maritime trade that were present at Batavia, see D. Lombard, J. Aubin, eds, *Asian Merchants and Businessmen in the Indian Ocean and the China Sea* (Delhi: Oxford University Press, 2000).

[21] Tonnage calculations are a better economic indicator than the number of vessels trading at Batavia, since they permit individual, annual and total trader groups' cargo capacity to be compared in a given market. While they have been calculated for trading participants at Batavia for the entire period, they are not presented for the sake of brevity.

[22] For a detailed discussion of Chinese merchant activity at Canton at this time, see Paul A. Van Dyke, *The Canton Trade: Life and Enterprise on the China Coast, 1700–1845* (Hong Kong: Hong Kong University Press, 2005).

[23] ARA, VOC 2868 to 3951, foreign vessel lists with trading details from 1755 to 1792.

[24] ARA, VOC 1382 to 3971, sales and purchases records or *Samengetrokken Lijsten* from 1693 to 1796.

commodities sold by the VOC to foreign traders was pepper, cinnamon, cloves, nutmeg, finished silk and diverse finished Indian cotton textiles, gold, silver, tin, lead, iron, Japanese and European copper and others. Chinese and Portuguese merchants were the primary buyers of pepper, cloves, nutmeg, silver, tin and sappanwood from the Company for the China market(s). Although of a lesser scale and dimension in comparison with the goods in demand for China, Manila demanded cinnamon, other spices and Asian textiles and had critical supplies of New World silver. This indirect trade was an important integral link in and an outlet for the VOC's intra-Asian trade. Portuguese and Spanish merchants, primarily, along with Armenian and Muslim/Moor merchants bought cinnamon, silk and diverse Indian cotton textiles, and undeterminable amounts of pepper, cloves and nutmeg from the Company at Batavia for Manila, where these goods were transshipped via the Manila Galleon to the New World.

The overall composition of the individual goods and commodities purchased by the VOC from Asian and other European merchants at Batavia was tea, raw silk and finished silk textiles, finished linen textiles, sappanwood, finished cotton textiles, silver, gold, cowries, copper, zinc and others. China supplied tea, raw silk and finished silk textiles, finished linen textiles and zinc. The trade in tea from China at Batavia was adversely impacted by the Company's decision in 1723 to initiate direct trading contacts from Europe to Canton.[25] Manila supplied silver, cowries, leather and sappanwood. Other markets supplied raw silk and finished silk textiles from Tonkin and India (Surat), finished cotton textiles, sappanwood (Bima and Thailand) and gold.

The total recorded quantity of the principal commodities sold by the VOC to foreign traders at Batavia in the fifty one annual reports examined for the period from 1693–1764 was 615,589 *picols*[26] and 5,965 chests. The total recorded sales value of all commodities sold by the VOC over the same period was 15,791,901 *rijksdaalers* (or 16,623,054 Chinese *taels* or 18,950,281 Spanish *pesos*).[27] This amount is an indicator of the relative order of magnitude of the Company's sales activity.[28]

---

[25] See J. de Hullu, 'Over den Chinaschen Handel der Oost-Indische Compagnie in de Eerste Dertig Jaar van de 18e eeuw', *Bijdragen tot de Taal-, Land- en Volkenkunde* 73 (1917), pp. 32–151.

[26] One *picol* equaled 133$\frac{1}{3}$ pounds.

[27] The conversion of *rijksdaalers* (rsd) to Chinese *taels* and Spanish *pesos* is: 1 rsd to 3 *guilders*, 2.85 *guilders* to 1 *tael* and 2.5 *guilders* to 1 *peso* of 8 *reales*.

[28] There are two observations about these sales reports related to the Company's modifications

Over the same period, the total recorded quantity of commodities purchased by the VOC from foreign traders at Batavia was 188,728 *picols*. The total recorded value of all the commodities reportedly purchased by the VOC was 5,137,375 *rijksdaalers* (or 5,407,763 Chinese *taels* or Spanish 6,164,850 *pesos*). Again, this amount is best employed as an indicator of the relative order of magnitude of the Company's purchases from the maritime activity of foreign merchants at Batavia.[29]

Based upon this detailed examination of these records from 1693–1764 and over the entire period, maritime trade at Batavia did meet the Company's predominant short-term commercial objective: to sell more goods than the VOC purchased. During the period from 1693–1764, the total recorded value of goods sold by the Company versus the goods they purchased at Batavia was 9,136,418 *rijksdaalers* (or 9,617,282 Chinese *taels* or 10,963,702 Spanish *pesos*). Over the entire period, in general, the longer term commercial objectives for maritime trade at Batavia for the VOC's Director's and the Company's administrators were also met and fulfilled. The Batavia market supplied commodities in the quality, quantities and at the price that the Company demanded and it was a market that provided an outlet for commodities in the quality, quantities and at the price that the Company wanted to sell to Asian and other European merchants. In the case of tea, as is commonly known,

in the preparation and inclusion of trade and non-trade related commercial data that had not previously been included in the report and/or favourably distort the actual figures for sales directly attributable to maritime trade at Batavia to Asian and other Europeans: (1) from 1748 to 1764, the Company included 1,978,751 rsd. from their annual sales by public auction at Batavia in these accounts; and (2) 5,965 chests of opium. Although these are significant quantities and values of sales income, it was decided not to suppress or exclude these amounts and values from this data.

[29] There is one observation about these purchase reports related to the Company's modifications in the preparation and inclusion of trade and non-trade related commercial data that had not previously been included in the report, which significantly distort the actual figures for purchases directly attributable to maritime trade at Batavia to Asian and other Europeans: (1) from 1758 to 1764, these reports included an additional total quantity of 927,009 *picols* or 4,559,606 rsd. of sugar, coffee, pepper and indigo purchased by the Company from the Java hinterland. In addition, significant quantities of Palembang pepper and Bangka tin (in total: 346,661 *picols* or 3,991,921 rsd.) were also registered. For pepper and cloves, see D. Bulbeck, et al., *Southeast Asian Exports since the 14th Century: Cloves, Pepper, Coffee, and Sugar* (Singapore: Institute of Southeast Asian Studies, 1998), pp. 17–106; and K. N. Chaudhuri, *The Trading World of Asia and the English East India Company. 1660–1760* (Cambridge: Cambridge University Press, 1978), pp. 313–328; for tin, see G. W. Irwin, 'The Dutch and the Tin Trade of Malaya in the Seventeenth Century', in *Studies in the Social History of China and South-East Asia*, eds J. Ch'en and N. Tarling (Cambridge: Cambridge University Press, 1970), pp. 267–87; and J. C. Jackson, 'Mining in 18th Century Bangka: The Pre-European Exploitation of a "Tin Island"', *Pacific Viewpoint* 10 (1969), pp. 28–54.

the Company's commercial strategy for Batavia did not work and the VOC had to re-initiate direct trading activities with China.[30] However, while the research on the principal foreign merchant groups trading at Batavia, primarily the Chinese, the Portuguese from Macao and the Spanish from Manila, is invaluable in the discussion of maritime trade at Batavia, in China's development and in the New World's global involvement, there is a danger that that work, unintentionally, negates or relegates the Company's maritime trade, commerce and intermediation of opium at Batavia and throughout the Indonesian Archipelago to a level of diminished importance. In order to better understand this observation, this essay will synthesise and recapitulate some of the salient features of the Company's maritime trade and commerce in opium at Batavia.

The Company initiated its commercial interest in Indian opium just before the middle of the seventeenth century. At that time, it exported small quantities of Malwa opium from Surat to Batavia. The Company shifted in the 1650s from opium sourced from Malwa to supplies from Bihar, which they began exporting from Bengal to Malabar and Batavia. It is from that date that the Company concentrated its dealings in opium supplied from Bihar, which became known as from Bengal, since it was shipped from Hugli in Bengal.[31] By the 1670s, although the Company continued to export the commodity from Bengal to Malabar, the trend overwhelmingly favoured exports of opium from Bengal to Batavia.

The Company ordered, purchased and exported opium from Bengal that was almost entirely sourced from Patna in Bihar. It was presented in a standardized format and purchase and sale prices and quantities were reported by chest.[32] The Company estimated in 1688 that 'the annual

---

[30] Christiaan J. A. Jörg, *Porcelain and the Dutch China Trade* (The Hague: Nijhoff, 1982).

[31] For a general introduction into opium cultivation and production in India, see S. Bose, ed., *Credit, Markets, and the Agrarian Economy of Colonial India* (Cambridge: Cambridge University Press, 1994); for cultivation and production in Malwa, see I. Habib, *The Agrarian System of Mughal India (1556–1707)* (Bombay, New York: Asia Publications House 1963); S. N. Gordon, 'Burhanpur: Entrepot and Hinterland, 1659–1750', *IESHR* 22 (1988), pp. 425–42; Idem, 'Forts and Social Control in the Maratha State', *Modern Asian Studies* 13 (1979), pp. 1–17; Idem 'The Slow Conquest: Administrative Integration of Malwa into the Maratha Empire, 1720–1760', *Modern Asian Studies* 11 (1977), pp. 1–40. For cultivation, production and early commercialization in Bengal, see O. Prakash, *The Dutch East India Company and the Economy of Bengal, 1630–1720* (Princeton: Princeton University Press, 1985); Idem, 'European Trade and the Economy of Bengal in the Seventeenth and Early Eighteenth Century', in *Trading Companies in Asia 1600–1830*, ed. J. van Goor (Utrecht: HES Uitgevers, 1986).

[32] The weight of each chest, including its contents, was standardized at 145 *ponden* and one Dutch *pond* was equal to 1.09 lbs. or 0.4 kilos.

output of opium in Bihar in a normal year at 8,700 *maunds* [595,950 *ponden* or 4,350 chests]' and the VOC's participation 'was approximately 1,000 maunds [500 chests], accounting for about 11.5 percent of the total output'.[33] The VOC's interest in this trade grew and the quantity of opium produced in Bihar, apparently, expanded significantly over the long eighteenth century. The VOC exported 67,831 chests from Bengal to Batavia from 1659 to 1771.

The VOC encountered and managed a variety of political and economic difficulties in their activities in Bengal long before the Battle of Plassey in 1757 and the implementation of the EIC's monopsonistic policies towards the procurement of opium by others in 1773.[34] One of their foremost problems was competition. The quantity of opium that the Company wanted purchased in Bengal on an annual basis was determined at Batavia. These orders may be interpreted as indications of the demand for opium at Batavia and throughout the consuming markets in the Indonesian Archipelago.[35] The evidence suggests that the Company was able to secure and purchase in Bengal the amount of opium ordered at Batavia only around a quarter of the time.[36] Indigenous[37] and other European private merchants, including the Portuguese,[38] Danes,[39]

---

[33] Prakash, *The Dutch East India Company,* pp. 57 and 58. One *maund* was 681/2 *ponden.*

[34] See Om Prakash, 'Trade and Politics in Eighteenth Century Bengal', in *On the Eighteenth Century as a Category of Asian History: Van Leur in Retrospect,* eds Leonard Blussé and Femme Gaastra (Aldershot, UK: Ashgate, 1998), pp. 237–60, especially, 251–56.

[35] For a discussion of the *eish* or order reports in general and their role in the Company's trade to Japan, see Minoru Omori, 'The *Eish Boek* in Dutch-Japanese Trade', in *Asian Trade Routes: Continental and Maritime,* ed. Karl Reinhold Haellquist (London: Curzon Press, 1991), pp. 199–208.

[36] Prakash's pioneering work examined the Company's order records for opium from 1659 to 1717, see Prakash, *The Dutch East India Company* pp. 150–51; for the 1719 to 1771 order records, see ARA, VOC 13575 to 13620, 'Kopie-eisen van gouverneur-generaal en raden aan de factorijen, met aantekeningen betreffende hetgeen naar Batavia is verzonden, 1719–1771'.

[37] See *GM,* III, 547, for the incorporation of Bengal opium in Mughal trading activities with neighbouring Arracan in the 1660s; for details on indigenous and European traders activities involving purchases of Bengal and sales at Bantam in the late 1670s and early 1680s prior to the Company's occupation of that port-city, see *GM,* IV, 18, 389 and 402 and J. M. J. de Jonge, compiler, *De Opkomst van het Nederlandsch Gezag in Oost-Indië,* 13 vols., (The Hague-Amsterdam, 1862–1888), VII, 9–10. For VOC complaints of Malay involvement in the trafficking of Bengal opium to Andragieri, Jambi, Palembang, Borneo and the ports of the Java north coast in the 1700s, see *GM,* VI, 431.

[38] For an example of the Portuguese involvement in exporting Bengal opium to the Malabar Coast in the 1690s, see George Bryan Souza, 'Portuguese Colonial Administrators and Inter-Asian Maritime Trade: Manuel de Sousa de Meneses and the *Fateh Moula* Affair', *Portuguese Studies Review* 12 (2004–2005), pp. 25–62.

[39] See *GM,* V: 758–761.

and, as well as other European companies, especially the English and French,[40] competed in procuring opium in Bihar and Bengal and selling it throughout Asia.

Since the Company could not establish direct control over the supply of opium in Bengal, it claimed a monopoly over the sale of opium in and throughout the Indonesian Archipelago and in parts of the Malay world. This monopoly was implemented via negotiation with the different indigenous state systems in the region.[41] It proved to be costly and burdensome on Company resources to enforce.[42] Commercialization by other merchant groups, what the Company considered smuggling, was rampant.

A trend analysis of the quantities of opium sold by the Company at Batavia from 1688 to 1789 is presented in Figure 1. Initially, there are an irregular number of reporting periods (the years 1688 to 1692, 1696 to 1698, 1701 to 1704 and 1711 to 1719). Average annual sales of chests of opium for these reporting periods were: 403, 745, 617 and 928. Subsequently, in this trend analysis, the reporting periods are for the decades from 1711 to 1789 in which sales of opium on an average annual basis per decade were: 928, 795, 897, 897, 1,100, 1,180, 739, 537 and 845 chests.

The Company's sales of opium in this period reached their apogee in the decades just before and after the Company decided to shift its primary channel of distribution at Batavia from public auction to the *Amfioen Sociëteit* (Opium Society).[43] Opium sales declined because of

---

[40] In specific years, English and French purchases and exports of opium from Bengal were significant or superior in comparison to the VOC's purchases and exports. The VOC reported in 1711, for example, that English purchases and exports were 850 chests in a year that the VOC exported 800 chests. French purchases and exports in 1714 were 4 to 500 chests in a year that the VOC exported 1,165 chests, see *GM*, VI, 719 and VII, 105–106.

[41] See J. E. Heeres and F. W. Stapel, eds, *Corpus-Diplomaticum Neerlando-Indicum*, 6 vols. (The Hague, 1907–1953); for the agreements granting the VOC the exclusive right to import Indian textiles and opium into, for example, Mataram (1677), Palembang (1678), Cheribon (1681), see *Corpus*, III, pp. 74–79, 140–42, 233–40 and 267–70. The VOC celebrated a similar treaty with Jambi in 1684; see *GM*, IV, p. 724. Despite a treaty with Palembang, the VOC reported indigenous shipping laden with textiles and opium in 1684; see *GM*, IV, 719.

[42] For example, on November 17, 1692, Company naval forces stopped a French ship at Phuket (Udjung Salang) and confiscated its cargo of opium, see *GM*, V, p. 591. Alexander Hamilton's ship was stopped and searched by VOC authorities at Melakka in 1712 and 18 chests of opium were confiscated, see *GM*, VI, p. 858. The *Raad van Justitie* at Batavia reviewed the Hamilton case in 1713 and upheld the actions of the VOC authorities; see *GM*, VI, p. 912.

[43] The *Amphioen Sociëteit* (Opium Society), a company within the Company, became responsible for marketing and financing the sales of opium to indigenous merchants in exchange for a guar-

Figure 1
Opium sales at Batavia, 1688–1789 (annual average number of chests/ reporting period)

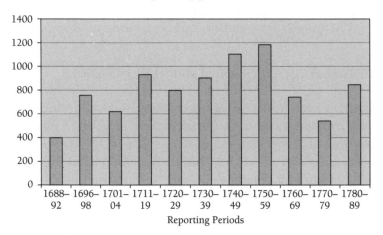

Reporting Periods

supply difficulties in Bengal, the eventual exclusion of the Company from purchasing and exporting opium from Bengal to Batavia by the English East India Company and wartime conditions between England and the Netherlands from 1775 to 1781. But, they recovered over the next decade.

The VOC continued its involvement in the trade by buying Bengal opium from whomever that could obtain and deliver it to them at Batavia and the Company continued to re-sell it to the *Amfioen Sociëteit*. From 1769 to 1792, for example, the Company purchased 5,850 chests of opium mostly from Bengal from British private traders at Batavia.[44] For the remainder of our period and beyond, the Company or Dutch colonial administration bought Bengal and increasing quantities of Levantine opium from diverse suppliers, including Danish, American and other private traders.[45]

anteed price on delivered volumes from the Company in 1745 and was active till 1794, when it was succeeded by the *Amphioen Directie*, see I.E. Mens, 'De Amphioen Sociëteit (1745–1794). Middel tot "redres" van de Compagnie of wellicht meer een middel to verijking van de Hoge Regering', unpublished, M.A. dissertation, Leiden University, 1987.

[44] See ARA, VOC 3252–3971; the total numbers of ships involved were 57 (51 English, 3 Portuguese, 1 French, 1 Prussian and 1 Armenian).

[45] Small quantities (90 chests in both years) of Levantine opium were sold by the VOC to the *Amfioen Sociëteit* at Batavia in 1753 and 1778, see Baud, 'Proeve van eene Geschiedenis ...', 151; there is increased activity in the delivery of Levantine opium, see the *Amphioen Sociëteit* (AS) documentation in the ARSIP (ARSIP, AS 1 to 34); for a discussion of the early nineteenth

Over 1677 to 1789, the Company reported total net revenues or profit earnings of 48,540,377 *florins* from the sale of opium at Batavia.[46] This figure may be converted and is the equivalent of 16,180,125 *rsd.*, which for the purpose of comparison of the magnitude of this figure is equal to 19,416,150 Spanish *pesos* and 17,651,046 Chinese *taels*.

COMPTOIR ACCOUNTS AND IMPERIAL FINANCES

Within the Company's imperial organization and accounting practices, the local *comptoir* was the administrative unit, in general, that reported its overhead and operating expenditures and its income or revenues for a specific geographical area. These expenditures and incomes were prepared in an annual report covering an operating period from the 1st of September till the 31st of August of the following year. Batavia, one imagines, might have been considered an exceptional case, since as the Company's imperial administrative centre, it carried and registered significant overhead and operating expenditures relating to defence, personnel, preparing and maintaining shipping and others. But, there was no variation in this accounting practice or exemption for Batavia.[47]

A significant number (61), nearly two-thirds of these accounts for the Batavia *comptoir* have been examined for the eighteenth century. In modern accounting terms, they are a combination of a profit and loss balance sheet and an income and expenditure report. They are denominated in *florins* or *guilders*. The conversion of *florins* or *guilders* to the *rijksdaalder* was 3 to 1 over the period. Care must be taken in the evaluation of the magnitude of the values in these accounts. The revenues or profits from opium in these accounts are in agreement with Baud's figures. Examples and distribution of these accounts are nearly evenly distributed over this period with the exception that there were no records found or consulted in the decade of the 1760s. It is argued that the potential for significant skewing or deviation statistically in one

century trade of Levantine opium, see Jan Schmidt, *From Anatolia to Indonesia: Opium Trade and the Dutch Community of Izmir, 1820–1940* (Istanbul: Nederlands Historisch-Archaeologisch Instituut, 1998).

[46] See Baud, 'Proeve van eene Geschiedenis, pp. 216–19.

[47] ARA, VOC 1603 to 3609: Annual Batavia *comptoir* reports, 1697–1781. For supplementary details or breakdown of the *Jacatra* payments for 1722, 1723, 1725– 1729, 1734 and 1736, see ARA, VOC 2005 to 2398.

Figure 2
Batavia comptoir accounts, 1702–1796: Income and expense distribution
florins ('000's)

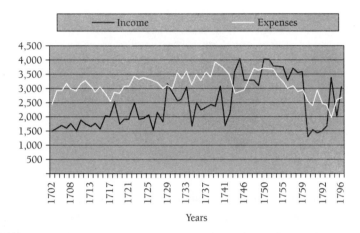

direction or another in the absence of an example for that time period is minimal in the trend and other analysis that was performed on these accounts.

In the first instance, as shown in Figure 2, the examination and analysis of these accounts reveal that regardless of the Company's control over extraordinary wealth, expenditures were usually greater than income revenues or in deficit in the Batavia *comptoir's* annual accounts for most of this period. The salient point being for the development of our argument is not that the accounts were usually in deficit and they were covered by the Company. Neither the existence of a deficit, *per se*, nor the method of how the Company covered this deficit is of interest or importance to the development of our argument in relation to opium. These deficits existed and they were covered. The point is to imagine or calculate the size of the deficit in these accounts if opium had not been traded and/or if it had not been as profitable for the Company as these accounts attest.

In the second instance, the composition of the Company's income or revenues was three-fold. It was derived from (a) trade (in essence, from sales revenues and profits from maritime trade including opium); (b) tax farming or Jacatra tax payments; and (c) other sources. Figure 3 graphically presents the breakdown of these three revenue streams by category, total value and percentage over the period. As it may be seen,

Figure 3

Batavia comptoir accounts, 1702–1796: Income sources and distribution (Total in florins and percentages)

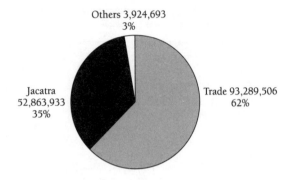

revenues from trade generated slightly under two-thirds; tax farming or Jacatra payments slightly over one-third; and the other category generated an insignificant 3 per cent of the Batavia *compoir*'s revenues.

In the third instance, a detailed examination of the composition of the quantities and net revenues or profits from the trade revenue receipts confirms that the sales of opium and all other Company-controlled and commercialized commodities from maritime trade by the Company to Asian and other European merchants at Batavia did enter this *comptoir*'s accounts. The breakdown of the revenues generated by trade, their composition and percentage distribution by individual major commodities and category groupings of goods (opium; cinnamon; pepper; other spices; Asian textiles, predominantly, Indian; Indian goods, such as saltpetre and others; and Fatherland or European woollen textiles and other goods) is shown in Figure 4. And they generally agree with the sales and purchases reports for maritime trade at Batavia. That opium sales and profits figured prominently in the *comptoir*'s commercial accounts was to be expected, but that opium sales generated over one-half of the net income from trade in the *comptoir*'s accounts is a major contribution. It is so sizeable that it is difficult to imagine the counter-factual scenario mentioned earlier: how or from what other sources of revenue would the Company have kept the Batavia *comptoir* deficits down and covered them? By the 1690s, although the Company would continue to commercialize textiles, the sales values of Bengal opium surpassed those of Indian cottons, silks and all other Asian textiles at

Figure 4
Batavia comptoir accounts, 1702–1781: Trade revenue
(composition and percentage distribution)

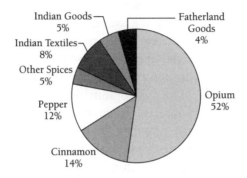

Batavia. One of the two real surprises in these accounts is that the sales profits from Sri Lankan cinnamon at Batavia generated 14 per cent of the *comptoir*'s revenue from trade. After opium, cinnamon was the second most important and largest individual commodity contributor to the Batavia *comptoir*'s financial results from trade.

In the fourth instance and the second surprise in the revision of these accounts are the volume and the value of the revenue contributed to the *comptoir* from tax farming revenues. They accounted for slightly over one-third of all the revenues accruing to the *comptoir* in the eighteenth century. Described in the accounts as contributions or payments from Jacatra, it should be remembered that this was the term that the Company used for Batavia and its environs after seizing the site from the *Pengeran* of Jacatra in 1619. This revenue farming system or *pacht*, the Dutch term for a rented monopoly privilege, was not new; 'they represented 27 per cent of total revenues of the VOC in Asia in 1653'.[48] While there is additional detailed serial data in the archives indicating the composition and contribution of the individual tax farms and revenues that were collected at Batavia, it is sufficient to observe for the purpose and space constraints of this essay that these revenues grew significantly over the latter half of the seventeenth and eighteenth centuries in absolute value and volume and as a percentage from 27 to 35 per cent of total Company revenues.

---

[48] See Reid, 'The Origins of Revenue Farming' p. 75.

CONCLUSION

By examining the structure, composition and participation of the Company, Asian and other European merchants in maritime trade and the composition of the Company's *comptoir* operating expenditures and revenues derived from maritime trade (including opium), tax farming and other sources at Batavia, opium's importance to the Company was discussed in this essay. Through a series of traditional economic analyses, the commercialization of Bengal opium was shown to have been a dramatically important source of revenue for the Company's imperial headquarters—the Batavia *comptoir*. It dwarfed all other individual or groups of commodities that were available to the Company to sell profitably on Java and in the Indonesian Archipelago over the long eighteenth century. Its sales revenues kept the deficits in the *comptoir's* accounts to a lesser level than they otherwise might have been. The repercussions of these historical developments and antecedents directly and significantly contributed to the emergence of opium farming, which as James Rush has shown became a major source of revenue in the colonial administration of the Dutch East Indies in the nineteenth century.[49]

The commercialization of opium, as Els Jacobs has capably discussed, was relatively unimportant and insignificant in the overall commercial results of the Company in the eighteenth century. This contrast between macro versus micro views of the importance of opium to the Company raises additional implications about the role and nature of commodities and of commerce at this time. Locality was certainly of importance as were consumer proclivities towards the value and utility and the nature and availability of individual commodities in shaping the early modern global economy. Despite the commercial expertise of the trading capabilities of early modern European commercial institutions—the Dutch and English East India Companies, neither of these institutions could find or develop alternatives in European or Asian commodities to the profits that could be made in trafficking opium in Southeast Asia and China, although Indian raw cotton exports to China in the late eighteenth into the early nineteenth century were a temporary exception to this claim. The same observation is true of other local

[49] See James R. Rush, *Opium to Java: Revenue Farming and Chinese Enterprise in Colonial Indonesia, 1800–1910* (Ithaca, NY: Cornell University Press, 1990).

and regional profit maximization competitors and collaborators of the Companies, indigenous and European private traders as individuals, groups and networks. Of additional importance, as our examination of the revenues of the Batavia *comptoir* reveal, neither could the Dutch East India Company escape from its dependency on revenues generated from the commercialization of monopolized nor monopoly claimed commodities. Finally, while relating consumer to commercial behaviour is always difficult, the emergence and the proclivity to consume opium by smoking in Southeast Asia and China, which did not occur to the same degree or intensity elsewhere in the early modern world, created the opportunity for the trade in this commodity to become distinctive from other parts of the globe. This first transformation of opium and its consumption was significant. Much later, there would be subsequent transformations in the history of opium history beyond being smoked with the development of heroin and alternate intravenous delivery systems that would expand its consumption beyond the markets that emerged in Southeast Asia and China in the early modern period.

A brief reference was made in the introduction to this essay that an examination of the social life or biography of opium as a vehicle or artifice could and should be usefully employed in a broader examination of the economic and social history of Southeast Asia—especially, on Java and elsewhere throughout the Indonesian Archipelago—in the long eighteenth century. While this essay did not concentrate upon developing this approach, it did, however, establish the commercial primacy of this commodity in the economy on Java, which was the necessary first step prior to developing opium's social life or biography. With opium's primacy established in the commercial and economic lives of rulers, merchants, growers, producers and consumers, it is now possible to develop the social biography approach further and incorporate and employ it in a broader, economic, social and cultural examination of opium at Batavia, in Southeast Asia and in global history.

6

The Mughals, the Sufi Shaikhs and the Formation of the Akbari Dispensation

Muzaffar Alam*

——— • ✦ • ———

Introduction

The authority exercised by the Mughal dynasty over much of northern India in the sixteenth, seventeenth and eighteenth centuries depended in part on various forms of legitimacy that were provided to it from outside the narrow sphere of elite politics. To be sure, the Mughals were also able to rule for so long and with such success because they successfully managed a composite political elite made up of elements both from northern India and from the Deccan (as well as other 'peripheral' regions), and migrants from Central and West Asia. However, as with a number of dynasties of the Muslim world in the period, a crucial element in the strategies of rule that they adopted were their relations with religious figures of various sorts. This essay is an attempt to understand the changing relationship between the Mughal rulers and the Sufi shaikhs, focusing on the early days of the formation and consolidation of the Mughal state in India. The question of the Mughal–Sufi equation, as we

* In several ways in the course of conversations over the years, Simon Digby, J. G. J. ter Haar and Sanjay Subrahmanyam have helped me write this essay. Sanjay Subrahmanyam also made significant comments on an earlier draft. I have also benefited from the suggestions of Stephen Dale, Sunil Kumar and Munis Faruqui. Rajeev Kinra and Hajnalka Kovacs's help was valuable in rechecking some of the important references. I am thankful to them all.

know, has generally been discussed with reference to the Naqshbandi order. Scholars have devoted particular attention to Shaikh Ahmad Sirhindi (d. 1624), the founder of the Mujaddidi branch of that order, his disciples and his ideology. Their questions have revolved around the extent and the nature of the influence of this group on seventeenth-century Mughal Indian politics.[1] There is no denying of the importance of this debate, and as a matter of fact, the present essay was initially motivated by the desire to contribute to it. In the course of my study of the relevant materials, however, I realized that I would be in a better position to re-evaluate this subject if I placed Mughal–Sufi relationships within a larger sixteenth-century context and not limit the discussion to the Naqshbandi shaikhs alone.[2]

The essay thus reviews the career, politics and ideology of Sufis who occupied a central position in the social and cultural life of Indian Muslims in the early sixteenth century, the time when the Mughals conquered India and began to build up their power. Here I will describe in brief the political and doctrinal life of Shaikh 'Abd al-Quddus Gangohi (d. 1537), a leading Chishti shaikh of the time. Gangohi was the *pir* or preceptor, very nearly the royal *pir*, of the Afghans, the archrivals of the Mughals. How then did the Mughals deal with him? How did he reconcile himself with the new situation?

---

[1] This is true of almost all modern historians. Whether they have highlighted evidence to support, qualify or reject the validity of this proposition; the contours of the proposition, itself, has not shifted. See for example I. Habib, 'The Political Role of Shaikh Ahmad Sirhindi and Shah Waliul-lah', *Enquiry* 5 (1961), pp. 36–55; Aziz Ahmad, *Studies in Islamic Culture in the Indian Environment* (Oxford: Oxford University Press, 1964), pp. 182–90; K. A. Nizami, 'Naqshbandi Influence on Mughal Rulers and Politics', *Islamic Culture* 39 (1965), pp. 41–52; Yohanan Friedmann, *Shaykh Ahmad Sirhindi: An Outline of His Thought and a Study of His Image in the Eyes of Posterity* (Montreal: McGill University, 1971); Fazlur Rahman, *Islam*, 2nd edition (Chicago: Chicago University Press, 1979), p. 148; J. G. J. ter Haar, *Follower and Heir of the Prophet: Shaikh Ahmad Sirhindi as a Mystic* (Leiden: Het Oosters Instituut, 1992); David W. Damrel, 'The "Naqshbandi Reaction" Reconsid-ered', in *Beyond Turk and Hindu: Rethinking Religious Identities in Islamicate South Asia*, eds David Gilmartin and Bruce Lawrence (Gainesville: University Press of Florida, 2000), pp. 176–98.

[2] S. A. A. Rizvi, 'Sixteenth century Naqshbandiyya Leadership in India', in *Naqshbandis: Historical Development and Present Situation of a Muslim Mystical Order*, eds Marc Gaborieau, Alexandre Popovic and Thierry Zarcone (Istanbul-Paris: Institut Français d'Etudes Anatoliennes d'Istanbul, 1990), pp. 153–65; Stephen F. Dale, 'The Legacy of the Timurids', *Journal of the Royal Asiatic Society*, 3rd Series 8 (1998), pp. 43–58; and Arthur F. Buehler, 'The Naqshbandiyya in Timurid India: The Central Asian Legacy', *Journal of Islamic Studies* 7 (1996), pp. 209–28, all do provide useful details on the Naqshbandis' relations with the early Mughals. However, they do not dis-cuss the complexities of the Mughals' encounters with Indian Sufis, while Damrel's discussion of some Chishti Sufi rites and practices with reference to Sirhindi, is essentially meant to show his connections with the Chishtis and the similarities in their 'politics' and Sufi practices. Compare Damrel, 'The "Naqshbandi Reaction" Reconsidered'.

Was there any change in his position, or later after his death, in the position of the other people and institutions related to the Chishti order? Can we explain the changes that did occur in terms of the evolving conditions in the wake of the establishment and consolidation of the Mughal empire? What was the response of the Mughals and why did it take the form it did? The essay also discusses the visit of the Central Asian Naqshbandi shaikhs to the Mughal court. Here besides some details of their relations with the early Indian Mughals, I also draw attention to the nature of their relations with the Timurid rulers in Central Asia. This has been done in an attempt to understand the problems that came up in the wake of their visits. I have thus asked if, with the Mughal conquest of India, these Naqshbandis shaikhs also saw the prospect of an extension of the domain of their power and if the legacy of the ideology and practice of Central Asian Naqshbandi *tasawwuf* hindered the progress of the building of the Mughal state in India, and created difficulties for the Mughals. I have hence examined in particular the connections between Akbar's new administrative measures on the one hand, and the Sufi shaikhs (whether Chishtis or Naqshbandis), on the other.

In the last section of the essay, I examine whether in the new conditions of Akbar's India, the Naqshbandis rearticulated their *tasawwuf* in a bid to renegotiate their relationship with the Mughals. It should be noted at the very outset that several details critical for our argument have been developed earlier, in particular by scholars of Central Asia. However, these same elements are reinterpreted here in the perspective of the development of Mughal Indian politics and religious culture. It is hoped that this will provide a more useful context for the questions often asked by historians of Mughal India.

THE CHISHTI SHAIKHS, THE AFGHANS AND THE MUGHALS

In the mid-1520s, when Zahir al-Din Muhammad Babur entered northern India with a plan to establish Mughal power in the subcontinent, Shaikh 'Abd al-Quddus Gangohi, a member of the Sabiri branch of Chishti order, was probably the most noted Sufi shaikh there, with his deputies (*khalifas*), disciples (*murids*) and ordinary associates (*mutawassils*) spread over almost the entire upper northern Indian plain. They belonged to diverse groups, ranging from lowly weavers and peasants to the very high members of the political class, including the reigning monarch and many of his courtiers, nobles and commanders.[3] Gangohi's early career was in Rudauli, in Awadh, where he was initiated into the Sabiri line of the Chishti order by Shaikh Muhammad, a grandson of the eminent Chishti Sabiri saint, Shaikh Ahmad 'Abd al-Haqq of Rudauli (d. 1434). He moved to the Punjab in the wake of Rajput uprisings in Awadh following the death of Bahlol Lodi (r. 1451–88) and settled in the Afghan-dominated town of Shahabad, near Karnal, north of the Yamuna river. In Shahabad, Gangohi spent the most important period of his life, living there for over 38 years, building intimate affinity with the ruling Afghan king of the Lodi dynasty and his nobility. He had close relations with, and a special appreciation for, Sultan Sikandar Lodi (r. 1488–1517), for he, according to Sufi accounts at least, was generous to the *'ulama* and the pious, so that in his reign 'in fear of his dreadful and dazzling sword, and because of the grandeur of his exalted kingly power, sinners and mischief mongers were totally annihilated (literally: disappeared into the darkness of night and inexistence)'.[4] We may however also note here that Sikandar Lodi, as the later chronicler Muhammad Qasim Firishta reports, was the first Muslim king to create facilities for Hindus to learn Persian, and thus be trained to take charge of several offices under the Persianate Muslim government.[5]

Gangohi, like many Afghan nobles of the time, was however unhappy with Ibrahim Lodi (r. 1517–26), though unlike them he did not welcome the Mughals, whom he saw as a divine scourge, set loose as a divine retribution in the world of the sinful Afghans. Indeed, the flourishing Afghan town where he lived with his family turned desolate with the news of the feared Mughal invasion of the region. He left Shahabad, moved farther to settle in Gangoh, on the eastern bank of the Yamuna river, away from the route of the invaders. But as he was nearly the sole royal *pir* of the Afghans, he was persuaded by his disciples to join with them in the Afghan camp, in order to bless them and pray for them in their imminent fight against the Mughals under Babur. Gangohi anticipated

---

[3] For the weavers (*ha'ikan and safed-baf*) of Saharanpur and Thanesar as Gangohi's disciples, see Muhammad Akram ibn Shaikh Muhammad 'Ali ibn Shaikh Ilah Bakhsh, *Sawati' al-Anwar*, British Library, India Office Library Ms, Ethé 654, fols. 370a and 385b.

[4] Shaikh Badhan ibn Rukun *alias* Miyan Khan ibn Qiwam al-Mulk Jaunpuri, *Maktubat-i Quddusiya* (Delhi: Matba' Ahmadi, 1287 AH./1870), p.45.

[5] Muhammad Qasim Firishta, *Tarikh-i Firishta*, Vol. I (Puna: Dar al Imarah, 1217 AH/1832), p. 344; Urdu trans. 'Abdul Hay Khwaja (Deoband: Maktaba-i Millat, 1983), p. 552.

the Afghan defeat, thought of fleeing, but eventually managed only to send his family away to Gangoh. He was constrained to stay back with Ibrahim Lodi's army together with his eldest son, Shaikh Hamid and his servitor (*khadim*), Sayyid Raja. With the Lodi Sultan's defeat and death, the Sufi fell into the hands of the Mughals, who first forced him to undo his turban, which they then threw around the necks of his son and *khadim*. The elderly *pir* of the Afghans was then forced to walk on foot from Panipat to Delhi, a distance of some forty miles, while his son and *khadim* were tied to the saddle of a horse by the long turban of the Shaikh.[6] Soon after, he was released, and he then spent the last eleven years of his life in Gangoh, where he died in 1537.

In 1530, when Babur died, the Afghan struggle to regain their lost power was still unabated. According to the *Lata'if-i Quddusi*, the most detailed and reliable *tazkira* of the Shaikh, throughout the years of the Afghans' fight against Babur's son and successor, Humayun, Gangohi remained opposed to the Mughals. He even allegedly had support and admiration for Sultan Bahadur Shah of Gujarat, the arch-enemy of Humayun on the western frontiers of his domain. It is interesting to note here the details of two visions of one Dattu Sarwani, a noted Afghan disciple of Gangohi. One of these visions pertains to Humayun's campaigns in Gujarat. According to the *Lata'if-i Quddusi*, one night, when Sultan Bahadur Shah was in the port of Diu and Humayun had gone to Gujarat, threatening to capture that kingdom, the Shaikh appeared in Dattu's dream, commanding him to go to Gujarat, convey his greetings to the *pirs* there and give them the following message:

> Humayun Padishah is destroying Islam. He makes no distinction between infidelity and Islam, plunders it all. I have come to the aid of Islam, and to your aid, and if you agree, I shall come there, join you, and drive Humayun out of the country of Gujarat; and if it pleases you I shall go to the country of Mandu to drive him out from there and you may drive him out from Gujarat, so that Islam may have peace and rest.

Accordingly, Dattu reached Gujarat, and delivered the Shaikh's message first to Hazrat Shah Manjhan and then to Shaikh Ahmad Khattu, the two major Sufi divines of the region. They both welcomed and endorsed the Shaikh's mission, promised their support, and requested him to come to them 'so that we may together drive away Humayun from both the

---

[6] Shaikh Rukn al-Din, *Lata'if-i Quddusi* (Delhi: Matba' Mujtaba'i, 1311 AH/1894), p. 64.

country of Mandu and the country of Gujarat, in order that Islam may grow strong and there may be stability in the land'.[7]

The other vision concerns Sher Shah's battle against Humayun, in which the Afghans defeated the Mughals and made them finally flee from India in 1540. The text of the *Lata'if* reports (through the voice of Dattu):

> When Sher Shah Sur and Humayun Padishah opposed each other on the banks of the Ganges, Humayun Padishah was on the side of the *qasba* of Bhojpur and Sher Shah was on the other side. In a general gathering, Humayun Padishah said, 'If this time I am victorious and the Afghans are defeated, I will not leave a single Afghan alive, even though he might be a child'. When I heard this story I was very worried. After this Humayun Padishah had a bridge of boats bound together, crossed the Ganges, and encamped on the bank of the river. I continued worrying. Suddenly in a dream my *pir* and helper, Hazrat-i Qutb-i 'Alam appeared and said, 'Dattu, look at the way the royal tent of Sher Shah is now standing'. I saw that it was standing very high, but that the pegs of the tent ropes were undone in the camp of Humayun Padishah, and that the royal tent of Humayun Padishah had fallen down, so that the Mughals were scattering and fleeing. Humayun Padishah was rallying them, while saying 'Don't leave me alone'. He was lamenting and wandering around in a distressed and stunned state. 'Have you seen the state of the Padishah?' Hazrat-i Qutb-i 'Alam asked. 'I have seen it', I submitted. He then said, 'Victory is Sher Shah's, defeat is Humayun's. The support of the *pirs* is on the side of Sher Shah'.[8]

These visions reflect a kind of consciousness of the opportunities to try and upset the Mughals' position in Gujarat, Malwa or eastern India—opportunities which the most persistent of their Afghan opponents, including the dreamer Dattu, must have been observing with interest.[9] However, the fact that they were incorporated into Gangohi's *tazkira* and continued to be an integral part of it, shows the image of the Shaikh that Gangohi's descendants and disciples preferred to keep, even when,

---

[7] *Lata'if-i Quddusi*, pp. 79–80. For an English translation, see Simon Digby, 'Dreams and Reminiscences of Dattu Sarvani, a Sixteenth Century Indo-Afghan Soldier', (in 2 Parts), *The Indian Economic and Social History Review*, 2 (1965), pp. 71–72. My translation of some of the words and phrases is different.

[8] *Lata'if-i Quddusi*, p. 83; Digby, 'Dreams and Reminiscences', pp. 180–81.

[9] Compare Digby, 'Dreams and Reminiscences', p. 80n.

as we will see later, they vied with their rivals, the Naqshbandis, to have some influence in Mughal official circles.

Gangohi, however, also seems to have periodically tried to develop good relations with Mughal conquerors. We possess letters written by him to Babur, Humayun and also to a Mughal noble, Tardi Beg. Besides the routine contents that such letters transmit, namely exhortations for pious acts and generous care for the learned and the saintly, in his letter to Babur, Gangohi particularly projects himself as an orthodox Sunni advocate of a rather narrow and bigoted juristic version of the *shari'a*.[10] To some extent he contradicts here an earlier position elaborated in his *Rushd Nama*.[11] Not much however can really be made of his apparently changed position, especially if we take into context the fluid and ambiguous political conditions in which these letters were written. Features of indigenous devotional religion in fact continued to be part of his *tasawwuf*. He also never gave up teaching the *Rushd Nama* to his disciples.[12]

As someone recovering from the trauma and humiliation of Mughal captivity, Gangohi's uncompromisingly bigoted position in his letter to Babur could also have been intended to reinstate himself as a pious *pir*, with an unstated assertion that his close affinity with the erstwhile rulers had been for a purely religious objective, unconcerned with anything profane and this-worldly. Whether he succeeded in his effort or not is a moot point. There is not much evidence in the existing contemporary sources—either from courtly circles or Sufi fraternities—to show his, and for that matter of any other Chishti shaikh's, regular and sustained connections with the early Mughals. The position of *pir* to Babur and Humayun was still a preserve of the Naqshbandis of Mawarannahr (Transoxiana).[13] Humayun showed interest in some Indian saints, but

---

[10] *Maktubat-i Quddusiya*, pp. 224–25 and 335–39.

[11] Simon Digby, 'Abd al-Quddus Gangohi (1456–1537 CE): The Personality and Attitudes of a Medieval Indian Sufi, in *Medieval India—A Miscellany*, Vol. 3, pp. 1–66, in particular pp. 34–66; S. A. A. Rizvi, *A History of Sufism in India*, Vol. I (Delhi: Munshiram Manoharlal, 2003 reprint), pp. 339–49.

[12] Digby, 'Abd al-Quddus Gangohi'; see also Iqtidar Alam Khan, 'Shaikh Abdul Quddus Gangohi's Relations with Political Authorities: A Reapparaisal, in *Medieval India: A Miscellany*, Vol. 4, pp. 73–90.

[13] Babur however did pay homage to the tombs of Qutb al-Din Bakhtiyar Kaki and Nizam al-Din Auliya in Delhi. Compare Zain Khan, *Tabaqat-i Baburi*, trans. Syed Hasan Askari (Delhi: Idarah-i Adabiyat-i Dilli, 1982), p. 92; Stephen F. Dale, *The Garden of the Eight Paradises: Babur and the Culture of Empire in Central Asia, Afghanistan and India, 1483–1530* (Leiden: Brill, 2004), pp. 199 and 331. Babur also visited the shrines of some other saints, like the one of Shaikh Sharf al-Din Yahya Maneri in Bihar (Dale, p. 444). Yahya was however a Firdausi Suhrawardi and

they, as will see below, were not Chishtis. Much later in Akbar's reign the emperor's ideologue and historian, Abu al-Fazl, however, mentions that Humayun with some of his companions used at times to visit the shaikh, and spend some time in his divinely inspired and animated assembly to experience truth and gnosis.[14] This mention was then copied with obvious additions and hyperbolic effects in almost all the later Chishti *tazkiras* and also in some Mughal chronicles. Among the principal Sufi *tazkira* writers who did so was the noted seventeenth-century scholar, 'Abd al-Rahman Chishti, the author of the *Mir'at al-Asrar*.[15] 'Abd al-Rahman Chishti, like Gangohi, was also a Sabiri and came from Rudauli. Interestingly the authority that 'Abd al-Rahman cites for this report is Abu al-Fazl's *Tazkirat al-Auliya*, which obviously means the chapter entitled *Auliya-i Hind* (saints of India) in the *A'in-i Akbari*. How and why were these images of Mughal–Chishti connections formulated in the course of the consolidation of Mughal imperial power under Akbar? For an understanding of the Mughals' rather late appreciation of the need to build close contacts with India-specific Sufis, it will be useful if we first considered the trajectory of their relations with their erstwhile Mawarannahri *pirs*, in Transoxiana and also in India.

NAQSHBANDI SHAIKHS AND TIMURIDS IN MAWARANNAHR

In the late fourteenth century, the Mughals' great ancestor Amir Timur himself is reported to have maintained close relations with Amir Kulal, the *pir* and preceptor of Shaikh Baha al-Din Naqshband, after whom the Sufi *silsila* came to be known subsequently.[16] This was principally a

---

not a Chishti saint, as Dale suggests. For his life see S. A. A. Rizvi, *A History of Sufism in India* (Delhi: Munshiram Manoharlal, 2003 reprint), Vol. 1, pp. 228–40.

[14] Abu al-Fazl Allami, *A'in-i Akbari*, ed. Sayyid Ahmad Khan (Aligarh: Sir Syed Academy, Aligarh Muslim University, 2003 reprint), p. 214.

[15] Compare 'Abd al-Rahman Chishti, *Mir'at al-Asrar*, British Library, Ms. Or. 216, fol. 483; Muhammad Akram ibn Shaikh Muhammad 'Ali ibn Shaikh Ilah Bakhsh, *Sawati' al-Anwar*, fol. 381 a. For an analysis of *Mir'at al-Asrar*, see Bruce B. Lawrence, 'An Indo-Persian Perspective on the Significance of Early Sufi Masters', in *Classical Persian Sufism from its Origins to Rumi*, ed. Leonard Lewisohn (London: Khanqahi Nimatullahi Publications, 1993), pp. 19–32; Bruce B. Lawrence and Carl W. Ernst, *Sufi Martyrs of Love: Chishti Sufism in South Asia and Beyond* (New York: Palgrave Macmillan, 2002), pp. 58–64. For 'Abd al-Rahman Chishti see also Shahid Amin, 'On Retelling the Muslim Conquest of India', in *History and the Present*, eds Partha Chatterjee and Anjan Ghosh (New Delhi: Permanent Black, 2002).

[16] Hamid Algar, 'A Brief History of the Naqshbandi Order' and 'Political Aspects of Naqshbandi

routine spiritual relationship of a *murid* (seeker, disciple) with a *murshid* (guide, preceptor). In the fifteenth century, however, things changed with the emergence of Khwaja 'Ubaid-Allah Ahrar (d. 1490), the second great figure in the *silsila* after Baha al-Din, with whom the Naqshbandis expanded the frontiers of their influence far beyond Mawarannahr into Iran and Ottoman territory. Now, the relationship between a Naqshbandi master and his disciples, in particular the ones associated with power, also acquired a special social and political significance. Khwaja Ahrar was not only the spiritual preceptor (*pir*), but also a kind of paramount political patron of his disciples, amongst whom were a large number of the Timurid rulers and their nobles in Central Asia. He and several of his descendants and disciples claimed that they were not simply their spiritual masters, but also a source of strength and help in politics and power struggles.

Mulla Fakhr al-Din ibn Husain Wa'iz al-Kashifi, the author of *Rashhat 'Ain al-Hayat*, the renowned *tazkira* of the Khwaja and his associates, devotes a full chapter to describe the Khwaja's interventions in politics with an objective of setting the record straight, as he thought it ought to be. The chapter entitled 'an account of the miracles of Hazrat-i Ishan that pertain to his bestowal of conquering power to the kings, rulers and the others of his time' (*zikr-i tasarrufat-i ki hazrat-i Ishan betaslit-i quwwat-i qahira nisbat besalatin wa hukkam waghair-i ishan az ahl-i zaman pish burda and*) contains numerous anecdotes of his support or opposition to one or the other ruler of his time.[17] It is useful to quote here one anecdote that also shows in some detail the Khwaja's avowed mission and method.

> Hazrat-i Ishan had a vision (*dar waqi'a dida budand*) that it was with his help that the *shari'a* would acquire strength, which in turn, he thought, was to be achieved through the support of rulers. He then came to Samarqand to meet Mirza 'Abd-Allah bin Mirza Ibrahim bin Shahrukh, the Sultan of the city. I (the author) had also accompanied the Hazrat. On arriving in Samarqand, the Hazrat told one of the nobles who had come to meet him, that the purpose of his visit to the city was to meet with the Sultan and that it would be very good if he helped him in this matter. In

History', in *Naqshbandis: Historical Developments and Present Situation of a Muslim Mystical Order,* eds Marc Gaborieau, Alexandre Popovic and Thierry Zarcone (Istanbul-Paris: Institut Français d'Etudes Anatoliennes d'Istanbul, 1990), pp. 3–44 and 123–52.

17 Fakhr al-Din 'Ali ibn Husain Wa'iz al-Kashifi, *Rashhat 'Ain al-Hayat*, ed. 'Ali Asghar Mu'iniyan (Tehran: Bunyad-i Nikukari-i Nuriyani, 1977), pp. 516–69 for stories about Ahrar's relations with Sultans 'Abd-Allah, Abu Sa'id, Mahmud and Babur, for instance.

a rude way the noble said: 'Our Mirza (ruler) is young and carefree. It is difficult to have an audience with him. And what do dervishes have to do with such tasks?' The Hazrat lost his temper and said: 'We have not come here on our own. We have been commanded [by God and the Prophet] to be in touch with the rulers (*beikhtilat-i salatin amr karda and*). [We] will bring another [ruler], if your Mirza is unconcerned'. When the noble left, the Hazrat wrote his [the Sultan's] name on the wall, then erased it with his saliva and said: 'Our mission cannot be carried out by this rule and his nobles'. The Hazrat left for Tashkent the same day. The noble then died after a week, and a month later Sultan Abu Sa'id Mirza marched from Eastern Turkestan against Mirza 'Abd-Allah and slaughtered him'.[18]

Ahrar thus saw himself as having been divinely ordained to protect the Muslims from the evil of oppressors (*Musalmanan ra az sharr-i zalama nigah darim*) and to help them achieve their purpose (*maqsud-i Muslimin bar-awurdan*).[19] This he thought he could achieve by 'trafficking with kings and conquering their souls' (*ba padshahan bayast ikhtilat kardan wa nufus-i ishan ra musakhkhar kardan*). There was thus a clear awareness of a political role that he believed he has been assigned to play. As a matter of fact, in the prevailing conditions, he believed that it was not correct for him to just sit on a street-corner, devoting his time to routine prayer and the spiritual training of disciples that a regular shaikh would normally do.[20] The chronicler Khwandamir thus reports that Sultan Abu Sa'id and his son, Sultan Ahamd sought his advice in important state matters.[21] Whether this meant the elevation of political activity to the level of a kind of principle of the Naqshbandi *silsila* is not so important as the fact that all this was with a view to ensuring the implementation of the cause of the *shari'a*. This was something *new* and *different* from a mere loyalty to the *shari'a* which earlier Shaikh Baha al-Din had insisted upon.[22]

---

[18] *Ibid.*, pp. 518–19.

[19] *Ibid.*, p. 295.

[20] *Ibid.*, p. 329. See also Jo-Ann Gross, 'Multiple Roles and Perceptions of a Sufi Shaikh: Symbolic Statements of Political and Religious Authority', in *Naqshbandis*, eds Gaborieau, Popovic and Zarcone pp. 109–21.

[21] Khwandamir, *Habib al-Siyar* (Tehran: Khayyam, 1352 Shamsi/1973), vol. 4, pp. 87 and 109.

[22] I intend to maintain a distance here from the scholars who think that all through their history the Naqshbadi Sufis have been involved in one or the other sort of political activity. I have therefore emphasized the words 'new' and 'different'. See also Algar, 'Aspects of Naqshbandi History', pp. 123–52, and Jo-Ann Gross, 'Multiple Roles of a Sufi Shaikh', pp. 109–21.

Ahrar's power and triumph is to be explained perhaps more in terms of his enormous wealth and organizing skill than his spiritual and sufi qualities, howsoever unusual and unprecedented such wealth and skill might have been. He was probably the biggest single landowner of Central Asia of his time. He possessed thousands of acres of the best irrigated lands in Tashkent, Samarqand, Bukhara, Kashkadaria and other places. Besides, he also owned sixty four villages surrounded with irrigating canals, thirty out-of-town orchards, eleven town estates and scores of commercial establishments and artisanal workshops, numerous arcades of shops and commercial stalls, town baths and water mills.[23] These properties were critical for the system of protection and patronage that Ahrar developed, and which included an economic network made up of these holdings and also his trading activities, both regional and international. There were a large number of people and officials involved in this network, working with Ahrar himself at the central *khanqah*, and also spread out in various places all over Turkestan, Mawarannahr and Khurasan, to maintain and administer these properties. Many of them were not even his formal spiritual disciples. With this organized wealth, Ahrar was able to help both commoners and rulers in time of their financial difficulties.[24] It was in this way that he rearranged the forces of the Naqshbandi *silsila* to an unprecedented degree, building and consolidating his overriding position and uncontested power in the region.

The nature of Ahrar's unusual relations with the rulers of the region is illustrated from the behaviour of Sultan Ahmad Mirza who along with some of his nobles was initiated by him into the Naqshbandi order. The Sultan was not simply extraordinarily respectful and overawed in the presence of Khwaja Ahrar. He never placed one knee over the other before the Khwaja, and on occasion would start trembling and sweating out of fear in his presence (*az haibat wa dahshat-i majlis-i Hazrat-i Ishan gosht-i shana-i wai mi larzid wa qatrat-i arq az jabin-i wai mi chakid*).[25]

---

[23] Compare O.D. Chekhovich, *Samarqand Documents* (Moscow, 1974), pp. 67, 72, 125, 244 and 247; al-Kashifi, *Rashhat*, pp. 227, 228, 246 and 328. See also Jo-Ann Gross, 'Economic Status of a Timurid Sufi Shaikh: A Matter of Conflict or Perception', *Iranian Studies* 21 (1988), pp. 84–104. For Ahrar's estates in Kabul see also, Stephen F. Dale and Alam Payind, 'The Ahrari Waqf in Kabul in the Year 1546 and the Mughul Naqshbandiyyah', *Journal of the American Oriental Society* 119 (1999), pp. 218–33.

[24] Cf. Jürgen Paul, 'Forming a Faction: The Himayat System of Khwaja Ahrar', *International Journal of Middle Eastern Studies* 23 (1991), pp. 533–48.

[25] Zahir al-Din Muhammad Babur, *Baburnama*, English trans. A. S. Beveridge (Delhi: Oriental Reprints, 1970), pp. 33. Also see Wheeler M. Thackston's translation, (New York: Modern Library, 2002), p. 53; al-Kashifi, *Rashahat*, p. 531.

In return, he received the Khwaja's full support and, according to Babur's own testimony, even if he was a man of ordinary intelligence he was successful only because 'his, highness, the Khwaja, was there accompanying him step by step'.[26]

Babur's own father 'Umar Shaikh Mirza was also a disciple of the Khwaja, who often visited the Mirza and treated him as his son.[27] According to Abu al-Fazl, 'the king ('Umar Shaikh) was always of a dervish mind and inclined to the society of religious persons and asked for wisdom at the doors of the hearts of the God knowing, especially the holy Nasir al-Din Khwaja 'Ubaid-Allah, known by the name Khwaja Ahrar'.[28] The Khwaja is also reported to have given substantial amounts of money to the Mirza, once 250,000 *dinars* and on another occasion 70,000 *dinars*, to relieve the tax burden of the Muslims of Tashkent.[29] A measure of the Khwaja's intimacy with the Mirza was the fact that at Babur's birth, he, his father-in-law, Yunus Khan, the ruler of Moghulistan, and Maulana Munir Marghinani, one of the major theologians of the time, who had composed the chronogram of the birth of the prince, 'begged his Holiness' (writes Mirza Haidar Dughlat), 'to choose a name for the child and he blessed him with the name of Zahir al-Din Muhammad. [But]t that time the Chaghatai were very rude and uncultured..., and not refined ... as they are now; thus they found Zahir al-Din Muhammad difficult to pronounce, and for this reason gave him the name of Babur'.[30] In the words of Abu al-Fazl the 'weighty appellation with its majesty and sublimity, was not readily pronounceable or current on the tongues of the Turks, the name Babur was [thus] also given to him'.[31] In Farghana, the Khwaja also had a close association with the important families of the nobles and high officials. One such was the family of 'Abd-Allah who made use of the joint name of Khwaja-Maulana-Qazi

---

[26] *Baburnama*, trans. Beveridge, pp. 33 and 34, trans. Thackston's, pp. 53–54.

[27] *Ibid.*, trans. Beveridge, p. 15, trans. Thackston, p. 41.

[28] Abu al-Fazl Allami, *Akbarnama*, Vol. I, ed. Agha Ahmad 'Ali and 'Abdur Rahim (Calcutta: Asiatic Society, 1877), p.84, English trans. H. Beveridge, (Delhi: Low Price Publications, 2002 reprint), p. 219. See also *Baburnama*, trans. Beveridge, p. 15, trans. Thackston, p. 9.

[29] S. A. A. Rizvi, *A History of Sufism in India* (Delhi: Munshram Manoharlal, 2002 reprint), vol. II, p. 177. Rizvi cites *Samarq and Documents* and a Tashkent Ms. of a *tazkira* of Ahrar, *Maqamat-i Khwaja Ahrar*.

[30] *A History of the Moghuls of Central Asia Being the The Tarihk-i Rashidi of Mirza Haidar Dughlat*, English trans. E. Denison Ross (London: Curzon Press, New York: Barnes and Noble, 1972 reprint), p. 173.

[31] *Akbarnama*, Vol. I, p. 87, English trans. p. 225.

because he combined in his house the positions of *muqtada* (religious guide), *shaikh al-Islam* and *qazi*.[32]

THE MAWARANNAHRI SHAIKHS AND THE EARLY MUGHALS

Although associated with the moment of his birth, Khwaja Ahrar had died by the time Babur rose to power. But the prince nevertheless attributes several of his achievements to the Khwaja's blessings. Shortly before he took Samarqand in 1501, he had seen the Khwaja in a dream. He writes:

> His Highness Khwaja Ubaid-Allah seemed to come; I seemed to go out to give him honourable meeting; he came in and seated himself; people seemed to lay a table-cloth before him, apparently without sufficient care and, on account of this, something seemed to come to his Highness Khwaja's mind. Mullah Baba (?Pashagari) made me a sign; I signed back, 'Not through me the table-layer is in fault'. The Khwaja understood and accepted the excuse. When he rose I escorted him out. In the hall of that house he took hold of my right or left arm and lifted me up till one of my feet was off the ground, saying in Turki, 'Shaikh Maslahat has given (Samarkand)'. I really took Samarkand a few days later.[33]

As a matter of fact, in that town the followers of the Khwaja held a considerable position at the turn of the century. They did not pay any levies to the government under the Khawja's principle of *himayat* and they sometimes even dictated who should have the supreme power in the town. For only a brief while, in 1494, they had some difficulty when Sultan Mahmud Mirza was for a few months in possession of the town, made new regulations, and treated them with harshness and oppression.[34] Khwaja Ahrar's son Khwaja 'Abd-Allah (better known as Khwajagi Khwaja) and Khwaja Muhammad Yahya were their leaders. Earlier, in 1499, when Babur intended to capture the town, he was told by the *begs* to approach Khwaja Yahya with whose consent, they thought 'the town may be had easily without fighting and disturbance'. In Babur's own understanding too, the matter was to be resolved when Khwaja Yahya would decide to 'admit us to the town'.[35] The issue thus was not

---

[32] *Baburnama*, trans. Beveridge, pp. 89–90, trans. Thackston, p.65.

[33] *Ibid.*, trans. Beveridge, p. 132, trans. Thackston, p. 98–99.

[34] *Ibid.*, trans. Beveridge, p. 41, trans. Thackston, p. 28.

[35] *Ibid.*, trans. Beveridge, p. 124, trans. Thackston, p. 93.

simply one of spiritual power; Khwaja Yahya was clearly involved in the politics of the town. Earlier, in 901 AH, when the Tarkhanis of the town had revolted against Baisunghar Mirza and raised his half-brother Sultan 'Ali Mirza to supreme power, Khwaja Yahya blessed the latter and became his *pir*. But interestingly enough, the rebels could not lay hands on Baisunghar as he had taken refuge in the house of Khwaja 'Abd-Allah.[36] Babur noted and actually appreciated this political involvement. He writes:

> Through these occurrences, the sons of His Highness Khwaja Ubaid-Allah became settled partisans, the elder (Muhammad Ubaid-Allah, Khwajagi Khwaja) becoming the spiritual guide of the elder prince, the younger (Yahya) of the younger.[37]

Later, when the Uzbek ruler Shaibani Khan conquered Samarqand, he had apprehensions about Khwaja Yahya and therefore dismissed him, with his two sons, Khwaja Muhammad Zakariya and Khwaja Baqi, towards Khurasan. Some Uzbeks followed them and near Khwaja Kardzan killed both the Khwaja and his two young sons. Babur strongly resented this incident.[38] As a ruler of Mawarannahr, however, Shaibani Khan could not afford to be indifferent to the great Naqshbandi lineages as such. While he harshly treated the descendants of Khwaja Ahrar, he offered prayers at the shrines of Khwaja 'Abd al-Khaliq Ghijduwani (d. 1220) and Shaikh Baha al-Din Naqshband (d. 1389), along with a large number of his nobles, the *'ulama* and Sufis, who included several noted Naqshbandis of the time.[39] Later, Shaibani Khan's nephew 'Ubaid-Allah Khan, restored the major part of the Ahrar family lands. Still later, the descendants of Khwaja Yahya became the *shaikh al-Islam* of the city of Samarqand, combining with it the trusteeship of rich endowments settled on the tomb of Khwaja Ahrar.[40]

It is well known that between 1500 and his conquest of India, Babur came into contact with Shah Isma'il Safavi and with his help

---

[36] *Ibid.*, trans. Beveridge, pp. 61–63, trans. Thackston, p. 45.

[37] *Ibid.*, trans. Beveridge, pp. 61–63, trans. Thackston, p. 45.

[38] *Ibid.*, trans. Beveridge, p. 128, trans. Thackston, p. 96.

[39] Fazl-Allah ibn Ruzbihani Isfahani, *Mihman-nama-i Bukhara*, ed. Manuchehr Satudeh (Tehran: Bungah-i Tarjuma wa Nashr-i Kitab, 1341Shamsi/1962), pp. 43 and 61. See also Annemarie Scimmel, 'Some Notes on the Cultural Activity of the First Uzbek Rulers', *Journal of Pakistan Historical Society* 8 (1960), pp. 149–66. Ghijduwani was separated by five links in the *silsila* before its crystallization under the auspices of Baha al Din Naqshband.

[40] Algar, 'A Brief History of the Naqshbandi Order', pp. 15–16.

avenged himself upon the Uzbeks for the devastation they had wreaked on the Timurids and their associates in Central Asia. Because of his close relations with the Safavid Shah, who was not an orthodox Shi'a but a zealous propagator of heterodox Shi'ism, Babur is also alleged to have temporarily developed Shi'a leanings. It is also reported that a Naqshbandi shaikh of the time, Ahmad ibn Jalal al-Din Khwajagi admonished him for his seeking help from the Shah of Iran and asked him instead to accept Shaibani Khan as a *khalifa*.[41] Be that as it may, Babur nevertheless remained a lifelong devotee of Khwaja Ahrar. Of interest here is an anecdote pertaining to Babur's victory over Ibrahim Lodi in the battle of Panipat in 1526. The anecdote is reported by a seventeenth-century historian, Muhammad Sadiq. Sadiq writes that as Babur's army was too small in opposition to a huge and near-countless Afghan brigade, he felt overwhelmed and feared that he might lose the battle to the enemy. He then contemplated the image of Khwaja Ahrar as he had heard it described. All at once there appeared a horseman dressed in white, fighting against the Afghans, who were thereupon completely routed. Later, after the fight, he narrated the incident to one of his nobles. The noble told Babur that according to his description, the horseman in white was Maulana Ahmad Khwajagi. The same day, Babur sent one of his close courtiers to Khwajagi with several gifts together with a portrait drawn on a piece of paper. Babur, according to Sadiq, included the following verses too in the letter he wrote to the saint:

Dar hawa-i nafs gumrah umr zayi' karda-im

pish-i ahl-i faqr az atwar-i khud sharminda-im

Yak nazar bar mukhlisan-i khasta dil farma ki ma

Khwajagi ra manda aknun Khwajagi ra banda-im.

I have wasted my life in pursuit of what my misguided soul desired
I am ashamed of my conduct in front of the ascetics

---

[41] See Fazl-Allah ibn Ruzbihani Isfahani, *Suluk al-Muluk*, British Library, London Ms. Or. 253, Preface, fol. 3a. Isfahani writes that with Babur's help, heresy, which is to say Shi'ism, spread in Mawarannahr and that he, like the Iranian Shi'i leaders played a detestable role in bringing the mosques and other religious centres of the region beyond the river Jihun under the control of the heretic Shi'as. The region was thus afire with their mischief (*fitna*). All this happened because he invited the red-capped Safavid *qizilbash* to come to his help in his fight against the Uzbeks to recover Samarqand and Bukhara. But for 'Ubaid-Allah Khan's gallant struggle (*jihad*), the rites and symbols of the true faith would have been completely routed in the region. See also the printed edition of this text by Muhammad 'Ali Muvahhid (Tehran: Intisharat-i Khwarzimi, 1362 Shamsi/1983), p. 50. For an English translation of this work, see Muhammad Aslam, *Muslim Conduct of State* (Islamabad: University of Islamabad Press, 1974), pp. 31–33.

Please spare a glance for your infirm devotees

I am now a slave of Khwajagi, who[se directives] I had neglected.[42]

The saint seems to be the same Ahmad Khwajagi who had earlier resented Babur's seeking help from the Safavid Shah. The letter sounds like a statement of repentance for his earlier comportment and a reaffirmation of his devotion to Khwajagi Ahmad, in particular, and to the Naqshbandi saints in general.

Although Babur himself does not mention this incident, his continuing faith in and loyalty to the Naqshbandi order is pretty clear. On 6 November 1528, when he fell ill in India, he decided to render into poetry a treatise of Khwaja Ahrar entitled *Risala-i Walidiya* with a belief that this was how he would be able to cure himself of the disease. He writes:

> I laid it to heart that if I, going to the soul of His Reverence for protection were freed from this disease, it would be a sign that my poem was accepted (...). To this end I began to versify the tract (...). Thirteen couplets were made in the same night. I tasked myself not to make fewer than ten a day; in the end one day had been omitted. While last year every time such illness had happened, it had persisted at least a month or forty days, this year by God's grace and His Reverence's favor, I was free, except for a little depression, on Thursday the 29th of the month (November 12). The end of versifying the contents of the tract was reached on Saturday the 8th of the first Rabi (November 20th). One day 52 couplets had been made.[43]

From their usual residence in Samarqand, Babur also invited to Hindustan Khwaja Ahrar's grandsons Khwaja Khawand Mahmud (also known as Khwaja Nura) and Khwaja 'Abd al-Shahid (the second son of Khwajagi Khwaja), and his great-grandson Khwaja Kalan (a grandson of Khwaja Yahya). The last two were guests of honour at a feast that Babur gave in Agra on 18 December 1528. On this occasion, they sat at his right and received rich presents.[44] However, they did not choose to stay in India. On the other hand, Khwaja Khawand Mahmud set

---

[42] Muhammad Sadiq, *Tabaqat-i Shahjahani*, British Library, India Office Library Ms., Ethé 705, fols. 192b–193a. Khwajagi Ahmad, a disciple of Maulana Muhammad Qazi, who was a disciple of Khwaja Ahrar, died in 949 AH He is buried in Dehbid.

[43] *Baburnama*, trans. Beveridge, pp. 619–20, trans. Thackston, p. 420; Dale, *The Garden of the Eight Paradises*, pp. 176–77.

[44] *Baburnama*, trans. Beveridge, pp. 632 and 641–42, Thackston trans., pp. 426 and 432; Dale, *The Garden of the Eight Paradises*, pp. 427–28. Dale also mentions one unidentified Khwaja Chishti.

out for India only in the spring of 1530, but before his arrival, Mirza Haidar Dughlat writes, Babur had died. He was nevertheless received in Agra with great honour by the new ruler, Humayun.[45] Soon however, 'for some [unspecified] reasons', he left for Kabul and died there.[46] In Dughlat's account, there is a vague clue suggesting the reason why he did not stay at Humayun's court. Khwaja Khawand had apparently come with the intention of occupying the exclusive position of the royal spiritual master. But while Humayun welcomed and showed respect to him, he was also simultaneously devoted to a Shattari Sufi saint, Shaikh Phul. Dughlat writes:

> At that period there had arisen in Hindustan a man named Shaikh Phul. Humayun was anxious to become his disciple, for he had a great passion for the occult sciences—for magic and conjuration. Shaikh Phul having assumed the garb of a Shaikh, came to the Emperor and taught him that incantation and sorcery were the surest means to the true attainment of an object. Since doctrines such as these suited his disposition, he became at once the Shaikh's disciple. Besides this person there was Maulana Muhammad Parghari who, though a Mulla, was a very [irreligious] and unprincipled man, and who always worked hard to gain his ends, even when they were of an evil nature. The Shaikh asked the aid of Mulla Muhammad and, in common, by means of flattery, they wrought upon the Emperor for their own purposes, and gained his favour.
>
> Not long after, I went to visit the Emperor (...), but I could never gather that he had learned anything from his *pir*, Shaikh Phul, except magic and incantation. But God knows the best. The influence of Shaikh Phul thus confirmed, Maulana Muhammad, or rather the Emperor and all his following, neglected and slighted Khwaja Nura, who had a hereditary claim to their veneration. This naturally caused the Khwaja great inward vexation.[47]

The sorcery and magic that Dughlat mentions were the Sufi prayer and litanics known as *da'wat-i-asma'-i hasana*, in vogue among the Shattaris in India. The practice involved the observation and study of stars and other heavenly bodies. Humayun's fascination with the Shattari

---

[45] *A History of the Moghuls of Central Asia*, p. 398; *Akbarnama*, Vol. II, p. 194, English trans. p. 301.

[46] *A History of the Moghuls of CentralAsia*, p. 398; Samsam al-Daula Shahnawaz Khan, *Ma'asir al-'Umara*, Vol. II (Calcutta: Bibliotheca Indica, 1891), p. 575.

[47] *A History of the Moghuls of Central Asia*, pp. 398–99. See also Persian text edited by Wheeler M. Thackston, (Cambridge, MA: Harvard University Press, 1996), pp. 345–47.

saints, we may guess, could have been because of his own interest in astronomical sciences. Later in the century, the chronicler 'Abd al-Qadir Bada'uni writes that he had great devotion to and trust in Shaikh Phul (or Bahlul) and his younger brother, Shaikh Ghaus of Gwalior and had learnt from them the method of *asma'*. In 1540, when during his campaigns in eastern India against Sher Khan, he heard the disturbing news of his brother Mirza Hindal's plan of rebellion, he sent Shaikh Bahlul to try to talk to him on his behalf to seek reconciliation. Hindal and the other nobles in his retinue, however, suspected the Shaikh to be acting in collusion with the Afghans. He was thus killed by one of Hindal's associates.[48]

As for Khwaja Khawand, he seems to have left for Lahore at the invitation of another of Humayun's brothers, Mirza Kamran. By this time, Mirza Dughlat also arrived in Lahore to have the honour of 'kissing his feet'. While they were in Lahore, the Safavid ruler Shah Tahmasp invaded Qandahar and captured it. This obviously caused Kamran 'immense grief' and when Dughlat at his request told the Khwaja about his misfortune, the latter is reported to have said to him: 'I have seen His Holiness [Khwaja Ahrar] in a vision. He asked me, 'Why are you sad?' I replied: 'On account of Kamran Mirza, for the Turkomans have taken Kandahar. What will come of it?' Then His Holiness advanced towards me and taking me by the hand said: 'Do not grieve; he will soon recover it'. And thus, indeed, it came to pass, for Kamran Mirza marched against Kandahar, and the troops of Tahmasp Shah gave up the city to him in peace'.

Dughlat's account shows not simply his anguish over Humayun's treatment of the Khwaja. It reiterates the Timurids' continuing faith in and their devotion to the family of Khwaja Ahrar. Humayun, therefore, was also perturbed over the Khwaja's decision to depart from his court, and begged him to stay, but the latter would not listen to his entreaties. He then sent Maulana Muhammad Parghari to Lahore to persuade the Khwaja to return, and on his continued refusal, the Maulana begged his

---

[48] 'Abd al-Qadir Bada'uni, *Muntakhab al-Tawarikh*, ed. Kabiruddin Ahmad, Ahmad 'Ali and W.N. Lees (Calcutta: Bibliotheca Indica, 1869), Vol. III, pp. 4–5; *Ma'asir al-'Umara*, Vol.II, pp. 575–76. Humayun remained close to Shaikh Muhammad Ghaus until he lost the empire to the Afghans and fled to Iran. The Shaikh then left for Gujarat. When Humayun regained power he returned to Delhi. The emperor, however, died soon afterwards and the saint was disappointed at his reception by Bairam Khan, the regent of the young emperor, Akbar. He then retired to Gwalior where he died in 970 AH. See also K. A. Nizami, 'Shattari Saints and Their Attitude towards the State, in *Medieval India Quarterly*, Vol. 1, No. 2 (1950), pp. 56–70.

sins to be forgiven and beseeched him to write a reply to the letter from Humayun. The Khwaja in response reportedly wrote only the following verse:

Humai gu mafigan saya-i sharaf hargiz

daran dayar ki tuti kam az zaghan bashad

Say, O Huma [bird], never cast thy noble shadow

In a land where the parrot is less accounted than the kite.

Dughlat further writes that in this response, there was a curious pun, for Humayun Padishah eventually did not come to throw his shadow in the country (India) where the parrot was rarer than the kite. Dughlat also notes that in those days, he often heard the Khwaja say: 'I have seen in a vision, a great sea which overwhelmed all who remained behind us in Agra and Hindustan; while we only escaped after a hundred risks'; and Humayun's defeat at the hands of Sher Shah eventually came about three years later, just as the Khwaja had predicted.[49]

The unfortunate Humayun thus missed the blessings of both the Naqshbandi Khwaja of his ancestral homeland, Mawarannahr, and the great Chishti Shaikh of Hindustan. Later his relations with Khwaja Khawand appear to have been restored somewhat. In 1546, during an illness of the Emperor in Kabul, the Khwaja and his son Khwaja Mu'in were the only ones besides his personal attendant allowed to visit him.[50] Humayun also had some contacts in Kabul with Maulana Zain al-Din, an eminent Naqshbandi of his time, and with Khwaja 'Abd al-Bari, a great-great-grandson of Khwaja Ahrar.

It is also worth noting here that the Mughals were connected with some of the great Naqshbandi lineages matrimonially. A daughter of Babur was married to Nur al-Din Muhammad, a descendant of Khwaja 'Ala al-Din 'Attar, who was the first *khalifa* (or disciple) of Khwaja Baha al-Din Naqshband. Their daughter, Salima Begam, as we will see below, was later married to the powerful Mughal noble Bairam Khan. Humayun's younger son, Mirza Muhammad Hakim, the ruler of Kabul, gave his sister, Fakhr al-Nisa in marriage to Khwaja Hasan Naqshbandi, a descendant of Baha al-Din Naqshband, after the death of her first

---

[49] *A History of the Moghuls of Central Asia*, pp. 399–400; *Ma'asir al-'Umara*, II, 575. Ross's translation of the phrase 'wa sargardan raft' here is confusing. He adds the name of Maulana Muhammad in square brackets and translates the phrase as '[Maulana Muhammad] returned stupefied'.

[50] *Akbarnama*, Vol. I, p. 253, English trans. pp. 493–94.

husband, Abu al-Ma'ali. Khwaja Hasan thus became very powerful in Kabul for a time in the later sixteenth century.[51]

In the early phase of Mughal settlement in Hindustan, the presence of certain Naqshbandi saints as *pirs* (but not necessarily as the royal *pir*) and as important members of the Mughal elite, is unmistakable. The second phase of Timurid contact with the subcontinent begins with Humayun's return from his exile in Iran. Humayun, as we know, died soon after his return and resumption of power in Delhi. The process of recovery of the lost territory, its consolidation and further expansion only took place in Akbar's time. We may now turn to how the Naqshbandi Khwajas figured at this critical juncture of the shaping of Mughal power.

Akbar Encounters the Naqshbandis

At the beginning of Akbar's reign (1556–1605) Khwaja 'Abd al-Shahid, who had earlier visited Babur's court, arrived anew from Samarqand. Akbar received him 'with respect and kindness' and granted him the *pargana* of Chamari in Punjab. There the Khwaja lived for about two decades, 'with piety and severe austerities, striving much in the path of holiness as a compendium of all such perfection as man can attain to'. He was widely respected and people from all walks of life visited him acquiring grace from his 'precious utterances', 'being directed thereby in the path of righteousness and godly living'. The Khwaja, according to the chronicler Bada'uni, was a symbol based on the earlier model of Khwaja Ahrar. In 1561, when the Mughal commander Husain Quli Khan chasing the rebel Mirzas (who had risen up against Akbar) arrived at Chamari, he received from the Khwaja an assurance of his own victory, and the holy man's dress as a present. Bada'uni concludes: 'The result of this prayer was that having arrived by forced marches in Tulambah

---

[51] *Muntakhab al-Tawarikh*, Vol. II, p. 72. Commenting on Khwaja Hasan's absolute power some of the wits of the period used to say:

If our Master be Master Hasan
We shall have neither sack nor rope left.

For his and other Naqshbandis position at Mirza Hakim's court in Kabul, see Sanjay Subrahmanyam, 'A Note on the Kabul Kingdom under Muhammad Hakim Mirza (1554–85)', *La Transmission du savoir dans le monde musulman périphérique, Lettre d'information* 14 (1994), pp. 89–101; Munis D. Faruqui, 'The Forgotten Prince: Mirza Hakim and the Formation of the Mughal Empire in India', *Journal of the Economic and Social History of the Orient* 48 (2005), pp. 487–523.

he (Husain Quli) gained a glorious victory'.[52] In 1574, however, the Khwaja left India, also according to Bada'uni, following a premonition of his fast approaching death. 'The time of my departure is drawn nigh', the Khwaja is reported to have said, 'and I have been commanded to convey this handful of bones, of which I am composed, to the burying place of my ancestors in Samarqand'. He died shortly after his arrival in Samarqand.[53] However, the real reason and occasion for the Khwaja's departure seems to have been the rapid decline of the Naqshbandis from the favour of the Emperor. To gain a clearer sense of this decline, we may examine the career of another noted Naqshbandi, Sharaf al-Din Husain, who also visited Akbar's court early in his reign.

Sharaf al-Din Husain was the son of Khwaja Mu'in and a grandson of Khwaja Khawand Mahmud. He had lived with his father in Kashghar, where the latter had made a fortune as a merchant dealing in precious stones.[54] He was sent by the ruler of Kashghar to offer condolences on the death of Humayun in 1556 and to congratulate Akbar on his accession.[55] Sharaf al-Din came with this mission accompanied by Khwaja 'Abd al-Bari, who had earlier been sent by Humayun to Kashghar at the time of his expedition to reconquer India. Khwaja 'Abd al-Bari also belonged to 'the noble line of the Naqshbandi Khwajas', and we learn that he was 'son of Khwaja 'Abd al-Khafi, son of Khwaja 'Abd al-Hadi, son of Khwajagan Khwaja, son of Khwaja Ahrar—may his grave be holy'.[56]

Now, Sharaf al-Din soon rose in eminence in the Mughal court through the influence of Maham Ananga and Adham Khan, important figures of the early years of Akbar's reign. He received the high rank of *amir*, and was given *jagir*s in Ajmer and Nagor. During the fifth year of his reign, the Emperor gave him his half-sister Bakhshi Banu Begam in marriage. In the seventh year he was deputed to capture the fort of Mertha. Abu al-Fazl notes that he was assigned a high *mansab* of 5000.[57] In the eighth year, his father Khwaja Mu'in 'hearing of his son's exaltation and grandeur', also arrived from Kashghar. The Emperor received him with respect, gave

---

[52] *Muntakhab al-Tawarikh*, Vol. III, p. 40; *Ma'asir al-'Umara*, Vol. II, p. 379; *Akbarnama*, Vol. II, p. 127, English trans. p. 195.

[53] *Muntakhab*, p. 40.

[54] *Akbarnama*, English trans. Vol. II, p. 194–95, English trans. pp. 301–02; *Ma'asir al-'Umara*, Vol. III, p. 234. Khwaja Mu'in had the monopoly of jade trade with China.

[55] *Akbarnama*, Vol. II, p. 195, English trans. pp. 302–03; *Ma'asir al-'Umara*, Vol. III, p. 234.

[56] *Akbarnama*, Vol. II, p. 21, English trans. p. 37.

[57] *Akbarnama*, Vol. II, p. 128, English trans. p. 197; *Ma'asir al-'Umara*, Vol. III, pp. 234–35.

him 'honourable quarters and treated him with favours such as kings show to dervishes'.[58] The Naqshbandis at this stage were hence held 'in great esteem', to the extent that Mulla Mubarak, whom Bada'uni portrays as a man opportunistically inclined doing what was most rewarding at a given moment, 'adapted himself to their rule'.[59] It has been noted that Bairam Khan's wife, Salima Sultan Begam also came from a Naqshbandi family. She was a 'daughter of Nur al-Din Muhammad, Nur al-Din was son of 'Ala al-Din Muhammad, who was son of Khwaja Hasan, commonly known as Khwajazada Chaghaniyan. This Khwajazada was grandson of Khwaja Hasan 'Attar, who again was a direct descendant of Khwaja 'Ala al- Din, the first *khalifa* of Khwaja Baha al-Din Naqshband. We should also keep in mind that Khwajazada Chaghanian was son-in-law of Sultan Mahmud, son of Sultan Abu Sa'id Mirza".[60]

Soon after, however, the Naqshbandis' position seems to have declined, even though some of them held a couple of offices until about the end of the 1570s. One 'Abd al-'Azim, better known as Sultan Khwaja, the son of a disciple of Khwaja 'Abd al-Shahid, was selected to be the *amir-i hajj* in 1576. He returned from Mecca in 1578 and then held the office of the *sadr* until his death in 1584.[61] In 1578, another Naqshbandi, Khwaja Muhammad Yahya, a direct descendant of Khwaja Ahrar was appointed *amir-i hajj*.[62] After the 1570s, however, we have only Sultan Khwaja with a position of some eminence at Akbar's court, as his daughter was even married to Prince Daniyal in 1588.[63] But Sultan Khwaja's seems to be an altogether peculiar case. His position, according to a report, owed to his 'conversion' in support of Akbar's religious innovations of the time, which meant unquestioned obeisance to the Emperor and a nearly total deviation from the Naqshbandi Ahrari tradition.[64]

[58] *Akbarnama*, Vol. II, p. 195, English trans., p. 303; *Ma'asir al-'Umara*, Vol. III, pp. 235–36.

[59] Bada'uni writes that he followed 'many and various rules of life. For some time during the reigns of the Afghan emperors he used to keep company with Shaikh 'Ala'i, and in the beginning of the Emperor's [Akbar's] reign, when the Naqshbandi order was held in a great esteem, he adapted himself to their rule, and for some time he was attached to the Hamadani Shaikhs, and at last when the Iraqis were in great favour at the Court he spoke as one of their religion'; *Muntakhab al-Tawarikh*, English trans. Vol. III, p. 74.

[60] *Akbarnama*, Vol. II, p. 64, English trans., p. 97; *Ma'asir al-'Umara*, Vol. I, p. 375.

[61] *Ma'asir al-'Umara*, Vol. II, p. 380.

[62] *Muntakhab al-Tawarikh*, Vol. II, p. 267.

[63] *Ma'asir al-'Umara*, Vol. II, p. 381.

[64] *Muntakhab al-Tawarikh*, Vol. II, p. 340–41. According to Bada'uni, Sultan Khwaja requested the Emperor at the time of his death to intern him in a grave with a special lamp and to fix a

A major factor behind the turn in the Emperor's attitude could have been the revolt of Sharaf al-Din Husain himself in 1560s. Akbar decided to tackle this with uncompromising firmness. He refused to listen even to Khwaja 'Abd al-Shahid's recommendation on the matter,[65] which must have disappointed the Khwaja and forced him to leave for Samarqand. This appears to be a major reason for what happened—and not simply a wish to die in Samarqand as Bada'uni would have us believe of his departure in 1574. In fact, Bada'uni gives this hagiographical explanation while writing the biographical notices of the saint in the third volume of his history. In the context of his description of the incident in the second volume, however, he himself provides a clue to the real reason for the saint's departure. He writes that the saint 'felt much grief at the refusal [to accept his advice] and left much saddened, even though the Emperor did not neglect any marks of due honour and respect, and publicly even read the *fatiha*'.[66]

THE SUFI SHAIKHS AND THE FORMATION OF AKBARI DISPENSATION

The seemingly disproportionate grief of the Khwaja reported by Bada'uni, might have been a consequence of the new developments at Akbar's court, where, he realized, there would be little place left for the Mawarannahri Naqshbandis to live in their erstwhile style. In several modern writings on Mughal India, we have excellent accounts of the details of these developments.[67] We need not repeat them all here, even

---

grill facing the sun so that the light thereof might obliterate his sins. He willed so to please the Emperor and because he was a follower of the new faith *Din-i Ilahi* in which light and the Sun had a special sacred place. The author of the *Ma'asir al-'Umara* (Vol. II, pp. 381–82) dismisses this story as an instance of Bada'uni's bigotry.

65 *Muntakhab al-Tawarikh*, Vol. II, p. 171; *Akbarnama*, Vol. II, p. 195, English trans., p. 303 for Sharaf al-Din's revolt.

66 *Muntakhab al-Tawarikh*, Vol. II, p. 171. Badau'ni also reports that the Khwaja commanded immense respect among the rulers of Kabul and Central Asia. On his way to Samarqand when he arrived at Kabul 'it happened that Mirza Shah Rukh had just taken the people of Kabul captive, and was returning with them to Badakhshan. By means of the intercession of the Khwaja nearly 10,000 persons obtained deliverance. . . .'. Compare *Muntakhab al-Tawarikh*, Vol. III, p. 40.

67 Compare, for instance, John F. Richards, 'The Formulation of Imperial Authority under Akbar and Jahangir', in *The Mughal State, 1526–1750*, eds Muzaffar Alam and Sanjay Subrahmanyam (Delhi: Oxford University Press, 1998), pp. 126–67; Iqtidar Alam Khan, 'The Nobility under Akbar and the Development of his Religious Policy, 1560–1580', *Journal of the Royal Asiatic*

if it may not be pointless to briefly mention some of them. The most momentous of these was the emperor's marriage with a Rajput princess early in his reign, and together with it a number of administrative measures such as the abolition of pilgrimage taxes and the hated *jizya*, and giving up of the practice of forcibly converting prisoners-of-war to Islam. By the mid-1560s there had also evolved a new pattern of emperor–noble relationship, which suited the needs of a new Mughal state, to be defended now by a nobility of diverse ethnic and religious groups, amongst whom the Hindus and the Shi'as came to occupy a significant position. The Mughals were originally Hanafi Sunnis and Akbar too, until the 1570s at least remained faithful to this tradition. On the other hand, the new non-Muslim and non-Sunni recruits into Mughal state service were not asked to abandon their old customs and beliefs. On the contrary, several non-Muslim rituals began to be integrated into an evolving Akbari political culture of governance. All this was evidently not compatible with the Naqshbandi Khwajas' perception of a Muslim state. A major task of the ruler with whom they had contact, as is illustrated from Khwaja Ahrar's relations with the rulers of his time, was not simply to ensure the comfort (*asa'ish*) and welfare (*rifahiyat, khair*) of the Muslims, but also to discourage and abolish the customs of strangers (*rusum-i biganagan*). In their view, Muslim society was to be totally free from the evil (*sharr*) of non-Muslim social practices.[68] Earlier Shaikh Baha al-Din Naqshband (d. 1389) had proclaimed that the distinctive feature of his *silsila* was a total conformity and obedience to the traditions of the Prophet and his venerable companions (*chang dar zail-i mutaba'at-i sunnat-i Mustafa zada im wa iqtida ba asar-i sahaba-i kiram-i u namuda*), and that his followers formed a community of the perfect (*kamilan-i mukammal*), having attained high status because of their adherence to the path of the Prophet, and that best and the fastest way to the Truth was to provide relief to the heart of the Muslim.[69]

Society (1968) Parts 1–2 pp. 29–36; I. A. Khan, *The Political Biography of a Mughal Noble: Mun'im Khan Khan-i-Khanan, 1497–1575* (Delhi: Orient Longman, 1973), Introduction, pp. ix–xx.

[68] Compare *The Letters of Khwaja 'Ubayd Allah Ahrar and His Associates*, Persian text (ed.), Asom Urunbaev, English translation with notes by Jo-Ann Gross, Introductory essays by Jo-Ann Gross and Asom Urunbaev (Leiden: Brill, 2002), pp. 114, 128, 143, 145, 146, 166 and 169, letters nos. 49 (50), 59 (62), 282 (286), 284 (288), 304 (308) and 306 (310). See also Jürgen Paul, 'Forming a Faction', pp. 540–41. *Biganagan* means strangers, foreigners, which in the context implied the customs and practices introduced and established by the Mongols.

[69] Compare Khwaja Muhammad Parsa, *Qudsiyya (Kalimat-i Baha al-din Naqshbad)*, ed. Ahmad Taheri Iraqi (Tehran: Kitabkhana-i Tahuri, 1356 Shamsi/1975), p. 61 (text), 51 (Introduc-

Although it is difficult to accept the understanding of some recent historians regarding the so-called 'highly centralized absolutism' or 'highly systematized administration' under Akbar, there is no denying the fact that the years between 1560 and 1575 saw a rapid change in the position of the Chaghatai nobles and this, in the main, was intended by the emperor to buttress the power around his person. The revolts by the old guard—the Mirzas, the Qaqshals and the Atka Khail, for instance—which followed and also precipitated measures aimed at weakening their strength, showed the intensity of their disapproval and resistance to this change. Their *jagirs* that they had hitherto held concentrated in a region were dispersed, while nearly all the civil and financial offices were now being staffed by the non-Chaghatai groups.[70] The fortunes of the Naqshbandis, who had an established affinity with the Chaghatais, according to one report, were ensured because of the high and unmatched strength of the latter in the early years of Akbar's reign.[71] Their preeminence then would very likely suffer a serious setback in the wake of the increasing corrosion in the power of the Chaghatai nobles.

From the mid-1570s, we see the unmistakable signs of Akbar moving away from the pattern of Islamic rulership of the erstwhile Timurids, shared on occasion and in a measure with members of the nobility and the Naqshbandi Sufi lineage. Instead, Akbar favoured a kind of universal kingship, emphasizing an undisputed and all-encompassing power for the ruler. He now had a new capital of his empire, Fathpur Sikri, built in large measure in deference to the place's association with a saint, but it was he, the emperor, not the place or the saint, who was to be lauded as the centre of authority in the new Timurid polity in India.[72] Critical as it was, this feature of the evolving Akbari dispensation of power clashed with Naqshbandi ideas regarding authority and kingship.

We have already summarized some key features regarding the position of Khwaja Ahrar. After him too, there were some other saints of the lineage who combined wealth with spiritual accomplishments to strengthen their intervention in the political domain. Khwaja Ju'ibari and Khwaja Mushtari, two members of the same family of Naqshbandi shaikhs in Uzbek-ruled Mawarannahr, were celebrated for

tion); 'Abd al-Rahman Jami, *Tariqa-i Khwajagan*, ed. 'Abd al-Hayy Habibib (Kabul: Intishrat-i Anjuman-i Jami, 1962), p. 89.

[70] I. A. Khan, *The Political Biography*, Introduction.

[71] *Ma'asir al-'Umara*, Vol. II, pp. 584–85.

[72] John F. Richards, 'The Formulation of Imperial Authority'.

their legendary wealth; and according to one report, from Turkestan to Khurasan, there was not a single city, desert or place where these Khwajas had not built a canal. One of them enjoyed a yearly income equal to the entire revenue collected by the Uzbeks from Samarqand, the other held over 2,000 pieces of property, administered by his expert personal employees. They dominated the grain market, owned over 100 shops in Bukhara alone, and their joint property is said to have surpassed even that of Khwaja Ahrar.[73] In another case, Makhdum-i A'zam (d. 1543), a disciple of Maulana Muhammad Qazi (d. 1516), a noted *khalifa* of Khwaja Ahrar established an ascendancy over the ruler of Kashghar in the same way as had Khwaja Ahrar over Sultan Abu Sa'id, and the power in his family remained for decades, until in 1678 one of his descendants, Khwaja Afaq managed to dislodge the ruler in Yarkand and became the ruler himself.[74] The power to terminate and appropriate the authority of a king was thus within the realm of a Naqshbandi shaikh's political activity. We have already noticed how disobedience to Khwaja Ahrar led to the elimination of Mirza 'Abd-Allah, the ruler of Samarqand. We may also note the following statement attributed to him by the author of *Rashhat 'Ain al-Hayat*:

> If we acted only as a shaikh in this age, no other shaikh would find a disciple. But another task has been assigned to us, to protect the Muslims from the evil of oppressors, and for the sake of this we must traffic with kings and conquer their souls, thus achieving the purpose of the Muslims. *God Almighty in His grace has bestowed on me such power that if I wish I can, with a single letter, cause the Chinese emperor who claims divinity to abandon his monarchy and come running over thorns to my threshold.* But with all this power I await God's command: whenever He wills, His command reaches me and is executed.[75]

---

[73] Compare David W. Damrel, 'Forgotten Grace: Khwaja Khawand Mahmud Naqshbandi in Central Asia and Mughal India', Unpublished Ph.D. Dissertation, Department of Religon, Duke University, 1991, pp. 80–81. Damrel cites Mansura Haider, 'Agrarian System in Uzbek Khanates of Central Asia', *Turcica*, 7 (1974), pp. 157–78, and Haider, 'Urban Classes in the Uzbek Khanates, XVI-XVII Centuries' in *Central Asia: Papers Presented at the 30th International Congress of Human Sciences in Asia and North Africa*, ed. Graciela de la Lama (Mexico City: El Colegio de Mexico, 1976); Richard C. Foltz, *Mughal India and Central Asia* (Karachi: Oxford University Press, 1998), pp. 97–99.

[74] Compare Robert Barkley Shaw, 'The History of Khwajas of Eastern Turkistan' (ed. N. Elias), *Journal of the Asiatic Society of Bengal*, 66 (1899), and René Grousset, *Empire of the Steppe*, cited in Algar, 'Political Aspects of Naqshbandi History', p. 128.

[75] Cited in Algar 'The Naqshbandi Order: A Preliminary Survey of Its History and Significance', *Studia Islamica*, 44 (1976), pp. 123–52. Emphasis mine.

Later Naqshbandi Ahrari shaikhs, who had a strong memory of a share in power, would then have found it difficult to adjust to a political environment where the king did far more than simply assert his sole authority. Akbar, for example, had the audacity to throw overboard the shaikh's recommendation, and that too when it came from a scion of the great Naqshbandi lineage. Quite noticeably, therefore, Akbar moved away from the Naqshbandis. The emperor had lately begun to see the seeds of a formidable challenge to his plan for power and political preeminence in the activities of several supporters of the Naqshabandi lineage at the court of his half-brother Mirza Hakim, in Kabul. A glimmering of these sentiments is evident from events in the 1580s. While his nobles and deputies were assigned the task of suppressing serious rebellions. In Gujarat and the east, Akbar, himself, commanded the expedition to deal with Mirza Hakim in the Punjab.[76] We will see below that Kabul served as the centre for relaunching the Naqshbandi order in India, even after the termination of Mirza Hakim's regime.

In the late 1570s Akbar had favoured the Chishti order. This is not to suggest that the Chishti saints' concerns were purely spiritual, with no taste whatsoever for power and politics. Their past too had seen cases of their conflict with rulers.[77] A significant feature of their politics had, however, been their support to rulers in their endeavour to adjust the nature of Muslim power to the Indian environment.[78] Again, no Chishti shaikh ever amassed wealth comparable to that of Khwaja Ahrar, with a mission to reform a political regime, reward those who would listen to his exhortations and become submissive, and punish the ones who dared act independently. On the contrary, the Chishtis had generally pleaded for a kind of asceticism, and preferred to advise and bless the political authorities from a distance. Indeed, their *tasawwuf* has been based on a doctrine, that is *wahdat al-wujud*, which had hitherto facilitated the process of religious synthesis and cultural amalgam. In some Chishti treatises of Akbar's time, the doctrine was expressed and elaborated in a much more forceful tone, even with a plea for the illegitimacy of

---

[76] Subrahmanyam, 'A Note on the Kabul Kingdom'; Faruqui, 'The Forgotten Prince'.

[77] Digby, 'The Sufi Shaykh and the Sultan: A Conflict of Claims to Authority', *Iran* 27 (1990), pp. 71–81; Sunil Kumar, 'Assertions of Authority: A Study of the Discursive Statements of Two Sultans of Delhi' in *The Making of Indo-Persian Culture: Indian and French Studies*, eds M. Alam, F. N. Delvoye and M. Gaborieau (Delhi: Manohar, 2000), pp. 37–65.

[78] For a discussion around this question, see Muzaffar Alam, *The Languages of Political Islam: India 1200–1800* (New Delhi: Permanent Black, 2004), pp. 81–114.

considering Islam as superior to any other religion. 'The whole world is a manifestation of love ('*ishq*)', to quote from one such treatise,

> and we see everything as perfect (...). As you begin *iradat* (become a *murid* and join the order) you stop quarrelling over *kufr* and *iman*. There is no precedence of one religion over the other (...). After you experience the limitlessness of unbounded Beauty you can see His Grace present both in a *kafir* and a Muslim.[79]

Nothing could have provided a stronger support to 'Akbar's dream'.

Akbar's visits to the shrine of Khwaja Mu'in al-Din, the founder of the Chishti *silsila* in India best illustrates his fascination with the order. Here it is also interesting to note the circumstances in which the emperor, according to Abu al-Fazl, was drawn towards the Khwaja. One night, while on a hunting expedition, Abu al-Fazl writes, he heard people singing Hindi verses in praise of the Khwaja, in a village near Agra. The emperor was impressed by the saint's popularity, would often discuss his 'perfections and miracles', and developed a 'strong inclination' to visit the shrine.[80] As we know, the emperor undertook several journeys to Ajmer, one of which was also on foot, all the way from Fathpur to the holy city of the saint. He also constructed several buildings around the shrine, arranged for its management and provided grants for the care and comfort of the visitors. Furthermore, in 1564 in Delhi, he visited the tomb of Nizam al-Din Auliya, while in 1569 he began the construction of palaces in Fathpur Sikri. This was selected as the site of his new capital, a token of respect for a living Chishti saint, Shaikh Salim Chishti, through whose prayers he believed he was blessed with a son who was named after the Shaikh.[81]

By the 1570s, Akbar thus appeared as an exclusive devotee of the Chishti saints, both dead and alive. In 1581, on his way to the Punjab he visited the *khanqah* of another major Chishti saint of the period, Shaikh

---

[79] Compare Mir 'Abd al-Wahid Bilgrami, *Sab' Sanabil*, Urdu trans. Muhammad Khalil Barakati (Bheondi, Maharashtra: Rizwi Kitabghar, 1981), pp. 330–31. Bilgrami wrote the treatise in Persian, of which the original is still unpublished, in 969 AH/1562. Later in 974/1567 he compiled the better known, *Haqa'iq-i Hindi*, in which he gave Islamic meanings to the words and expressions explicitly 'Hindu'.

[80] *Akbarnama*, Vol. II, p. 154, English trans., p. 237; P. M. Currie, *The Shrine and Cult of Mu'in al-Din of Ajmer* (Delhi: Oxford University Press, 1989). p. 100; K. A. Nizami, *Akbar and Religion* (Delhi: Idarah-i-Adabiyat-i-Dilli, 1989), p. 104.

[81] Richards, 'Formulation of Imperial Authority'; Currie, *The Shrine and Cult of Mu'in al-Din*, pp. 99–102 and 152–54; Nizami, *Akbar and Religion*, pp. 104–05, 111 and 117.

Jalal al-Din, in Thanesar. This visit is of special importance for us, since the grand old shaikh was a noted *khalifa* of Shaikh 'Abd al-Quddus Gangohi. Akbar was accompanied by the brothers Abu al-Fazl and Faizi. They had a long conversation with the shaikh, discussed with him the secrets of Divine Realities and mystical sensibilities (*haqa'iq wa ma'arif*). The emperor, as the recorded memory in later Chishti *tazkiras* remember, was so impressed with the shaikh's response that he even expressed a desire to give up kingship. The shaikh, however, dissuaded him from doing so. He is reported to have said:

> First you find a person who can match you and sit [on the throne] in your place, and then come for this work (...). Your justice for an hour is better than the prayers of a thousand of saints. Piety and sainthood for you lies in your being just to God's people (*khalq-i Khuda*) and in conferring benefits upon them. Remember God. Kingship does not prevent you from remembering Him.[82]

Did Akbar recognize the Chishtis then as royal *pir*s? There is nothing in our sources to suggest an answer to this in the positive. What did Akbar expect a Sufi to be? Which Sufis did he like to be close to? We are provided an answer to these questions in the following remark by Abu al-Fazl on Mirza Sharaf al-Din's revolt (which we have noticed above). This remark also supports and in a measure reiterates the reasons that were given above for the decline of the fortunes of Naqshbandis. He writes:

> It is an old custom for the divinely great and for acute rulers to attach to themselves the hearts of dervishes and the sons of dervishes. And they have exhibited this tendency, which is both an intoxicant which destroys men, and sometimes as a means of testing their real nature. If the matter be looked into with the eye of justice, it will be evident to the prudent and awakened-hearts, that the favour shown by the Shahinshah to this father and son exhibited both motives. Accordingly the concomitants of His Majesty's fortune withdrew in a short time the veil from the face of Mirza Sharaf al-Din Husain's actions, and his real worthlessness and insubstantiality became manifest to mankind. When God, the world-protector, wills to cleanse the site of the eternal dominion from the evil and black-hearted, and to deck it with the sincere and loyal, a state of things spontaneously arises which could not be produced by a thousand planning. The hypocrites depart from the threshold of fortune by the

---

[82] *Sawati' al-Anwar*, fols. 389b- 390b; *Mir'at al-Asrar*, Or. 216.

efforts of their own feet and fall into destruction. Such was the evil-ending case of Mirza Sharaf al-Din Husain, who by influence of the man-throwing wine of the world did not remain firm of foot, but left his place, and into whose head there entered thoughts of madness and melancholy.[83]

It is time now for us to return to the question that was posed at the end of the first section of this essay. We know that Abu al-Fazl wrote his history, in which he included a brief, three-line, description of 'Abd al-Quddus Gangohi, in the 1590s, a time when the Akbari dispensation had in a sense been fully formed. While he does not neglect regards for the truth, the basic duty of a historian, his portrayal of the developments of the earlier years in several cases is influenced by the particular ideology and concerns of this late phase of Akbar's rule. We also know that he was not a mere chronicler. He had his own philosophy of life and social order, and propounded, promoted and defended the ideology of this dispensation. He wrote history with a mission. Now, in order to appreciate the significance of this particular case we may also note the following points. Firstly, the description of the shaikh as noted above is very brief indeed. Secondly, one line of this brief notice, which comprises the information about Humayun's visit and his meeting with the shaikh, begins with the word *guyand*, that is they say or it is said,[84] which in a measure implies it is based on a kind of hearsay or on something remembered and constructed by the associates of the shaikh himself. This also means that while Abu al-Fazl wants his audience and posterity to take note of what is recounted, he is not particularly concerned with its truth. Again, we know that Gangohi was the royal *pir* of the enemies of the Mughals, supported them and on that count suffered humiliation at the hands of the Mughals. The memory of these details, already recorded, and incorporated in the *tazkira* of the shaikh written by his son, repeatedly read in the circle of the shaikh's associates and followers, threatened to affect adversely the good relations that Akbar had developed with the Chishtis and

---

[83] *Akbarnama*, Vol. II, p. 195, English trans. p. 303.

[84] '*Guyand Jannat Ashyani ba barkhi az kar agahan bezaviya-i u dar shudi va anjuman-i agahi garmi pizirafti*'. Abu al-Fazl generally seems to be very meticulous in his choice of words to indicate the evidence and degree of authenticity of what he describes. While describing a person's descent and family line, for instance, if he is certain about it he prefers the simple, '*ast*' or '*and*', that is to say: is or are. In cases for which he wants to remain non-committal, he would use expression like '*khud ra az (...) nazhad bar shamurd*', i.e. 'he counted himself Saiyid-born' Cf *A'in-i Akbari*, pp. 211 and 214, for example.

which Abu al-Fazl applauded. There was however also the memory of the shaikh's efforts to restore his own relations with the Mughals, as we can guess from the letters he wrote to Babur, Humayun and Tardi Beg. The shaikh also seems to have visited Agra in 1537 for a brief stay just before his death.[85] And, it is not unlikely that the efforts in this direction continued in the changed political atmosphere to create conditions of friendship with the new rulers, and that in the process there also emerged stories of the emperor's meeting with the shaikh. Since the Mughal court's contact with the Chishtis was in practice an endorsement of Abu al-Fazl's own ideology, he promotes the memory of this anecdote bearing on an intimate contact between the two. He does not even allude to anything from the shaikh's life pertaining to the time of the Afghan rule, for he wants his readers to forget everything that invoked the memory of the Mughals' distance from him. His aim is to emphasize the necessity and significance of the Mughal court's good relations with the Chishtis. If at all a king needed—which in Abu al-Fazl's view, he did indeed—to 'attach to himself the hearts of dervishes', such dervishes in India should be the Chishtis, and certainly not the Mawarannahri Naqshbandis.

Interestingly, Abu al-Fazl is the sole authority cited for this anecdote in the later Chishti *tazkiras*, as if his was a piece of contemporary evidence, by an eyewitness to the event. Obviously, in these *tazkiras* were added words and phrases, implying that Humayun had regular meetings with the shaikh, the same way as the earlier Afghan rulers had had.[86] A seventeenth-century non-Chishti account, however, mentions the anecdote without referring to Abu al-Fazl.[87] It is relevant here also to note that in the oft-cited Mughal–Sufi *tazkira*, written by Shaikh 'Abd al-Haqq Dehlavi (d. 1642) about the same time as Abu al-Fazl wrote his history, this anecdote finds no place, even though Dehlavi's account of Gangohi is pretty detailed, comprising over 1,400 words.[88] This may be because Dehlavi did not share Abu al-Fazl's concern, and also his primary connection was with the Qadiri *silsila*.

---

[85] Compare Digby, 'Shaikh Abd al-Quddus Gangohi'.

[86] *Mir'at al-Asrar*, fol. 427; *Sawati' al-Anwar*, fol. 381a.

[87] Muhammad Sadiq Isfahani, *Tabaqat-i Shahjahani*, British Library, India Office Ms., Ethé 705, fol. 195b.

[88] Shaykh 'Abd al-Haqq Dehlavi, *Akhbar al-Akhyar* (Deoband: Kutubkhana Rahimiya, n.d.), pp. 227–30.

Akbar for his part retained his faith in Khwaja Mu'in al-Din, and thereby remained in contact with the Chishtis, even after what Bada'uni and some Naqshbandis projected as the emperor's rejection of Islam.[89] In return the emperor too received noticeable appreciation from Chishti circles. If Abu al-Fazl is to be believed, on the occasion of one of his visits to Ajmer, the people connected with the shrine told the emperor that they saw the Khwaja in a dream saying: 'If he (Akbar) knew the amount of his own spirituality, he would not bestow a glance on me, the sitter-in-the dust of the path of studentship'.[90] At the time of his visit to Shaikh Jalal al-Din in Thanesar, the old shaikh, who because of his advanced age would generally keep lying in bed, in a half conscious state, asked his attendants to give him support to stand up and welcome the emperor, 'the Caliph of the age'. In the seventeenth-century Chishti *tazkiras*, Akbar is remembered and mentioned as a just and pious king, devoted to Khwaja Mu'in al-Din, and also on occasion with the Arabic phrases such as *rahima-hu Allah* (may God bless him) and *anar Allahu burhana-hu* (may God illumine his proof),[91] which are generally used for saints.

THE RETURN OF THE NAQSHBANDI SHAIKHS

We have seen that the Naqshbandis came to India along with the Mughals. But far from being the royal *pir*s as they had been in Central Asia, they could not manage to maintain good relations with the Mughal rulers. In the society outside the charmed circle of the ruling class too, they made little mark as notable Sufi shaikhs. In the Indian conditions, they noticed that the other shaikhs, the Chishtis most prominently, had greater appeal and that the Naqshbandis' heritage of explicitly combining power (or *wilayat*) with rulership had, in a measure, stood in the way of their achieving the high position they wanted and aspired to. They thus had to reckon with the existing popular Sufi orders, assert and establish the supremacy of their own order and emphasize how it

---

[89] *Mutakhab al-Tawarikh*, Vol. II, pp. 272–3.

[90] *Akbarnama*, Vol. II, p. 324, English trans., p. 477. This incident, characterized by Nizami as sycophancy (*Akbar and Religion*, p. 104), could also be taken as an illustration of how Akbar gradually grew antithetical to Sufism. For a discussion around this dimension of Akbar's politics, see Bruce Lawrence, 'Veiled Opposition to Sufis in Muslim Asia', in *Islamic Mysticism Contested: Thirteen Centuries of Controversies and Polemics*, eds Frederick de Jong and Bernd Radke (Leiden: Brill, 1999), pp. 436–51.

[91] *Mir'at al-Asrar*, fol. 236a; *Sawati' al-Anwar*, fol. 389b.

was the best, and that how even in matters relating to the principle and practice of poverty and asceticism (*faqr, tark-i dunya*) they were really far ahead of the Chishtis. They always remained within the limits of the traditions of the Prophet, and stated that their primary task was to achieve 'the purpose of the Muslims', even as they engaged with worldly politics and trafficked with kings.

Two further major Naqshbandi saints, Khwaja Khawand Mahmud 'Alavi Husaini (d. 1652) and Khwaja Baqi-Billah (d. 1603), came to India and established their *khanqahs* during Akbar's reign. Khawand Mahmud was perhaps the first to be directed by his *pir*, Shaikh Muhammad Ishaq Dehbidi (d. 1599) to come to India to propagate the Naqshbandi mission. Thereupon he joined a caravan and set out for Lahore. When he arrived in the town of Gujarat in the Punjab where the road bifurcated, one path leading to Kashmir, the other to Lahore, he fell into a mystic trance and his horse took the route of Kashmir. After he regained consciousness, he decided to continue his journey in the direction of Kashmir, thinking that this was what God and his master would have wanted. He settled in Kashmir, and though initially he had some difficulty, succeeded in establishing the order on a firm footing in the Valley. His son and successor, Khwaja Mu'in al-Din (d. 1674) also was a prominent saint in the Valley. Khawand Mahmud's influence, despite his efforts to come close to some nobles in Delhi and Agra, did not really extend beyond the Valley.[92]

It was hence Khwaja Muhammad Baqi-Billah—a member of the family of Khwaja Ahrar from his mother's side—who took up the challenge of reinstating the Naqshbandi order in the heartland of Mughal Hindustan. He came to settle in Delhi from Kabul in 1599, inspired and perfected in the order by Khwaja Muhammad Muqtada Amkinagi (d. 1600). He had earlier been to India, lived and wandered in Sambhal, Lahore and Kashmir. He lived very briefly in Delhi, for slightly over 4 years, but before his premature death in 1603 he had virtually reinstated the Naqshbandi order.[93] He left behind four major *khalifas*, Shaikh Ilahdad (d. 1640), Shaikh Husam al-Din (d. 1633), Shaikh Taj al-Din Sambhali

---

[92] S. A. A. Rizvi, *A History of Sufism*, Vol. II, pp. 181–85. For a comprehensive discussion of Khawand Mahmud's career, see Damrel, 'Forgotten Grace: Khwaja Khawand Mahmud Naqshbandi in Central Asia and Mughal India'. See also Shamsuddin Ahmad, *Hazrat Khwaja Naqshband aur Tariqat-i Naqshbandiya* (in Urdu) (Srinagar: Gulshan Publishers, 2001), pp. 358–407.

[93] Rizvi, *A History of Sufism*, Vol. II, pp. 185–93; Rizvi, 'Sixteenth Century Naqshbandiyya Leadership in India', in *Naqshbandis*, eds Gaborieau, Popovic and Zarcone, pp. 153–65.

(d. 1642) and Shaikh Ahmad Sirhindi (d. 1624). Of these, the last two occupied prominent positions in strengthening and propagating the teachings of the order in India and abroad in the Islamic lands in the seventeenth century. Sirhindi, we know, also founded a new branch, the Mujaddidi, of the order.[94]

There is plenty of information about the nature of Baqi-Billah's *tasawwuf* and *karamat* in the contemporary and near-contemporary writings of his disciples and *khalifas*, and also in the *tazkiras* compiled during the seventeenth and early eighteenth centuries. For the following discussion, however, I have drawn, in the main, on his own writings, that is, *malfuzat* (table-talk) and *maktubat* (letters) and poetry, edited and published together with his poems in one volume, by two leading twentieth-century Naqshbandi–Mujaddidi scholars.[95] I will select a few issues here, which in his view were the distinctive features of the order and are in a measure also illustrative of a rather combative overtone. He compares the features of his order with those of the other orders, the Chishti in particular, pointing succinctly to the flaws of the latter. He emphasizes and stresses on the dimensions of mystical sensitivity (*wajd, zauq*), without losing contact with mundane power. Regarding the *pir*, for instance, he observes that according to the Naqshbandi order there could be more than one *pir*. For the *pir* as the Chishti and the Suhrawardi shaikhs understood it was not simply the one from whom the seeker received *khirqa* (robe). There were other two categories of *pir* as well, which he characterized as the *pir-i ta'lim* who gives training in litanics, and the *pir-i suhbat* whose company resulted in general benefit and in enabling the seeker to appreciate the diverse avenues of spiritual progress.[96] Baqi-Billah thus was keen to initiate into his *silsila*, even those who already had their *pirs*, of the Chishti, Suhrawardi or any other lineage, in India. This amounted to making a bid to extend the domain of his own order, even if it meant violation of generally accepted Sufi practice. In this connection it is interesting to note the following passage, which explains why he did as above:

> Someone reported in the presence of Hazrat-i Ishan (Baqi-Billah) that a certain person [the author hints at Nizam al-Din Thanesari, a leading Chishti shaikh, but does not mention his name] says that Hazrat-i Ishan

---

[94] Rizvi, *A History of Sufism*, Vol. II, pp. 195–263 and 336–38.

[95] Khwaja Muhammad Baqi-Billah, *Kulliyat-i Baqi-Billah*, ed. Abul Hasan Zaid Faruqi and Burhan Ahmad Faruqi (Lahore: Din Muhammad and Sons, n.d).

[96] *Kulliyat-i Baqi-Billah*, Section *Malfuzat*, pp. 31–32.

emancipates seekers from having faith in former *pirs* and insists that they receive teaching only from him. He (Baqi-Billah) said this was not the case. 'But if I find some of the seekers in two minds, I advise them to concentrate on one path (...)'. Then he said that the faith that he had in the shaikhs of the other *silsilas* is hardly found among them. In particular, the people of India's beliefs about their *pirs* verge on idolatory.[97]

But while for him, and for that matter for any other *shaikh* of his order, it was legitimate to allure the followers of other *silsilas*, he did not allow the *murid* of a Naqshbandi to seek guidance from any other *pir* in India. Elaborating on the relationship between the seeker and the preceptor, he wrote to his *khalifa*, Shaikh Taj al-Din:

> And similarly in the moral conduct (*adab*) of the Naqshbandi Ahrari path you should be firm like a mountain, never mixing it with the path of the other (...). Whoever is your *murid* is *your* murid *only*. Train and teach him according to Naqshbandi path only (...). Of what interest is the person who receives the light from you and then attends upon a Shattari [shaikh]?[98]

With reference to the discourse on *tauhid* and *wujud*, we are aware that the Chishtis in India followed Ibn al-'Arabi (d. 1240) and maintained that the position of 'Ala al-Daula Simnani (d. 1336), who contested Ibn al-'Arabi's stand and propounded a contrary view, was not correct. Baqi-Billah for his part took a different stand. He proposed that both Ibn al-'Arabi and Simnani were right. Still, while he tried to reconcile the two views and suggested that the difference between them was only in words rather than in deeper substance, he argued that Simnani was closer to the truth:

> His (Simnani's) *shuhud* (perception) is the most perfect *shuhud*. The difference is that a group of the '*ulama* [read: Indian Sufis] believe that things do not exist objectively and that their external appearance is only like the appearance of the reflections in a mirror. In sum, they recognize only one existence. The shaikh [Simnani] with his power of perception (*shuhud*) and its pre-eminence recognized the objective existence of things too.[99]

Further, Baqi-Billah firmly rejected the Chishtis' understanding of *tauhid*. He openly challenged Shaikh Nizam al-Din Thanesari— nephew

---

[97] *Kulliyat-i Baqi-Billah*, Section *Malfuzat*, p. 35.

[98] *Kulliyat-i Baqi-Billah*, Section *Ruq'at*, p. 77.

[99] *Kulliyat-i Baqi-Billah*, Section *Ruq'at*, p. 123.

and son-in-law of Jalal al-Din Thanesari, who after the latter's death was virtually the sole spokesman of the Sabiri branch of the Chishti order—to debate him about the matter and prove his position if he was right, in an assembly of *'ulama* and Sufis. In the circle of his associates, the belief was that Thanesari, even if he was considered to be the most perfect Indian dervish, did not possess adequate knowledge and mystical sensitivity to appreciate Simnani's observations on Reality, and that his understanding was based on wrong and misleading translations and interpretations. Baqi-Billah was aware of the intensity of such offensive opinion (*gustakhi*). But he asserted that he was constrained to express himself thus with the sole objective of disseminating and protecting the position of the true sect and bringing forth the correct meanings of the utterances of the great shaikhs. He wanted, or so he claimed, to save the people from being misled and thus sinking into the whirlpool of mistaken belief. He wrote further that often the illumination experienced by a Sufi in an early stage of his mystical journey was taken as the real epiphany (*tajalli*). This was an error and was just a reflection of, and not the real light of, *tajalli*.[100] This assumes special import considering that the Mawarannahri Naqshbandis, including the great Ahrar and Shaikh 'Abd al-Rahman Jami, were mostly *wujudis*.[101]

Baqi-Billah's competitive attitude towards his contemporary Chishti shaikhs is further illustrated from his observations on *sama'* or Sufi music. *Sama'* had come to be an integral part of Chishti Sufi life, and was regarded as a means to experience and achieve the spiritually sublime; in this, the order drew support from the life and teachings of the early great saints, whose Sufi accomplishments the Naqshbandis also recognized. Baqi-Billah however contested their reading and interpretation of their predecessors. He took up the case of Shaikh Nizam al-Din Auliya, since his practice was the most oft-cited evidence

---

[100] *Kulliyat-i Baqi-Billah*, Section Ruq'at, p. 118.

[101] Algar, 'A Brief History', and J. G. J. ter Haar, 'The Naqshbandi Tradition in the Eyes of Ahmad Sirhindi', in *Naqshbandis*, eds Gaborieau, Popovic and Zarcone pp. 21 and 89–90 for references to the *wahdat al-wujudi* leanings of Khwaja Baha al-Din Naqshband's disciple, Khwaja Muhammad Parsa, 'Ubaid-Allah Ahrar and his disciple, 'Abd al-Rahman Jami (d. 1492). The majority of Jami's writings involve either commentaries on Ibn al-'Arabi or elaborations in prose or poetry of his ideas of *wujud*. See for instance, Jami's *Naqd al-Nusus fi Sharh Naqsh al-Fusus*, ed. William C. Chittick (Tehran: Mu'asses Pazhohish-i Hikmat wa Falsafa-i Iran, 1991), Editor's Introduction. See also, James Winston Morris, 'Ibn 'Arabi and His Intrepreters, Part II: Influences and Intrepretations', *Journal of the American Oriental Society*, 107 (1987), pp. 101–19; Claude Addas, *The Quest for the Red Sulphur, The Life of Ibn 'Arabi* (Cambridge: The Islamic Text Society, 1993), p. 291.

in support of musical practices, and remarked that in his *malfuzat* where Nizam al-Din discussed the legality of *sama'*, he appended the condition that the listener should be a true lover of God. This evidently meant, Baqi-Billah added, that he disapproved of its practice. True love of God, Baqi-Billah added, required total and unqualified submission to the path (*sunna*) of the Prophet. A true follower of his path would never indulge in an act for which there was no precedent in the life of the Prophet. The Prophet never listened to music nor did he ever permit its performance.[102] The Indian Sufis failed in getting at the correct meaning of the discourses in the texts composed in India too, as they misunderstood and misinterpreted Ibn al-'Arabi and Simnani. Islam in India was to be as Baqi-Billah saw it, whatever its practice in the past.

In all this obviously lay the critique of basis of the prevailing understanding of *tasawwuf*. 'Our *tariqa*', Baqi-Billah noted, 'is based on three things: an unswerving faith (*rusukh*) in the truth of the beliefs of the Sunni community (*ahl-i sunnat wa jama'at*), knowledge, gnosis (*agahi*) and prayer ('*ibadat*). Laxity in any one of these throws one out of our *tariqa*'.[103] The principal duty of a seeker, according to him, was to follow the *shari'a*. 'Correct beliefs', he reiterated, 'regard for *shari'a* and sincere attention to God are the greatest wealth. No mysticism (*zauq, wijdan*) is comparable with this'.[104] Indeed, the ultimate aim for him was to achieve what the earlier shaikhs of his lineage characterized as *musalmani*. When a seeker asked him about its implications, he said: '*Musalmani* is the *murad* [the desired goal, but it] is difficult'. It is achieved only with divine grace, and is beyond the circle of human effort. To become a *musalman* is the very reality (*haqiqa*) of mysticism (*ma'rifa*).[105] In one of his letters, he elaborates on the question saying that beauty (*jamal*) and perfection (*kamal*) in a seeker follows from his submission (*bandagi*), which meant prayer, fasting, alms-giving, *hajj*, war with the infidels, regard for the rights of the parents and others, and justice.[106]

Furthermore, Baqi-Billah pleaded for the need to insist on maintaining the distinction between infidelity (*kufr*) and faith (*iman*). He dismissed

---

[102] *Kulliyat-i Baqi-Billah*, Section *Malfuzat*, pp. 42–3.
[103] *Kulliyat-i Baqi-Billah*, Section *Malfuzat*, p. 25.
[104] *Kulliyat-i Baqi-Billah*, Section *Malfuzat*, p. 36.
[105] *Kulliyat-i Baqi-Billah*, Section *Malfuzat*, p. 29 and Section *Ruq'at*, p. 137.
[106] *Kulliyat-i Baqi-Billah*, Section *Ruq'at*, p. 139.

as heretic (*zandaqa*) and extremely stupid (*ablahi*, *safahat*) the idea that encouraged words implying abandoning of the *shari'a*, admiration of unbelief and emphasis on the basic unity between a believer and an infidel.[107] A measure of the intensity in his attitude on the matter was reflected in his resistance to the idea of treatment by a Hindu physician during his illness. He relented as he was told that this was only arranged at his mother's wish. Still, he did not like the presence of the physician and turned his face away from him when he visited.[108]

It is however significant that together with these statements— addressed to the Indian shaikhs, in the main, in a rather uncompromising and aggressive tone—he also disapproved a Sufi's direct involvement in power and money making. He thus discouraged a feature of Ahrari *wilayat*, which had hitherto legitimated the drive of a Naqshbandi shaikh to aspire for a position alongside the ruler, at least, if not above him. As we have already noticed, this was one of the factors that alienated the Mughal emperor Akbar. To Baqi-Billah, *musalmani* or the highest stage in *tasawwuf* was to be accomplished with poverty (*faqr*) and negation of self (*nisti*),[109] and not with power and wealth. He showed no direct concern for power politics; but he was in close contact with people at the helm of affairs, and spared no chance in recommending the cases of his associates and disciples.

Among others, he recommended the case of Shaikh Ahmad Sirhindi for an adequate cash grant.[110] Of the eighty six of his letters available to us, no less than thirteen were addressed to people engaged in state service and trade. His addressees included Shaikh Farid Bukhari, who according to a report bore all the expenses of his *khanqah*,[111] Mirza 'Aziz Koka and the *sadr al-sudur*, Miran Sadr-i Jahan Pihani. Some of these recipients have been mentioned by the compiler as his sincere devotees (*az 'umara-i mukhlis*), but it is not clear if they really became his *murids*.

Baqi-Billah used all his strength and accomplishments to reinstall the Naqshbandi *silsila* as a great, if not the greatest, mystic order in Mughal India. He joined issue with the contemporary saints of the other orders,

---

[107] *Kulliyat-i Baqi-Billah*, Section Ruq'at, pp. 122–23.

[108] *Kulliyat-i Baqi-Billah*, Section Malfuzat, pp. 49–50.

[109] *Kulliyat-i Baqi-Billah*, Section Malfuzat, pp. 130–31.

[110] *Kulliyat-i Baqi-Billah*, Section Malfuzat pp. 91, 93, 98, 105, 107, 118, 120, 130, 133, 134 and 135.

[111] *Kulliyat-i Baqi-Billah*, Section Malfuzat, p. 36.

and tried to demonstrate the supremacy of his order. He disapproved of several features of prevailing Sufi culture that lent strength to some important features of the Akbari dispensation. He also hinted that it was purification of things Indian and their redefinition that the mission of his coming to Hindustan was. Nowhere, however, did he actually comment upon their legality or illegality, let alone pronouncing a verdict on the very faith of the emperor. On this question, his approach seems to be different from the one we generally associate with his noted disciple, Shaikh Ahmad Sirhindi. Can we assume that this was because he died prematurely, leaving his mission incomplete while still mobilizing his strength? We are discouraged from following this line of speculation by the fact that Sirhindi, howsoever powerful he may have been, was not the sole spokesman of the Naqshbandi order after his death. But this is a major question which still demands careful examination, and which should be dealt with elsewhere.

CONCLUSION

This essay has traced the relationship between the Mughal dynasty in India and various groups of Sufi shaikhs over the course of the sixteenth century. Rather than focusing exclusively, or even largely, on the Naqshbandi–Mujaddidi tradition of the early seventeenth century, we have attempted to look to the competition between various orders of Sufis for influence over the Mughals. In this, the central role is played by the competitive axis between the Chishtis and the Naqshbandis, the former having exercised considerable influence over the Afghans while the latter were, in a manner of speaking, the 'ancestral' saints of the Central Asian Timurids. We have seen how the mainstream of the Ahrari Naqshbandi tradition from Transoxiana failed eventually for a number of reasons to consolidate its hold in India during the reign of Humayun, leading to the brief ascendancy of the Shattari order. Eventually, after a phase of Chishti reassertion that characterizes the early years of Akbar's rule (and his relations with both Ajmer, and the more proximate figure of Shaikh Salim Chishti), the Naqshbandis were able to rally themselves. This is in no small measure because of the key role played by Khwaja Baqi-Billah, the master of the celebrated Shaikh Ahmad Sirhindi, in reinventing both an aspect of their theology and their concrete functioning as an order.

A fuller consideration of Mughal–Sufi relations would naturally take us to a proper examination of events and processes of the seventeenth century, which lack of space has prevented me from doing here. That consideration would also require a further, careful investigation of the role played by members of the Chishti order in the seventeenth century, including the key personage of 'Abd al-Rahman Chishti (mentioned only in passing in this essay). It is only by examining the full range of materials produced both by different orders about themselves, and about each other, while keeping the political compulsions that shaped the choices of the Mughal emperors and their elites, that we may grasp the intricacies and complexities of this field. This essay has thus been a modest first step in the direction of a far larger enterprise.

7

Notes on Political Thought in Medieval and Early Modern South India

VELCHERU NARAYANA RAO

AND

SANJAY SUBRAHMANYAM*

———— • ✦ • ————

In these days, when we don't have any kingdoms worth the name, texts on statecraft are of no use for ruling the state, and they are useful only for historians of *shāstra* texts.

—*Veturi Prabhakara Sastri*

This country has seen the conflict between ecclesiastical law and secular law long before Europeans sought to challenge the authority of the Pope. Kautilya's *Arthashāstra* lays down the foundation of secular law. In India unfortunately ecclesiastical law triumphed over secular law. In my opinion this was the one of the greatest disasters in the country.

—*B. R. Ambedkar*

* This essay is a shorter version of a more extended analysis of *nīti* and *dharma* texts in medieval and early modern South India, which may eventually take a monographic form. Early versions of this essay have been presented at St. Antony's College (Oxford), the Haus der Kulturen der Welt (Berlin), the Centre for the Study of Social Sciences (Kolkata), the University of British Columbia, the EHESS (Paris), the Humanities Institute (Wisconsin-Madison) and the Center for India and South Asia (UCLA). For critical comments and suggestions, we are particularly grateful to Partha Chatterjee, Don Davis, Carlo Ginzburg, Claude Guillot, Roland Lardinois, Patrick Olivelle, Anthony Pagden and S. R. Sarma.

INTRODUCTION

Past works on the nature and content of state-building in medieval South India have focused largely on the inscriptional corpus, and a limited set of narrative accounts, in order to support classic formulations of such ideas as the 'segmentary state' and 'ritual kingship'.[1] In this essay, we return to some of the questions raised by our colleagues and predecessors in the field, but with a view to looking at ideological and ideational issues far more than concrete institutional arrangements. We should note at the outset that the specter of a perpetually receding horizon of universal concepts—those that can be used with equal confidence, say, for the analysis of pre-1800 societies in Europe, Asia and Africa—has taken something of a toll in recent decades. Is it at all legitimate to assume that 'money' existed in all or even most of these continents?[2] What of the 'economy' itself, or even 'society'? Is the notion of 'art' applicable everywhere? Can 'religion' be found in most societies?[3] It is well known by now that many postcolonial theorists wish to claim that 'history' was certainly not present in any more than a tiny fraction of the societies they study, until European colonial rule apparently created the conditions for its worldwide spread as a hegemonic discourse. In other words, it is claimed often enough now that no fit whatsoever existed between these and other '-etic' categories of the humanities and social sciences (with their uniquely Western origins and genealogy) and the highly varied '-emic' notions that may be found in different locales and times in the world of the past, a claim that has become a source of anxiety for some, a source of indifference for others, and a ground for rejoicing

---

[1] Burton Stein, 'All the King's *Mana*: Perspectives on Kingship in Medieval South India, in *Kingship and Authority in South Asia*, ed. J. F. Richards (Delhi: Oxford University Press, 1998), pp. 133–88 (with a brief mention of some Jaina *nīti* texts on pp. 144–45). For a succinct critique of Stein's formulations on the period under consideration here, see Sanjay Subrahmanyam, 'Agreeing to Disagree: Burton Stein on Vijayanagara', *South Asia Research* 17 (1997), pp. 127–39.

[2] For anthropological perspectives, see Jonathan Parry and Maurice Bloch eds, *Money and the Morality of Exchange* (Cambridge: Cambridge University Press, 1989); C. A. Gregory, *Savage Money: The Anthropology and Politics of Commodity Exchange* (Amsterdam: Harwood Academic, 1997); Stéphane Breton, 'Social Body and Icon of the Person: A Symbolic Analysis of Shell Money among the Wodani, Western Highlands of Irian Jaya', *American Ethnologist* 26 (1999), pp. 558–82.

[3] On the problem of religion, see Talal Asad, 'The Construction of Religion as an Anthropological Category' in Asad, *Genealogies of Religion: Discipline and Reasons of Power in Christianity and Islam*, (Baltimore: John Hopkins University Press, 1993), pp. 27–54; drawing on the earlier work by Wilfred Cantwell Smith, *The Meaning and End of Religion: A New Approach to the Religious Traditions of Mankind* (New York: Macmillan, 1962).

for still others who see a positive virtue in 'incommensurability', which they perhaps view as akin to a (necessarily virtuous) claim for species diversity.[4] Related to this is the recurrence of older formulae on the notoriously difficult subject of translation, both from those historians and from those social scientists who claim—on one extreme—that everything is translatable, and those who are eager to sustain equally extreme claims of 'malostension' or 'radical mistranslation' as a perpetual condition, rather than a contingent (and even potentially reversible) consequence of specific procedures and circumstances.[5]

It is of interest that even in this welter of relativistic claims, one category that few have sought to challenge in its universal applicability is that of 'politics'. Why has this been so, we may ask? Perhaps the reasons lie not only in an embarrassment with the charged, and patronizing, largely Marxist category of the 'pre-political', but also in the fact that to deny the existence of 'politics' would be tantamount to denying the existence somewhere in collective human existence of 'power', a move that few if any in the academy today would wish to risk.[6] To be sure, we could follow Benedict Anderson in relativising power, and argue that the 'idea of power' in, say, Java was not the same as that in the West; but this would be quite different to denying its very existence or utility as a concept for analysis.[7] In the case of India, almost any universal concept that one can mention has recently been challenged in its applicability to the present or past situation of that area, with the notable exception of 'politics'. Indeed, it is instructive in this regard to turn to an essay produced by a leading relativist amongst Indian social theorists, Ashis Nandy, who would argue that 'politics' is practically the only category that one can use as a constant to speak of the past 2,000 years in India.[8] Yet, this argument, first defended by

[4] Thomas N. Headland, Kenneth L. Pike, Marvin Harris eds, *Emics and Etics: The Insider/Outsider Debate* (Newbury Park: Sage Publication, 1990).

[5] See the useful discussion in Ian Hacking, *Historical Ontology* (Cambridge, MA: Harward University Press, 2002), pp. 152–58.

[6] The category of the 'pre-political' appears most famously in Eric Hobsbawm, *Primitive Rebels: Studies in Archaic Forms of Social Movement in the 19th and 20th Centuries* (Manchester: Manchester University Press, 1959).

[7] Benedict R.O'G. Anderson, 'The Idea of Power in Javanese Culture', in *Culture and Politcs in Indonesia*, eds Claire Holt, Benedict R. Anderson and James T. Siegel (Ithaca, NY: Cornell University Press, 1972), pp. 1–69; also the earlier essay by Anderson, 'The Languages of Indonesian Politics', *Indonesia* 1 (1966), pp. 89–116.

[8] Ashis Nandy, 'The Culture of Indian Politics: A Stock Taking', *The Journal of Asian Studies* 30 (1970), pp. 57–79. Also see Nandy, 'The Political Culture of the Indian State', *Dædalus*, 118 (1989), pp. 1–26.

him over three decades ago, came paired with an important caveat. For Nandy wished to argue that politics in twentieth-century India was in fact a split field. If on the one hand there were those who practiced politics in the 'Western' mode, drawing upon concepts and notions that were all-too-familiar to Western political scientists and theorists, others continued to understand and practice politics through a deeply 'emic' set of lenses, which is to say while using concepts that had no familiar equivalents in the Western political vocabulary. To understand these concepts, and the working of this other field, Nandy went on to argue, it was necessary to return to a series of texts produced in the Sanskrit language in ancient India, which alone could explicate this deep-rooted and culturally specific vocabulary, involving (usually substantive and untranslatable) terms such as *dharma, karma, kāma, artha, sanyāsa* and the like.

In making this argument, Nandy was paradoxically drawing above all upon a claim that was first set out in colonial India, namely that the only source of 'authentically indigenous' concepts could be found in ancient texts in Sanskrit. To his credit, however, it must be stated that he at least posed the problem of whether a possible field of political thought or political theory might have existed in India before colonial rule. Later writers, even those who were comfortable with the notion that concepts of 'politics' could be applied to study moments in the pre-colonial Indian past, have rarely returned to this problem.[9] Those who have done so have usually drawn upon Persian-language materials, and a learned tradition that has consistently maintained that in Islamic societies at least, the idea of 'politics' had long existed under such heads as *siyāsat*.[10] This view is lent credence by a genealogical claim, wherein the common Hellenic roots of Western and Islamic thinking on the issue can be pointed to; the problem then would arise with that part of India where Arabic and Persian did not ever come to dominate as the languages of intellectual discourse.[11]

---

[9] For example, see V. R. Mehta and Thomas Pantham eds, *Political Ideas in Modern India: Thematic Explorations* (New Delhi: Sage Publication, 2006).

[10] Patricia Crone, *Medieval Islamic Political Thought, c. 650–1250* (Edinburgh: Edinburgh University Press, 2004). The most important recent exercise on Indo-Islamic polities, and exploring the genre termed *akhlāq*, is that of Muzaffar Alam, *The Languages of Political Islam: India 1200–1800* (Chicago: University of Chicago Press, 2004).

[11] Our problem thus parallels in some measure that faced by historians of political thought in China. For some examples, see Roger T. Ames, *The Art of Rulership: A Study in Ancient Chinese Political Thought* (Honolulu: University of Hawaii Press, 1983), and Hsiao Kung-chüan, A

This is the heart of the issue that this essay seeks to address. We wish to argue that in reality a quite substantial and varied body of material can be found in South India between the fourteenth and the late eighteenth centuries that attempts to theorize politics, while doing so neither in Persian nor in Sanskrit, even if it may bear traces of contact with bodies of material in these two 'classical' languages.[12] These materials may be found instead in the Indian vernacular languages, of which we shall focus on a particular body, that in Telugu (though a similar exercise could easily be attempted with materials in Kannada or Marathi).[13] Secondly, we suggest that most writers who have looked into the matter (and they are a mere handful, as noted above) have usually misidentified the location of such materials, by seeking it solely in the corpus known as *dharmashāstra*. Thirdly, we will attempt to show how the materials that we are fundamentally concerned with, and which usually term themselves texts on *nīti* rather than *dharma* (although there is some overlap in the two usages), changed over the centuries with which we are concerned. Nīti may be glossed here by such terms as 'pragmatics', 'politics' or 'statecraft'.[14] Finally, we shall briefly rehearse an argument on how the status of these materials was transformed in the nineteenth century, when British colonial rule reclassified them in ways that were at odds with their place in the universe of knowledge in India in earlier times.

We should begin perhaps with a rapid and schematic survey of the political history of the region with which we are concerned, namely the southeastern part of peninsular India, in which Telugu had emerged already by 1300 CE as a major literary language. A series of kingdoms can be found here, some of modest size and pretensions, others that can be classified as veritable imperial structures. To summarize, the early

History of Chinese Political Thought. Volume 1, From the Beginnings to the Sixth Century A.D., trans. F. W. Mote (Princeton: Princeton University Press, 1979).

[12] By focusing on the vernacular traditions, we seek to distinguish ourselves from a few earlier attempts which remain focused on Sanskrit; see, for example, Upendra Nath Ghoshal, *A History of Indian Political Ideas: The Ancient Period and the Period of Transition to the Middle Ages* (Bombay: Oxford University Press, 1959); and more recently the disappointing essay (again deriving from a secondary literature, but referring to Sanskrit materials) by Bhikhu Parekh, 'Some Reflections on the Hindu Tradition of Political Thought', in *Political Thought in Modern India*, eds Thomas Pantham and Kenneth L. Deutsch (New Delhi: Sage Publication, 1986).

[13] See, for example, Ramacandra Pant Amatya, *Ajñapatra*, ed. Vilas Khole (Pune: Pratima Prakasana, 1988).

[14] We should note in passing that the word *nīti* is etymologically related to *netā*, the most common North Indian word in use today for 'politician'.

fourteenth century sees the demise of the rule of a fairly substantial regional polity, that of the Kakatiyas of Warrangal, and the emergence of a set of far smaller kingdoms.[15] After a hiatus, the fifteenth century then sees the emergence of the great empire of Vijayanagara, which dominates the region (as indeed much of peninsular India) until the late sixteenth century.[16] The collapse of Vijayanagara power means in turn that the two centuries from 1600 to 1800 are marked by a complex period of contestation, without a single stable and hegemonic polity. The Mughals eventually come to play a substantial role in the region, but indirectly rather than as a centralized political structure.[17] In short, we can see an alternation, with two cycles of fragmented political formations sandwiching an extended central moment of a century and a half of imperial consolidation that is associated with Vijayanagara.

Although it was famously termed a 'forgotten empire' by Robert Sewell in 1900, it is clear that the memory of Vijayanagara remained very alive in South India as late as the beginning of the nineteenth century.[18] However, the lack of adequate lines of communication between a society that already possessed a centuries' long set of continuous intellectual traditions, and a new political power that had assumed the role of 'civilizing' a group of ostensibly uncivilized or partially civilized nations, was never more striking than at this early juncture of colonial Indian history. For the traditionally educated Indian intellectual of the early nineteenth century whom the East India Company might have consulted, India certainly had a sophisticated discipline termed *nīti*, beginning from early texts such as the *Arthashāstra* and continuing until their time. There was a whole range of texts on *dharma*, beginning with Manu's *Dharmashāstra* (and dating perhaps from the early centuries CE),

---

[15] For a recent examination of this period, see Cynthia Talbot, *Precolonial India in Practice: Society, Region, and Identity in Medieval Andhra* (Delhi: Oxford University Press, 2001).

[16] For Vijayanagara's relationship to (and memory of) earlier polities in the region, see Hermann Kulke, 'Maharajas, Mahants and Historians: Reflections on the Historiography of early Vijayanagara and Sringeri', in *Vijayanagara–City and Empire: New Currents of Research*, 2 volumes, eds A.L. Dallapiccola and S. Zingel-Avé Lallemant (Stuttgart: Franz Steiner Verlag, 1985), Vol. I, pp. 120–143.

[17] On Mughal involvement in the region, see Sanjay Subrahmanyam, *Penumbral Visions: Making Polities in Early Modern South India* (Delhi/Ann Arbor: Oxford University Press/University of Michigan Press, 2001).

[18] Robert Sewell, *A Forgotten Empire—Vijayanagar: A Contribution to the History of India* (London: Swan Sonnenschein & Co., 1900; reprint, Delhi: Publication Division, Ministry of Information & Broadcasting, Govt. of India, 1962).

and also continuing through the medieval period both in terms of a manuscript tradition and by way of extensive commentaries.[19] But the British administrators and their native assistants in early colonial South India were primarily looking for 'moral instruction'.[20] Of the two concepts in the Indian tradition that come close to the idea of morals—*dharma* and *nīti*—*dharma* was seen as somewhat unsuitable for moral instruction because it was too close to the religious world. Manu's celebrated *Dharmashāstra* was also deeply embedded in the *varna* and *jāti* order, and discussed legal matters relating to marriages, property rights, and so on. Law courts needed these texts, to administer justice to Indians according to their indigenous laws. The story of Sir William Jones's efforts in this direction and Henry Thomas Colebrooke's translation of legal digests for use in the British courts is too well known to be repeated here.[21]

At the same time, it was also easy enough to argue that there was a direct line of ascent between the medieval regional language *nīti* texts and the *Arthashāstra* of Kautilya, and thus to conclude that the regional language texts were derivative and, if anything, bad copies of an original (however elusive that original was in purely philological terms) and therefore not particularly interesting. Another problem was that since the authors of *nīti* texts invariably claimed to be poets, literary scholars of late nineteenth and early twentieth centuries, influenced by notions deriving from Western literary models, began by rejecting any formal literary merit in their texts and then showed no interest in analysing them seriously for their content. Doubly neglected, the regional language *nīti* texts were relegated to a sort of intellectual no-man's land. Yet, as noted above, native schools still needed moral instruction, and in the absence of an Indian equivalent of the Ten Commandments, or similar codes of virtue, teachers often turned to *nīti* texts to fill the need.

---

[19] Patrick Olivelle, *The Law Code of Manu* (Oxford: Oxford University Press, 2004), p. xxiii: 'the composition of the MDh may be placed closer to the second century CE'.

[20] On this early interaction, also see the essay by Phillip Wagoner, 'Precolonial Intellectuals and the Production of Colonial Knowledge', *Comparative Studies in Society and History* 45 (2003), pp. 783–814, which however appears to us far too influenced by the model of 'dialogic interaction' put forward in Eugene F. Irschick, *Dialogue and History: Constructing South India, 1795–1895* (Berkeley: University of California Press, 1994).

[21] The classic study remains J. D. M. Derrett, *Religion, Law and the State in India* (London: Faber & Faber, 1968). Also see, more recently, Richard W. Lariviere, 'Dharmaśāstra, Custom, "Real Law" and "Apocryphal" Smrtis', *Recht, Staat und Verwaltung im Klassischen Indien*, ed. B. Köelver (München: R.Oldenbourg, 1997), pp. 97–110.

The principal focus of this essay is the transformation and development of *nīti* discourse from classical Sanskrit texts to early modern Telugu texts and their later use in the colonial period. Our interest is to show, first, that these texts demonstrate a lively change with time and context as guides to practical wisdom, and strategies of success; and second, that they are not concerned with religion and are therefore mostly 'this-worldly' (*laukika*) or 'secular' in character. A third point that is developed in the analysis is of how the late nineteenth century colonial interest in teaching morals in schools gave selective, and one might say, distorted attention, to some *nīti* texts while ignoring the bulk of the others. The sources of the discussion are mainly from Telugu with a few examples from Sanskrit and Persian.

Some Ur Texts

No Indian text from ancient times has arguably been as used and misused in the context of the twentieth century as the *Arthashāstra* of Kautilya.[22] The first edition of this text, from 1909, was produced in Mysore by R. Shama Sastri from a single manuscript (with a commentary by a certain Bhattasvamin) originating in the Tanjavur region. It had already been preceded by a first translation (in the pages of the *Indian Antiquary*) from 1905 by the same scholar. The text quickly attracted massive attention, and a number of other manuscripts came to light, mostly in southern India (in Grantha and Malayalam characters), with one of the rare northern Indian manuscripts being from Patan, from a Jain collection. The confident initial assertion that the text's author was 'the famous Brahman Kautilya, also named Vishnugupta, and known from other sources by the patronymic Chanakya', and that the text was written at the time of the foundation of the Maurya dynasty, has of course been considerably eroded over the course of the twentieth century. Despite the relative rarity of manuscripts, it is clear that the text was known to the medieval tradition in various forms, and that its author was considered to be one of a series of important ancient authors of *nīti* texts. The Vijayanagara-period work, *Rāyavācakamu*, tells us that the king Vira Narasimha Raya in the early sixteenth century was

---

[22] The standard work is R P Kangle, ed. and trans., *Kautilya's Arthaśāstra*, 3 Vols. (Bombay: University of Bombay, 1965–72), but there is a vast secondary literature.

accustomed to hearing recitations from various texts including Canura's *Nīti*, with 'Canura' being a distortion of Canakya.[23]

The text of the *Arthashāstra* in its modern critical edition, which was not necessarily the received version in the medieval tradition, is of course quite astonishing in its ambition and coverage.[24] It is a highly detailed text, and not one that simply contents itself to enunciate vague general principles. The text also quotes earlier authors, often pointing to the difference between its author's own opinions (in the third person, as 'Kautilya') and those of others. A striking and oft-remarked aspect of the work is that a great deal of its content is markedly 'secular'. To be sure, in the initial part, the text invokes Sukra and Brahaspati, and then the Vedas; but thereafter, such location devices or references seem to disappear from the text. The first chapter discusses the overall contents, and Chapter 2 (*adhyakshapracārah*) then begins by noting that there are normally four *vidya*s: philosophy; the three Vedas; agriculture, cattle rearing and trade (collectively *vārtā*) and law-and-order (*daṇḍa-nīti*). According to Kautilya, there are however those who follow the Brahaspati's line of thinking, believing that there are only three disciplines (*vidya*s) and the Vedas are really a mere façade. We then get a version of the *āshrama* system of social ordering followed by a description of material life, with no reference thereafter in this extensive chapter to anything that might be understood as 'religion'. This is once again the case in later chapters on judicial and legal matters, criminals and how to deal with them, secret matters (*yogavrittam*), and the manner of dealing with other kings and kingdoms (the themes of Chapters 6 and 7, respectively, *maṇḍalayonih* and *shāḍguṇyam*). The highly circumscribed place of *dharma* in the text has recently been summed up as follows by Charles Malamoud:

> The originality of the *Arthashāstra* is that the science of government, the doctrine of royal conduct, is set out there in a perspective where *artha* appears in a highly limited form and not, as in the Epics or the Laws of Manu for example, where it is assimilated to the perspective of 'duty' (*dharma*). The question in the *Arthashāstra*, is not that of knowing how, while obeying his 'duty of state', the king contributes to order in the

---

[23] Phillip B. Wagoner, *Tidings of the King: A Translation and Ethnohistorical Analysis of the 'Rāyavācakamu'* (Honolulu: University of Hawaii Press, 1993), pp. 182, 197. This Telugu text bears a close and interesting resemblance to a Kannada text of the same period, *Shrī Krishnade-varāya Dinacari*, ed. V.S. Sampatkumara Acarya (Bangalore: Svatantara Mudranalaya, 1983).

[24] We have used Kautilya, *Arthashāstram*, ed. Pullela Sriramacandrudu (Hyderabad: Sri Jayalakshmi Publications, 1999) with Balanandini commentary, in Telugu script.

world and in society, or even how he guarantees it, but rather of what he should do to attain his ends: conquer territory and hold on to it. To be sure the two perspectives are not wholly incompatible, and many of the 'Machiavellian' precepts of the *Arthashāstra* also appear in texts that layout the norms of *dharma*; and there are even some passages in the *Arthashāstra* that recall some principles regarding the final ends which are *dharmic* in nature. But all in all, the *Arthashāstra* does not justify the means by the ends: the means and the ends appear at the same level, and each means is a provisional end. The treatise sets itself the task of laying out in detail the modalities of royal action and to evaluate them in relation to its sole objective: to succeed.[25]

Unfortunately, we do not know a great deal about the history of the book's subsequent use until far later. The speculation of the past few decades is that it may date from the fourth century CE, but it is really quite difficult to make a definitive pronouncement on the matter. Buddhist sources seem to have been quite negatively disposed both to the text—on account of its alleged amorality—and to its author as a personage.[26] We may note that the *Kāmandaka* or *Nītisāra* also comes from broadly the same period, but slightly later, and that its author Kamanda states that he knows the *Arthashāstra*, specifying that the text's author was Kautilya, also known as Vishnugupta. Kamanda also appears to be the source for the confusing claim that Kautilya was the one who broke the power of the Nandas. In a similar vein, the author of the *Mudrārākshasa*, the Sanskrit play of Vishakhadatta from about 600 CE, seems to have known and used the *Arthashāstra*.

Unlike later medieval texts that we will discuss below, the *Arthashāstra* is not aphoristic in nature. Its literary quality is in fact rather interesting, being written mostly in short prose sentences with some occasional *shlokas* in the middle, and one or sometimes more than one *shloka* at the end of each chapter, and yet it is composed in a way that does not lend itself to easy oral transmission in this form. It seems largely meant

[25] Charles Malamoud, 'Croyance, crédulité, calcul politique: Présentation et traduction commentée de l'Arthaçâstra de Kautilya, livre XIII, chapitres I et III' in *Multitudes*, 1997 (http://multitudes.samizdat.net/Croyance-credulite-calcul.html).

[26] Thomas Trautmann has in particular attempted to date the text from linguistic evidence. See Thomas R. Trautmann, *Kautilya and the Arthaśāstra: A Statistical Investigation of the Authorship and Evolution of the Text* (Leiden: Brill, 1971). Also see K. J. Shah, 'Of Artha and the Arthaśāstra', *Contributions to Indian Sociology*, N.S., 15 (1982), pp. 55–73, and H. Scharfe, *Investigations in Kautilya's Manual of Political Science* (Wiesbaden: Harrassowitz, 1993).

for readers of a written book, and once more demarcates itself from later texts in the fact that 'Kautilya' himself, whoever he is, still poses and is regarded as an authoritative author. We shall have occasion to contrast this with the strategy of later texts, which seek legitimacy from their acceptability rather than invoking and using a notion of authority.

A second text from the early period that merits some mention, and seems to slightly postdate the *Arthashāstra*, is Kamanda's *Nitisāra*, briefly noted above. This work is shorter and also far less detailed than that of Kautilya, but follows it largely in terms of tone and general content, being partly advisory and partly authoritative.[27] Again, this text is written in the form of Sanskrit *shlokas*, not particularly easy for memorization or oral transmission, but perhaps intended more for reading. This text survived far more clearly into the medieval tradition, appearing in a Telugu version in the late sixteenth century (about 1584) as the *Āndhra Kāmandaka*, with some additional material that the Sanskrit 'original' does not contain.

NĪTI AND ITS OPPONENTS DURING THE MEDIEVAL PERIOD

A very active interest in creating *nīti* texts is found in Telugu from the Kakatiya period in Andhra, which is to say the period from about the twelfth to the mid-fourteenth centuries.[28] The emergence of a powerful dynasty of major rulers from the great centre of Warrangal and the conditions that existed for a general upward mobility among many communities in the Deccan apparently motivated many writers to produce such works in Telugu. Some of the authors of *nīti* books of this period were themselves kings or their ministers, and many were associated with people of power in some manner or the other. The *Sakala-nīti-sammatamu* (hereafter *SNS*), a major anthology of selections from a number of *nīti* texts in Telugu, is of particular interest to us because it demonstrates the popularity of *nīti* as a subject in medieval Andhra.[29] The compiler of this anthology, Madiki Singana, was a poet

---

[27] Kamanda, *Nīti-sāra*, ed. with a Telugu translation by Tadakamalla Venkata Krishna Rao (Madras: Vartamanatarangini Mudraksarashala, 1860).

[28] See Talbot, *Precolonial India in Practice*.

[29] Madiki Singana, *Sakala-nīti-sammatamu* eds, Nidudavolu Venkataravu and P. S. R. Apparao (Hyderabad: Andhra Pradesh Sahitya Akademi, 1970) (this includes a facsimile of the 1923 edition by M. Ramakrishna Kavi).

in his own right. In his preface to the book, he declares that *nīti* should have equal circulation everywhere like a coin with the stamp of the Sultan (*suratāṇi*) and appropriately enough he calls his book 'Nīti acceptable to everyone'.

Singana lived in a period when a number of *nīti* texts were already popular, perhaps each one in a different subregion or community. In his preface to the anthology, he hence expresses a desire to produce a digest of *nīti* and lists the names of books from which he has collected his selections. He thus notes that his compilation is of some 982 selections from 17 distinct *nīti* texts by known authors (we may note in passing that many of the texts that were available to Singana are now lost), several verses from oral tradition, some verses by unknown authors, and his own verses as well. Among the known authors from whom Singana quotes, some are either kings themselves or ministers closely associated with kings. Rudradeva I (1150–95), who wrote *Nītisāramu*, was a king of the Kakatiya dynasty; Sivadevayya (1250–1300), who wrote *Purushârthasāramu*, was the adviser and minister of Kakatiya king, Ganapatideva, and Baddena, also known as Bhadrabhupala, who wrote a particularly celebrated book called *Nīti-shāstra-muktāvali*—better known as *Baddenīti*—is considered by modern Telugu scholarship to have been a king, from the Telugu Cola family.[30] Not much is known about this last poet-savant who addresses himself in his verses with royal epithets, except that he lived sometime before Singana (who himself flourished in about 1420), and that by the early fifteenth century, his book had acquired considerable popularity, as is indicated by the short title which Singana uses when he quotes from it. The other *nīti* writers whom Singana quotes are mostly unknown, with the exception of Appappamantri who wrote a Telugu version of Bhoja's *Cārucarya*, a book of advice about healthy habits for wealthy people to follow.

Singana classifies his selections under 47 categories covering a range of topics related to kings as well as commoners—courtiers, physicians, pundits and of course accountants and scribes (*karaṇams*). Two things stand out from Singana's anthology. In the first place, it does not invoke an other-worldly authority in any place. The goal is mundane, this-worldly, and the only thing that counts is success in any profession. However, it is not an 'amoral' text, as the desire for success is considered acceptable as part of

---

[30] Baddena, *Nīti-shāstra-muktāvali*, ed. M. Ramakrishna Kavi (Tanuku: Sri Narendranatha Sahityamandali, 1962).

a good human life, and it is implicit that success should be achieved within the framework of ethical conduct. The only concept that might suggest a Hindu 'world-view' of some sort is that a certain number of the verses refer to the scheme of the four goals of life, the *caturvidha purushârthas* (that is, *dharma, artha, kāma* and *moksha*) of which *artha* and *kāma*, profit and pleasure, are the most significant areas upon which *nīti* texts focus. Even this reference, from the tone of its use, does not seem to be particularly religious in the context. While we do not have access to Sivadevayya's text in its entirety to see if it deals with the other two *purushârthas,* that is *dharma* and *moksha*, we know that no other extant *nīti* text deals with them, and in the use of later texts, for instance, the *Sumati-shatakamu*, the phrase *purushârtha-parudu* simply means a successful person.

It should also be noted that *SNS* for its part does not include even a single verse from the thirteenth-century *dharmashāstra* work, Ketana's *Vijñāneshvaramu*, a Telugu work based on the Sanskrit *mitâkshara* commentary of Vijnanesvara to the *Yajñavalkyasmriti*. This, we suggest, emphasizes the conceptual separation that already operated in these authors' minds of *nīti* from *dharma*.[31] For Ketana's work, we should note, followed in the standard, rather Brahmanic, *dharmashāstra* tradition of normative texts. Its author was a close relative (probably the nephew) of the celebrated Tikkana, who seems to have instructed him and guided him in writing this text.[32] Ketana was also the author of two other texts, one a *Dashakumāracaritramu*, an entertaining book of stories, and a grammar of Telugu, *Āndhrabhāshābhūshanamu*. He, like Tikkana, seems to have been creating an intellectual culture of a conservative and 'revivalist' kind, as we see from a close reading of the huge *Mahābhārata* that Tikkana produced at much the same time in Telugu.

To gain a sense of Ketana's *Vijñāneshvaramu* it may be useful to turn to the *vyavahārakānda* section of his text, which—though a relatively short section of the whole—starkly brings out the contrast we wish to develop between *dharma* and *nīti* texts. Here is a passage where he sets out his conception of rulership:

---

[31] Ketana, *Vijñāneshvaramu*, ed. C.V. Ramachandra Rao (Nellore: Manasa Publications, 1977). Ramachandra Rao in his preface to the work already notes that Singana does not include Ketana's work in his anthology, but assumes that this is be due to the lack of 'popularity' of the latter during his time. Also see Ketana, *Vijñāneshvaramu*, ed. C. Vasundhara (Nellore: Manasa Publications, 1989).

[32] On Tikkana, see V. Narayana Rao and David Shulman, *Classical Telugu Poetry: An Anthology* (Berkeley: University of California Press, 2002).

A king, without becoming greedy or angry,
with *dharma* in his own heart,
should decide issues of *dharma*,
in the company of competent, well-known and scholarly Brahmins.
In that group, he should have those
learned in Veda, truthful,
versed in the *dharmashāstras*,
and not given to love or hatred.
Such Brahmins should be members of his council.
In number, they should be seven,
or five, or three,
and if the king cannot attend,
he should send a scholar of the *dharmashāstra*,
who is a good judge.
And if the king does something unjust,
and is supported by his council,
they will be drowned in sin (*papambuna munuguduru*).[33]

So we see here the clear evocation of the idea of *pāpa* (sin) as the ultimate punishment for incorrect action even in the context of statecraft. At times however, as noted by Malamoud in the classical context, the texts of *nīti* and *dharma* do converge, as when certain procedures are discussed (for example, on how to collect evidence in the context of a trial, or some other practical affairs). However, often enough, even the flavour of judicial considerations matters considerably, since texts like that of Ketana imply a strong caste variation in trials and punishments, and even seem directly to echo ideas from the Manu *Dharmashāstra*. Thus, we have the following example:

If a Brahmin commits a crime
deserving capital punishment,
this is what should be done:
Shave his head,
Mark his forehead with the sign of a dog's paw,
Confiscate his money,
sit him on a donkey,
and drive him out of town.
This is as good as killing him.

---

[33] Ketana, *Vijñāneshvaramu*, ed. Ramachandra Rao, p. 24, Verses 1–5.

But if a lower-caste person commits a crime
that deserves capital punishment,
taking his life
is quite appropriate.[34]

Where then, may we ask, do *dharma* and *nīti* texts in fact overlap without a great deal of tension? This is on those rare occasions when *dharma* texts deal with rather concrete commercial matters, such as the passage in Ketana dealing with how to write a promissory note (*patra*).

Mark the year, month, the fortnight,
the number and name of the day,
and the place.
Write the name of the lender,
Along with his father's name,
Then that of the borrower,
with his father's name too.
Then write the sum of the loan,
And the rate of interest,
And the witnesses must then write:
That they know and certify the facts.
The borrower should sign his name,
Saying that he has received the money,
and agrees to the conditions.
At last, the executor of the note must sign
to make what civilized people (*nāgarika*) call a trustworthy note.[35]

In general, however, Ketana's text is everywhere marked by a manner of thinking that reflects the *dharmashāstras*, and is consequently anxious above all to protect and defend the caste hierarchy as the most important aspect of the functioning of the polity. Nowhere is this clearer than in the passages where he gives ways of testing the four *varṇas*, to see if they are telling the truth or not.

If it is a Brahmin,
first weigh him in scales
with a certain number of bricks.
Save the bricks,
and on the day of the test,
bring them back,

---

[34] Ketana, *Vijñāneshvaramu*, ed. Ramachandra Rao, Verse 42, p. 27.
[35] Ketana, *Vijñāneshvaramu*, ed. Ramachandra Rao, Verse 109, p. 32.

worship the scales,
invoke the lords (*dikpālas*) of the eight directions,
and have him sit facing east.
Put the same bricks back,
and call upon the gods (*daivambulāra*) saying:
If he speaks the truth, lift him up,
and if he lies, pull him down.
And when the judge says this, if the pan rises,
he does not lie.

In contrast to this somewhat soft treatment, Kshatriyas on the other hand are to be tested by fire, Vaishyas by water and Sudras by poison. Thus, for Kshatriyas:

An iron ball of a certain weight
should be properly worshipped.
The person to be tested
should stand facing east.
In his palms, seven *pīpal* leaves should be placed,
and tied with seven twists.
The red hot iron ball should be brought with tongs,
and placed in his hands by a judge,
who all the while chants *mantras*.
If on account of the leaves,
his hands are not burnt,
the man is truthful.[36]

It is hence clear that different tests are to be administered to different castes, a feature that markedly does not appear in *nīti* texts. The division of property among children finds extensive mention in Ketana, as well as the proper limits to its use in daily life.

If someone wishes to dig a well,
or build a tank,
on someone else's land,
for the welfare of the people,
he still must ask the owner's permission.
and if the owner refuses,
he is obliged to stop.[37]

---

[36] Ketana, Vijñāneshvaramu, ed. Ramachandra Rao, pp. 33–34, Verses 117–21.

[37] Ketana, Vijñāneshvaramu, ed. Ramachandra Rao, p. 36, Verse 149.

Thus, the difference between the *vyavahārakāṇḍa* of a *dharma* text like that of Ketana and sections dealing with similar matters in a typical *nīti* text are rather clear. Divine intervention (*daivas*) is constantly invoked in the former, the notion of sin (*pāpa*) is brought in and punishments are explicitly hierarchized by caste. Even judgement is a ritual, requiring the chanting of *mantras*. In general, we may note that in this vision of things, punishments suggested with regards to castes lower down in the hierarchy (including scribal groups) are very heavy, and most of the discussions, including even those on how murders should be investigated, wind up having a strongly *dhārmic* flavour about them. The example below demonstrates this amply:

> If a person of a low caste
> forces himself on the wife
> of a man of higher caste
> he should be killed for it.
> that is the *dharma* of a king.
> If a man forces himself
> on a housewife of his own caste
> fine him a thousand *paṇas*.
> But if a man of high caste
> makes love to a woman of lower caste
> fine him five hundred *paṇas*.
> If a lower caste man
> makes love to a higher caste virgin
> he should be killed.
> But if he is a higher-caste man
> and the virgin loves him,
> the two should be married.[38]

The role of the king is hence clear enough; he is, in large measure, the guarantor of the caste hierarchy and the protector of upper-caste males, but also the defender of their virtue—even against themselves. The examples below make this perfectly clear, and reinforce our notion that we are dealing with a socially conservative text.

> If a Brahmin makes love to an untouchable (*caṇḍāla*) woman,
> the drawing of a vagina should be inscribed on his body,
> he should be fined,

---

[38] Ketana, *Vijñāneshvaramu*, ed. Ramachandra Rao, pp. 21–22, Verses 107, 108 and 110.

and driven out the country.
That's appropriate for a king to do.[39]

The text does occasionally adopt a mildly humorous—or if one prefers, 'realistic'—tone, but this is far more exception than the rule. One example of this appears in the same section.

If a woman is found with an illegitimate lover,
and tries to claim that he is a burglar,
he should still be fined five hundred
as an illegitimate lover.[40]

At the same time, Ketana is a strong defender of royal authority, which he sees as requiring defence with an iron hand and the most severe of deterrent punishments. Hence:

If someone insults the king,
Or reveals the royal secrets,
His tongue should be cut out
And he should be driven out of town.[41]

All in all, then, this is a text that is remarkable for its censorious tone, and marked desire to regulate the moral life of society, rather than the harmonious combination of its parts in some form of social equilibrium. Virtue, for Ketana, must be produced, and if that production requires pain—whether physical or financial—so be it. Even gossips and malicious speech are seen by him as requiring regulation in some form, and that too by the king.

If a person lacks one limb,
or if he has a deformed limb,
or if one limb is badly diseased,
one should not talk ill of them.
And those who ridicule them by saying:
'How well formed he is',
'No one compares to him',
should pay a fine of three *rūkas*.[42]

In a similar vein, ethnic slurs, or insults based on caste, are not to be allowed, in this most 'politically correct' of utopias.

---

[39] Ketana, *Vijñāneshvaramu*, ed. Ramachandra Rao, p. 23, Verse 126.
[40] Ketana, *Vijñāneshvaramu*, ed. Ramachandra Rao, p. 23, Verse 129.
[41] Ketana, *Vijñāneshvaramu*, ed. Ramachandra Rao, p. 23, Verse 134.
[42] Ketana, *Vijñāneshvaramu*, ed. Ramachandra Rao, p. 16, Verse 42.

If someone says that people from Murikinadu are stupid,
that the Arava [Tamil] people are quarrelsome (*penaparulu,*)
or that Brahmins are greedy,
and abuses people by country, language or caste,
such a person should be fined a hundred *paṇas*.[43]

In other sections, notably the *ācāra-kāṇḍa*, many passages seem to bear
a close resemblance to Manu's *Dharmashāstra*, at times literally and at other
times in spirit. A great preoccupation of the author, Ketana, is with the
mixing of castes and the potentially negative effects of this phenomenon.
Further, the gender roles are distinctly asymmetrical in this vision of
things, all the more so in the context of intercaste relations. Thus:

If a high caste woman
Makes love to a *shūdra* man,
She may become pure again
by ritual punishment (*prāyascitta*).
But if she becomes pregnant,
her husband should leave her.

Further, unlike what would find in *nīti* texts, it is understood that the
rights of women are far more limited, and that they can be unilaterally
disciplined for a number of faults, often merely on the basis of accusation.
A last verse from Ketana below demonstrates how thorough-going and
consistent a vision he embodies.

If a woman drinks,
and has a sharp tongue,
if she wastes all the money,
if she hates men,
or if she is barren,
or if she only has female children,
if she is sick,
if she is a termagant,
then the man can leave her, and marry again.
there is nothing wrong in that.[44]

To develop the contrast, and the opposed visions that we have been
suggesting inhere in the different genres, we should now turn to the
nīti tradition of roughly the same period. In the *nīti* texts that were

---

[43] Ketana, *Vijñāneshvaramu*, ed. Ramachandra Rao, p. 17, Verse 56.
[44] Ketana, *Vijñāneshvaramu*, ed. Ramachandra Rao, p. 10, Verse 113.

written during the Kakatiya period, by such writers as Sivadevayya and Rudradeva, the localized nature of the king and his kingship is quite evident. Even though the king they address is portrayed as a strong monarch, he is not an emperor ruling over multiple regions or extensive domains. The advice given relating to the protection of *durgas* (fortresses), for dealing with spies, and for invading the enemy's territory, the conduct of battle, and so on, is not on a scale anywhere suggesting a large empire. Yet, the advice is practical and clearly derived from real experience of the administration of a kingdom. We may take for instance, the following excerpts from Singana:

- A king who does not command, is like a king in a painting, (good only for looks). If a king doesn't punish anyone who defies his command—even if the wrongdoer is his own son—he does not rule long.
- To allow merchants to take as much as they want is to ruin your people.
- If you don't make scales and measures uniform, it means you effectively permit thieves to go scot-free.
- If a king increases taxes, that effectively prevents (foreign) goods from entering his country.
- Wherever a letter might come from, a king should never disregard it. It is only through letters that a king knows everything—from alliances to enmities.
- Not killing a criminal amounts to killing a host of gentle people. All that you need to do in order to kill cows is to spare a tiger.

Some of the quotations in the *SNS* are clearly influenced by a traditional Sanskrit model of kingship, for example when the king is equated with god, quoting Manu's *Dharmashāstra*:

- The king is godly, and that is what Manu says, and he should be treated as such and wise people should not treat him otherwise.
- Even if he is a boy, a king should not be treated like an ordinary mortal. He is god, and that's how he should be treated.
- The king may be bad, but the servant should serve his interests.
- If he [the servant] should leave his master for another to make a better living, the new master will never respect him for his loyalty.

However, in the same anthology we find some advice regarding bad kings. It is interesting to note that this advice comes from writers who perhaps served kings themselves in various capacities such as scribes (*karaṇams*), or soldiers.

- If anyone has caused you harm, go and complain to the king. But if the king himself harms you, who can you complain to?
- If serving a ruler causes incessant pain to the servant, the servant should leave such a master right away.
- He may be rich, born in a good caste, a strong warrior beyond comparison, but if a king is an ignoramus, his servants will no doubt leave him.
- If a king does not distinguish between the right hand and the left, a precious diamond and a piece of glass, it is humiliating to serve such a king—no matter how great a warrior you are.
- A bad king surrounded by good people turns out to be good. But even a good king is difficult to serve if his advisers are bad.
- A king who enjoys hearing stories of others' faults, who enjoys putting people through trouble and steals other men's wives, brings calamity to his people.

The authoritative figure of Baddena is generously quoted in the *SNS*, and has some fascinating instructions to a king in his *Nītishāstramuktāvaḷi*. Contrary to the later importance *karaṇams* acquired in managing the affairs of the kingdom as ministers and scribes, Baddena strikes a note of caution against too much dependence on the minister. In his words:

- A king should not direct his people and his servants to his minister for all their needs. The king should be his own minister and treat the minister as an assistant.

The major writers on *nīti* whom Singana quotes in his *SNS* are already aware of the whole *nīti* tradition before them, including the Sanskrit *Arthashāstra* text. Besides, closer to hand, we find medieval texts from the Deccan, such as the *Mānasollāsa* of the twelfth-century Calukya king, Someshvara III.[45] Such works as these can certainly be seen to participate in a culture of political realism, and thus give the lie to those who have argued that pre-colonial politics in India was conceived along purely idealist lines. At the same time, the genre of the 'Mirror for Princes' is well known in the Indo-Islamic context, where a number of such texts exist both from the time of the Sultanate of Delhi, under the later

---

[45] See Someshvara, *Mānasollāsa*, 3 Vols., ed. Gajanan K. Shrigondekar (Baroda: Oriental Institute, 1925–61).

Mughals, and from the regional Sultanates such as those of the Deccan.[46] Such texts, often written in Persian, are themselves at times influenced by Indic models such as the *Pañcatantra*, known in the Islamic world through its translation as the *Kalila wa Dimna*. Yet, they also bear the clear imprint of the non-theological perspective on kingship that had emerged in the Islamic lands in the aftermath of the Mongol conquests, when Muslim advisers and *wazīrs* struggled with the problem of how to advise *kāfir* rulers and princes on the matter of government, without taking them into murky and controversial theological waters.[47] The 'Mirror for Princes' genre ranges wide, and attempts to do everything from forming the prince's musical tastes, to refining his table manners, but the core of the matter is usually politics, both in the sense of diplomatic relations between states, and relations between a prince and his companions, or between different elements in a courtly setting.[48]

The authors included in the *SNS* appear to be aware of these different traditions, and even draw upon them quite explicitly.[49] Yet, in contrast to the typical 'Mirrors for Princes', these authors offer a top-down, hands-on vision, partly rooted in pragmatic experience, partly creatively adapting the existing literature of *nīti*-statecraft. This is no armchair pontificating but a largely practical synthesis reflecting the political, economic and institutional changes of the fifteenth century. Still, highly individualized statements that can be attributed directly to the book's author Singana, do alternate with verses that seem to be lifted from

[46] Linda T. Darling, '"Do Justice, Do Justice, for That is Paradise": Middle Eastern Advice for Indian Muslim Rulers', *Comparative Studies of South Asia, Africa, and the Middle East* XXIII (2002), pp. 3–19. Also see Wagoner, *Tidings of the King*, pp. 182, 197; and especially his 'Iqta and Nayankara: Military Service Tenures and Political Theory from Saljuq Iran to Vijayanagara South India', unpublished paper presented at the 25th Annual Conference on South Asia, Madison, WI, 18–20 October, 1996. In this latter essay, Wagoner presents convincing evidence for the influence of Persian-Islamic political thought on Baddena.

[47] On this thorny issue, see Jean Aubin, *Émirs mongols et vizirs persans dans les remous de l'acculturation* (Paris: Association pour l'aivancement des études iraniennes 1995).

[48] For a recent, and stimulating, reconsideration of the genre, see Jocelyne Dakhlia, 'Les Miroirs des princes islamiques: Une modernité sourde?', *Annales HSS* 57 (2002), pp. 1191–1206.

[49] For an earlier translation, see A. Rangasvami Sarasvati, 'Political Maxims of the Emperor-Poet Krishnadeva Raya', *Journal of Indian History* IV (1926), pp. 61–88; also the later rendition (with the Telugu text of the *rāja-nīti* section) in *Further Sources of Vijayanagara History*, 3 Vols, eds K. A. Nilakantha Sastri and N. Venkataramanayya, (Madras: University of Madras, 1946). We have already dealt at length with this text in V. Narayana Rao, David Shulman and Sanjay Subrahmanyam, 'A New Imperial Idiom in the Sixteenth Century: Krishnadeva Raya and His Political Theory of Vijayanagara,' in *South Indian Horizons: Felicitation Volume for François Gros on the Occasion of his 70th birthday*, eds Jean-Luc Chevillard and Eva Wilden (Pondicherry: Institut Français de Pondichéry, Ecole Française d'Extrême Orient, 2004), pp. 597–625.

standard *nīti*-texts about politics and kingship. Nonetheless, we are left with a total impression of a unique concoction of pragmatic wisdom, specific constraints, an inherited normative politics.

AN IMPERIAL INTERLUDE: KRISHNADEVARAYA

Singana wrote in the fifteenth century and the immediate textual heritage he had available to him came from the period of the Kakatiyas. These were rulers who had dominated a relatively well-defined regional space in the eastern Deccan and their preoccupations were very much reflective of that fact. In the case of Singana, we may suspect that the political landscape had fragmented even further, and that the kings he referred to were ruling over domains that would qualify a few centuries later as no more than *zamīndārīs*. But this was certainly not the case by the latter half of the fifteenth century, when a new, diverse and complex polity had emerged to control much of peninsular India south of the Tunghabhadra river, namely the state that is normally known as Vijayanagara (from the name of its capital city).

Normative texts on kingship, or statecraft, are hard to come by for fifteenth-century Vijayanagara. But we are far better served for the sixteenth century, and the times of the Third (Tuluva) and Fourth (Aravidu) Dynasties that ruled over Vijayanagara. A particular high point in terms of literary production, including that within the *nīti* genre, is the reign of the Tuluva monarch Krishnadevaraya (d. 1529).[50] When Krishnadevaraya ascended the throne in 1509 it is clear that a number of crucial problems regarding political management still remained to be resolved.[51] One major concern in the mind of the king was to make himself generally acceptable, and secure an area that encompassed more than one region, one language and one religion. The king's self-perception given to us eloquently in his major work, *Āmuktamālyada*, suggests that he sees himself as a Kannada Raya, a Kannada king, while the god to whom he had dedicated his book was a Telugu Raya, a

---

[50] There is, unfortunately, no recent biography of this monarch. See, however, the works of Oruganti Ramachandraiya, *Studies on Krsnadevaraya of Vijayanagara* (Waltair: Andhra University, 1953), and N. Venkataramanayya, *Krishnadevarāyalu* (Hyderabad: Andhra Pradesh Archeological Series, 1972).

[51] For the succession dates of Krishnadevaraya and his coronation, see P. Sree Rama Sarma, *A History of Vijayanagar Empire* (Hyderabad: Prabhakar Publications, 1992), p. 133.

Telugu king. Without anachronistically invoking regional nationalisms and language loyalties in the context of the sixteenth-century Deccan, we can still see local polities conflicting with each other and wary of dominance by someone from the outside.

Another way to formulate the dilemma that this king confronted is in terms of an enduring tension between local and trans-local forces. There is a consistent effort to conceptualize some basis for a trans-local polity that could extricate the state from its constant resubmergence in diffuse local contexts. A striking element in this conceptual effort lies in the king's own dynastic origins in one of the most marginal, and recently conquered localities—the western coastal plain of Tulunad. A kind of upstart, whose own family inheritance dictated that he prove himself outside the family context, finds himself articulating, at times somewhat inchoately, a vision of trans-regional, highly personalized loyalties.

Once a trans-regional state system is conceivable, its ruler runs up against its external boundaries. The *manyam* forest regions (especially the northern and northeastern frontiers but also implicitly to the south-west in Kodagu, or Coorg, and the Western Ghats) thus figure prominently in the *Āmuktamālyada*'s section on *rāja-nīti* and require special treatment. External boundaries, however, coexist with the internal wilderness, as we see in a verse about a farmer marking off his field and then slowly making it free of stones and other impediments. But the text is also marked by a consistent suspicion, at times bordering on hostility or even contempt, for peoples like the Boyas and the Bhils, who could be found both at the border regions of the empire (in the north-east) and at the internal frontier. A prose passage within the *nīti* section thus advises the listener: 'Allay the fears of the hill-folk, and bring them into your army. Since they are a small people, their loyalty or faithlessness, their enmity or friendship, their favour or disfavour, can all easily be managed'. Another passage, this one in verse, runs as follows:

> Trying to clean up the forest folk
> is like trying to wash a mud wall.
> There's no end to it. No point in getting angry.
> Make promises that you can keep and win them over.
> They'll be useful for invasions, or plundering an enemy land.
> It's irrational for a ruler to punish a thousand
> When a hundred are at fault.

This then is *rāja-nīti* for building an empire, composed by a rather introspective, yet by now quite experienced king, who has been on the throne for perhaps a decade. In certain key respects, the author departs from conventional wisdom. For example, he recommends posting Brahmins as commanders of forts, *durga* and the fact that this was practical advice is shown by studies of the prosopography of the notables of the empire in that time.[52]

Make trustworthy Brahmins
The commanders of your forts
And give them just enough troops,
to protect these strongholds,
lest they become too threatening.

Brahmins, in this view, have certain clear advantages over non-Brahmins, even though this caste is theoretically at least not to be associated with warrior functions (though numerous exceptions, both in the epics and earlier historical instances could be found):

The king will often benefit by putting a Brahmin in charge,
for he knows both the laws of Manu and his own *dharma*.
And from fear of being mocked
by Kshatriyas and Sudras,
he will stand up to all difficulties.

Beyond this, however, lies the Brahmin's relative freedom from local attachments. At the same time, these Brahmins are clearly trained by now in military ways and engaged in worldly activities.

The potential for conflict between kings and ministers, that would be a staple of the histories and treatises produced by the *karaṇams*, the class from which the ministers themselves came, is also ever-present here, though its resolution is rather more to the king's advantage. The following extended passage makes this clear enough:

Employ Brahmins who are learned in statecraft,
who fear the unethical, and accept the king's authority,
who are between fifty and seventy,
from healthy families,
not too proud, willing to be ministers,
capable of discharging their duties well.

---

[52] Cynthia Talbot, 'The Nayakas of Vijayanagara Andhra: A Preliminary Prosopography', in *Structure and Society in Early South India: Essays in Honour of Noboru Karashima*, ed. Kenneth R. Hall (Delhi: Oxford University Press, 2001), pp. 251–75.

A king with such Brahmins for just a day
can strengthen the kingdom in all its departments.
If such ministers are not available,
a king must act on his own,
and do whatever he can.
If not, a bad minister can become
like a pearl as large as a pumpkin—
an ornament impossible to wear.
The minister will be out of control,
and the king will live under his thumb.

EARLY MODERN VARIATIONS

The post-Krishnadevaraya period in Vijayanagara changes the context of such writings, in particular once we enter the period of the dominance of the Aravidu family. The growing role of Aravidu ('Aliya') Ramaraya's relatives and his extended family spread out in smaller kingdoms all over the Deccan already marks a significant shift in this respect. The *nīti* of the empire, articulated by Krishnadevaraya, again gives way to the *nīti* of small kingdoms, most of which survive with the help of kinship relations and support from the extended family. While this also creates the usual family intrigues, rivalries and battles, the new political conditions also give rise to opportunities for upward mobility. The emergence of the Nayakas from the flexible and uncertain political conditions in the post-Krishnadevaraya period is reflected in the *nīti* texts of this time.[53]

The *Āndhra Kāmandakamu* by Jakkaraju Venkatakavi was written in 1584, and is of crucial interest to us in this context. Venkatakavi was employed in the court of Kondraju Venkataraju, himself a small king from the Aravidu family. The personal history of this Venkataraju is interesting, especially because he is reputed to have renovated the Ahobilam temple, when it had been ruined by the Turks (*turakalu*). Even so, the *nīti* book Venkataraju has authored does not have any mention of Muslims, either disapproving or approving. What is instead

---

[53] On the emergence of the Nayaka polities, see Velcheru Narayana Rao, David Shulman and Sanjay Subrahmanyam, *Symbols of Substance: Court and State in Nayaka-Period Tamilnadu* (Delhi: Oxford University Press, 1992); and for a study based on the inscriptional record, Noboru Karashima, *A Concordance of Nayakas: The Vijayanagar Inscriptions in South India* (Delhi: Oxford University Press, 2002).

noteworthy for us now is the regional and 'secular' (in the sense of non-sectarian) nature of *nīti* in the *Āndhra Kāmandakamu*. Even though the author states that his work is a translation of the earlier Sanskrit *Kāmandakiya* or *Nītisāra*, the later work in fact includes a number of *nīti* statements that are not to be found in the original, making it more an early modern *nīti* text rather than a simple restatement of a classical *nīti* vision. For instance here is a passage concerning the treatment of relatives and other political allies.

> Sons of your maternal uncle and aunt, and your nephews and your maternal uncle himself, sons of your mother's sister's sons—these people are allies by blood (*aurasa-mitrulu*).
>
> Your sons-in-law, brothers-in-law, your wife's brothers and sisters, are allies by marriage (*sambandha-mitrulu*).
>
> Kings of the lands on the other side of the country with which you share a border are allies from a related foreign land (*deshakramāgatulu*).
>
> Kings who seek your protection in time of need are protected allies (*rakshita-mitrulu*).
>
> A king should take note of these four kinds of allies and nurture their friendship.[54]

We have already noted that the relationship between kings and their ministers had been a matter of concern for both Baddena and Krishnadevaraya, both of whom have some words of caution to the king regarding the choice of his ministers. Venkatakavi goes a step further and describes the corrupt practices that bad ministers could adopt in order to enrich themselves. The verse below gives several kinds of bribes a minister could take:

> If the minister comes to a festival, what he gets is called *kānuka*. What he receives by way of things he appropriates from people is called *porabaḍi*.
>
> If he gets kickback in cash it is called *paṭṭubaḍi*. The money he gets privately in return for taking care of their business is called *lañcam*.
>
> A king should make sure that his minister does not take any of the above, and such a person should work for the king and receive his livelihood only from the king.[55]

[54] Jakkaraju Venkatakavi, *Āndhra Kāmandakamu*, ed. Veturi Prabhakara Sastri (Tanjore: Tanjore Sarasvati Mahal Library, 1950), Verse 2.112.

[55] *Ibid.*, Verse 2.82.

NĪTI AND *KARAṆAM* CULTURE

The political landscape we have described changes again from the seventeenth century onwards. A new group of people who made writing their profession emerged as a politically and culturally important group. In Andhra, Karnataka and Orissa, these people were often called *karaṇams*, and they were considered to be the counterparts of the *munshīs* in northern India.[56] Often seeing themselves as *mantris* or ministers of kings, the *karaṇams* perceive themselves broadly as managers of public affairs. Most members of this group were not connected with major empires or powerful kings, but they nevertheless had an enormous influence in running small kingdoms, *zamīndārīs* and petty principalities. They were also successful managers of properties, accountants, poets and historians. They prided themselves in their multiple language skills, their ability to read scripts of many languages and above all their skill at calligraphy. They were also at the same time accomplished at writing a highly unintelligible cursive script, which could be read only by other *karaṇams*. They came mostly from Brahmin castes, and in Andhra they were mostly Niyogi Brahmins— as opposed to the Vaidikis.[57] The former managed public affairs while the latter specialized in ritual texts and ritual performances, even though both wrote poetry. *Karaṇams* used the pen for their power and prestige. They were writers in the true sense of the word as we understand it today.

The self-image of the *karaṇams* is fascinating. They have left behind a large body of writings about themselves, their code of conduct and training, in addition to a number of historical texts. Here is what some of the verses tell us about a *karaṇam*:

> By good fortune a person become intelligent.
> By his intelligence, he receives the king's respect.
> When the king respect him, he becomes his adviser,
> and begins to manage public affairs.
> And when he becomes his chief adviser, he runs the kingdom.
>
> He writes, reads and speaks intelligently.
> He listens to what people say.

[56] We return here to a set of themes treated in Velcheru Narayana Rao, David Shulman and Sanjay Subrahmanyam, *Textures of Time: Writing History in South India, 1600–1800* (New York: Other Press, 2003).

[57] Komarraju Venkata Lakshmana Rao, 'Āndhra brāhmaṇulaloni niyogi-vaidika-bheda kāla nirṇayamu', in *Lakshmanarāya vyāsāvaḷi*, 2nd edition (Vijayawada: Adarsa Granthamandali, 1965), pp. 1–17.

He interprets foreign languages to the king, and
calms the assembly when it is out of control.
He says the right words at the right time, and brings people together,
and sees, right away, honesty from trickery.
He is capable of bringing people together and separating them too.
Or favouring enemies and offering them the throne.
He is humble, dignified, skilled and giving.
That's what a good *mantri* should be.

When the king is against you,
You need to make friends with the scribe.
When the god of death, Yama was angry and declared a person dead,
gatāyu, didn't Citragupta, his scribe make him live a hundred years, a
shatāyu, by changing *ga* to *sha*?

Included in a list of thirty two legendary ministers is a certain Rayani
Bhaskarudu, who appears most frequently in manuscript sources. Here
are a few poems about him from tradition.[58]

There should be twelve *bhāskaras* (suns) in the sky, Why do I see only
eleven? One of them is now serving as a minister on earth.
You mean the famous minister Bhaskara? I don't see a thousand hands
(rays) on him.
You see them when he gives to people, when he kills enemies, and when
he writes.

When Rayani Bhacadu writes,
sitting in front of his king Kataya Vema,
the sound of his pen gives
chills to his enemies
and shivers of joy to the poets.

Even when he was learning his alphabet,
Rayani Bhacadu did not join *la* and its e-curve
or write *da* and make a loop on its side.
The letters together would make, *ledu*, which means 'no'.
That was how generous he was to those who asked him for help.[59]

---

[58]   Veturi Prabhakara Sastri, ed., *Cāṭu-padya-maṇi-mañjari*, Vol. II (Hyderabad: Veturi Prabhakara Sastri Memorial Trust, 1988) (including the 1913 edition), section entitled *mantrulu*, pp. 251–308. Also see the section on *Sabhāpati-vacanamu*, in *Cāṭu-padya-maṇi-mañjari*, Vol. I, pp. 283–89.

[59]   Prabhakara Sastri, ed. *Cāṭu-padya-maṇi-mañjari*, Vol. II, p. 257. The combinations of vowels and consonants are now described in their graphic terms such as *ĕtvamu, kŏmmu*, rather than as phonological terms such as *ĕkāra*, and *ukāra*.

We also find a verse concerning a minister inscribed on the front gate of the Gopinathasvami temple in Kondavidu.

He built the town of Gopinathapuram
with incomparable walls on all sides.
Compelling in gentle power, he conquered
the Yavanas and all their armies.
He installed the deity, Gopika-vallabha and
organized his worship in a regular order.
He ruled over the Andhra *maṇḍala* area
with a name for law and justice.
He is the one who is praised among
the best of *mantris* of the best of kings,
who worked for the honor and good of Acyutadevaraya
He is Ramayabhaskara, brilliant as the mid-day sun.

We can see that a number of developments led to the growing importance of *karaṇams* in the affairs of the state. The increased use of Persian as a language of administration, and the presence of multiple languages in which smaller kings had to correspond with their political allies and neighbours, the availability of pen and paper, and the elaborate new accounting responsibilities made the position of scribes far more important in society than what it had been before. Now scribes were employed in jobs of higher status and power than simply serving as persons who could take down dictation or copy manuscripts. Reality is now what was written down, and not as earlier, what was uttered. We can see a corresponding change even in the popular mythology and Hindu iconography. The goddess of language and arts, Sarasvati was now endowed with a book in one of her hands, in addition to a vīṇa, the stringed musical instrument. Yama, the god of death, acquires an assistant Citragupta, who keeps accounts of living beings in separate files, and as in the poem that was quoted earlier, can even become more powerful than Yama himself.

The people who called themselves ministers (*mantris*) were not always ministers of a ruling king. *Mantri* was in a sense more an honorific caste title rather than a fixed position or office. Often these 'ministers' were themselves independent chiefs of a locality or even a village. However, in keeping with the convention that a king should be a warrior, the minister who has taken independent control of an area, also describes himself in military terms. But by the seventeenth century there was a significant shift in the values of peninsular Indian society. Greater importance was given to *dāna*, charity, rather than *vīra*, valour in battle. The possibility of acquiring wealth in the form of cash created conditions of upward mobility, that were different from those created by simple military conquest. The emergence of the left-hand caste Balijas as trader–warrior–kings as evidenced in the Nayaka period is a consequence of such conditions of new wealth. This produces a collapsing of two *varṇas*, Kshatriya and Vaishya, into one. Acquired wealth, rather than status by birth in a family now leads to an entirely new value system where money talks. The *Sumati shatakamu* records this change rather cynically:

> Never mind if he is born in a low caste,
> never mind if he is timid,
> never mind if he is son of a whore.
> If he has money, he is king.

The presence of cash also generates charity. Members of the nobility are now constantly advised to excel in charity. In keeping with the changes in the social values, *nīti* is no longer regarded as a matter that simply concerns kings and courtiers. It is for everyone, and in particular for anyone who desires status and social recognition. *Nīti* is now told in the form of stories rather than aphorisms and *shāstric* statements. Kuciraju Errana's *Sakala-nīti-kathā-nidhānam*, a book of stories that teaches *nīti*, indicates an early recognition of this change.[60] Errana adopts a number of stories from *Betala-pañca-vimshati* and other *kathā* sources, both from Sanskrit and from Telugu. The main thrust of the stories is to teach the individual wise and tactful ways of handling oneself, and thus maximizing one's chances for success.

One book that codifies the conduct of *karaṇams* is the *Sumati shatakamu*.[61] Written by an unknown author probably in the eighteenth century, this book is variously attributed to Baddena and to an even more

---

[60] Errayya, *Sakala-nīti-kathā-nidhānamu*, ed. T. Chandrasekharan (Madras: Government Oriental Manuscripts Library, 1951). The exact date of Errayya (or Errana) is not known and the suggestion by the editor Chandrasekharan that he belongs to late-fifteenth century seems to be too early.

[61] The text of the *Sumati shatakamu* has been printed many times with a number of variations, some of them indicating that the text itself changed with time, including a bowdlerized edition by Vavilla Ramasvami Shastrulu & Sons (Madras), and reprinted it many times. The edition we have used is dated 1962. But also see Macca Haridasu, *Tathyamu Sumati* (Hyderabad: Andhra Pradesh Sahitya Akademi, 1984). In the nineteenth century, C. P. Brown collated a number of verses from manuscripts and translated them, for which see C. P. Brown, *Sumati Shatakam*, ed. C. R. Sarma (Hyderabad: Andhra Pradesh Sahitya Akademi, 1973).

ancient Bhimana. Perhaps both authorships were ascribed by *karaṇams* to make the text serve two different purpose. Baddena's authorship serves the interests of the *karaṇams* in claiming political legitimacy among kings and other aspirants to rule an area, and the Bhimana authorship makes the text speak with a voice of the authority of an ancient, god-like poet to serve the interests of the same community when they desire legitimacy among the people in general. The *Sumati shatakamu* elevates the role of the minister (*karaṇamu*) and treats it is more crucial for the maintenance of the order of the kingdom than that of the king himself.

> A kingdom with a minister runs smoothly with its strategy intact.
> And a kingdom without a minister breaks down like a machine with a
> critical part missing.
> A king without a minister is like an elephant without a trunk.

It also gives practical wisdom for ordinary people such as the following:

> Don't live in a village where you don't have a moneylender, a doctor, and
> a river that does not dry up.

> If you don't spend the money you earn for your pleasures,
> part of it goes to the king and the other part is lost into the earth.
> That's very much like the honey that bees gather in the forest—
> part of it goes to people who collect honey and part of it falls to earth.

> The lord of the wealth Kubera is his friend, but Siva still begs for his living.
> What you have is your wealth, not what your friends or relatives have.

> Don't ever trust the tax-collector, the gambler,
> the goldsmith or the whore. Don't trust a merchant
> or a left-handed person, that is not good for you.

> Listen to everyone, but wait to think through what they say.
> Only one who accepts things after ascertaining truth or falsehood, is a
> wise man.

> A wise man is stronger than a man who is only physically strong.
> A slim rider controls an elephant big as a mountain.

> A snake has poison in its head.
> A scorpion has poison in its tail.
> An evil person has poison all over his body, head to toe.

Despite such practical advice, the *Sumati shatakamu* is at bottom a cynical (rather than simply an amoral) text, which believes women are not trustworthy, that kings never keep their word, and friends last only as long as you have money. In the hard world it depicts, you have to take care of yourself—no one else helps.

CONCLUSION

When the British government and its native employees wanted 'morals' to be taught in the early nineteenth century, the Telugu equivalent that their pundit informants could find was *nīti*. This was based on a rather curious misunderstanding: for even if there are some ethical teachings and moral statements in these texts, they are not exactly the kind of moral code that one would apply to all people. Vennelakanti Subbarao (1784–1839), translator for the *Sadr 'adālat* of the Madras Presidency, a Telugu Niyogi Brahmin who rose to the highest post a native could aspire to in the East India Company administration at the time, and who commanded competence in about half a dozen Indian languages in addition to English, was one of the more prominent of the Company's interlocutors already from an early time. When he was appointed member of the Madras School Book Society, he submitted a report in 1820 on the state of teaching in schools, in which he wrote that children in schools were taught neither adequate grammar nor morals. So they came out of their schools with no real ability in using the language and they were not trained to become upright members of their society either. Therefore, he recommended—addressing the need for teaching morals—that 'tales extracted from different books composed chiefly of morals written in modern languages' be prescribed for study.[62]

In this context, Ravipati Gurumurti Sastri also put the *Pañcatantra* stories into Telugu prose and taught them at the College of Fort St. George in Madras. This was soon followed by another translation of *Pañcatantra* by the very influential Paravastu Cinnaya Suri.[63] Now the *Pañcatantra* was not in fact a 'Book of Morals'; rather, it was statecraft taught by means of animal fables. When the first generation of colonial

---

[62] Vennelakanti Subbarao, *The Life of Vennelacunty Soobarow (Native of Ongole) As Written by Himself* (Madras: C. Foster, 1873), pp. 65–75.

[63] On Cinnaya Suri, see Velcheru Narayana Rao, 'Print and Prose: Pandits, *Karanams*, and the East India Company in the Making of Modern Telugu', in *India's Literary History: Essays on the Nineteenth Century*, eds Stuart Blackburn and Vasudha Dalmia (New Delhi: Permanent Black, 2004), pp. 146–66.

schoolboys needed a textbook, Puduri Sitarama Sastri, a pundit in Madras wrote a text called *Pĕdda Bāla Siksha* (The Big Book of Lessons for Children), which was published in 1847. This work contains a number of items such as basic arithmetic, the names of the weekdays, months, and years according to the traditional lunar calendar, and many items of conventional wisdom, a few stories, and aphorisms modelled after the statements from *nīti* texts, to teach '*nīti*' (now translated in an unproblematized way as 'morals') to school boys. To be sure, in every *nīti* text, there were occasional statements that looked like teachings of virtue, which were carefully selected and included in school textbooks. Verses from Bhartrahari, which were translated into Telugu by several poets during the medieval period, came in handy. Even the *Sumati shatakamu*, which, as we have seen, is actually a handbook for *karaṇams*, yielded some nice and acceptable moral statements.[64] Because of the simple language in which the *Sumati shatakamu* was written, it came to be particularly popular in school moral curricula. Soon enough, lines from these verses came to adorn classroom walls and copybooks. Thus, in the end, books on statecraft and worldly wisdom could serve as acceptable substitutes for the Ten Commandments.

Our central purpose in this essay has been to widen the rather narrow conception within which 'political thought' has hitherto been studied in an Indian context. We would only caricature very slightly if we were to say that the usual strategies espoused by analysts are two: either they assume that modern politics in India was a pure product of the interaction with colonialism and colonial modernity, or at best, they leap over the intervening centuries to classical India and its materials. In this context, we welcome the development of interest in recent times in the Indo-Persian corpus, and what it might tell us about both institutional arrangements and political thought at the time of the Sultanate and the Mughals. The problem does remain however of that part of India where Persian was not the principal language in which such thought was expressed. The example of the Maratha polity in the

---

[64] For instance, the following verse:
A good deed in return for another—
That's nothing special.
Doing good in return for harm—
Think about it: that's really good strategy.
This verse, actually stated as a form of political strategy, is now interpreted as an altruistic moral statement.

seventeenth and eighteenth centuries brings this home, even though the Marathi used by them was heavily inflected by Persian. It is clear from the researches of Hiroyuki Kotani and Narendra Wagle, however, that the eighteenth-century Maratha Deccan continued to witness a struggle between precisely the forces we have set out in this essay, that is between the proponents of *nīti* on the one hand (who no doubt drew on the Indo-Persian corpus as well) and those who remained fiercely attached to the highly *dharmashāstra*-oriented vision of social ordering and political functioning. The continued presence of terms such as *dosha* and *prāyascitta* in the vocabulary of the Maratha polity possibly testify to the waning influence of the *nīti* tradition in that system.[65]

A celebrated reflection on the 'history of concepts' written some thirty five years ago proposed to historians of Europe that they needed to go beyond their preoccupation with social (and political) history to look at both individual concepts, and groups of concepts, to clarify that which underlay the functioning of the political and social systems in the societies they studied. In that context, Reinhart Koselleck wrote:

> The relationship between the history of concepts (*Begriffsgeschichte*) and social history (*Sozialgeschichte*) appears at first sight to be very loose, or at least difficult to determine, because the first of these disciplines primarily uses texts and words whereas the latter only uses texts to deduce facts and movements which are not contained in the texts themselves. It is thus that social history analyses social movements and constitutional structures, the relations between groups, social strata and classes; beyond the complex of events, it tries to come to terms with medium or long-term structures and their changes (...). The methods of the history of concepts are very different.[66]

---

[65] Hiroyuki Kotani, '*Doṣa* (sin)-*Prāyascitta* (penance): The Predominating Ideology in the Later Medieval Deccan', in *Western India in Historical Transition: Seventeenth to Early Twentieth Centuries*, ed. Hiroyuki Kotani (New Delhi: Manohar, 2002); N. K. Wagle, 'The Government, the Jāti, and the Individual: Rights, Discipline and Control in the Pune Kotwal Papers, 1766–94', *Contributions to Indian Sociology*, N.S., 34 (2000), pp. 321–60. Cf. the earlier pioneering work of V.T. Gune, *The Judicial System of the Marathas* (Pune: Deccan College, 1953). Also of interest to this discussion is Sumit Guha, 'An Indian Penal Régime: Maharashtra in the Eighteenth Century', *Past and Present 147* (1995), pp. 101–126.

[66] '*Begriffsgeschichte und Sozialgeschichte*', *Kölner Zeitschrift für Soziologie* 16 (1972), translated in Reinhart Koselleck, *Le Futur Passé: Contribution à la sémantique des temps historiques*, trans. Jochen Hoock and Marie-Claire Hoock (Paris: Ecole des Hautes Etudes en Sciences Sociales, 1990), p. 99.

We would hardly wish to be so immodest as to claim to be introducing the history of concepts (*Begriffsgeschichte*) into the study of the Indian past. However, in this collaboration between a historian and analyst of literature, and a social and economic historian, we hope to have opened a window into a neglected, and yet highly significant, corpus.

We began this essay with two quotations, one by a scholar and editor of forgotten texts, lamenting the loss of importance suffered by the *nīti* tradition, the other by one of the most important political figures in twentieth-century India. B. R. Ambedkar was, we are aware, a keen student of the Indian past, and had even studied with R.P. Kangle, an authority on the *Arthashāstra*. The remark by him that we quote refers precisely to the tension between the *nīti*- and *dharma*-oriented traditions that have lain at the heart of this essay. He glossed these respectively as 'secular law' and 'ecclesiastical law', and there are many—especially among the growing number of 'anti-secularist' intellectuals in India—who would immediately object to these translations.[67] But perhaps Ambedkar was not so wrong after all in his use of the term 'secular' (however problematic the word 'ecclesiastical' might be). Not as cavalier in his disregard of the Indian past—or dismissive of history—as writers such as T. N. Madan and Ashis Nandy have usually been, it may well be that his view of a struggle between different conceptions of political and social arrangements in pre-colonial India might shed light on the deeper roots and more profound purchase that 'Indian secularism' has, than that of a mere transplant from distant climes. To explore that line of inquiry would take us, however, beyond the confines of this essay.

---

[67] Most notable amongst these are Ashis Nandy, 'An Anti-Secularist Manifesto', *Seminar* 314 (1985), pp. 14–24; T. N. Madan, 'Secularism in Its Place', *Journal of Asian Studies* 46 (1987), pp. 747–59. The debate is summed up in Rajeev Bhargava ed., *Secularism and Its Critics* (Delhi. Oxford University Press, 1998).

8

Becoming Turk the Rajput Way:

Conversion and Identity in an Indian Warrior Narrative

Cynthia Talbot[*]

———— • ✦ • ————

Introduction

In 1974, John F. Richards noted, 'Muslim expansion into South Asia is one of the most important and prolonged instances of cultural encounter to be found in world history'.[1] Considerably more is known today about the processes of Muslim expansion in the subcontinent than when these words were written, over thirty years ago. However, much of the scholarship on the spread of Islam is from the vantage point of Muslim courts and the Persian literature they produced; alternatively, it examines the process of Islamization only on a large scale. In this essay I adopt a different approach, one that is microhistorical. Relying primarily on a single text, I explore how an Indian Muslim gentry community represented their past and articulated their present identity. The text is the *Kyamkhan Rasa* (henceforth KKR), composed between

[*] I am indebted to Rupert Snell for explicating several difficult verses in Braj Bhasa, and to the anonymous reviewer of *Modern Asian Studies* for his/her thoughtful critique. I am also grateful for the comments made by participants at the conference on 'Expanding Frontiers in South Asian and World History' held at Duke University in September 2006 and by my Austin colleagues, Susan Deans-Smith and Julie Hardwick.

[1] John F. Richards, 'The Islamic Frontier in the East: Expansion into South Asia,' *South Asia* 4 (1974), p. 91.

c. 1630 and 1655 at Fatehpur, a town in the Shekhavati region of northern Rajasthan.[2] Its author Nyamat Khan used the pseudonym Jan Kavi in writing this poem in Braj Bhasa, the literary language of Hindi, that covers the history of his lineage, the Kyamkhanis, so named after the ancestor who is supposed to have converted to Islam in the fourteenth century.[3]

By the late sixteenth century, the Kyamkhanis were a well-established community with two main branches. The senior branch was entrenched in the town of Fatehpur (in modern Sikar district, Rajasthan), founded c. 1450 by Fateh Khan, the senior grandson of Kyam Khan, the founder of the clan.[4] A junior branch had been established in the nearby town of Jhunjhunu (in modern Jhunjhunu district) by Kyam Khan's second son.[5] Other relatives were settled in various places in the vicinity.[6] The community presumably also included the descendants of Kyam Khan's brothers, two of whom are also said to have become Muslims.[7] Although there were frictions within the group at times, the KKR portrays the Kyamkhanis as generally cooperating with each other, especially when faced with an outside threat.

The Kyamkhanis were important enough in their corner of the Mughal empire to have their presence noted in *Ain-i Akbari*, the official report compiled by Abu'l Fazl in the 1590s. In his statistical survey of the territories under imperial control, Abu'l Fazl sometimes provided figures that related to military matters, along with information on revenue and the like. He listed the Kyamkhanis as the main gentry community of Fatehpur and Jhunjhunu, and one of three communities in Nahar (modern Jhunjhunu district, to the north-east of Jhunjhunu city). We also learn that Fatehpur and Nahar both had 500 horsemen and 2,000 foot soldiers apiece, whereas Jhunjhunu had 2,000 cavalry and 3,000 infantry; all three towns had stone forts.[8] These numbers

---

[2] Jan (Kavi), in Dasaratha Sharma, Agarcand Nahata and Bhamvarlal Nahata eds, Hindi trans. Ratanlal Misra, *Kyamkhan Rasa*, 3rd ed. (Jodhpur: Rajasthan Pracya Vidya Pratishthan, 1996).

[3] In KKR, Jan Kavi states that his father was Alaf Khan, but does not give his own name; it is provided in another of his poems, however. He was the second of five sons (Dasaratha Sharma, 'Kyamkhan Rasa ke Kartta Kavivar Jan aur Unke Granth,' in *Kyamkhan Rasa*, by Jan Kavi, pp. 2–3).

[4] KKR, vv. 377–81.

[5] Dasaratha Sharma, 'Kyamkhan Rasa ke Kartta,' p. 45.

[6] KKR, vv. 317, 328–29.

[7] KKR, v. 121.

[8] Abu al Fazl ibn Mubarak, *Ain i Akbari*, trans. H. Blochmann and H. S. Jarrett (Osnabruck. Biblio Verlag, 1983), Vol. 2, pp. 194 & 277.

represent the militia troops under Kyamkhani command, demonstrating that they were a formidable power at the locality level.[9] Their military strength was a reflection of their dominant position as controllers of land and its income in this small section of northern Rajasthan.

The family history of the Kyamkhanis provides us with an unusual glimpse into the self-conceptions and memories of an Indian Muslim warrior group who were moderately successful, a strata of early modern South Asian society that we seldom have the opportunity to study first-hand. I begin my analysis by looking at two narratives that tell the story of how their forefather became a Turk—that is, a Muslim—and then proceed to consider the significance of political allegiance and patron-client ties in motivating conversion to Islam in the pre-Mughal era. I also explore the seventeenth-century political and literary contexts which the author of KKR inhabited and the reasons for his choice of Braj Bhasa as the medium of poetic expression. The final section of the essay explores the numerous Rajput aspects of Kyamkhani identity and rhetoric in the KKR, focusing on their genealogy and alleged heroic actions. By revealing that Indian Muslims could be strongly embedded in their regional societies and cultures even while participating in the cosmopolitan world of the Mughal empire, this seventeenth-century text suggests that local affiliations were by no means eradicated or weakened by an allegiance to Islam, with its more global reach. By foregrounding other aspects of Kyamkhani identity more forcefully, it also reminds us that religion is but one of many attributes that comprise a sense of self.

HOW KARAMCAND BECAME A TURK: NARRATIVES OF CONVERSION

The change in faith and fortunes resulting from Kyam Khan's conversion was perceived as sufficiently significant that his descendants adopted his name and thereby created a new social identity for themselves. I, therefore, begin my analysis with a summary of the KKR's account of this momentous event.

---

[9] Jos J. L. Gommans, *Mughal Warfare: Indian Frontiers and High Roads to Empire, 1500–1700* (London & NY: Routledge, 2002), p. 74. For more on the significance of these statistics, see Sumit Guha, 'The Politics of Identity and Enumeration in India, c. 1600–1990,' *Comparative Studies in Society and History* 45 (2003), pp. 151–52.

One day the young Karamcand goes hunting in the forest with a large group of people. Engrossed in their search of animals, the others wander far off. The tired young boy sits down under the shade of a tree and promptly falls asleep. Meanwhile, the sultan of Delhi, Firuz Shah [Tughluq] is also hunting in that forest and comes upon the young boy sleeping. It is an astonishing sight—Karamcand is enveloped in a cool, deep shade, even though it is high noon and no other trees around cast any shadow. The Delhi sultan—usually called *patsah* or emperor in this text—summons his companion Saiyid Nasir, who agrees that the boy must be a great being. But when they awaken the boy, they are perplexed to discover that he is a Hindu. Since Hindus have no miraculous powers (*karamat*), how had the boy obtained such a boon? The Saiyid surmises that he would adopt the path of the Turk (i.e., become a Muslim) in the end.

Firuz Shah renames the boy Kyam Khan and takes him back to Hisar. When Karamcand's father arrives in Hisar, informed by messenger of his missing son's whereabouts, the sultan insists on keeping the boy. 'Don't worry about him becoming a Turk', the sultan reassures Karamcand's father, 'I'll treat him like a son'. After receiving gifts from Firuz Shah, the father returns home.

The young Kyam Khan is entrusted to the care of Saiyid Nasir and, after many days of instruction, completes his studies. The Saiyid tells Kyam Khan he should now get circumcised, say the prayers (*namaz*) and embrace the Islamic faith (*din*). Kyam Khan hesitates, however, for his mind is troubled. His heart longs for the faith, he says, but he is worried that no one would subsequently trust (*sak*) him and his family—in other words, that their reputation or good name would be ruined. Kyam Khan's anxiety about his social standing after conversion concerned mainly the marriage alliances, for Saiyid Nasir promptly predicts that great kings of the future—including a Rathor Rajput king of Mandor and Bahlul Lodi, a Delhi sultan—will marry their daughters into his lineage. With his fear of being shunned by others alleviated, Kyam Khan takes the plunge and becomes a 'pure, orthodox Musalman'.

Saiyid Nasir then takes Kyam Khan to Delhi, the capital city, and presents him to the sultan, who is mightily pleased. Some time later, Saiyid Nasir is taken ill and asks the sultan to regard Kyam Khan, more capable than his true sons, as his successor. Upon Saiyid's death, Kyam Khan receives his lands and goods and becomes a trusted noble at the Delhi court.[10]

---

[10] The story of how Karamcand became a Turk is narrated in KKR, vv. 122–62.

Several aspects of this description of Kyam Khan's conversion to Islam are noteworthy. The process begins with a miracle, a supernatural act that brings Karamcand to the attention of the Delhi sultan. Karamcand is no ordinary person, or he would not have possessed *karamat*, a word that can be translated not only as miraculous power but also as signs of nobility.[11] Both his future greatness and adoption of Islam are represented as predestined to happen, in other words. The initial stage of Karamcand's metamorphosis to a different persona is signified by the new name the sultan bestows on him, a name that is Turco-Mongol rather than Indic in origin. Kyam Khan is now nominally a Turk but he is not yet a Muslim. He must be educated first, presumably in the tenets of Islam, and he must also be circumcised. Unlike names, which had no legal standing and could thus potentially be altered frequently, circumcision was an irreversible sign of Muslim identity. It was a way of literally inscribing difference on the male body in a South Asian world where most men were not circumcised. Social markers of his new affiliation were not enough, however, for Kyam Khan also had to publicly profess the Islamic religion by reciting prayers. With that, Kyam Khan's transformation was complete, and he could be presented at the sultan's court in Delhi.

A second version of how Kyam Khan became involved with the Delhi court is provided by Mumhato Nainsi, the celebrated chronicler from western Rajasthan.[12] Nainsi, who long served the Rathor rulers of Jodhpur, included many genealogies and tales relating to the major warrior families of the region in his *Khyat*, compiled between 1637 and 1666.[13] Nainsi's account says nothing explicitly about Kyam Khan's conversion to Islam. Instead, he reports that Saiyid Nasir was a military governor of the Hisar region who, one day, raided the town of Daraira. In the aftermath of his attack, two baby boys were found abandoned, one a Cauhan and the other a Jat.[14] Given to Saiyid Nasir as an offering (*nazar*), the boys were first raised by his elephant driver, then by his

---

[11] Chase F. Robinson, *Islamic Historiography* (Cambridge: Cambridge University Press, 2003), p. 150.

[12] Mumhata Nainsi, in Badriprasad Sakariya ed., *Mumhata Nainsi ri Khyat,* Vol. 3 (Jodhpur: Rajasthan Pracya Vidya Pratisthan, 1993), pp. 273–74.

[13] Richard D. Saran and Norman P. Ziegler, *The Mertiyo Rathors of Merto, Rajasthan: Select Translations Bearing on the History of a Rajput Family, 1462–1660* (Ann Arbor: University of Michigan Centers for South and Southeast Asian Studies, 2001), Vol. 1, pp. 10–11.

[14] The Cauhans and Jats are both major landholding communities in the Haryana region. Cauhans, as members of the broader Rajput category, are typically ranked higher in social status than Jats.

wife, and finally by a Sufi teacher. Upon Saiyid Nasir's death, the now grown-up boys went to see the ruler of Delhi, Bahlul Lodi, who decided that the Cauhan was more capable than any of Saiyid Nasir's sons. The Cauhan was named Kyam Khan and inherited Saiyid Nasir's position at the court (mansab). After serving for some time as the military governor of Hisar, Kyam Khan decided it would be good to have a home base (thikana) of his own and he, therefore, founded the towns of Jhunjhunu and Fatehpur (in northern Rajasthan).

Although the two narratives correspond in a number of particulars, Nainsi is considerably less complimentary. Both texts identify Kyam Khan as a Cauhan from a place with a similar name (Dadreva/Daraira), whose political mentor was a man called Saiyid Nasir of Hisar (in Haryana, about 100 miles north-east of Fatehpur), a town created by Firuz Shah Tughluq. Because the Delhi sultan found Kyam Khan more capable than the actual sons, Kyam Khan eventually inherited Saiyid Nasir's position. Kyam Khan is, hence, similarly characterized as a talented young man whose merits were recognized by the Delhi political elite. But Nainsi imputes more dubious social origins to Kyam Khan, an orphan who would never have risen to prominence without the intervention of Saiyid Nasir. Nainsi's insinuation that Kyam Khan was an upstart is strengthened by two couplets (doha) appended to the prose narrative, which may have been drawn from a common pool of verses that circulated among Rajasthani bards. According to Nainsi's verses, Kyam Khan, who was first a Hindu and then became a Turk, lost stature as a consequence. He and his descendants were inferior, having been dependants (or slaves) of Saiyid Nasir from the outset.[15]

The conflicting assessments of Kyam Khan's background found in KKR and Khyat, two chronicles compiled in almost exactly the same time period, reflect the different vantage points of their authors. Nyamat Khan, writing under the pseudonym Jan Kavi, was a member of the senior Kyamkhani lineage and thus had a vested interest in both portraying Kyam Khan as coming from a long-established noble lineage

---

[15] This is a loose translation, based on the Hindi rendition provided by Sakariya, *Khyat*, Vol. 3, p. 275. The word I gloss as dependant is *bandi*, which can mean prisoner or slave; it may also here be a variant of *banda* (slave, servant, dependant). Another label applied to Kyam Khan in the *Khyat* verses is *gola*, a term that implies a condition of servitude, as well as inferiority (Ramya Sreenivasan, 'Drudges, Dancing Girls, Concubines: Female Slaves in Rajput Polity, 1500–1850,' in *Slavery & South Asian History*, eds Indrani Chatterjee and Richard M. Eaton (Bloomington & Indianapolis: Indiana University Press, 2006), p. 144.

and in identifying his political patron as the Delhi sultan himself, rather than a mere governor. Nainsi was a Jain in the service of the Rajput ruler of Jodhpur, in western Rajasthan; both he and his father held the highest administrative post in the Jodhpur kingdom.[16] Nainsi's perspective is that of an outsider, whose allegiance was to a more powerful dynasty that sometimes came into conflict with the Kyamkhanis. The Kyamkhanis clearly were of some consequence in the region or their history would not have been included among the numerous narratives of ruling lineages in Nainsi's *Khyat*, which focused especially on western Rajasthan.[17] Given the incessant jockeying for position among warrior groups and the growing emphasis on aristocratic background in seventeenth-century Rajput culture, it is not surprising that Nainsi might denigrate the origins of a rival, if less powerful, family.[18] Although a lofty pedigree had always been an asset, it became increasingly important for Rajput lineages once they became incorporated into the Mughal empire, partly due to Mughal interest in their own ancestry but also because genealogy was a factor in the competing claims of the various branches of larger Rajput lineages and clans to political leadership under the Mughals.

The production of historical narratives like the KKR and *Khyat* in Rajasthan occurred in this context of growing insistence on noble descent and competition among rival groups in service to the Mughal empire. Although the writing of genealogies, martial tales and the like had been going on for some centuries, the seventeenth century witnessed an outpouring of historiographic literature.[19] Not only did the accounts of a single lineage or dynasty, such as the KKR, increase in number, but new genres of historical writing also emerged. One such genre was the *khyat*, a compilation of prose narratives and poems detailing the ancestry and accomplishments of one or more warrior lineages, of which Nainsi's text is the oldest surviving example.[20] The illustrious past of a particular group could be demonstrated in a chronicle or dynastic history, both in

---

[16] For biographical details on Nainsi, see Saran and Ziegler, *Mertiyo Rathors*, Vol. 1, pp. 15–24.

[17] Saran and Ziegler, *Mertiyo Rathors*, Vol. 1, p. 11.

[18] Dirk H. A. Kolff, *Naukar, Rajput and Sepoy: The Ethnohistory of the Military Labour Market in Hindustan, 1450–1850* (Cambridge: Cambridge University Press, 1990), pp. 72–74.

[19] For a discussion of some of the historical texts, both literary and visual, produced at the seventeenth-century Mewar court, see Cynthia Talbot, 'The Mewar Court's Construction of History,' in *The Kingdom of the Sun: Indian Court and Village Art from the Princely State of Mewar*, ed. Joanna Williams (San Francisco: Asian Art Museum, 2007), pp. 12–33.

[20] Norman P. Ziegler, 'Marvari Historical Chronicles: Sources for the Social and Cultural History of Rajasthan,' *Indian Economic and Social History Review* 13 (1976), pp. 231–33.

terms of its bloodline and its actions. That is, a lineage could assert the antiquity and seniority of its descent and also the exemplary conduct of its members by this means. Whereas the Mughal model of a flourishing historiographic milieu surely acted as a stimulus, Norman P. Ziegler has pointed out that the rise of historical writing in Rajasthan also resulted from the desire to establish the order of ranking between and among different warrior groups, in response to the new circumstances created by Mughal dominance. Consciousness of ranking, and the rivalry over it, were accentuated by the formality of the Mughal imperial system, in which the status of officers was hierarchically graded and enacted publicly at court.[21]

The considerable effort that Jan Kavi expends on providing a lengthy and exalted genealogy for his family in the KKR suggests that Nainsi might not have been alone in disdaining their ancestry. I will discuss the Kyamkhani genealogy at greater length in another part of this essay, but the salient point for the moment is that it forestalls any allegation of humble origins in respect to Kyam Khan. A long section of Kyam Khan's biography in the KKR can also be interpreted as a defence against the charge that he was a slave or dependant. Almost sixty verses are devoted to the conflict between Kyam Khan and an important figure at the Delhi court, Mallu Khan (also known as Iqbal Khan), a former slave/servant.[22] According to a recent history of the Delhi sultanate, Mallu Khan became influential in the 1390s, first as the power behind the Delhi throne and later in his own right. He had managed to achieve pre-eminence over his rivals only weeks before the Central Asian king Timur sacked Delhi in 1398 and continued to be a major contender for power after Timur's departure from India. Mallu died in battle in 1405, fighting against the forces of Khizr Khan (Khidar Khan in Braj Bhasa), who in 1414 would establish the Sayyid dynasty of the Delhi sultanate.[23]

In the KKR, Kyam Khan rails against Mallu Khan's assumption of power on the grounds that a slave (*cera*) should never sit on the imperial throne. Intelligence (*buddhi*) varied according to heredity (literally, clan), he says, and no amount of effort could improve the baseborn (*kul-hin*). Moreover, no one could gain lustre through service

---

[21] Ziegler, 'Marvari Historical Chronicles,' pp. 233–35, 240–44.

[22] KKR vv. 184–242.

[23] Peter Jackson, *The Delhi Sultanate: A Political and Military History* (Cambridge: Cambridge University Press, 1999), pp. 306–13, 318–21.

(*cakar*) to a slave.[24] The ministers then offer the throne to Kyam Khan, since seven of his ancestors had previously been emperors of Delhi (alluding to Prithviraj Cauhan and others of the royal lineage based in Sambhar-Ajmer during the eleventh and twelfth centuries). But Kyam Khan declines, citing the fleeting nature of power and the sorrow that inevitably ensued from its loss. Jan Kavi thus seized the opportunity, when covering these events, to reiterate that the Kyamkhanis were of aristocratic stock in contrast to Mallu Khan's lowly origins. The poem's vehemence in denouncing slaves as unworthy of high political position appears somewhat excessive, since many of the most influential posts in the sultanate army were occupied by slaves and ex-slaves. Jan Kavi was writing during the Mughal period, when the employment of slaves in military service was no longer customary or approved; nonetheless, he seems unduly incensed over this issue unless we take into account Nainsi's accusation that Kyam Khan was not a free political agent but rather indebted or enslaved to Saiyid Nasir.[25]

We have seen that the biographies of Kyam Khan presented in Jan Kavi's KKR, a poem in Braj Bhasa, and in Nainsi's *Khyat*, a work of prose composed in Middle Marwari, are broadly in agreement regarding his political career. Whereas they differ considerably on the question of Kyam Khan's social origins, both authors share in common a belief that family background and free/unfree status were major factors in shaping the quality of an individual. Much less concern for heredity is displayed by a third chronicler from the seventeenth century, who similarly covers events set in the fourteenth century. The *Mirat-i Sikandari*, a Persian history of the Gujarat region written in 1611, describes Saharan, the father of Zafar Khan and Shams Khan, who were the founders of the Gujarat sultanate and the smaller principality of Nagaur in Rajasthan, respectively.[26] Saharan was clearly no more than a well-off villager at

---

[24] KKR vv. 187–8, 192–3.

[25] There was a range of unfree statuses in medieval India, making it difficult to translate words like *banda* or *cera*; nor were the boundaries between free and unfree status entirely clear. Richard M. Eaton has advanced the following definition of slavery: 'the condition of uprooted outsiders, impoverished insiders—or descendants of either—serving persons or institutions on which they are wholly dependent' ('Introduction,' in *Slavery & South Asian History*, eds Indrani Chatterjee and Richard M. Eaton [Bloomington & Indianapolis: Indiana University Press, 2006], p. 2). An important feature of slavery was an individual's alienation from his/her natal family, a situation that was true for Kyam Khan in both KKR and *Khyat*.

[26] The following summary is based on the English translation by Edward Clive Bayley (*The Local Muhammadan Dynasties: Gujarat* [London: W. H. Allen and Co., 1886], 67–72) and a Hindi

best, coming from a community described as degraded *ksatriyas* whose ancestor had been outcasted due to his use of alcohol. Although the author Sikandar bin Muhammad denies that Saharan was himself a brewer of alcohol, an occupation regarded as extremely base, he does so in a perfunctory manner. Instead, he ends his discussion of Zafar Khan and Shams Khan by stating, 'Whatever they were, they were men of high and noble spirit, whose charities and deeds of kindness to the people of God were beyond number.'[27] Perhaps because of the Islamic view that lordship was determined by God's will rather than being an attribute of certain bloodlines, Sikandar clearly does not regard birth as important as a person's character and actions. Jan Kavi's emphasis on aristocratic genealogy is thus more in line with other histories from Rajasthan composed in Indic languages than it is with a Persian chronicle such as the *Mirat-i Sikandari*.

THE SULTAN AND CONVERSION IN THE PRE-MUGHAL ERA

The figure of the Delhi sultan appears in both versions of Kyam Khan's conversion: although Nainsi identifies the ruler as Bahlul Lodi (r. 1451–89), Jan Kavi asserts it was Firuz Shah Tughluq (r. 1351–88). Scholars have uniformly accepted the KKR's chronology for Kyam Khan, placing his conversion in Firuz Shah Tughluq's reign rather than following Nainsi's time frame. The main reason for this consensus is the references to a Qawam Khan in Yahya ibn Ahmad Sirhindi's *Tarikh-i Mubarak Shahi*.[28] This Indo-Persian chronicle completed in 1434 states that Qawam Khan was executed in 1419 for conspiring to overthrow Khizr Khan, the vanquisher of Mallu Khan and future founder of the Sayyid dynasty of Delhi sultans.[29] We are not given any information about Qawam Khan's early life; he first appears in the text in 1407, at which time he was commander of Hisar district, a locality Kyam

---

translation (Iskandar ibn Muhammad Manju, *Mirate Sikandari* [Jaipur: Sabd Mahima Prakasan, 2002], pp. 1–6).

[27] Bayley, *Local Muhammadan Dynasties*, p. 72.

[28] References to Qawam Khan appear in *Tarikh-i Mubarakshahi*, trans. K. K. Basu (Baroda: Oriental Institute, 1932), pp. 182, 183, 186, 195.

[29] The date of the text is given in Peter Hardy, *Historians of Medieval India. Studies in Indo-Muslim Historical Writing*, 2nd ed. (New Delhi: Munshiram Manoharlal, 1997), p. 56.

Khan is associated with in both KKR and *Khyat*.[30] The identification of Qawam Khan with Kyam Khan is lent credence by the large number of verses KKR devotes to events of the 1390s and early 1400s, as well as its allusion to Khizr Khan's suspicions of Kyam Khan.[31] As during the period of Mallu Khan's ascendance, Kyam Khan is described in KKR as a strong, independent player who maintains his position at Hisar against the demands of Khizr Khan. Although the two are close for some time, Khizr Khan eventually comes to distrust Kyam Khan. One day Khizr Khan suddenly shoves him into a river, but Kyam Khan does not retaliate, believing that fighting with an emperor was a breach of righteous conduct (*dharm ki hani*). This ends the text's treatment of Kyam Khan's life, with the exact manner of his death left unexplained.

Whether Kyam Khan actually was converted at the instigation of Firuz Shah Tughluq is unclear, however. Even if we accept that the Qawam Khan of *Tarikh-i Mubarak Shahi* was indeed Kyam Khan, the events covered in the Persian chronicle occurred several decades after Firuz Shah's death. KKR's chronology seems doubtful, moreover, as it states that Kyam Khan died when he was 95, an impossibly old age for a man described as actively engaged in politics and warfare up to the time of his death. What little is said about Firuz Shah's reign in KKR also appears to be inaccurate. The most likely scenario is that Kyam Khan rose to a position of some power during the turbulent decades after Firuz Shah Tughluq died, when the Delhi sultanate rapidly declined due to internal strife and external attack. If so, Firuz Shah may have been introduced into the KKR primarily because he could symbolically validate the political authority assumed by Kyam Khan.

Firuz Shah Tughluq was a logical choice for Kyamkhani historical memory to associate with their forefather, since he was the last legitimate ruler of the Delhi regime when it still held sway over much of North India. He was also well known to have encouraged conversion by offering 'presents and honors' to those who embraced Islam.[32] It was at the

---

[30] Approximately 120 verses of the KKR cover the period from Firuz Shah Tughluq's death to Kyam Khan's death, out of a total of 1,045 verses. Alternatively, Jan Kavi may have been familiar with Indo-Persian historical literature and/or traditions and fleshed out this portion of his text with their help, although the considerable divergence in particulars makes this scenario less plausible.

[31] KKR vv. 242–303; cf. Jackson, *Delhi Sultanate*, pp. 321–22.

[32] See the extract from *Futuhat-i Firuz Shahi*, a text intended to be made public as an inscription, in H. M. Elliot, in John Dowson (ed.), *The History of India as Told by Its Own Historians*, (Delhi: Low Price Publications, 1996), Vol. 3, p. 386.

instigation of Firuz Shah, for instance, that the leader of the Khanazada ruling lineage of Mewat is said to have converted.[33] Additionally, there are several examples of recent converts or their offspring who rose to high office at court while Firuz Shah was sultan. The pre-eminent position of vizier (*wazir*), for instance, was occupied by a brahmin convert from Telangana, formerly known as Kannu. He changed his religious allegiance along with his political loyalty, after the downfall of the Kakatiyas at the hands of Delhi's armies, and received his new name Maqbul from Firuz Shah's predecessor as sultan, Muhammad Tughluq.[34] Zafar Khan and Shams Khan, whose history was told in the previously mentioned *Mirat-i Sikandari*, were the sons of a Hindu convert who had attached himself to the young Firuz Shah. Once Firuz Shah ascended the throne, he promoted Zafar Khan and Shams Khan to the trusted post of cupbearer (*sharabdari*). Zafar Khan was later appointed as governor of Gujarat and eventually founded the sultanate of Gujarat, which lasted until 1573, whereas his younger brother, Shams Khan, established the smaller kingdom of Nagaur (fl. 1405–1536) in Rajasthan.[35]

The patronage of Firuz Shah Tughluq had, in fact, elevated a number of young men to positions of authority, just as he was said to have done in KKR where Kyam Khan's encounter with the Delhi sultan radically altered the course of his life. Even in Nainsi's narrative, in which the governor Saiyid Nasir plays a major role, it is the sultan who gives Kyam Khan his new name and position—that is, his new identity. We cannot take these accounts at face value, of course, for more than two centuries had lapsed since the events that they ostensibly recorded. Yet it is significant that the pasts of certain Indo-Muslim elites—lineages that wielded military and political power—should be remembered as commencing with, or at least transformed by, their contact with royal authority. As described in KKR, Kyam Khan's conversion was motivated not by any conviction in Islam's superiority as a faith but by a political allegiance to a Muslim ruler. In return for the honour of Firuz Shah's favour, Kyam Khan demonstrated his commitment by adopting his patron's religion.

---

[33] Shail Mayaram, *Against History, Against State: Counterperspectives from the Margins* (NY: Columbia University Press, 2003), p. 23.

[34] For more on Maqbul's career, see R. C. Jauhri, *Medieval India in Transition—Tarikh-i-Firuz Shahi, a First Hand Account* (New Delhi: Sundeep Prakashan, 2001), pp. 221–34.

[35] For the political history of Shams Khan of Nagaur and his descendants, see Saran and Ziegler, *Mertiyo Rathors*, Vol. 2, pp. 439–42.

Indeed, on a couple of occasions Jan Kavi implies that the main difference between Turks and Hindus is the former's greater reliability as political allies. It is surprising, given its lengthy treatment of Karamcand's transformation into Kyam Khan, that the KKR has so little to say about the binary sets of identities—Hindu/Muslim and Hindu/Turk—that it has laid out. The word 'Muslim' (in its Persian variant, Musalman) appears only twice in the entire text, 'Turk' six times, and 'Hindu' eight times in all.[36] For the most part, Jan Kavi ignores religious faith and affiliation, choosing to instead emphasize the warrior identity of the Kyamkhanis. In this context of warriors supporting the military and political agenda of Muslim rulers, however, we do find a couple of pejorative references to Hindus. The Kyamkhanis, for instance, are said to have ignored Bahlul Lodi until he complained about their leader, saying, 'is he a Hindu that he doesn't come to meet me?' This impelled the Kyamkhani chief Fateh Khan to join Bahlul Lodi in his expedition against the fortress of Ranthambhor in eastern Rajasthan. Some generations later, Jan Kavi informs us that the Mughal emperor Akbar gave Kyamkhani Fadan Khan supervisory responsibilities over some local chiefs whom he didn't trust because 'Hindus tend to go astray (in their allegiance).'[37]

That Islam was appealing because it was the religion of the politically dominant has long been recognized as an important factor in its expansion. Richard M. Eaton describes this as the 'Religion of Patronage' thesis, which asserts that 'Indians of the premodern period converted to Islam in order to receive some non-religious favor from the ruling class—relief from taxes, promotion in the bureaucracy, and so forth'.[38] Aside from the economic benefits, opportunities for social mobility are also thought to have encouraged conversion to Islam in environments where power was in the hands of Muslims.[39] Because entry into the circles of imperial power was difficult for non-Muslims during the thirteenth and fourteenth centuries, conversion could potentially open up avenues for political advancement for those who were dependent in

---

[36] Musalman appears in vv. 14 & 153; Turk (*turak*) in vv. 120, 122, 131, 140, 816, 859; and Hindu in vv. 14, 121, 130, 385, 429, 511, 640, 818.

[37] KKR vv. 385, 640. See also v. 816.

[38] Richard M. Eaton, *The Rise of Islam and the Bengal Frontier, 1204–1760* (Berkeley: University of California Press, 1993), p. 116.

[39] Marshall G. S. Hodgson, *The Venture of Islam, Vol. 2: The Expansion of Islam in the Middle Periods* (Chicago: University of Chicago Press, 1974), p. 538.

some fashion on a Muslim lord. Many of those who became Muslims in the sultanate era were of humble backgrounds, because the Delhi rulers routinely sought to amass followers who did not have conflicting allegiances to other lords. Large numbers of slaves who then became Muslims were purchased by the sultans—the chronicler Shams Siraj Afif reports, for instance, that Firuz Shah Tughluq had 180,000 slaves, more than any other Delhi sultan before him.[40] 'Social menials', as Sunil Kumar calls individuals from low-status groups, similarly lacked ties to the nobility and were recruited as royal servants or clients,[41] typically converting in the process. There may have been an element of coercion involved in becoming a Muslim in such instances, but Islam was also attractive in this setting due to its social and political ramifications.

However, the Kyamkhani example reminds us that converting may not always have had positive social consequences. We cannot, of course, be sure when Kyam Khan became a Muslim—the process of conversion is often more informal and drawn out than described by the KKR, sometimes taking place gradually over centuries.[42] In the retrospective understanding of Jan Kavi, Kyam Khan's conversion is presented as a necessary prerequisite to his induction into the sultanate military service; as it enabled him to prove himself as a warrior, becoming Muslim can be interpreted as a political asset. If not in the Delhi sultanate period, then at least during the Mughal era when Jan Kavi was writing, conversion clearly also involved a certain amount of social dislocation. The anxiety over the reaction of his social peers that Jan attributes to Kyam Khan is a telling indication that changing one's religion could lead to social rejection. Only after Saiyid Nasir's prophetic vision assures him that great kings would give their daughters to his family in the future does Kyam Khan finally profess the Islamic faith, in the KKR. By itself, the conversion did not, it would seem, elevate the social status of the Kyamkhanis.

Whatever other motivations may have led warriors and their families to adopt Islam in medieval India, we should recognize that conversion

[40] Jauhri, *Tarikh-i-Firoz Shahi*, pp. 158–59.

[41] 'Service, Status, and Military Slavery in the Delhi Sultanate: Thirteenth and Fourteenth Centuries,' in *Slavery & South Asian History*, eds Indrani Chatterjee and Richard M. Eaton (Bloomington & Indianapolis: Indiana University Press, 2006), pp. 97–102; see also Iqtidar Husain Siddiqui, 'Social Mobility in the Delhi Sultanate,' in *Medieval India 1*, ed. Irfan Habib (Delhi: Oxford University Press, 1999), pp. 27–28, 37–42.

[42] For recent scholarship on conversion as an often ambiguous and protracted process, see Rowena Robinson and Sathianathan Clarke eds, *Religious Conversion in India* (Delhi: Oxford University Press, 2003).

could also have a strong political resonance. For the Kyamkhanis, their forefather's 'becoming a Turk' signified his worthiness as a warrior as well as his loyalty to a political patron. Thus historical chronicles like KKR and *Mirat-i Sikandari*, which concern themselves primarily with warrior elites, present quite a different insight into the process of Islamic expansion than does the Sufi literature. Numerous hagiographies recount the fourteenth-century migrations of Sufi leaders to areas along the trade routes radiating from Delhi to the east and south.[43] Muslim settlers often accompanied these Sufis as they established themselves in new areas, forming small communities of faith in overwhelmingly non-Muslim environments. According to this immigration or transplantation model, the cultural frontier of Islam was extended through the colonization of the hinterland by urban residents who were already Muslim. Although modern scholarship often credits Sufi teachers for the propagation of Islam in the subcontinent, KKR reveals another means by which Islam gradually spread into the countryside, as rural warrior households were recruited or lured by the Indo-Muslim political elite entrenched in cities and induced to become Muslims.

Despite Kyam Khan's transformation into a Muslim subordinate of the Delhi sultanate, the KKR describes him as residing outside the capital throughout most of his career. Only for a short while does he stay in Delhi, looking after affairs for the sultan who is away pursuing a military campaign. Firuz Shah Tughluq dies soon thereafter and is succeeded in rapid succession by two other members of his dynasty. Once the former slave Mallu Khan becomes dominant, however, Kyam Khan retreats to Hisar where he remains based until his death; in the next generation his descendants make the permanent move from Hisar, in Haryana, to the Shekhavati area of northern Rajasthan. Settled at some distance from the main centres of Islamic power and culture, the Kyamkhanis maintain contact with Delhi but also establish links with neighbouring warrior groups.

The simultaneous participation of the Kyamkhanis in both the world of the metropole and that of the hinterland can be best illustrated by the marriage alliances mentioned in the KKR. The first offer of marriage comes from Raja Jodha (r. 1453–89), the Rathor Rajput ruler of Mandor

---

[43] Simon Digby, 'Before Timur Came: Provincialization of the Delhi Sultanate through the Fourteenth Century,' *Journal of the Economic and Social History of the Orient* 47 (2004), pp. 302–25.

and Jodhpur, in fulfilment of Saiyid Nasir's prophesy to Kyam Khan immediately before his conversion. However, Fateh Khan, chief of the senior Kyamkhani lineage at this time, cannot forgive Jodha's family for previously attacking Fatehpur and, therefore, refuses. Instead, Shams Khan of the junior Kyamkhani lineage based at Jhunjhunu accepts Raja Jodha's daughter. Soon afterward, the Delhi sultan Bahlul Lodi (r. 1451–89) proposes an exchange (*adal-badal*) of brides, but once again the alliance takes place with a member of the Jhunjhunu branch rather than with the Fatehpur Kyamkhanis (supposedly because the latter had no unmarried daughters available). This marriage proposal too had been foreseen by Saiyid Nasir. Raja Lunkaran (r. 1505–26), a Rathor Rajput from Bikaner, also offered a daughter; this time the Fatehpur branch of the Kyamkhanis follows through with the marriage.[44]

The web of marriage alliances established by the Kyamkhanis thus included lords from Delhi and Rajasthan, Hindu as well as Muslim. The Kyamkhanis were by no means unique in straddling the marital boundary between Hindu and Muslim in this era, as a number of powerful warrior lineages did so.[45] But intermarriage is but one instance of how the Kyamkhanis, as Indian Muslims who lived in a primarily non-Muslim rural environment, partook in multiple, overlapping social and cultural spheres.

JAN KAVI'S MUGHAL PRESENT

The loyalty to the supreme Islamic ruler of North India that KKR advances as a central feature of Kyamkhani identity may reflect the conditions of Jan Kavi's present time more than the reality of the past. During Jan Kavi's lifetime, the Mughal empire attained its greatest strength and extent, and the Kyamkhanis had prospered due to their ties with this large, powerful Muslim dynasty, just as Kyam Khan had supposedly benefited from his affiliation with the Tughluq dynasty of Delhi sultans.

The Kyamkhanis had not always been clients of an imperial power. In the many decades from the fragmentation of the Delhi sultanate in

---

[44] The marriages are mentioned in KKR, vv. 433–5, 438–44 and 581–2, respectively. For the dates of Jodha and Lunkaran, I have relied on Saran and Ziegler, *Mertiyo Rathors*, pp. 194 and 256.

[45] Norman P. Ziegler, 'Action, Power and Service in Rajasthani Culture: A Social History of the Rajputs of Middle Period Rajasthan' (PhD dissertation, University of Chicago, 1973), pp. 61–63.

the early fifteenth century to the consolidation of the Mughal empire by Akbar in the late sixteenth century, the Kyamkhanis had instead operated largely as an independent group. In Jan Kavi's account of the six Kyamkhani leaders who spanned this period, one finds occasional references to the major rulers of North India such as Bahlul Lodi, Babur and Sher Shah. For the most part, however, the activities of the Kyamkhanis took place in a geographically circumscribed world bounded by Hisar in the north, Nagaur in the south-west and Amber to the east. Within this sub-regional arena, the Kyamkhanis participated in the armed struggles between more powerful warrior lineages, including the Khans of Nagaur, the Ranas of Mewar and the Rathors of Jodhpur, but their alliances constantly shifted.

The Kyamkhanis were one of many martial gentry communities recruited by the Mughal empire, enabling it to expand the size of the army and extend the boundaries of the empire. The incorporation of rural gentry also prevented unrest in the countryside, by aligning the main possessors of armed force with the imperial state. Among the warriors inducted into the Mughal imperial service during Akbar's reign was Taj Khan, of the senior Kyamkhani branch from Fatehpur.[46] The fact that the Kyamkhanis were Muslims of Indian origin is acknowledged in the suffix Khatria (from the Sanskrit word *ksatriya* or warrior) appended to Taj Khan's name in the *Ain-i Akbari*, probably to differentiate him from another Taj Khan of Central Asian origin. Taj Khan was by no means eminent—when the *Ain* was compiled: he held the rank (*mansab*) of 200, the lowest level of officer whom Abu'l Fazl named.[47] Even so, Taj Khan must have had some acquaintance with the cosmopolitan, multi-ethnic culture of Akbar's court, if only through contact with its major nobles.[48]

---

[46] According to KKR, the first Kyamkhani to have contact with the Mughals was Daulat Khan I, whom Babur supposedly visited and described as one of the three most renowned men in Hindustan (vv. 517–31). This is highly implausible. KKR also states that Fadan Khan, Taj Khan's father, was honoured by both Humayun and Akbar and gave a daughter in marriage to the latter (vv. 627–42). While this is possible, Fadan Khan is not mentioned in any Mughal sources.

[47] Taj Khan Khatria is No. 404 in the list of mansabdars in *Ain-i Akbari* (Vol. 1, p. 526), whereas the other Taj Khan is No. 172 (Vol. 1, p. 457).

[48] It should be noted that numerical *mansab* ranks were considerably lower during Akbar's reign than in later times. The *Ain-i Akbari* lists only 57 mansabdars at 1,000 zat or higher, another 145 in ranks from 900 down to 250 zat, and 81 at 200 zat; for a total of 283 men (Shireen Moosvi, *The Economy of the Mughal Empire c. 1595* [Delhi: Oxford University Press, 1987], Table 9.2 on p. 214). Hence, despite his seemingly low rank, Taj Khan was a member of a very select circle. The rankings initially indicated the number of horsemen that an officer was supposed to maintain for

Alaf or Alif Khan, Taj Khan's grandson and successor, achieved sufficient success that he attained noble status. Starting out at the rank of 700 at the outset of emperor Jahangir's reign in 1607, Alaf Khan rose steadily and by 1623 had reached the rank of 2,000.[49] This placed Alaf Khan well within the circles of the nobility (*umara*), defined as rankholders (*mansabdar*) at the level of 1,000 or above. There were approximately 350 such nobles in 1628.[50] According to the KKR, Alaf Khan fought in the campaigns against the Sisodiya ruler of Mewar led by Jahangir while he was still a prince, and in the Deccan expedition against Malik Amber. Alaf Khan was sent repeatedly to Mewat and to the Kangra hills to quell minor rebellions; additionally, he served in the Lakhi jungle area of the Panjab. He died in battle in 1626. Roughly a quarter of KKR is devoted to the exploits of Alaf Khan, the father of the text's composer, Jan Kavi or Nyamat Khan.

Daulat Khan II, Alaf Khan's successor, was never to rise as high at court as his father; he ended his career at the 1,500 rank.[51] Like his father, at one point he held the position of warden (*qiledar*) of Kangra fortress. In the 1640s, he and his son Tahar Khan were involved in pacifying the city of Nagaur, after its lord Amar Singh Rathor was killed in Agra. The two Kyamkhanis also participated in the disastrous Mughal campaign of 1646–47 against the Uzbeks in Balkh; the young Tahar Khan tragically died during it. Daulat Khan died of fever a few years later in Kandahar, which Mughal forces were attempting for the third time to recover from Shah Abbas II of Safavid Iran.[52] Tahar Khan's son Sardar Khan became the next head of the Kyamkhanis, and with this detail the text ends. Although Jan Kavi informs us that the main portion of the text, culminating in Alaf Khan's death, was completed in 1634,[53] the last section on Daulat Khan was evidently added after he died in 1653.

---

the imperial service, but inflation in the rankings during the seventeenth century led to the introduction of complicated ratios between *mansab* rank and the required level of troop support.

[49] Alaf Khan's highest rank was 2,000 *zat*/1,500 *sawar* (M. Athar Ali, *The Apparatus of Empire: Awards of Ranks, Offices and Titles to the Mughal Nobility, 1574–1658* [Delhi: Oxford University Press, 1985], pp. 80, 84). He is mentioned in Jahangir's memoirs, sometimes with the suffix Qiyamkhani (Jahangir, *The Jahangirnama: Memoirs of Jahangir, Emperor of India*, trans. Wheeler M. Thackston [Washington, DC: Freer Gallery of Art, Arthur M. Sackler Gallery; NY: Oxford University Press, 1999], pp. 94, 180, 353, 374–75, 381, 410).

[50] Firdos Anwar, *Nobility under the Mughals (1628–1658)* (Delhi: Manohar Publishers, 2001), p. 21.

[51] Daulat Khan's highest rank was 1,500 *zat*/1,000 *sawar*, achieved in the 1640s. Mention of him in Mughal sources is noted in Athar Ali, *Apparatus of Empire*, pp. 100, 147, 169, 194, 216.

[52] John F. Richards, *The Mughal Empire* (Cambridge: Cambridge University Press, 1993), pp. 132–33.

[53] KKR, v. 939.

The geographical horizons of the Kyamkhanis had expanded enormously by the time Jan Kavi completed his history of the lineage. Rather than being confined to a small section of Haryana and Rajasthan, warriors from this community had fought as far afield as modern Uzbekistan and Afghanistan, as well as in the Deccan and in numerous localities bordering the imperial heartland. The social horizons of the Kyamkhanis had similarly grown larger, for Alaf Khan and Daulat Khan were part of the ethnically diverse Mughal noble class, along with Central Asians, Iranis, Afghans, Indian Muslims from other regions and Hindu Rajputs. A cosmopolitan artistic culture that drew from the elements of both Indic and Persian traditions flourished in the cities of seventeenth-century India, at least among the most elite circles. The extent to which this cosmopolitan culture penetrated smaller towns like Fatehpur and Jhunjhunu is unclear. Although scholars have studied the Mughal noble class as a whole, and select high-ranking lineages within it, little work has been done on individual gentry communities. Even if the more rustic gentry did not participate in many aspects of Mughal courtly culture, their leaders who held rank at the noble level had to attend court on occasion and must have had some familiarity with its artistic patronage.

In that context, it is significant that Alaf Khan's son, Jan Kavi or Nyamat Khan, composed poems in Braj Bhasa rather than Persian, the prestigious language of the Mughal court. The Persian language had been introduced into North India along with the Delhi sultanate in the thirteenth century, and spread even more widely after Akbar made it the language of administration for the Mughal empire in the late sixteenth century. Even non-Muslims who worked as scribes or accountants had a working knowledge of Persian in seventeenth-century North India.[54] In Jan Kavi's day, Persian was without doubt the literary language employed by most educated Muslims in India. If Jan was not himself conversant in Persian, someone in his household or entourage certainly was, as he wrote a Braj Bhasa version of a Persian text (Amir Khusrau's *Divalrani Khizr Khan*).[55] It is quite possible, therefore, that Jan deliberately opted for Braj Bhasa despite knowing Persian.

---

[54] Muzaffar Alam, 'The Pursuit of Persian: Language in Mughal Politics,' *Modern Asian Studies* 32 (1998), pp. 323–30.

[55] He also prepared a Braj Bhasa version of the Sanskrit *Pancatantra* animal fables, which was presented to emperor Shah Jahan (Sharma, 'Kyamkhan Rasa ke Kartta,' pp. 3, 6, 9).

Braj Bhasa was a newer language, used for literary purposes in North India primarily since the sixteenth century. Because it was derived from the vernacular, it had less cachet and less circulation than either Persian or Sanskrit, the subcontinent's two cosmopolitan languages. This was particularly true in the beginning of Braj Bhasa literary production, when most compositions were devotional poems about the god Krishna. During the seventeenth century, the language was also increasingly used for non-religious topics such as poetic theory or royal eulogies, in texts that were produced from a courtly context.[56] Among the biggest patrons of Braj Bhasa poets were the rulers of local Rajput kingdoms such as Orcha, where the poet Kesavdas flourished in the late sixteenth and early seventeenth century, and Amber, where Biharilal composed his famous *Satsai* at about the same time as Jan Kavi wrote KKR.[57] Another contemporary of Jan Kavi was Raja Jasvant Singh of Jodhpur, a powerful Rajput lord who produced works on rhetoric, the *Bhagavad Gita*, and metaphysics.[58]

Kyamkhani patronage of Braj Bhasa literature thus followed the overall pattern of Rajput kingdoms in Rajasthan and Central India. However, literary production at Fatehpur was quite limited, as it seems to have been restricted solely to Braj Bhasa, in contrast to most sub-imperial court settings where Sanskrit and other Indic languages also flourished. Jan Kavi himself composed about eighty poems in it between c. 1613 and 1644, many on romantic themes.[59] Two other Braj Bhasa poets from Fatehpur mention Kyamkhani Alif Khan and his successor, and likely received patronage from them.[60] Braj Bhasa compositions

---

[56] For more on these two genres in Braj Bhasa literature, see Allison Busch, 'The Anxiety of Literary Innovation: The Practice of Literary Science in Hindi/Riti Tradition,' *Comparative Studies of South Asia, Africa and the Middle East* 24 (2004), pp. 45–60; Idem, 'Literary Responses to the Mughal Imperium: The Historical Poems of Kesavdas,' *South Asia Research* 25 (2005), pp. 31–54.

[57] R. S. McGregor, *Hindi Literature from Its Beginnings to the Nineteenth Century* (Wiesbaden: Otto Harrasowitz, 1984), pp. 126–29, 173–74.

[58] Rupert Snell, *The Hindi Classical Tradition: A Braj Bhasa Reader* (London: School of Oriental and African Studies, 1991), p. 43.

[59] Two volumes of Jan's poems have recently been published (Vina Lahoti et al. eds *Jan Granthavali, Vol. 3: Premakhyan Sangrah,* [Jodhpur: Rajasthan Pracya Vidya Pratishthan, 2004]; Vandana Singhvi et al. eds *Jan Granthavali, Vol. 4: Premakhyan Sangrah,* [Jodhpur: Rajasthan Pracya Vidya Pratishthan, 2005]). A good number of Jan's poems (some of which are quite short) are classified as *premakhyans* or romantic adventure tales. Unlike the famous romances written earlier in Avadhi by Jayasi and others, however, Jan's poems do not reveal any Sufi influence (Om Prakash Sharma, 'Foreword,' in *Jan Granthavali, Vol. 3*, p. vi).

[60] Dasaratha Sharma, 'Kyamkhan Rasa ke Kartta,' pp. 3, 11–12.

on religious themes were also produced in Fatehpur during the mid seventeenth century by Sundardas, a major poet of the Dadu sect whose printed works comprise over a thousand pages. Dadu (d. 1604) was a Rajasthani saint belonging to the *sant* tradition, which rejected formal religion and worshipped a god without attributes. Like the most famous *sant* leader, Kabir, Dadu probably came from a Muslim family of humble origins; his sect was soon taken over by high-caste Hindus, however. Although Dadu's teachings were to eventually spread to other parts of North India, the majority of his followers remained concentrated in Rajasthan.[61] Dadu's disciple Sundardas and the Muslim lord (*nawab*) of Fatehpur reputedly had a number of conversations, and we can assume that Sundardas received support from some Fatehpur notables if not the Kyamkhanis themselves.[62]

Regardless of their leaders' status as Mughal nobles, the Kyamkhanis of the seventeenth century behaved like local lords in their cultural activities, patronizing a literature that was, at least originally, primarily regional and Hindu in character. The regional and Hindu nuances lessened over time, however, as Braj Bhasa literature increasingly found favour in a variety of courts, including those of the Marathas and Mughals. Despite the continuing prestige of Persian and Sanskrit, the seventeenth century was a time of growing popularity for Braj Bhasa and other literary languages based on Indic vernaculars. One reason for this phenomenon was the flexibility of Braj Bhasa, which could accommodate a range of linguistic registers from the highly Persianized to the highly Sanskritized, thus offering a common ground that could not be found in the radically different classical languages. The many translations of texts from Persian and Sanskrit into the north Indian vernaculars from the late sixteenth century onwards attest a gradual shift in literary preferences towards the Indic vernaculars, among which Braj Bhasa in particular came to assume a transregional role.[63]

Nor was it unknown for Muslims like Jan Kavi to compose poetry in Braj Bhasa, although they were generally also accomplished in other

---

[61] The information on Sundardas and Dadu in the previous sentences has been taken from Monika Thiel-Horstmann, *Crossing the Ocean of Existence: Braj Bhasa Religious Poetry from Rajasthan* (Wiesbaden: Otto Harrassowitz, 1983), pp. 3–14.

[62] Dasaratha Sharma, 'Kyamkhan Rasa ke Kartta,' pp. 11–12.

[63] A pioneering study of the transregional character of Braj Bhasa is Allison Busch, 'The Courtly Vernacular: The Transformation of Braj Bhasa Literary Culture (1590–1690),' PhD dissertation, University of Chicago, 2003.

languages. A prominent example is Abd Al-Rahim Khan-i Khanan (1556–1624), one of the most powerful nobles at Akbar's court, who composed works in several different languages. The linguistic versatility of educated Indo-Muslims is displayed in Muhammad Afzal's *Bikat Kahani*, written in 1636 in a combination of both Persian and dialects of western Hindi, as well as in Mirza Khan's *Tuhfatu'l Hind* (c. 1675–1700), which contains a bilingual Persian–Braj Bhasa dictionary.[64] A few Muslims had written exclusively in Indic languages, like the early sixteenth-century Jayisi and others who composed Avadhi works that wove Sufi themes into Indian folk romances. These Sufi poets had lived in an era between empires, when regional states sometimes employed regional languages, not in Jan Kavi's expanding Mughal world where Persian was resurgent. Another well-known Braj Bhasa poet, Raskhan, was a former Muslim who had become a devotee of Krishna.[65]

Even in a milieu where Muslims chose more and more to communicate poetically in an Indic language, Jan Kavi was somewhat unusual, however. Few other Muslim authors wrote only in an Indic language during the Mughal period, especially if they were not Sufis or converts to Krishna worship. Furthermore, his adoption of a pseudonym with both Sanskrit and Persian roots was a conscious act that effectively masked his religious affiliation, whatever its intended purpose. (Nyamat Khan constantly referred to himself as Jan in KKR, a name that was poetically useful because it rhymed with so many Braj Bhasa words.) Although the world of Indian Muslim elites was suffused by Persianate culture, as a poet Jan dwelt in a literary sphere that was distinctly Indic and much less cosmopolitan than Persian. The various Hindi languages were indeed utilized by the Muslim literati precisely because they evoked the feminine, the domestic and the rustic.[66] Jan Kavi/Nyamat Khan did so, I believe, because he wished to participate in the literary universe inhabited by his warrior neighbours, the Rajput lords of Rajasthan and its vicinity.

---

[64] On *Bikat Kahani*, see Shantanu Phukan, "'Through Throats Where Many Rivers Meet": The Ecology of Hindi in the World of Persian,' *Indian Economic and Social History Review* 38 (2001), pp. 37–41; on *Tuhfatu'l Hind*, see R. S. McGregor, 'The Progress of Hindi, Part I: The Development of a Transregional Idiom,' in *Literary Cultures in History: Reconstructions from South Asia*, ed. Sheldon Pollock (Berkeley: University of California Press, 2003), pp. 942–44.

[65] Snell, *Hindi Classical Tradition*, pp. 33–34, 39–40.

[66] Phukan, "'Through Throats Where Many Rivers Meet",' pp. 43–48, 54.

ACCEPTING THE GLOBAL/AFFIRMING THE LOCAL

Jan Kavi, as best we can tell from the evidence of his literary products, was a man with a foot in two worlds. One was the universe of Islam, which stretched as far west as Morocco and as far east as island Southeast Asia during the seventeenth century. The other was a more localized realm within South Asia, where Braj Bhasa literature flourished and Hindus were in the majority. Jan acknowledged the reality that he was living in a society with two major religious faiths at the outset of his poem, when, as appropriate in a historical narrative, he begins with the origins of humanity. In two verses, he tells us:

> All the people who've existed in this world, says Jan (the poet),
> Are descendants of Adam, Hindu and Musalman.
> One origin for both of them, no difference in blood or skin,
> But their deeds don't coincide, so their labels are distinct.[67]

This is a firm declaration of the fundamental unity of all mankind, divided though it is into two groups. Whereas Hindus and Muslims do not differ in origin or in essence, in Jan Kavi's view, they have become differentiated through their separate deeds (*karni*)—probably referring to religious activities or ritual acts.

The story of Karamcand becoming a Turk was a crucial moment for Jan Kavi's folk, the point at which they diverged from the mass of Hindus around them. In the remainder of KKR, however, little is made of this religious difference. The word 'Muslim' does not occur again, nor is there any mention of mosques or the *sharia*. Only three features in the bulk of the text give any indication that its author was a Muslim: the occasional reference to a supreme being (*karta, paramatma*), the assertion that a saint called Qutb protected Kyam Khan, and the glorification of Alaf Khan's tomb-shrine (*dargah*). Jan's disinterest in religion extends, by and large, to Hinduism as well. The elision of religion and religious affiliations may be partly due to the genre chosen by Jan Kavi, the *rasa* or *raso*, typically a tale of martial exploits. In the idealized portrayal of warriors found in martial narratives, it was their heroic actions that mattered and not their religious faith. Additionally, we should not discount the possibility that Jan Kavi deliberately downplayed religious differences because his main objective, as we shall see, was to present

---

[67] KKR, vv. 14–15.

the Kyamkhanis as exemplary within a regional warrior culture shared with many Hindus.

Why then did Jan spend so much time in his narrative on the episode of Karamcand/Kyam Khan? From Jan's vantage point in the seventeenth century, this was the series of events that led to the formation of his unique community, the Kyamkhanis. Kyam Khan had set himself apart from others not only by adopting Islam but also by establishing himself as a trustworthy political subordinate to the Delhi sultan. Two of his three brothers also converted, we are told, and presumably supported Kyam Khan in his political career and military activities. Even in successive generations, the various lineages that branched off from the senior line settled near each other and often suppressed their conflicting interests for a common political good. Kyam Khan was the progenitor from whom they were all descended and he had defined them, not only as Muslims, but as capable and loyal warriors who were worthy of lordship, even if only as the subordinates of others. The KKR's extensive coverage of Karamcand/Kyam Khan was probably not meant to emphasize the Kyamkhani's Muslim affiliation so much as their distinctiveness as a community.

The Kyamkhanis were but a small clan, however, and Jan Kavi foregrounds their affiliation with a larger social category in the KKR. The identity that is most insistently proclaimed for the Kyamkhanis is that of Cauhan, a term that figures at least 136 times.[68] We learn that the Kyamkhanis are Cauhans as early as the fifth verse of this poem of 1,046 verses; and it is as a Cauhan that Karamcand identifies himself when Firuz Shah Tughluq asks who he is. Cauhan often figures as part of the name of a Kyamkhani ancestor, as when we are told that Daulat Khan Cauhan crushed the pride of the Nagauri Khan. Or Cauhan may be used in place of a personal name, for example, 'after this victory the Cauhan attacked Chopala village'.[69] Although Cauhan is also a label applied to an exogamous lineage or other social unit within many communities, the primary reference is to one of the thirty six royal clans of the Rajput class of Hindu warriors. Jan Kavi makes it clear that this is the meaning he has in mind when he states that the Cauhan clan (*got*) is the best among all kinds (*jat*) of Rajputs.[70] He also applies to the Kyamkhani

---

[68]   The word Rajput appears in KKR, vv. 68, 605, 635, 1041.

[69]   KKR, vv. 458, 557.

[70]   KKR, v. 68.

leader Alaf Khan the epithet 'lord of Sambhar', harkening back to the twelfth-century Cauhan kings of the Ajmer region.[71] Whatever other allegiances and identities the Kyamkhanis possessed, in Jan Kavi's mind they were Cauhans first and foremost.

Jan Kavi faced something of a predicament in situating the Indic Cauhan identity of the Kyamkhanis within the larger framework of universal history with which he felt obliged to begin his text. Some Indian texts of the *purana* genre also begin with the creation of the cosmos, but Jan was here following a widespread convention in Islamic historiography. *Akbarnama*, the official biography of emperor Akbar composed by Abu'l Fazl, for instance, contains a similar account of mankind's origins that starts with Adam, the first human.[72] In the ninth generation after Adam, according to Jan Kavi's version of early human history, came Nuh, better known to the Western world as Noah. Just as in the Jewish and Christian traditions from which it borrowed, in the Islamic view of human beginnings, all existing races could be traced back to one of the three sons of Nuh/Noah. This conception has been labelled 'Mosaic ethnology' by Thomas R. Trautmann, who has shown how it inspired Sir William Jones and other Orientalist scholars of the late eighteenth and early nineteenth centuries to classify the multiple varieties of people in the world into three categories with a shared origin.[73]

In standard Indo-Muslim historical texts, we are told that Nuh's oldest son Sam (Shem) was the progenitor of the Arabs and Persians, among others. The middle son, Ham, was ancestor of Hind (Indians) and others including, in our text, the Uzbeks and Habshis (Abyssinians). From the youngest son, Yaphas (Japhet), were descended the Turks, the Mughals (Mongols) and the Chinese.[74] The KKR makes an unusual addition to this scheme, however. Classified under the offspring of Nuh's oldest son, Sam, are not only the Arabs and Persians, but also the Pathans and Cauhans.[75] In Jan Kavi's text, in other words, the Cauhans are represented as a category of people who go back to the same stock as the Arabs and

[71] KKR, vv. 895, 936.

[72] Abu al-Fazl ibn Mubarak, *The Akbarnama of Abu-l-Fazl,* trans. H. Beveridge (Calcutta: Asiatic Society, 1897), Vol. 1, pp. 155–69.

[73] Thomas R. Trautmann, *Aryans and British India* (Berkeley: University of California Press,1997), pp. 28–61.

[74] Trautmann, *Aryans and British India,* p. 53.

[75] KKR, v. 32.

Persians—the most prestigious of all ethnic groups in the diverse Indo-Muslim world. By this means, Jan Kavi deftly inserts an undeniably Indic social identity into an Islamic classificatory scheme and links his regional society to the larger universe of Islamic civilization.

Jan Kavi does not stop there. Having grafted the Cauhans onto this Judeo-Christian–Islamic family tree, Jan Kavi continues on with a detailed line of descent. He enumerates twenty three generations stemming from Nuh's son Sam—all men with Indian names, including some well-known figures from classical Sanskrit mythology like the sage Jamadagni and Parasurama, an incarnation of Vishnu. We finally arrive at the figure of Cauhan, the eponymous founder of the clan, followed by a few verses praising the Cauhan clan. Just as the (Hindu) god Indra is the most eminent among all deities, the moon among all stars, the rose among flowers, etc., so too is the clan of the imperial Cauhans superior among all kings. The Cauhans are compared to the wish-fulfilling tree of Indian myth, with its many branches. After a catalogue of these branches (*sakh*) of the Cauhan clan (*bams*) comes a list of the seven Cauhan emperors who ruled from Delhi, ending with Prithviraj (of the late twelfth century). Jan Kavi then returns to the ancestor Cauhan, first of the line, and names the twenty one forefathers from him to Karamcand, who became a Turk and took the name Kyam Khan.

One of these last twenty one progenitors is Guga, a folk deity whom both Hindus and Muslims used to revere.[76] Guga (or Goga) Cauhan is still widely worshipped today in the villages of Rajasthan, Haryana, Panjab and western Uttar Pradesh for his ability to control snakes. His supernatural powers are commemorated in a folk epic with many variants, in some of which he is described as fighting Mahmud of Ghazni, the famous Turkic king who made numerous raids into the subcontinent c. 1000.[77] Guga Cauhan is also called Guga Pir or Zahir Pir, and some devotees claim he became a Muslim.[78] Although the KKR does not highlight Guga's presence in the Kyamkhani genealogy, it later specifies the hometown of Mote Ray, Kyam Khan's father, as Dadreva. Since this is the place in Curu district (Rajasthan) where Guga allegedly

---

[76] KKR, vv. 110–111.

[77] G. W. Briggs, *Gorakhnath and the Kanphata Yogis* (Delhi: Motilal Banarsidass, 1973 [1938]), pp. 235–6; Elwyn C. Lapoint, 'The Epic of Guga: A North Indian Oral Tradition,' in *American Studies in the Anthropology of India*, ed. Sylvia Vatuk (New Delhi: Manohar, 1978), pp. 281–308.

[78] William Crooke, *The Popular Religion and Folklore of Northern India*, 2nd ed. (Delhi: Munshiram Manoharlal, 1968), Vol. 1, pp. 211–13.

lived, the connection between the Kyamkhanis and Guga Cauhan is pointed out a second time.[79] Guga is an appropriate heroic predecessor for the Kyamkhanis, for he too traversed religious boundaries but did not stray outside the regional culture of North-western India.

Despite a view of the human past that in its broad outlines was derived from Islamic tradition, we have seen that Jan Kavi chose to stress a more localized Indic ancestry for his community. To be sure, the elaborate Cauhan genealogy in KKR was embedded within a larger Islamic narrative of human origin that is expansive in character, encompassing the known races of the world. Jan Kavi demonstrated not only his awareness of the large-scale perspective of Islamic civilization, but also his acceptance of its basic premises. He was part of the global culture of Islam, yet at the same time he was most interested in affirming an identity that was meaningful only within a specific region of India, just as he had selected a language of expression that could only be comprehended within more or less the same area. In this regional culture, declaring that the Kyamkhanis were Cauhans of exalted lineage was simultaneously an assertion of their local origins and their high status as warriors. Jan Kavi's intent in KKR was clearly to establish the Kyamkhanis as equivalent in prestige and prowess to the leading warrior lineages of Rajasthan, Haryana and western U.P.

It was not only their descent from an ancient, distinguished clan that made the Kyamkhanis comparable to other Rajput warriors, but also the warrior spirit they reportedly exhibited. In its martial ethos and rhetoric, the KKR is virtually indistinguishable from the literature produced at Hindu Rajput courts during this era. Jan Kavi's text abounds with formulaic vignettes of warrior bravado. A Kyamkhani hero will issue a sharp warning to a troublemaker to mend his ways, and the scoundrel will refuse with great bluster. Once our hero marches out with his army, his adversary seldom stays to fight but instead runs away—no distinction is drawn in the text between cowardly flight and strategic retreat. This scenario is repeated dozens of times in a mechanical and predictable

---

[79] E.g., Nainsi identifies Daraira/Dadreva as Guga's residence (John D. Smith, *The Epic of Pabuji* [Cambridge: Cambridge University Press, 1991], pp. 72, 488). Dadreva appears to have long been under Cauhan sway, for an inscription there dated 1217 CE cites a Cauhan lord who appears four generations before Karamcand's father, Mote Ray, in the Kyamkhani genealogy (Dasaratha Sharma, *Early Chauhan Dynasties*, 2nd ed., [Delhi: Motilal Banarsidass, 1975], p. 365). Scholars have placed considerable credence in the genealogy because of its correspondence with the inscription, without considering the possibility that the Kyamkhanis were somehow aware of the inscription's contents.

fashion. Similarly, if urged to withdraw when faced with severe odds in a battle situation, our Kyamkhani heroes never agree. 'How can I shame Hammir and flee?', are the words the poet puts in Alaf Khan's mouth, alluding to the celebrated Cauhan warrior Hammir of Ranthambor, who gave up his life in a valiant struggle against the Delhi sultan Ala al-Din Khalji around 1300.[80] Much is made of the 'sense of shame' (*laj*) or honour possessed by Kyamkhani warriors.[81]

Dying in battle is the greatest virtue of all in the KKR, as in many Rajput works. This is one reason Alaf Khan receives so much attention in the KKR, for he lost his life in the Panjab hills while fighting for the Mughal emperor.[82] The fifty verses narrating his last battle highlight Alaf Khan's fearless and resolute nature: most of his army has been dispatched elsewhere yet Alaf Khan has no misgivings about confronting the enemy, even after his two wing commanders abandoned the battlefield. Over and over, the poet stresses that a warrior should be prepared to give up his life; he adds that the Supreme Being gives victory to the one who dies on the battlefield.[83] As might be said about a heroic Hindu warrior, Alaf Khan is described as ascending to the god Vishnu's heaven, Vaikuntha, upon his death. As a Muslim, however, Alaf Khan was buried in a tomb, which is extolled as a shrine (*dargah*) that could cure all one's ills.[84]

By Jan Kavi's lifetime, there had been prolonged contact between warriors from the Rajasthani countryside and others whose origins were in regions to the west of India. In terms of dress, military equipment, or style of warfare, there was little to differentiate the Hindus and Muslims who occupied high posts in the imperial service.[85] An important value held in common was loyalty to the overlord, what Jan Kavi calls *svamdharma* or service to the master.[86] Jan Kavi's employment of an Indic

---

[80] KKR, v. 740. Other references to Kyamkhani greatness as a result of their descent from Hammir and Prithviraj Cauhan are found in vv. 612 and 1032.

[81] On *laj*, see Saran and Ziegler, *Mertiyo Rathors*, Vol. 1, p. 96 n. 120. The word *raj*, meaning pride in one's bravery or honourable reputation, is sometimes paired with *laj* in KKR (vv. 881, 952).

[82] KKR, vv. 879–928.

[83] KKR, vv. 879, 927.

[84] KKR, vv. 934, 936–7.

[85] Stewart Gordon, 'Zones of Military Entrepreneurship in India, 1500–1700,' in *Marathas, Marauders, and State Formation in Eighteenth-Century India* (Delhi: Oxford University Press, 1994), pp. 189–92.

[86] KKR, v. 936. See John F. Richards, 'The Formulation of Imperial Authority under Akbar and Jahangir,' in *Kingship &Authority in South Asia*, ed. John F. Richards (Madison: South Asian Studies, University of Wisconsin-Madison, 1978), pp. 253–54, 271–72.

idiom in this, as in many other instances, is noteworthy. Although his immediate family certainly participated in a multi-lingual, multi-cultural courtly society, Jan Kavi consistently remains within the bounds of a cultural discourse that is distinctly Rajput in the KKR. Alaf Khan's last battle is a case in point. It is compared to the great war of the Kauravas and Pandavas described in the *Mahabharata* epic. So many warriors lay dead on the ground, it is said, that the fierce female deities (*yoginis*) gathering their skulls were bowed down with the weight—another frequent allusion in Rajput literature. Only one thing is missing that might be found in a Hindu Rajput warrior narrative: any mention of *sati*, the voluntary suicide of a widow on her warrior husband's funeral pyre.

This analysis of the KKR—the only 'history' of the family, produced by its sole author—leads us to characterize them as Rajputs whose Muslim religion led to slight deviances in culture from their non-Muslim brethren. Seventeenth-century literature from Rajasthan on occasion includes Muslims under the rubric of Rajput, although not the Kyamkhanis specifically.[87] Indian ethnographers working for the colonial census in 1891 also classified the Kyamkhanis in this way, stating that 'It is difficult to distinguish them from the Rajputs of eastern Marwar because there is only a very slight difference in their looks, dress, and speech.'[88] The Kyamkhanis of 1891 would not share food or drink with 'foreign' Muslims, but Rajputs in some places in Marwar and Shekhavati would share a hookah and food with them. In other words, the Kyamkhanis not only acted much like Hindu Rajputs, but were regarded as akin to themselves by local Rajputs. A more recent ethnographic account notes that the Kyamkhanis have long-standing patron–client relations with the Bhats, a caste of genealogists who traditionally served the (Hindu) Rajputs, in another clear indication of their Rajput-like status in local society.[89]

Like their Hindu Rajput counterparts, the Kyamkhanis were a community of warriors with considerable control over, and income from, agricultural land. The ruling lineages whose history was narrated in the KKR lost their lordship over Fatehpur and Jhunjhunu in the

---

[87] Ziegler, 'Action, Power and Service,' pp. 58–60.

[88] *Riport Mardumsumari Rajmarvar San 1891 Isvi: Marwar Census Report 1891* (Jodhpur: Sri Jagadisasingh Gahlot Sodh Sansthan, 1997), p. 77.

[89] B. K. Lavania et al. eds, *People of India, Vol. 38 pt. 2: Rajasthan* (Mumbai: Anthropological Survey of India & Popular Prakashan, 1998), p. 311.

1730s to the Shekhavat Rajputs, a branch of the Kachwaha clan.[90] However, Kyamkhanis continued to reside in the Shekhavat region, as well as in adjacent kingdoms such as Jodhpur—they numbered 28,340 individuals according to the 1911 census. Since Rajputana Agency (that is, much of modern Rajasthan with the exception of the Ajmer–Merwara territory) had a population of over 10 million, the Kyamkhanis were but a small, localized community.[91] During the nineteenth and twentieth centuries, the Kyamkhanis maintained their martial traditions by seeking employment in the army, police and as guards.[92] This differentiated them from other Muslim communities in Rajasthan like the Meos or Desawalis, who claimed Rajput ancestry but were engaged almost exclusively in cultivation.[93] Today, it appears that many, if not most, Kyamkhanis have left Rajasthan for Karachi and other places in Pakistan.

CONCLUSION

The KKR narrates the martial past of a warrior lineage. In common with many warrior tales worldwide, it sought to publicize the heroic deeds of members of the lineage, as well as their exemplary service to the ruler. A third feature of the KKR, its emphasis on an extensive and illustrious bloodline, reflected the genealogical concerns of its immediate milieu— the Rajput society of the Mughal era. More than any other social label, the Cauhan clan affiliation was accorded the most prominence in the KKR for it signalled the high status that the Kyamkhanis claimed within the local social order. Despite the embedding of the Cauhans within a

---

[90] Frances H. Taft, 'The Origins of the Shekhavat Thikanas of Jaipur,' in *Religion, Ritual and Royalty*, eds N. K. Singhi and Rajendra Joshi (Jaipur and New Delhi: Rawat Publications, 1999), pp. 289–95.

[91] Census of India 1911, Vol. 22 pt. 1, p. 253.

[92] *People of India: Rajasthan*, p. 510.

[93] The Meos are a much larger group than the Kyamkhanis, comprising 165,416 individuals in the 1911 census. Although they are considered a dominant landed caste comparable to rural Rajputs, they never possessed the elite status that is characteristic of the aristocratic Rajput lineages of Rajasthan. For more on the Meos, see Shail Mayaram, *Against History, Against State*, and Raymond Jamous, *Kinship and Rituals among the Meo of Northern India: Locating Sibling Relationships*, trans. Nora Scott (Delhi: Oxford University Press, 2003). For descriptions of a range of Muslim communities in Rajasthan, see S. Inayat A. Zaidi and Sunita Zaidi, 'Conversion to Islam and Formation of Castes in Medieval Rajasthan,' in *Art and Culture: Felicitation Volume in Honour of Professor S. Nurul Hasan*, eds Ahsan Jan Qaisar and Som Prakash (Jaipur: Publication Scheme, 1993), pp. 27–42.

larger Islamic understanding of humanity's evolution and the inclusion of a lengthy account of the founding father's conversion to Islam, the KKR manifests little interest in religious faith and only a muted sense of religious difference. The conversion episode, I have argued, was necessary to the narrative in order to explain the ethnogenesis of the Kyamkhani community—how they came to be differentiated from other warrior groups in their locality. It had the secondary purpose of demonstrating the depth of Kyamkhani commitment to the Muslim overlords who dominated much of north India.

The Kyamkhanis inhabited multiple social, cultural and political spheres concurrently, as mid-level gentry with entry into aristocratic imperial circles, as rural residents in a cosmopolitan culture centred on cities and as Muslims whose local peers were mainly Hindus, to give but a few examples. At times their many intersecting allegiances could come into conflict, as when the Kyamkhani leader Alaf Khan was dispatched by Jahangir, the Mughal emperor, to subdue Dalpat, the Rathor Rajput lord of Bikaner. Dalpat was on the verge of defeat when he sent Alaf Khan a request through an intermediary to cease his attack, reminding him of the numerous daughters the Rathors of Bikaner and Jodhpur had given to the Kyamkhanis in marriage. Thinking of these relationships, Alaf Khan should now protect him, Dalpat says, for who else could defend the honour of local landholders (*bhomiya*)? Alaf Khan heeds Dalpat's words and stops his assault, thereby rescuing Dalpat from harm.[94] This apparent disregard of imperial orders is glossed over by the text, which informs us that Alaf Khan later sent Dalpat to Jahangir, who received him happily; a surprising outcome in view of Dalpat's earlier transgressions. What this episode makes clear is that their local warrior loyalties were paramount for the Kyamkhanis, when push came to shove.

The Kyamkhanis differed from most elite Muslims in early modern South Asia in celebrating their Indian roots. Foreign immigrants, rather than Indian converts, were alleged to be the forefathers of most elite South Asian Muslims, an improbable scenario given their large number. The desire to link oneself genealogically to Arabia and other parts of the Middle East reflects the prestige of Islam's heartland, one of the side effects of the process of Islamization. That is, as the Islamic religion spread to various areas of the world, the culture of core Islamic territories such as Arabia and, in the case of the eastern Islamic world, Persia

[94]   KKR, vv. 710–717.

was increasingly held in high esteem and emulated where possible. Aspects of Arabic or Persian material culture that had nothing to do with religion—certain kinds of dress, cooking styles and architecture, for example—were disseminated widely, and adopted by many who did not accept the faith.

The expansion of Islam can, therefore, be analysed in much the same way as the more modern phenomenon of globalization, the accelerating movement of people, ideas and technologies, which is such a prominent feature of our current times. It too involved the migration of people, but more important was the transmission of values and practices that started out from a specific locale but came to be acclaimed as universal. The transmission was not always complete, of course, in the sense that some Muslim communities in South Asia and elsewhere maintained many local customs and beliefs. Lack of education in Islamic doctrine and norms is typically regarded, at least by modern reformist Islamist movements, as the reason why Indic social patterns and religious observances persist among some South Asian Muslims even today.

Yet the example of Jan Kavi suggests that the resilience of local, Indic identities may not have resulted solely from ignorance of the global culture of Islam. Although some members of the Kyamkhani community, comprised of numerous lineages, may have been uneducated and untravelled, that cannot have been the case for its senior lineage, whose leaders were part of the Mughal court circles. Moreover, Jan Kavi discloses his knowledge of Islamic traditions in his recounting of the descent of human races from the sons of Noah. In the past decade, social scientists have moved away from the view that globalization inevitably results in greater uniformity and instead begun considering the ways in which it can also reinforce local identities.[95] In a similar vein, scholars of South Asia might dedicate more attention to the diversity of local formulations that arose in earlier phases of the expansion of Islam, a diversity that is rapidly being erased today in the move to counter the globalization of Western culture with a monolithic Islamic alternative.

---

[95] A. G. Hopkins, 'Introduction,' in *Global History: Interactions between the Universal and the Local*, ed. A. G. Hopkins (Hampshire: Palgrave Macmillan, 2006), p. 6.

9

Nature and Nurture on Imperial China's Frontiers

Peter C. Perdue

— • ✦ • —

Introduction

John Richards' *The Unending Frontier* is a magisterial survey of the formation of a globally connected society in the early modern age.[1] For Richards, the main forces creating a global society were 'a critical conjuncture between two developments: the expansive dynamism of European early modern capitalist societies, and the shared evolutionary progress in human organization that appears to have reached a critical threshold across Eurasia, if not the entire world'.[2] These two forces— markets and states—drove the increasingly intensive exploitation of natural resources around the globe, uniting continents, empires and traders in a tighter network of trade and administration. It is a brilliant synthesis of environmental and political history, which will shape all future work on this period.

For Richards, frontiers are sites of penetration by outsiders seeking control over borders and productive natural resources. A relentless

---

[1] John F. Richards, *The Unending Frontier: An Environmental History of the Early Modern World* (Berkeley: University of California, 2003). This paper was also delivered at the Second International Conference on Environmental History held on 8–10 November 2006 and sponsored by the Institute of Taiwan History, Academia Sinica. I am grateful for the comments received by Profs. Liu Ts'ui-jung, Lin Man-houng and other attendees of the conference.

[2] *Ibid.*, p. 17.

process of warfare, consolidation, investment and exploitation of nature leads over the long run to heavy resource usage, and often exhaustion, driving the conquerors to push farther into the hinterlands in search of further gains. Native peoples of the frontier borderlands, for the most part, are merely victims of the much more powerful organized states and trading companies around them.

Although the nineteenth century is not the subject of this book, and the North American continent appears only in discussion of the fur trade, the ghost of Frederick J. Turner still hovers over Richards' work. It is now not a uniquely American story, but a global one, and it begins three centuries earlier. Still, the story of penetration of empty or underutilized lands and their increasingly intensive exploitation resonates with Turner's original account.

Although Richards would not use Turner's crude terms of 'civilization' and 'barbarism', he does argue that 'when pioneer settlers brought new land under sedentary cultivation, they made landscapes more productive in economic terms' and gives credit to the 'consistent, intelligent land managers' who brought this about. He does recognize that the domination of indigenous peoples, who were expelled, killed or enslaved by the new settlers, caused great suffering and cultural losses, but also notes that 'we too-readily romanticize the relationship between such peoples and nature'. Some of his case studies examine the responses of indigenous peoples to the pressures of the new settlers, but he argues that we cannot interpret this contact as simply tragic.[3]

From somewhat different approaches, other scholars have reached similar conclusions. Richards argues for the increasing capabilities of states and other organizations to bind their subjects together in material and political terms:

Across Eurasia and Africa (and perhaps the New World), human organizations were becoming larger, more complex, and more effective— especially states and quasi-state organizations. Having adapted and learned from continuing trial and error, rulers and elites in early modern states were more effective than their predecessors at providing basic public order within those territories they claimed. They mobilized and deployed larger armies and naval forces that were able to use the new gunpowder weaponry effectively. They did better than their predecessors

---

[3] *Ibid.*, pp. 12–13.

at unifying fragmented polities under one system of authority. They did better at collecting taxes rather than tribute, which they assessed on some notion of public policy and relative productivity and with greater predictability and regularity. They were better than their predecessors at articulating ideologies and principles that legitimated their authority and appealed to their subjects.[4]

This perspective is quite similar to that of Victor Lieberman, who has portrayed a general process of increasing administrative, economic and political integration across Eurasia over the eight centuries from 1000 to 1800 CE:

> In sum, between c. 1450 and 1830 across mainland Southeast Asia, in what became the Russian empire, in those territories that cohered as France, and in the Japanese islands we find parallel tendencies towards the consolidation of fragmented political units, more efficient systems of extraction and control, and more uniform cultural expression.[5]

Lieberman, however, does not see Western Europe as the unique stimulant of this integrative process. He also outlines a series of 'administrative cycles' of consolidation and decline during this period, with the seventeenth century marking a time of breakdown in many polities of Eurasia. Lieberman places less stress on exploitation of natural resources and more on inter-state competition and the conflict over centralization of states between rulers and their landed elites. He also attends more closely to cultural integration, regarding the early modern trends as a broad process of integration in many realms, not simply intensified economic productivity.

Lieberman's approach is less Eurocentric and more contingent, but like Richards, he puts considerable emphasis on frontiers as the critical sites where these processes of integration played out. One important group promoting integration were marginal frontier elites, the dynamic military and political entrepreneurs emerging from borderlands to take over and reinvigorate encrusted traditional regimes. In Lieberman's scheme, the frontier strikes back as much as it is taken over. Its peoples are active participants in the process, not simple victims.

---

[4] *Ibid.*, p. 55.

[5] Victor B. Lieberman ed., *Beyond Binary Histories: Re-imagining Eurasia to ca. 1830* (Ann Arbor: University of Michigan Press, 1999), p. 52. See also Victor B. Lieberman, *Strange Parallels: Southeast Asia in Global Context, c. 800–1830. Volume 1: Integration on the Mainland*, 2 vols., vol. 1 (Cambridge: Cambridge University Press, 2003) reviewed by P. C. Perdue in *Social History*, vol. 31 no. 3 Aug 2006, pp. 394–97.

These two works offer complementary perspectives for viewing frontier expansion as a key element in early modern world history. Lieberman focuses on the formation and coordination of centralizing states, while Richards focuses on the ecological processes driven by state formation on the frontiers. Lieberman allows for greater interaction between periphery and centre, while Richards puts more stress on the transformation of natural resources into productive resources for states and capitalists than on the internal political dynamics of the expanding states. Lieberman is more aware of the vulnerability of states to internal factionalism, external conquest, fiscal weakness and loss of legitimacy, while Richards puts more weight on the long-term material impact of war and commerce. Lieberman allows for fluctuations, irregularities and the simultaneous production of cultural difference and similarity, while Richards describes a nearly inevitable homogenizing process, turning less productive borderlands into settled fields.

Because of the size of the Chinese empire, which grew from 150 to 300 million people in this period, and its dramatic territorial expansion, nearly tripling its size, we might expect imperial China to feature strongly in any account of frontier development in the early modern age. In both studies, however, China plays a somewhat secondary role. Lieberman does not examine the empire at all, although he promises to devote some attention to China in the second volume of his work.[6] Richards does have two brief chapters on China, but European expansion dominates the book. This neglect suggests that scholars of China need to pay more systematic attention to frontier development, so that Chinese perspectives can be included more fully in comparative world historical analysis.

I would also suggest, however, that neither study gives enough attention to the residents of the frontier themselves. These frontiers were not empty lands, and those who inhabited the region before the arrival of state-supported settlers shaped the evolution of land use there. It is not really accurate to call them 'indigenous peoples', since many of the residents were themselves immigrants or conquerors who arrived before the next wave of pioneer settlers. But from the viewpoint of the Han

---

[6] Articles by Lieberman and myself in the journal *Social Science History* provide some comparative perspectives on China. See Victor Lieberman, 'The Qing Dynasty, and Its Neighbours: Early Modern China in World History', *Social Science History* 32 (2008), pp. 281–304. Peter Perdue, 'Strange Parallels across Eurasia', *Social Science History* 32 (2008), pp. 263–79.

peasantry who intruded into the new borders, the earlier settlers were 'natives', 'aborigines' or 'barbarians'. From their own point of view, the local peoples saw themselves as natives whose homelands faced threats from outside. In order to deepen our understanding of an important world historical process, we need to examine more closely how these peoples formed their collective identities while interacting with the expanding states. Recent comparative studies of European empires have begun to stress the interactions in both directions between metropolitan cores and frontier peripheries. Processes in frontier regions or imperial peripheries shaped politics at the centre just as much as the other way around.[7]

Historians of China have recently produced an abundant amount of scholarship on the frontier regions of the Qing empire (1636–1911).[8] These studies cover a variety of regions and time periods, but nearly all of them address the central issues discussed above: the impact of imperial expansion on frontier regions, formation of collective identities on the peripheries, the role of trade, war and religion in shaping border definitions, and how these processes shaped the late imperial Chinese state. Many of these historians devote a great deal of attention to ethnicity, since so many of the peoples of the frontiers embraced cultural traditions quite different from the Han culture of the core. They agree, however, that the current PRC definition of fifty six ethnic groups, or nationalities [minzu], is utterly inadequate to capture the contested, contingent formation of ethnic consciousness on frontiers.

---

[7] Frederick Cooper and Ann Laura Stoler eds, *Tensions of Empire: Colonial Cultures in a Bourgeois World* (Berkeley: University of California Press, 1997).

[8] For example, Pamela Kyle Crossley, *A Translucent Mirror: History and Identity in Qing Imperial Ideology* (Berkeley: University of California Press, 1999); Pamela Kyle Crossley, Helen F. Siu and Donald S. Sutton, *Empire at the Margins: Culture, Ethnicity, and Frontier in Early Modern China* (Berkeley: University of California Press, 2006); Mark C. Elliott, *The Manchu Way: The Eight Banners and Ethnic Identity in Late Imperial China* (Stanford: Stanford University Press, 2001); C. Patterson Giersch, *Asian Borderlands: The Transformation of Qing China's Yunnan Frontier* (Cambridge, MA: Harvard University Press, 2006); Stevan Harrell ed., *Cultural Encounters on China's Ethnic Frontiers* (Seattle: University of Washington Press, 1995); Laura Hostetler, *Qing Colonial Enterprise: Ethnography and Cartography in Early Modern China* (Chicago: University of Chicago Press, 2001); James A. Millward, *Beyond the Pass: Economy, Ethnicity, and Empire in Qing Central Asia, 1759–1864* (Stanford: Stanford University Press, 1998); Peter C. Perdue, *China Marches West: The Qing Conquest of Central Eurasia* (Cambridge, MA: Harvard University Press, 2005); John Robert Shepherd, *Statecraft and Political Economy on the Taiwan Frontier, 1600–1800* (Stanford: Stanford University Press, 1993); Emma J. Teng, *Taiwan's Imagined Geography: Chinese Colonial Travel Writing and Pictures, 1683–1895* (Cambridge, MA: Harvard University Asia Center, 2004).

Other historians pursuing the comparative history of empires have also invoked the frontier as a crucial site of imperial formation, and a number of recent works have included serious discussion of China along with other empires.[9] I will draw on these studies to give a few examples of what new insights we can gather by looking at these works comparatively.

The central questions I have in mind are: How do ecologies of production shape the character of peoples in border regions? How do states expanding into border regions classify the peoples they encounter, and how do these collective categories affect frontier policy? How do the residents of the frontier construct their own collective identities, and how do their conceptions of themselves interact with those of the settlers and officials? Can we adopt the working hypothesis that the sharper the distinction of productive ecologies between the frontier and the core settlers, the more distinct the lines which frontier residents and pioneers draw between each other? A long tradition of discourse on frontier issues from the classical texts of the first millennium BCE through the Qing dynasty indicates how rulers, officials and settlers in imperial China confronted these questions.

The Qing rulers sponsored a large corpus of works in Manchu, Chinese and other languages to describe the frontier territories which they conquered. These include memorials from officials to the emperor, essays on frontier policy, ethnographic albums portraying the customs of frontier people, maps and drawings, travellers' reports, literature, poetry and art. I will draw on only a few examples to illustrate some of the principal sites and issues of frontier control from the seventeenth and eighteenth centuries.

NATURE AND NURTURE IN CLASSICAL CHINESE THOUGHT

How is human character linked to location? The Chinese classics gave conflicting answers to this question. An essential principle of the

---

[9] Charles S. Maier, *Among Empires: American Ascendancy and its Predecessors* (Cambridge, MA: Harvard University Press, 2006); Annlavra Stoler, Carole McGranahan and Peter C. Perdue eds, *Imperial Formations and their Discontents* (Santa Fe, New Mexico: School for Advanced Research Press, 2007); Bradley J. Parker and Lars Rodseth eds, *Untaming the Frontier in Anthropology, Archaeology, and History* (Tucson: University of Arizona Press, 2005); Daniel Power and Naomi Standen eds, *Frontiers in Question: Eurasian Borderlands 700–1700* (New York: St. Martin's Press, 1998).

Confucian moral tradition is that all humans are endowed with equal potential from birth. They can all develop their positive qualities into genuine ethical understanding if they put effort into study and self-reflection on what is required to become a *junzi* [Confucian gentleman, or sage]. This universal humanist principle excludes no one from sagehood.

On the other hand, classical writers agreed that environments strongly influence human character. Mencius used the metaphor of a deforested mountain to illustrate how human impulses towards the good can be defeated by hostile surroundings, just as grass cannot grow sustainably on a mountain which is overgrazed and underwatered. Daoists more explicitly connected true understanding of the moral Way [*dao*] to the avoidance of the corrupting influences of state offices, cities and wealth. The ideal state described in the classic text *Daodejing* was a small, isolated village:

> Though they may gaze across at a neighboring state,
> and hear the sounds of its dogs and chickens,
> The people will never travel back and forth,
> till they die of old age.[10]

Other writers, like Legalists, believed that active transformation of nature, through large public works, for example, had positive effects on human character. By shaping nature to suit their own goals, humans also shaped themselves to fit into nature. Harmonising both the human and natural orders required active transformation on both ends.

In more practical terms, the incessant military competition of the Warring States period of the fifth to third centuries BCE led to intensive demands on natural resources, and the exhaustion of many of them. Even in time of peace, few Chinese were friends of forests or of elephants. Chinese settlement proceeded in inverse relationship to the survival of wild animal habitats. The diligent local official, dedicated to improving the welfare of his people, should do his best to 'exhaust the resources of the earth' [*jin dili*].[11]

What about peoples who were not so productive? Those who did not live on the intensively cultivated agrarian lands of the Han core found

---

[10] Lao-tzu, *Tao Te Ching [Daodejing]* trans., Victor H. Mair (New York: Bantam Books, 1990), 39[80] p. 30.

[11] Mark Elvin, *The Retreat of the Elephants: An Environmental History of China* (New Haven: Yale University Press, 2004); Peter C. Perdue, *Exhausting the Earth: State and Peasant in Hunan, 1500–1850* (Cambridge, MA: Harvard University Press, 1987).

a different form of production more suitable. They might be nomads living off animals in the grasslands, mountain peoples practicing swidden agriculture, or fishermen and hunters in forest and maritime environments. The core Chinese settlers generally called these peoples 'barbarians' and considered them to be at the margins of the civilized realm. The ancient states pushed outward into these regions in order to fortify themselves against their rivals and the unified empires continued the process. In China, state-promoted settlement, land clearance, population growth, suppression of frontier peoples and extension of control through military and commercial means go back to the first millennium BCE.

Two general modes of thinking about frontier peoples contended with each other over the centuries of the imperial era. The idea of 'transformation' [hua] allowed that all peoples could become 'civilized' in Chinese terms, if they adopted central elements of orthodox social and ritual practice. These included study of the classical texts, observation of rituals to honour ancestors, practicing settled agriculture and rural textile production, proper segregation and subordination of women, etc. This was usually the dominant view of officials and policymakers. The opposing view held that certain peoples, because of their location and environment, must be irrevocably cast out of the realm of civilization. They could not be transformed; the only options for the imperial state were coexistence or forcible extermination. This perspective, which repeatedly compared nomadic peoples to birds and beasts, assigned them to the natural order and not the human one. The most disturbing aspect of nomadic practice was their mobility. Since they lived off grasslands, they did not settle down; therefore, they could not be counted, taxed or drafted for military and public works.

Following the terminology of George Frederickson, we may distinguish these opposing perspectives as 'culturalism' and 'racialism'.[12] Frederickson argues that European imperialists used similar stereotypical descriptions both of the peoples they conquered and of Jews within Europe. Both perspectives saw the conquered peoples as inferior, but culturalists allowed for the possibility of raising up subject peoples

[12] George M. Frederickson, *Racism: A Short History* (Princeton: Princeton University Press, 2002). Further discussion in Peter C. Perdue, 'Erasing the Empire, Reracing the Nation: Racialism and Culturalism in Imperial China', in *Imperial Formations and Their Discontents*, eds Ann Laura Stoler, Carole McGranahan and Peter C. Perdue (Santa Fe: School of American Research Press, 2007).

through education, religious conversion and economic development, while racialists rejected these possibilities. Jonathan Lipman uses similar terminology to describe Qing attitudes towards Chinese Muslims.[13] I find it useful to apply this distinction more broadly towards Chinese ruling elite perceptions of peoples on the frontier.

Transformationalists, or culturalists, believed that it was possible to induce mobile peoples to become more settled, and thereby register them and incorporate them into the imperial realm. Cultural change could trump natural determinism. Racialists argued that the environment irrevocably stamped the 'essential character' [*xing*] of people and no cultural or political measures could change them. A Ming writer describing Mongols who raided along the northwest frontier explicitly invoked these naturalist tropes. He compared the campaign to defend the Ordos frontier to the legendary statesman Yu's controlling of the flood waters:

> I compare it [defense] to building a dike to stop flood waters. If one morning the dike breaks, a huge flood cannot be stopped. If we recover the Ordos by brandishing our military might, drive out the exterior cause of calamity, and create a barrier along the Yellow River..., the enemy's courage will be shattered, their wolfish glances will turn into a timid hush, and they will not dare to plunder for several hundred years. It will be like Great Yu controlling the flood using the sea as a ditch so that the water returns to its proper place, and does not flood. . . it will be an achievement that Han and Tang cannot equal.[14]

Thus, he viewed Mongols as simply forces of nature, bestial or physical.

Although both streams of thought coexisted through many dynasties, broadly speaking, dynasties ruled by Han-dominant elites, especially in periods of division, were most likely to embrace racialist perspectives. Dynasties ruled by conquest elites from Central Eurasia, generally expansive and unifying military forces, tended to embrace culturalism. The Song [960–1280 CE] and Ming [1368–1644 CE] dynasties represent the racialist perspective most strongly, while the Yuan [1281–1368 CE] and Qing [1636–1911 CE] display greater culturalism. The Han dynasties [206 BCE–220 CE], in their policy debates over handling the Xiongnu nomadic confederation, display an interesting mix of the two.

---

[13] Jonathan N. Lipman, '"A Fierce and Brutal People": On Islam and Muslims in Qing Law', in *Empire at the Margins: Culture, Ethnicity, and Frontier in Early Modern China*, eds Pamela Kyle Crossley, Helen F. Siu and Donald S. Sutton (Berkeley: University of California Press, 2006).

[14] Zeng Xian, *Mingchen zouyi*, Shanghai Yinshuguan, Shanghai (1935) 24: 18b–19a.

The Tang dynasty [618–906 CE], whose ruling elite was partly Han and partly Turkish, also embraced many of the culturalist perspectives of Central Eurasian conquerors.

Culturalism meant an effort to find common ground with alien peoples, so as to convince others that cooperation with the imperial centre could help join different peoples together in the interest of higher goals. Cultural policies looked for bridging mechanisms to create channels of communication, selecting shared elements of each culture. The culturalists took for granted that their own culture was more 'civilized', but they did not necessarily advocate complete assimilation of the inferior culture to their own. Extreme advocates of cultural transformation expected total assimilation in a distant future, but many policy makers were willing to accept the coexistence of distinct ethnic markers as long as bases for communication and peace were established. The search for bridging elements could include specific religious traditions, such as the Buddhist beliefs of Han, Manchus, Mongols and Tibetans, a general appeal to universal desires for peace and prosperity, or efforts to trace common genealogies of distinct peoples. The Manchus often appealed to Mongols by claiming that they belonged to the same 'family', and Hakkas, a distinct sub-ethnic group of the Han Chinese, liked to trace their ancestry to Tang dynasty elites.

Chinese racialism drew sharp distinctions between peoples, and almost always assumed a hierarchy of superiority and inferiority. Unlike much modern Western racism, however, these distinctions did not have to be based on skin colour or physiognomy and did not invoke genetic inferiority or pretensions to science. This racialist perspective had more environmental than genetic foundations, although separate genealogies could sometimes appear. Food, clothing, landscape, climate, marriage customs, mobility and other ways of life all created sharply distinct 'folkways' in this view.

The best known example of explicit racialist ideology is the seventeenth century writer Wang Fuzhi [1619–92], who declared, 'Barbarians and Chinese are born in different places, which are endowed with different atmospheres. Since the atmospheres are different, their habits must be different. Since their habits are different, their thinking and behavior must be different.'[15]

---

[15] Cited in Fa-ti Fan, 'Nature and Nation in Chinese Political Thought: The National Essence Circle in Early Twentieth-century China', in *The Moral Authority of Nature*, eds Lorraine Daston and Fernando Vidal (Chicago: University of Chicago Press, 2004).

Wang was loyal to the fallen Ming dynasty and firmly rejected the legitimacy of the conquering Manchu elite. His writings were suppressed under Manchu rule, but were revived in the late nineteenth century in order to energise anti-Manchu nationalist revolutionaries. Wang's ideas, however, survived as a simmering counter-ideology to the orthodox views of the Qing rulers.

In the early eighteenth century, the Yongzheng emperor [r. 1723–35] and an obscure scholar named Zeng Jing debated this question publicly.[16] Zeng Jing, a low-level degree holder from Hunan, had concluded that the Manchus had no legitimate right to rule China, because they came from a different territory and different cultural heritage. In his view, only Han rulers from the central plains or the south could rule the empire; other peoples were 'barbarians' who could never adapt to the civilized ways of the interior. Zeng Jing drew inspiration for his ideas from writers of the late Ming dynasty like Wang Fuzhi who had refused to serve the Manchus after the conquest. He wrote a letter to a leading Han general, proposing that the general lead an uprising to throw out the Manchu usurpers.

The general immediately revealed the proposed plot to the emperor and Qing officials rounded up Zeng Jing and his very small number of disciples. There was never a serious military threat to the empire, or even a threat of disorder. Yet, the emperor was so disturbed by this proposal that he had Zeng Jing interrogated severely, and under torture forced him to confess his errors. The emperor also wrote his own lengthy refutation of Zeng and insisted that it be made required reading in all the empire's schools.

Why was the emperor so disturbed? By furiously suppressing Zeng and by publicising his refutation, the emperor in effect put Zeng's ideas on a par with his own. He clearly feared that Zeng's conception of the Manchus as illegitimate might be more widely shared among the Han literati class. Zeng drew on elements of the classical tradition to build his argument that nature determined character. He rejected the idea of transformation, arguing that Manchus could not change their ways. Yongzheng, by contrast, did not base his claim to rule on the proposition that Manchus had become identical to the Han. He too, agreed that the two peoples were distinct. But the Manchus had 'wiped out the shame' of the Ming dynasty, which had failed to keep internal

---

[16] Further discussion in Perdue, *China Marches West*, pp. 470–76. An engaging narrative of the Zeng Jing case is Jonathan Spence, *Treason by the Book* (New York: Viking, 2001).

order. The Manchus had brought peace and prosperity, which benefited both peoples. The only people who needed to be 'transformed', in the emperor's view, were those diehard adherents of the vanished Ming dynasty who stubbornly refused to accept Manchu legitimacy. He devoted the massive resources of his bureaucratic regime to stamping out any traces of cultural resistance. Some scholars attribute this overkill to Yongzheng's paranoid character, but he may have had real reasons to fear subterranean resistance. There were indications of rumours and placards in some southern Chinese cities advocating open resistance to the Manchus, and the rulers could never be certain that Han literati entirely accepted them. Yongzheng purged some of his most loyal Han generals, out of fear that their successes might overshadow his power, or become too appealing to the Han subjects.

The Manchus, as a minority ruling elite, had strong incentives to reject racialist ideas of rule, but they also rejected complete assimilation with the Han. They selectively adopted certain Han cultural features, but maintained their separateness through religious ceremonies, the banner system and compulsory exercises in horsemanship and military drill.[17] They succeeded in preserving their difference through the end of the dynasty and even up to the present. Over time, the Manchu homeland became a key element in defining Manchu identity, even though most Manchus never lived there. The association of people with a territory and distinct landscape was deliberately strengthened during the Qing as a mechanism of preserving Manchu power. At the same time, the Manchus appealed to the common values shared with the Han to ensure that their rule would be accepted by the majority. Qing rule depended on preserving a delicate balance between conceptions of difference rooted in territory and folkways, and appeals to similarity based on universal values. The frontier origins of the Manchus were the underlying conditions that impelled them to develop this complex ideology of rule.

THE VIEW FROM BEYOND THE FRONTIER

What did those on the other side of the imperial boundary think? Although most of our sources give only the imperial Chinese point of view, sometimes we can detect analogous tensions among the frontier

[17] Elliott, *The Manchu Way*; Evelyn S. Rawski, *The Last Emperors: A Social History of Qing Imperial Institutions* (Berkeley: University of California Press, 1998).

peoples themselves. Some regarded cultural transformation as genuinely possible, either as a threat or a positive opportunity. Others insisted on segregation and protection of the distinct cultures of their region. Often, however, those who believed in the possibility of transformation saw it as a threat. Their main concern was to ward off Chinese 'soft power'. Through the window of Chinese writings about the Xiongnu nomadic confederation in the Han dynasty, we can see evidence of the 'five baits' used by the Han empire to weaken the resistance of the Xiongnu: 'elaborate clothes and carriages to corrupt their eyes; fine food to corrupt their mouths; music to corrupt their ears; lofty buildings, granaries, and slaves to corrupt their stomachs; gifts and favors for [those] who surrendered'.[18]

A Chinese advisor to the Xiongnu warned them against this seductive strategy:

> The strength of the Xiongnu lies in the very fact that their food and clothing are different from those of the Chinese, and they are therefore not dependent on the Han for anything. Now the Shanyu [Xiongnu chieftain] has this fondness for Chinese things and is trying to change the Xiongnu customs. Thus, although the Han sends not more than a fifth of its goods here, it will in the end succeed in winning over the whole Xiongnu nation. From now on, when you get any of the Han silks, put them on and try riding your horses through brush and brambles! In no time your robes and leggings will be torn to shreds and everyone will see that silks are no match for the utility and excellence of felt and leather garments. Likewise when you get any of the Han foodstuffs, throw them away so that people can see that they are not as practical or tasty as milk and kumiss![19]

In the eighth century CE, in the native language of the steppe, the Orkhon inscriptions in ancient Turkish blamed the disintegration of the Türk empire on seduction by Chinese ways.

Bilgä khaghan warned his people:

> They [the Chinese] give [us] gold, silver, and silk in abundance. The words of the Chinese people have always been sweet and the materials of the Chinese people have always been soft. Deceiving by means of their sweet words and soft materials the Chinese are said to cause remote

---

[18] Thomas J. Barfield, *The Perilous Frontier: Nomadic Empires and China* (Cambridge, MA: Basil Blackwell, 1989). p. 51.

[19] Sima Qian, *Shiji* (Taipei: Hangye Shuju, 1976), cited in Barfield, p. 52.

peoples to come close in this manner.. . . . Having been taken in by their sweet words and soft materials, you Turkish people were killed in great numbers. O Turkish people, you will die [if you settle close to the Chinese in the south]... If you stay in the land of Ötükän and send caravans from there you will have no trouble. If you stay in the Ötükän mountains you will live forever dominating the tribes.[20]

These writers did not actively embrace 'Sinicisation' or assimilation to the empire's demands, nor were they merely 'nostalgic' for vanished practices of the past. They saw Chinese imperial efforts at cultural change as a present, clear danger to their autonomy as people and as a state.

When conquest dynasties took control of core Han territory, similar debates broke out about how to preserve their own cultural core while also accommodating large numbers of Han Chinese. Often, the solution was to create two or more separate administrations for each region, distinct in institutional structure, personnel and policies. The Liao, Jin and Yuan dynasties established these types of dual administrations, as did the Qing in its own frontier regions, including the Manchu homeland.

But other social processes beyond administrative control always threatened to undermine policies of segregation. Migration of Han settlers to frontier regions caused great ambivalence. In the view of proponents of migration, the migrants could raise the productivity of cleared lands and increase the proportion of settled farmers, thereby raising the level of 'civilization' on the frontier. Opponents argued that mixing two distinct populations inevitably generated conflict, and that segregation was the way to ensure peace. In addition, these contrasting perspectives did not only apply to peoples on the 'interior' of the empire, or to nomads on the steppes. All the peoples and states on imperial China's borders constantly interacted with Han culture and took a variety of stances towards it. In this sense, Mongols, Koreans, Japanese, Vietnamese and Southeast Asian polities all faced similar issues.

How were these ethnic perspectives connected to environmental conditions? I would propose that, in general, the more radical the differences between ecologies of production of two peoples, the sharper the ethnic distinctions and the sharper the consciousness of difference. On the other hand, in borderlands between two sharply distinct ecologies, mixed settlement and cooperation often flourished. Settled

---

[20] Talat Tekin, *A Grammar of Orhhon Turkic* (Bloomington: Indiana University Press, 1968) pp. 261–62.

Han peasants in the core and their rulers saw very little in common with the most mobile nomads of the Central Eurasian steppes. Manchus and Han pioneers on the frontiers, however, shared certain features with their neighbours, like mobility and the use of horses, making greater cultural communication possible. Similarly, in the southwest, from the Chinese perspective, the 'raw' aborigines were too mobile and primitive to be controlled or even educated, while the 'cooked' peoples who learned Chinese, settled down and lived near to Han settlers could be transformed into civilized humans.[21]

But environments did not totally determine cultural change. Every empire could accommodate radically different ecologies and cultures. The accidents of war and expansion brought diverse peoples under one imperial gaze. Because imperial borders are not fixed by ethnic criteria, empires by their nature must be set up to accommodate and manage difference. As Charles Maier notes,

> Imperial and national frontiers—even if of similar outward type— usually enclose different processes of governance and institutional structuration within their respective territories. The nation-state will strive for a homogeneous territory. . . Because of their size, and their assumption of power over old states and communities, empires possess a far less administratively uniform territory.[22]

On the other hand, some regimes with the most similar production systems to the settled Han core had the most success in fighting off Han domination. The Vietnamese of the Red River valley, whose agriculture and social customs most resembled those of south China, had the greatest success in driving out Chinese rule in the tenth century and defeating Chinese invasions ever after. We need to look at particular political and military encounters in order to clarify the connections between frontier environments and ethnic interaction.

The three case studies that follow look at different types of frontier interactions leading to different categorizations of frontier peoples by the centre and different policies towards migration, settlement and the use of force.

---

[21] For further discussion, see Peter C. Perdue, 'From Turfan to Taiwan: Trade and War on Two Chinese Frontiers', in *Untaming the Frontier in Anthropology, Archaeology and History*, eds Bradley J. Parker and Lars Rodseth (Tucson: University of Arizona Press, 2005).

[22] Maier, *Among Empires*, p. 102.

MANCHUS AND MONGOLS IN THE SEVENTEENTH CENTURY

Manchus and Mongols played complementary roles in constructing their collective identities in the early seventeenth century. The Manchus did not exist as a single people until the military unifier Nurhaci named them in 1635. The term 'Mongol' also seldom referred to a single unified population. Various tribes, each with their own lineages and territorial attachments, moved across the grasslands and forests of Central Eurasia, interacting with the Han Chinese to the south. Most of those later to be called Manchus were forest dwellers, living off fishing, hunting and trade in forest goods, while some settled in river valleys and practiced agriculture. Nurhaci [1559–1626], the founder of the Manchu state, had obtained licenses to trade with Ming garrisons on the frontier, and he used the resources gained through trade to strengthen his position beyond the Great Wall. Nurhaci's conquests of his neighbours mainly kept him in the forest zone. His successor, Hong Taiji [1592–1643], expanded the state southward into the settled regions of Liaodong, bringing under his sway Han settlers escaping Ming taxation, runaway soldiers, traders, criminals and others. These 'transfrontiersmen' joined with the growing Manchu state and the newly established banner system, a combined military and administrative institution including many ethnic groups, gave them a place within it. From its origins, the Manchu state spanned several ecological zones and incorporated many different cultural groups. Some Mongols also joined the Manchus in the early period, but others remained apart. Some, like the Chahar Mongols, resisted Manchu rule, but lost to them in battle. Others joined when they observed the growing military strength of the new state.

The Mongols, spread over a vast area, did not share a common spoken language or religion. Most were nomads, but some had begun to settle down and Buddhist Mongols had established fixed monasteries since the late sixteenth century. The primary common allegiance of Mongols was to the heritage of Chinggis Khan. To obtain legitimacy as supreme Khan of the Mongols, one had to claim descent from Chinggis Khan's clan, the Borjigid and demonstrate superior military leadership. During the Ming dynasty, no Mongol could both claim to be Chinggis' descendant and win enough battles to unify all the Mongols. Several non-Chinggisids did create powerful confederations, but they lasted only for a short period of time.

The Manchu rulers of the Qing were well aware of these divisions and used them effectively to keep the Mongols divided. They won over early Mongol adherents and incorporated them into the earliest banner units. The Khalkha Mongols of eastern Mongolia came over to the Manchu side in 1691, after prolonged internecine warfare and invasion by the Oirat leader Galdan from the West. The Oirat Mongols, the federation farthest west, fought against Qing expansion tenaciously under leadership by the Zunghar leaders, but finally were subdued in 1760.

The appeal of the Kangxi emperor [r. 1662–1722] to the Zunghar leader Galdan [r. 1671–97] illustrates how the Qing appealed to universal ideals to consolidate its rule over the Mongols. By claiming common interests with the Dalai Lama as a patron of Buddhism, the Qing emperor attempted to bridge cultural divisions between the core of China and the steppe, stressing the benefits of peaceful relations. The Qing emperor asserted his ability to embrace multiple peoples under a single benevolent administration, while respecting the distinctive practices of each of his subjects. He gave the Mongols and other 'barbarians' credit for having comparable moral values, but also offered them a moral choice: they could accept submission to the Qing comprehensive imperial project, or else face extermination. The Kangxi emperor did not conceal his military power or willingness to use it if necessary. His embrace of culturalism combined the enticing benefits of peace, prosperity and mutual respect, but reserved the right to use the sword if these were rejected. When Galdan rejected the Kangxi emperor's tempting offer, the emperor conducted personal military campaigns designed to literally 'pull up the roots' of his regime.[23]

The Kangxi emperor, however, failed to eradicate the Zunghar state. It took sixty more years before his grandson, the Qianlong emperor [r. 1736–95] could extend Qing military rule over all of Zungharia, eliminating the Zunghar state and people. The Qianlong emperor took advantage of divisions among the Zunghars over succession to leadership. He intervened on the side of prince Amursana, who called in Qing troops to support his campaign against his rival. After Amursana's victory, the emperor made it clear that Amursana would not have sole power, as he expected, but share it with others. Amursana rebelled against the Qing, but lost to the final Qing campaigns in 1760.

---

[23] Perdue, *China Marches West*, pp. 141–52.

Qianlong's victory made possible more intensive settlement of the oases of Xinjiang and the conversion of grasslands to cultivated fields. The Qing state actively promoted transformation of the northwest territories in order to tie them more closely to the interior. The emperor also sponsored large-scale scholarly projects to map the region, classify its peoples and write its definitive history. The emperor, in his preface to the history of his military campaigns, gave the Zunghars a prominent role in the 'opening' of Xinjiang. He recognized their long-term presence, but attributed their loss to the Qing to abandonment by Heaven. He defined them as a separate group of nomads, carefully classifying them into their subordinate units. By systematizing the very confusing history of the Zunghar state, the Qianlong emperor granted them a distinctive character based on their domination of the grasslands of the west. Now the Qing, with Heaven's aid, had brought peace to the region, bringing prosperity to all its peoples. (The fact of deliberate extermination of many Zunghar warriors by Qing armies was omitted in this account.)

In the eighteenth century, Qing writers recognized that the particular landscape of Xinjiang (literally, the 'New Borderland') created a distinct kind of people. Some even thought that Han emigrants to the region could benefit from the austere conditions of life there, and that the frontier would reinvigorate the martial spirit of the Han people. Xinjiang also became a land of temporary exile for many officials convicted of crimes. Some literati sent to the region found the experience bracing. Far from seeing a wasteland, they portrayed the cities of Xinjiang as vibrant communities with their own particular songs, customs and ancient heritage. Xinjiang was neither just like the interior, nor was it empty. It was another special component of the differentiated space that comprised the sprawling Qing empire.

TAIWAN: NATIVES AND MIGRANTS

Taiwan, another region newly conquered by the Qing in the seventeenth century, had a very different ecology. Before the Qing arrival, the inhabitants of Taiwan were mainly peoples with Polynesian or Southeast Asian connections, practicing swidden agriculture and deer hunting in the deep tropical forests. Dutch colonial rule of the early seventeenth century promoted agricultural cultivation along flatter lands in the southern part of the island. The Zheng regime of 1661–83 further stimulated land clearance.

Qing settlement began from a baseline that already included aboriginal peoples, incipient agricultural development and colonial domination. All three interacted over the next two centuries of Qing rule.[24]

The writings of Lan Dingyuan [1680–1733], an official active in the promotion of the colonization of Taiwan, indicate how the native population participated in Qing penetration. Lan, like many Qing officials, regarded the aboriginal population as endemically warlike. The young men engaged in incessant feuds with other tribes, leaving them incapable of resisting the organized Qing forces. But migrants from mainland China also proved to be turbulent. They came from different regions of China, and often instigated feuds against each other for control of land, water and other resources. The settlers also resisted official efforts to tax them and mobilize their labour for public works. In 1721, the duck breeder Zhu Yigui, an immigrant from Fujian province, raised a rebellion against particularly abusive official demands. He attacked official headquarters and defeated the small Qing forces in southern Taiwan. Zhu also rallied anti-Manchu support by claiming to be a descendant of the Ming royal family, since he had the same surname. As the revolt spread more widely, panicked officials abandoned the capital of southern Taiwan in Tainan. Within two weeks, Qing control of nearly all the island had collapsed.

Lan joined the campaign to suppress Zhu's rebellion. The Qing leaders enrolled aboriginal troops on their side against Zhu's forces, offering the natives rewards of three taels for every rebel killed and five taels for every rebel leader. This incentive led the native troops to attack Han settlers indiscriminately, burning whole villages and slaughtering large populations. Lan concluded from this bungled policy that natives were by nature 'greedy, wild, and insatiable'. Regular Qing forces soon suppressed the rebellion and brought the native forces under control, but Lan blamed the rebellion on restrictions of Han immigration to the island. He aggressively advocated Han settlement in order to tame the aboriginal menace. Until this time, Qing officials had tried to restrict migration to the island, both to prevent feuds among the Chinese and to protect the aboriginal population, but Lan pushed hard for an assimilationist policy. Lan took the vision of cultural transformation to its extreme: large-scale Han immigration to the island and enforced settlement of aborigines

---

[24] Major studies include Murray A. Rubinstein, *Taiwan: A New History* (Armonk, NY: M. E. Sharpe, 1999), Shepherd, *Statcraft and Political Economy on the Taiwan Frontier*; Teng, *Taiwan's Imagined Geography*. See also the excellent summary in Richards, *The Unending Frontier*, pp. 89–111.

would make them give up violence and tribal hunting and adapt to settled Han ways. His aggressive views were not typical of most Qing officials. His arguments for increased immigration and aboriginal assimilation were rejected and the court continued to impose restraints on immigration.[25]

Although the emperors repeatedly reversed policies on immigration, over the long-term, a wave of Han settlers flowed there in defiance of imperial prohibitions. The aborigines who adapted to Han ways still proved helpful to Qing officials in putting down other rebellions by Han settlers in the late eighteenth century. Those who rejected the new settlers fled to more distant mountainous regions in order to continue slash-and-burn agriculture and hunting as means of subsistence.

In sum, on this frontier, some of the native inhabitants actively assisted Qing settlement, just as the cooperative Mongols had aided Manchu expansion in the northwest. Even though the ecologies of production differed radically at the outset, those aborigines who took up settled agriculture found common cause with Qing officials who enforced stable conditions of production, like the Mongols who praised the peace brought by Qing rule. Unlike Mongolia, however, the largest threat to social order came not from the 'wild' natives, but from groups of Chinese settlers themselves. Perhaps, because the old ways of swidden agriculture and deer hunting offered only limited opportunities on the narrow island in the face of increasing Han settlement, holding out against Qing control held less promise for aboriginal Taiwanese than for Mongols. Mongols still had vast spaces of grasslands to retreat to, and under Qing rule, they could still continue a constricted nomadic way of life. Aborigines had to convert totally to settled agriculture in order to convince Qing officials that they had become 'civilized'. Radical colonialists like Lan Dingyuan wrote off the entire aboriginal population as irredeemably aggressive, but more balanced officials used the converted aborigines to control unruly Han settlers. The mixed population on this frontier offered several opportunities for balancing different ethnic forces against each other.

FROM MIAO TO 'MIAO' IN SOUTHWEST CHINA

In Taiwan, Qing officials could identify loyal aboriginal populations and use them against troublesome Han migrants. On the southwest frontier,

---

[25] Lan Dingyuan, *Pingtai Jilue* (Taibei: Taiwan Yinhang, 1958).

it was more difficult to define exactly who the loyal populations were.[26] The Qing experience with 'Miao' peoples in western Hunan and Guizhou province illustrates this concern. The term 'Miao' embraced a variety of local populations who lived in mountainous regions on the peripheries of several provinces of south China. Although the Ming dynasty had placed garrisons in part of the region, significant control and penetration by Han migrants only came in the eighteenth century. Qing officials recognized that this region, even though part of the regular provincial administration, was different from the interior [*neidi*] and regularly referred to it as the 'Miao borderland' [*Miaojiang*]. As in Taiwan, they tended to blame disorder in the region on Han migrants who disturbed the peaceful activities of the innocent Miao, even using the term 'Han traitors' [*Hanjian*] to describe migrants who created disturbances. The culturalists argued for allowing migration, while promoting policies to protect Miao land rights and also accustom them to Han ways. Education, the adoption of Han dress, wearing of the queue and other external signs of acculturation would, in their view, reduce differences between the two populations and lead to peace. Pessimists, with a more racialist view, argued for keeping the populations distinct in order to prevent contamination of one by the other. They feared that the Han miscreants would provide hostile Miao with weapons and techniques of resistance to Qing rule, while also mistreating the Miao and creating resentment.

The Yongzheng emperor had promoted active migration in the 1720s, but the Qianlong emperor reversed this policy, arguing that the Miao needed to be left in peace. Efforts at quarantining the Miao, however, failed here as in Taiwan because of demographic pressures and the penetration of Han trade networks into the region. In the 1760s, rival Miao groups called in Qing troops to settle their feuds, but the Qing military officials rejected the orders to settle disputes according to Miao custom. Instead, they carried out brutal repression of all Miao, stimulating sharp resentments which burst out in a major revolt in 1795, led by Miao who spoke Chinese. Qing officials had radically misjudged the loyalty of the semi-acculturated Miao. As Donald Sutton notes:

> Eighteenth-century writings . . . did not distinguish between accultura-
> tion and assimilation. It was assumed that the hearts and minds of the

---

[26] Donald S. Sutton, 'Ethnicity and the Miao Frontier in the Eighteenth Century', in *Empire at the Margins: Culture, Ethnicity, and Frontier in Early Modern China*, eds Pamela Kyle Crossley, Helen F. Siu and Donald S. Sutton (Berkeley: University of California Press, 2006).

Miao had been (or were being) won over, and that talking and behaving like Chinese and receiving minimal Confucian education would make them loyal Qing subjects. But bilingualism in the three subprefectures [in western Hunan]... was forming and fortifying political identity, not weakening it. The fact that Miao of all three subprefectures and Songtao rose up almost in a body in 1795 suggests that their sense of common identity had been crystallized by the experiences of the preceding decades.[27]

Brutal repression put down the Miao rebels of Hunan after many years of military campaigning from 1795 to 1806, but in the mid-nineteenth century, revolts broke out in neighbouring Guizhou. This rebellion lasted from twenty years, from 1854–73, and it, too, required many years of devastating, and expensive, military campaigns. In this rebellion, however, the Miao themselves played only a subordinate role. As Robert Jenks argues: 'Many more Han than Miao were involved on the rebel side, despite the misleading name—to wit, "Miao" rebellion—that has been applied to this period of turmoil'.[28] The rebels included other hill peoples, Han militia groups, followers of sectarian religions, Muslims, martial arts experts, peasants resisting tax exactions, along with Miao and others protesting Han immigration to the province. Robert Jenks' excellent study gives a detailed narrative of the multiple revolts and military campaigns of this period. I will only comment that misperceptions by Qing officials of the ethnic composition of the province aggravated the problem of restoring order just as it had in eighteenth-century Hunan. By mischaracterizing the rebels as 'Miao' and by assuming that all Miao were stupid, aggressive and violent, the officials and military men simply polarized the population, making it impossible to find local allies. The inability to distinguish ethnic and religious loyalties on this very mixed frontier prolonged the control effort, and led to much merciless massacre and destruction. Some local officials recognized the complexity of the region, but their views did not carry the day.

It seems that the Manchus of the seventeenth and eighteenth centuries, who cleverly manipulated Mongols of the northwest and found local allies in Taiwan, lost their touch in the Miao borderlands in the nineteenth century. The development of a more racialist ideology

---

[27] *Ibid.*, p. 216.

[28] Robert Darrah Jenks, *Insurgency and Social Disorder in Guizhou: The "Miao" Rebellion, 1854–1873* (Honolulu: University of Hawaii Press, 1994), p. 72.

of separation had begun in the mid-eighteenth century, for a number of reasons. As the Manchus themselves came to fear losing their collective identity among the vast sea of Han whom they ruled, they began to promote policies to preserve Manchu identity based on genealogical descent and the special features of the Manchu homeland. This sharper definition of the Manchus led to defining other peoples of the empire in more rigid ways. By the late eighteenth century, on many borderlands, severe ethnic discontent sharpened Manchu and Han repression, leading them to create polarized images of loyal subjects and vicious rebels. As they lost their ability to distinguish among different local populations on a number of frontiers, they lost the ability to recruit local allies.

In the mid-nineteenth century, rebellions broke out around the empire on a much larger scale. Although population pressure, immigration and trade disrupted all the frontier regions, intelligent local policies could have prevented friction and forestalled revolt. The mid-nineteenth century rebellions had many causes, but one of them was the inability of Qing frontier officials to gather enough information about the multiple ethnic groups in their jurisdiction to make possible nuanced policies. In order to maintain peace, Qing rulers needed ethnic categorizations attentive to the diverse environments of the empire's frontiers. When they lost the ability to make these distinctions, they lost one of the keys to their enduring dominion.

10

The Frontiers of Memory:
What the Marathas Remembered of Vijayanagara

SUMIT GUHA*

———— • ✦ • ————

INTRODUCTION

Historians have long struggled with the task of interpreting narratives that although written in the past tense are yet hard, if not impossible to reconcile with each other or indeed, the modern historical sense of there having been a singular past. The usual response has been to 'mine' them for historical knowledge as 'such consciousness is not always visible and has to be prised from sources which tend to conceal it'.[1] Alternatively, we can treat historical texts as literary ones and allow them all to benefit from the suspension of disbelief available to the literary understanding. Thus, Hayden White proposed in 1966[2] to treat historical explanation as something that 'can be judged solely in terms of the richness of the metaphors which govern its sequence of articulation' because, after all, 'there is no such thing as a single correct view of any object'.[3]

* An earlier version of this essay was presented at a conference in honour of John Richards, Duke University, 29–30 September, 2006. I am indebted to the participants for many valuable comments and suggestions, and to Phillip Wagoner for a close reading and valuable information on Mackenzie and his collaborators. I have also benefited from the comments of an anonymous referee and the critical scrutiny by Indrani Chatterjee. Any remaining errors must, of course, be credited to me.

[1] Romila Thapar, *Interpreting Early India* (Delhi: Oxford University Press [1992] 1999), p. 137.

[2] Here and throughout the rest of this essay, the Common Era dates are inserted without specific marking; the calendrical system is indicated in all other cases.

[3] Hayden V. White, 'The Burden of History', *History and Theory* 5 (1966), p. 130.

Gabrielle Spiegel, an important scholar of pre-modern narrative has sought a middle ground between these opposed positions arguing that the 'alternative between seeing language as either perfectly transparent or completely opaque is simply too rigidly framed'. She then pointed out a vital difference between the way that historians and literary scholars needed to approach texts.

> But historical contexts do not exist in themselves; they must be defined, and in that sense constructed, by the historian before the interpretive work of producing meaning, of interpreting the past, can begin.....[4]

This can be done by seeking to answer the questions 'when?' and 'why?' Once this is achieved, there is an immense deepening of both our historical and literary understanding as is, for example, achieved by Sheldon Pollock when he draws out the historical research embodied in Chalukya inscriptions, that even such an accomplished scholar as Nilakanta Shastri had rejected as 'of no value for factual history'.[5] The positive processes by which memories have been generated have often been discussed—the accompanying processes of forgetting less so. But, as Prachi Deshpande recently pointed out, 'memory as a category of cultural history is more useful if employed to investigate the many contexts within which some representations become part of popular memory and *others do not*'.[6] This essay is concerned with those that do not achieve perpetuation. Finally, it shows how knowledge could be irrevocably lost as a consequence of that social choice.

In his pathbreaking *Time Maps: Collective Memory and the Social Shape of the Past*, Eviatar Zerubavel points out, 'not everything that happens is preserved in our memory, as many past events are actually cast into oblivion. Acknowledgedly, historical events still form only that small part that we have come to preserve as public memory'. Nor is the creation of this mnemonic archive a purely random process. Zerubavel shows also that groups consolidate themselves around the memories of a common past and that 'acquiring a group's memories and thereby identifying with its collective past is part of the process of acquiring

---

[4] Gabrielle M. Spiegel, *The Past as Text: The Theory and Practice of Medieval Historiography* (Baltimore: The Johns Hopkins University Press, 1997), pp. 51, xix.

[5] Sheldon Pollock, *The Language of the Gods in the World of Men: Sanskrit, Culture and Power in Premodern India* (Delhi: Permanent Black, 2007), pp. 155–61. Sastri cited on p. 160.

[6] Prachi Deshpande, *Creative Pasts: Historical Memory and Identity in Western India, 1700–1960* (New York: Columbia University Press 2007), p. 4. Emphasis added.

any social identity.[7] This, of course, becomes especially important when the bearers of one social identity supplant those of another. Over a half-century ago, Maurice Halbwachs analysed how 'Christian collective memory could annex a part of the Jewish collective memory by appropriating part of the latter's local remembrance while at the same time transforming its entire perspective of historical space'.[8]

Both these scholars were concerned with situations in which the boundaries of the relevant community were clearly defined. Zerubavel's units of analysis are mainly nation-states while the processes that Halbwachs' essay addressed occurred when the Christian church had effectively permeated the political structures of late Imperial Rome. Communities and identities in the South Asian setting are both more numerous and more fluid. This, in part, is what makes their study especially interesting. Twenty years ago, V. N. Rao made a major breakthrough in his consideration of the perceived veridical status of Telugu oral epics—narratives of a type that often cross to and through written text. Rao found that

> "[c]ommunities who tend to adopt a narrative as 'their story' give it a historical status, whereas communities who do not, regard it as fiction.... . The mere presence of identifiable historical elements, therefore, does not cause a narrative to be accepted as a 'true story'; it must also represent a world-view for a caste or a social group."[9]

Equally, we may see narrative texts as Sanjay Subrahmanyam proposed recently as being analysable 'in relation to the process[es] of state-building'.[10] So if individual autobiographic memory is teleologically structured to a later context, so is the collective memory that helps constitute the community that transmits it.[11] But historical

---

[7] Eviatar Zerubavel, *Time Maps: Collective Memory and the Social Shape of the Past* (Chicago: University of Chicago Press, 2004), pp. 2–3.

[8] 'The Legendary Topography of the Gospels in the Holy Land', in *On Collective Memory*, ed. and trans. Lewis A. Coser (Chicago: University of Chicago Press, 1992), p. 215.

[9] V. Narayana Rao, 'Epics and Ideologies: Six Telugu Folk Epics', p. 132, in *Another Harmony: New Essays on the Folklore of India*, eds Stuart H. Blackburn and A. K. Ramanujan (Berkeley: University of California Press, 1986), p. 132.

[10] Sanjay Subrahmanyam, 'Reflections on State-Making and History-making in South India 1500–1800', in *Penumbral Visions: Making Polities in Early Modern South India* (Delhi: Oxford University Press, 2001), p. 186.

[11] On autobiographical memory, see Craig R. Barclay, 'Autobiographical Remembering: Narrative Constraints on Objectified Selves', in *Remembering Our Past: Studies in Autobiographical Memory*, ed. David C. Rubin (Cambridge: Cambridge University Press, 1996), pp. 94–127.

memory is created both by memory and forgetting—the omission of events that 'would fit awkwardly, even seriously inconvenience, the neatly woven pattern'.[12] Indeed as Renan argued in 1882, forgetting— and even historical errors—were essential for the creation of a national consciousness, so much so that 'advances in historical research constitute a hazard for the nation'.[13] More recently, Indrani Chatterjee has studied the Mizo re-appropriation of an 1872 attack on an encroaching tea plantation as the providential event that began the Christianization of the Mizos and their own constitution as a community, to the exclusion of other elements of the story.[14] The cost of such exclusion can be, as I will show later in this essay, that memories once lost may become irrecoverable and be re-created in unrecognizable form. I will, therefore, essay to study the loss and re-invention of historical memory in the Marathi-speaking tradition.

Maratha power, as represented by the Bhosle dynasty, rose within the frame of the Sultanates of south India. It then came to an accommodation with the Mughal empire whose effective control it challenged on a sub-continental scale by the mid-eighteenth century. I will show how memory was constructed around the project of inheriting the legitimacy and power of that Islamicate empire. Vijayanagara was slighted. I will also lay out my understanding of why this was so. So, this essay will seek to establish what the Marathas remembered of Vijayanagara and then contextualize the nature of that memory in terms of the identity and world-view of the community that generated and transmitted it. It will try to establish that Vijayanagara had a peripheral place in their vision of the past through to the end of the nineteenth century before its re-discovery in the early twentieth century.

The great empire of Vijayanagara dominated the Southern half of peninsular India for over two centuries. Legends of about it bulked large in popular and scholarly memory for centuries after, leading to the careful construction of spurious narratives of its time, such as the *Rayavacakamu*

12 The quote is from Shahid Amin's 'Prologue' to *Event, Metaphor, Memory: Chauri Chaura 1922–1992*, (New Delhi: Penguin, 2006), p. xx.

13 Ernest Renan, '*Qu'est-ce qu'une nation?*' reprinted in *Oeuvres Completes*, Vol. 1, (Paris: Calmann-Levy, [1882] 1947), p. 891

14 Indrani Chatterjee, 'Captives of Enchantment?: Gender, Genre and Transmemoration' Seminar paper presented at the University of California Santa Cruz, Workshop on Comparative Feminisms, March 2005.

so brilliantly analysed by Phillip Wagoner.[15] Wagoner convincingly shows that the far-away rulers of Madura were still enthralled by Vijayanagara fifty years after its fall and an elaborate narrative was generated to link them to that empire. But the memory of Vijayanagara was not merely current among courtly literati. It also entered folk memory and crops up in many of the village histories and local histories collected for Mackenzie and excerpted in the *Sources of Vijayanagar History*[16] and *Further Sources of Vijayanagar History*. So, for example, when the barbers of Utukuru in the district of Pottapinadu had to justify their tax exemption (to the East India Company?) they explained that:

> Kondoju, the barber gave Ramaraja such a clean and comfortable shave at Vijayanagara that he won the royal approbation. Ramaraja granted him graciously a charter as mark of his approbation of Kondoju's workmanship. The *pannu* and *kanike* which the barbers had to pay. . . were made *sarvamanya* [tax-exempt].[17]

Vijayanagara was clearly a name to conjure within the lands south of the Tungabhadra.

This is in sharp contrast with Maratha memories of the same regime. They were scanty despite the fact that the Bhosle regime was to campaign in and govern large parts of the former Vijayanagara lands. Shahaji Bhosle, father of the *Chatrapati* Shivaji, was a prominent Maratha noble who had risen to the position of regent to the infant sultan of Ahmednagar in the last days before the kingdom was absorbed into the Mughal empire. In 1637, he was compelled by the joint pressure of the Mughals and the Adilshahi sultanate to accept the status of an Adilshahi *jagirdar*. He spent the last decades of his life in central Karnataka warring with local chiefs as well as Qutbshahi commanders.[18] If his panegyrist Jayaram Pindye is to be believed, one of those defeated by him was the Rayalu of Vidyanair (Vidyanagara—sixteenth century synonym of Vijayanagara). The poet claims that the *Chatri-jata* (warrior caste) of Vidyanair lost all

---

[15] Phillip B. Wagoner, *Tidings of the King: A Translation and Ethnohistorical Analysis of the Rayavacakamu* (Honolulu: University of Hawaii Press, 1993).

[16] S. Krishnaswamy Iyengar ed., *Sources of Vijayanagar History* (Madras: University of Madras, 1919).

[17] K. A. Nilakanta Sastri and N. Venkataramanayya, *Further Sources of Vijayanagar History* (Madras: University of Madras, 1946, 3 vols.), Vol. 3, p. 197.

[18] Govind Sakharam Sardesai, *Marathi Riyasat*, Revised and annotated edition (Mumbai: Popular Prakashan 1988, 8 vols.), vol. 1, p. 89–109.

shame and fled abandoning their strongholds.[19] By the early eighteenth century, Maratha rulers were established in or seeking to conquer a significant part of the former territory of that empire. A Bhosle dynasty ruled from the ancient city of Thanjavur, and the Chatrapati's warlords were striving to build appanages for themselves from the Krishna to Ramnad. In this they were reviving the example of Shahaji Bhosle who was forced out his ancestral lands in Ahmednagar sultanate by a pact between the Mughals and the Adilshahi sultans, and agreed to serve the latter as a warlord in the ruins of the former Vijayanagara empire. There can be little doubt that many of the same administrator Brahman families served both the Nayaka successors of Vijayanagara and their Maratha competitors (not to mention other local rulers).

But in contrast to the Telugu and Kannada countries, Maratha historical memory was largely impervious to the appeal of Vijayanagara as a repository of ancestral glory. Indeed, while Jayarama Pindye had at least been aware of the legend linking Vidyaranya with the founding of Vijayanagara[20]—hence his adoption of Vidyanagara as its name—the later generations of Marathi speakers even forgot that famous name and referred to the kingdom of 'Anegondi'. Anegondi or Anigondi is still an extant town on the northern bank Tungabhadra, about five kilometres from the ruined city itself. A tradition reported by Nuniz in the early sixteenth century was that Deva Raya (Harihara?) lived in the fort there before moving up the river to found Vijayanagara. Etymologically meaning the 'elephant pit' or 'elephant valley', Anegondi was evidently a suburb of the great city in the days of its prosperity. In the eighteenth century, it was the seat of a local Rayalu or king claiming descent from the Aravidu dynasty of Vijayanagara.[21] This ruler was recognized as the heir to Vijayanagara in Maratha tradition, but few concrete memories of that empire survived.

This is evidenced in the following entries in Molesworth's early (1831, 1857) *Dictionary* of the Marathi language. Molesworth lived and worked in western India for several decades and was assisted by seven

[19] Jayarama Pindye, *Radhamadhavavilasacampu* ed. Vishwanath K. Rajwade (Pune: Varda Books [1923] 1993), pp. 256–57.

[20] For background, see Hermann Kulke, 'Maharajas, Mahants and Historians: Reflections on the Historiography of Early Vijayanagara and Sringeri', in *Kings and Cults: State Formation an Legitimation in India and Southeast Asia* (Delhi: Manohar reprint, 2001), pp. 208–39.

[21] Natalie Tobert, *Anegondi: Architectural Ethnography of a Royal Village* (Delhi: Manohar for the American Institute of Indian Studies, Vijayanagara Research Project Monograph Series, Vol. 7, 2000), x–xii, pp. 192–96.

local *panditas* as well as John and Thomas Candy and the well-known orientalist John Wilson. The compilers began by employing Brahmans to collect words and phrases 'in several quarters of the Maratha territory'. These were then scrutinized by a group of seven or eight other Brahmans and finally checked by other Indian scholars sitting with either Molesworth or one of the Candy brothers.[22] The entry for Anegondi in it is, therefore, a good indication of the state of Marathi historical memory in the early nineteenth century.

> Anagondi *a[djective]* (From the name of a town of which, as the legend runs, the king or Raja used to call himself *sarvabhauma* or sovereign paramount, and divert himself with entering the revenues of the whole earth on the credit side of his ledger, expending them off again on the debit side.) Applied variously to as *Anagondi karkhana-karbhar-kharch-baksis-bolnem* & c. Disorderly business of proceedings; vast and foolish expenditures; lavish largesses or presents; wild extravagant speech & c. 2 *A[nagondi]ce rajya n[oun]* A name for any very confused and disorderly business or proceeding. *A[nagondi]ca raja* m. A term for a soft fellow ready to give whatever is asked from him.

Sic transit gloria mundi!

The decay of memory set in early. This is shown by a probably forged Sanskrit document produced by a learned Brahman family, the Padhyes of Golavalli about 1600 as evidence in a lawsuit. The Sanskrit text claimed to be a judicial verdict from *Sake* 1285 or 1362–63 and alluded to the rule of a Yadava Ramaraja—obviously an impossible echo of Ramacandradeva of the Yadava dynasty who had died in 1312 as a vassal of the Khalji sultans of Delhi. But the Marathi verdict rendered in 1600 seems to view it as a document originating from the much more recent Ramaraja of Vidyanagara or the Aliya Rama Raju, killed in 1565![23] The Sardesai family who contested the Padhyes' claim also invoked the authority of Vidyanagara (Vijayanagara) but claimed their original grant came from its fourteenth-century ruler Vijayanagara ruler, Bukkanna

---

[22] *Dictionary of Marathi and English* compiled by J. T. Molesworth assisted by George and Thomas Candy – Second Edition revised and enlarged by J. T. Molesworth [1857] 2nd Corrected Reprint Pune: Shubhada Saraswat 1982, Preface to the second edition, pp. xviii–xxi.

[23] D. V. Potdar and G. N. Mujumdar eds, *Sivacaritra Sahitya- 2* (Pune: BISM 1930), pp. 333–38; I located this reference via the valuable article by D. V. Potdar, 'Marathit Vijayanagara' in *Vijayanagara Smaraka Grantha (Marathi Avrutti)*, eds Dattatreya P. Karmarkar and Rajaram V. Oturkar (Pune: BISM 1936–37), pp. 338–50. The discussion of the rival narratives of the Sarde sai and Padhye households is taken from that essay.

who is said to have ruled the whole of south India north up to the Narmada river.[24] It is striking that both these literati lineages had little actual knowledge of the history and chronology of the empire.

These fading memories baffled the rare scholars who sought for some memory of that regime. This is evident in a compilation of Marathi verses in a manuscript belonging to Satipa Kondkar, a resident of Loni in Kadevala district. The manuscript was copied in 1738–39. It briefly narrates the story of Vidyanagara being founded under the patronage of Vidyaranya; mentions some of the successive rulers; and states that Sadasiva, son of Acyuta, moved the capital from Vidyanagara to Anagondi. His son was Rama, unskilled in war and given to dissipation. Dandu, the Turk lord was stupid by nature and could not learn Kannada. He knew that the emperor used to go on fixed days to bathe in the Krishna-tirtha at Rakshat-gadhi (sic). He gathered three others and killed the Rau with their swords. The army had no leader and was overcome by the Adal, Kutubaraya and Nizamashaha in 1354 [1431–32] paradhavi abda, on the fifth day in the bright half of Magha. But the author then adds 'the original manuscript is old and damaged; it does not match (other) evidence'. He then provides several Sanskrit chronograms and Marathi verses—presumably from other manuscripts, which give the following alternative dates:

> Saka 1414 [1491–92] paradhavi samvatsara Magha bright half 5th day, Friday
>
> Saka 1407 [1484–85] parabhava samvatsara magha bright half 5th day, Friday
>
> Saka 1467 [1544–45] parabhava samvatsara Magha bright half 5th day, Friday

All of these are wrong and it is evident that the event was remembered only by its astrological conjunction, that is, by the month, day and year of the 60-year cycle.[25] The present text represents a later attempt to work out the exact year. But the author evidently found few resources in Marathi or Sanskrit beyond a simple dynastic list and a tale of Muslim trickery. Likewise, in the later eighteenth century, the Marathi narrative of the rise of the Bhosles—the *Shivadigvijaya*—stated that Ramaraja left

---

[24] Cited in Potdar, 'Marathit Vijayanagara', pp. 339–40.

[25] Y. Khu. Deshpande, 'Vijayanagarce Rajanca ullekha' with notes by D. V. Potdar and S. N. Joshi, *BISMT* 10 (1929), pp. 113–15.

for the south, after nominating a (nameless) merchant (*vaishya*) to rule in his place. Six *Yavana* (Muslim) youths who had been raised by Ramaraja then decided to usurp the empire—they imprisoned the merchant and divided the empire among themselves, founding kingdoms at Anagondi, Bijapur, Bhaganagar (Hyderabad) Daulatabad, Amdabad (in Gujarat?) and Nagpur.[26] In this version, even the ruler of Anagondi was now classed as a Muslim usurper! The author clearly believed that the six Subahs, or governorships of the Dakhan in late Mughal times represented the original six parts into which the empire was divided but did not have an accurate list of these as they had existed under Aurangzeb. So he extemporized by inserting the names of prominent cities of his own time.

A similar disregard was shown by the successors of Vijayanagara even in lands that had been important parts of that empire. In 1803, the last Bhosle Maratha ruler of Thanjavur had his personal secretary Baburaya compose a long Marathi family history that was then inscribed on the wall of the Brihadishvara temple in that city where Vijayanagara-era frescoes still survive.[27] Yet even this southern ruler with a multilingual court slighted Vijayanagara in his origin myth.[28] It begins by stating that Bhosle family's original ancestor was the Lord Narayana. In his line was Suryanarayana, then Manu, then the King Iksvaku—and from him many kings renowned through the first three epochs (*yuga*). In the fourth epoch, *kaliyuga*, there descended the lord of Maharashtra, king Sambhu. In his line came Sarabharaje who pleased Somaskanda who appeared in a dream and gave him a powerful *mantra*. With this *mantra*, he so pleased the (nameless) *padshaha* (emperor) of the south who bestowed the *jahagira* of Bidalarhi. The family's rise to prominence then commenced.[29] Vijayanagara as point of origin—so important for many rulers of the same region—is here spurned in favour of an origin in Maharashtra and consequent affiliation to the anonymous *padshaha*. This choice was made despite the evident Sanskritization (Hinduization?) of Sharifji (Sarfoji) into *Sharabha*—in evident denial of the legend that Maloji's sons were named Shahaji and Sharifji after

---

[26] Potdar, 'Marathit Vijayanagara' pp. 343–44.

[27] S. Paramashivan, 'Vijayanagarakalina Citrakala', in *Vijayanagara Smaraka Grantha*, pp. 208–09.

[28] As Zerubavel points out, beginnings are highly significant. 'Origins help articulate identities, and where communities locate their beginnings tells us quite a lot about how they perceive themselves'. *Time-Maps*, p. 101, emphasis original.

[29] T. Sambamurti Row copied and published, *The Marathi Historical Inscription at the Sri Brihadeeswaraswami Temple at Tanjore* (Tanjore: The Editor 1907), pp. 1–2.

a Muslim *pir*, Shah Sharif.[30] In sum, therefore, the Maratha imperium invented little and knew less about their predecessors in the southern peninsula. Vijayanagara as point of origin does appear in an exceptionally contrarian narrative: the anonymous late eighteenth-century *More yanci choti bakhar*, glorifying Shivaji's enemy, Chandrarao More of Javli. It is probably a part of this contrarian stance that causes it to state that all the noble Maratha lineages were originally in the service of Krishnadevaraya at Vidyanagara. So also were those who were later to become Sultans— Ibrahim and Ali Yedilshaha and Bahirinizam. Ibrahim (Qutbshaha) was appointed governor of Telangana and, when out hunting on the banks of the Musi river, encountered a hare that attacked his hunting dogs. He then founded Golkunda.[31] Vijayanagara finds no further mention in this narrative.

But even when we turn to district hereditary officials (variously titled *qanungo, deshpande, nadkarni*, etc.)—the appointed custodians of popular memory all over the sub-continent—we find that precious little of the great empire had passed into Maratha historical memory. Thus in 1823–24, the officials of Anjanvel subdivision in the southern Konkan were required to compile a detailed memorandum of the past revenue administration of their district. The memorandum shows considerable knowledge of past tax rates and practices and was clearly based on both memory and written records going back several centuries. They certainly had some hazy recollection of the Anagondi raja as being the first ruler of their region. I translate the opening paragraphs of the document they produced.

> Administration of taluka Anjanvela Suru san 1214[32]—a true account of the previous kings' government [In the beginning there was] Kanada Ramaraja Chatrapati by caste (*jati*) Lingayat Vani—in his time there were no fortresses in the taluka. But then one Pawar, Maratha by caste built a small fort in the village of Gudhe, subdivision Valambe and created a province called Gudhe and established a market-town and governed from there. That was about 600 years ago. Under that government much of the land was uncultivated, and there was new settlement. The land

---

[30] Equally interesting but not relevant to the present theme is the systematic downplaying of Shivaji and his line.

[31] Incomplete text, without ascription, published as 'Aitihasik sphuta lekha' pp. 21–29, in *Itihasa Samgraha* 1 (1908–09).

[32] Internal evidence suggests that this was a copyist's error, and either the year was in *Fasli* or the number should perhaps be 1224. The regimes covered extend up to Sake 1739, or 1817–18.

tax was not assessed on the basis of area measurement but levied after an annual estimate in agreement with the peasants in accordance with the *taka bandi* system. In Pawar's time the following small forts existed in the subdivision:

1 Manikdurg in the village of Madki, subdivision Savarde

1 In the village of Sir, subdivision Valambe, a fort named Kasardurg.

2 (total)

Affairs were conducted thus for about 275 years and then came the rule of the Padshahs.

Ali Idalshah and Bahiri Nizyamshah these two brothers killed the Kanada Ramaraja in the camp of Anagondi and seated Ali Idalsha on the throne of Vijyapur *san salas [3] tisa [9?] maya [100] Shake* 1424 [1501–2 CE] *samvatsara* Dundubhi [current year should be 1502–3 so this is evidently elapsed year reckoning]

Account of that government (follows)

Ali Idalshah was himself present from Shake 1424 San *salas miya* to San *saman arbain va tisa maya* Shake 1469 [1546–7 CE] *samvatsara* named Kilaka. . .[33]

As must be evident, little information had been transmitted through the centuries. The dates are wrong and the indeed beyond the simple name 'Ramaraja' it is clear that the authors knew nothing of the great empire beyond its existence at some point in the hazy past. This despite the fact that its rule had extended north to the borders of the Konkani–Marathi speaking Phonda region of Goa where a Marathi inscription of 1412–13 (*Sake* 1335) recorded the grants of certain incomes to a temple at Bandivada.[34] This profound indifference was found even among the most learned. It is reflected in an entry in the list of Sanskrit law books known to the Pandits of Pune as prepared by Vamana Sastri Satya 'and corrected by reference to the Hindoo College and other Brahmuns who attended the distribution of the Dukshuna in 1825'. It lists the 'Madhwu', said to have been written by Sayunacharya or Widyaruneswamee [Vidyaranya svami], a Sunyasee Brahmun of Anagoondy about 1,000 years ago, and 'Nundurajakrit', by Nunduraja of Anagoondy, of the

[33] Datto Vamana Potdar ed., *Anjanvela Talukyaci Vahivata*, in Khanderav Cintamana Mehendale (ed.) (BISM Varshika Itivritta Sake 1835), pp. 318–20.

[34] Published by V. K. Rajavade and D. V. Apte in *ibid.*, pp. 169–75.

Kshutryu caste.[35] The reader should know that I have not selected these narratives as against better-informed ones: these are among the very few Marathi historical sources that mention Vijayanagara at all. The deeply learned Datto Vamana Potdar was forced to end his survey of the Marathi sources with an expression of chagrin at the confused and obscure state of their knowledge of Vijayanagara. 'In today's light this can only be a source of astonishment and regret.. . . . It is our duty now to remedy the errors of the past'.[36]

To sum up, then, Maratha power as represented by the Bhosle dynasty rose within the frame of the Sultanates of south India. It then came to an accommodation with the Mughal empire whose effective control it challenged on a subcontinental scale by the mid-eighteenth century. Memory was constructed around the project of inheriting the legitimacy and power of that Islamicate empire. Vijayanagara was slighted. Historical memory of it was lost and proved irrecoverable even when actively sought. This is evident in the scantiness of the information available in a Marathi text produced at the end of the eighteenth century. This was copied into a set of Modi manuscripts bound together and transported to the India Office. There is no author name or colophon to this portion of the text. It is titled simply '*Anego[n]dici kefiyat*' and occupies five folios in a neat scribal hand, unfortunately written on both sides of the paper. Phillip Wagoner has suggested in a personal communication that it might have been written at the instance of, or by Colin Mackenzie's assistant, Narain Rao who was in the Bellari region in 1806–07. I will present a free translation here:

> Kisandevraya (*sic*) ruled Vijayanagara, and the entire country to the south of the Narmada river was under him. He had an army of many lakhs, and Anegondi was a part of his dominion and a place where animals were stabled. Vijayanagara was densely peopled and thirty lakhs lived there. The King was very religious and—after having risen, bathed and refreshed himself—he used to meet distinguished ascetics and ask each of them of the secret of the magic marble.[37] Many days passed, lakhs of rupees were expended but the marble could not be produced. Finally, a great ascetic and his disciple came. The emperor entertained them and

---

[35] Arthur Steele, *The Hindu Castes Their Law, Religion and Customs* (Delhi: Mittal Publications, reprint 1989), pp. 4–5. This text is a reprint under a different title of *The Law and Custom of Hindoo Castes of the Dekhun Provinces*, first published in 1827.

[36] Potdar, 'Marathit Vijayanagara' p. 350.

[37] This is something that if held in the mouth gives supernatural powers to the holder.

raised the issue of the marble. The holy man promised to make one for him if given six months and all the equipment that he needed. The king was highly pleased, built a separate house for him, walled it around and visited him regularly for the six months needed to produce it. The magic pebble was prepared in a garden allotted by the king. When it was ready, the ascetic lay down for a nap before the king's visit that evening. His disciple took the marble in his mouth and using its power, flew off to see the world. When the *gosavi* woke, he found the marble and his disciple both missing and was deeply concerned. The king came in the evening, found that the magic marble had vanished and flew into a rage. He had the *gosavi's* eyes plucked out. Helpless, the ascetic remained in the garden. Fifteen days later, the disciple returned and the ascetic's eyes were restored by the marble being waved around his head. The gardener told the king that the ascetic he had had blinded had recovered his sight. The king was astonished and came to see for himself. The *gosavi* cursed him, saying there would never be more than one son born in his lineage and the two ascetics flew away into the sky. 'And to this day we never have more than one son among our children'.

The king made many more efforts to secure the magic marble but never succeeded. Then Ramdevarayala was born in Kisandevraya's family. He used to be called Ramaraja. He reserved the water in the city tank in the morning hours. At that time, Ali Adalshah, Kutubshahaji and Nijyamshah—who were cousins—were personal attendants of Ramaraja. Except for these three, there was no Muslim raja anywhere near. The king was very fond of these three and trusted them. He made Ali Adalshah steward of the law court,[38] Nijyamshah steward of the gift menagerie and Kutubshah of the beverages.[39] They appointed deputies for their tasks and stayed constantly in attendance on the raja. So they became great favourites. Even though the king would not look at any Muslim in the morning, he gave them high appointments with the command of thousands of soldiers.

Then a fakir who had wandered down from Hindustan came to Vijayanagara. He wandered through the whole city and found no Muslim.

[38] *adl* means justice; *adalat* meaning court of law was assimilated into Marathi. The function of Adal-shah is thus fancifully reconstructed from the dynastic title. *Bahiri-sasana* is the Marathi for peregrine falcon—hence the occupation of the Nizam Shah!

[39] An echo of the derogatory tradition found in the *Rayavacakamu*: 'a fellow named Barid of Bidar. . . began to rule. . . His hawk keeper came to be known as Nizam Shah, his water-pot bearer became known as Adil Shah, and the man who was in charge of keeping the dogs became known as Qutb Shah. Each of the three was given charge over a province.. .', Wagoner trans. *Tidings of the King,* p. 123.

Tired and thirsty, he went to a lake to drink and dived into it. The watchmen seized him, beat him and brought him to the king. Enraged, the king ordered him beheaded. Then Ali Adalshah and the others stood before the king with their hands bound and pleaded that the fakir was not one of their Muslims but had come from Hindustan. He did not know the rules. Let him be freed on our account. Then the fakir had one hand cut off and was released. The Muslims tended him for a few days and then let him go. He went to Delhi where he told the padshah that if he failed to cut off the Vijayanagara king's head, he was no Muslim but a *kufar* (*sic*) [infidel]. Then the emperor prepared for a campaign. This news was transmitted to Vijayanagar by the Raya's envoy. Ramaraja ordered lakhs of soldiers to assemble and hold the fords of the Narmada river. The (Delhi) emperor hearing this was perplexed and began to make enquiries. Then he wrote treasonous letters to Ali Adilshah, Nijyamshah and Kutubshah telling them if they would return to the faith (*din*) and send Ramaraja's head to him he would gift them the whole of the South. But the king still regarded them as trustworthy.

So it happened. The king had risen at dawn and, having washed himself, was sitting alone when the three went to salute him in the second hour. Adilshah came from behind and cut off his head and sent it off to the emperor. Then they gathered their soldiers and opened fire on the royal camp. The soldiers there then fled. Then they gathered soldiers up to sixty or seventy thousand and subdued the country, making a sort of *taluqdari* [tax-farming] settlement of taxes. Some chieftains fought them and were subdued, others submitted and received a share of the territory. They shared out the country: Ali Adilshah received Bijyapur kingdom and Kutubashah got Bedar and all its forts. So the three became kings by the favour of chance.

At that time, Vijayanagara was deserted, and the descendants of Ramaraja came and settled at Anegondi. In our fathers' time, the account papers for the entire realm of the South used to be regularly prepared. This was the situation when Ramaraja's descendant, Yenkatapati Rayal left Anegondi because of Tipu's harassment and came to Kharapur.

A few points are evident: this manuscript was produced by a Maratha clerk associated with the Rayal's household and is written in the first person. The audience is clearly the British government: perhaps the object was to make a case for some claim in the aftermath of the fall of Tipu. It is also likely that the story of the ascetic's curse is introduced in order to discredit rival claimants to the family name. In these circumstances, one would expect every historical resource to be deployed. Yet the writer had no information at his disposal beyond two legendary names and essentially produced a rather thin pastiche of folklore and wonder tale. Molesworth's legend about the tax revenues of the earth being accounted for by the Anagondi Raja is clearly echoed in the closing paragraph.

By the late nineteenth century, and especially after the publication of Sewell's *A Forgotten Empire* (1900), some Maratha historians were seeking 'Hindu' rather than Mughalesque roots for Maratha imperial formation. This was the path also taken by some of the earliest Tamil historians of the Vijayanagara empire.[40] At the same time, they were engaged in finding 'indigenous' sources of history to refute both the contemporary colonial as well as the medieval Persian sources of the Dakhani history. The next narrative that I will discuss came to light as a part of both these efforts. The incomplete Marathi text of this narrative was first published by G. K. Chandorkar in the second annual volume of the *Proceedings of the Bharata Itihasa Samshodhaka Mandala* in 1914. He lacked the first few pages, and they have never been found. In the 1990s, neither the Nagari press copy nor the original manuscript used by Chandorkar could be located. Therefore, the Nagari printed text of 1914 is the only available copy of the Marathi version as it appeared in the early twentieth century.[41] Then various Kannada versions of what seemed to be the same story began to be located.

S. Krishnaswamy Iyengar located a Kannada manuscript titled *Ramrajana Bakhairu* in the Oriental Manuscripts Library, Madras. The Kannada text was printed in 1922. Iyengar suggested that Chandorkar's Marathi work was an abridged translation of the Kannada original, which itself was written within a year of the great battle itself. He published a summary in the *Proceedings of the Indian Historical Records Commission* in 1925. [42] An English translation from Kannada had been made for Colin Mackenzie, but lay unpublished in the India Office collection. In 1946, a Kannada text and English translation appeared in *Further Sources of*

---

[40] An excellent survey is in Burton Stein, *Vijayanagara* (Cambridge: University Press, New Cambridge History of India, I.2, 1989), pp. 4–7.

[41] This information is derived from the introduction to the reprinted text in Avinash Sovani ed., *Aitihasika Bakhari- Khand phhila* (Pune: Shabdavedha Prakashan 1998), p. 12 (preface); pp. 13–23 (text).

[42] S. K. Iyengar, 'The Bakhair of Rama Raja' in *Proceedings of Meetings* (Poona Calcutta: Government Central Press, 1925), Vol. 7, pp. 53–63. See also Rajaram V. Herwadkar, *A Forgotten Literature: Foundations of Marathi Chronicles* (Mumbai: Popular Prakashan 1994), pp. 12–13; idem, *Marathi Bakhar* (Pune: Venus Prakashan, Revised enlarged edition, 1974), pp. 40–41.

Vijayanagara History.[43] Meanwhile, the 1922 Kannada text had been studied by N. S. Rajpurohit as a guide to the location of the battlefield. He translated several passages into Marathi and paraphrased the rest. This appeared in the *BIS Traimasika* in 1929.[44] I have compared this with the English and Marathi versions. This work titles itself *'Ramarayana bakhairu'* (the *bakhar* of Ramaraya). I will not enter into the necessary minute comparisons here, but it appears evident that several Kannada versions going back to at least the late eighteenth century were extant. Internal evidence and major inconsistencies show that none of these texts were even remotely contemporary to the battle. The late seventeenth century seems the earliest likely period for their composition. They differed in some details from each other and from the Marathi version. Given this distribution of manuscript sources, it is most probable that, as Iyengar suggested, the original was written in Kannada and a single Marathi recension was produced later—perhaps as a result of Mackenzie's enquiries around 1800, perhaps even to satisfy Chandorkar after 1900![45] The Marathi language of Chandorkar's version shows a style and vocabulary that clearly do not date before the 1670s or 1680s at the earliest.[46] Its Kannada moorings are suggested by the list of worthies that it mentions and more especially by the list of fortresses to which commanders are dispatched concluding the combat of the fatal battle itself. But there are suggestions that it was compiled after Maratha power began to be felt in the region. So, for example, the 'Rayegad' listed here may be a reference to the fortress capital built by Shivaji. On the other hand, if these officers are being projected as the founders of Nayaka kingdoms, then the list implicitly placed the ruler of Anegondi as a Nayaka rather than the heir to Vijayanagara that the Marathi language traditions were to identify him as. This once again suggests a southern and non-Marathi origin for this narrative.

Ramachandra Narttakasi to Chandragad   Virapa Naik to Ilori

---

[43] *Further Sources,* Vol. 3, pp. 204–42. Note on p. 205 refers to the Mackenzie translation as India Office Mss no. X.

[44] Na. Shri. Rajpurohit, 'Rakshas-Tangdiya *rananganaca sthalanirnya', Bharata Itihasa Samshodhaka Mandala Traimasika,* Vol. 10, No. 1 (1928–29), pp. 17–22.

[45] Phillip Wagoner (personal communication) suggests that it might even have been written for, or at the behest of, Colin Mackenzie in 1809–10 when his research assistants, Narrain Row and Ananda Row were both in the vicinity of Bellari.

[46] I have translated and discussed this text in 'Literary Tropes and Historical Settings: A Study from Southern India', in *Rethinking a Millennium: India from the Eighth to the Eighteenth Centuries,* ed. Rajat Datta (Delhi: Aakar Books, 2008).

Lakshmana Naik Treasurer to Rayegad	Amrit Naik to Kadnoli
Chikanna Naik to Shahadurg	Bhojraj to Chandavar [?Thanjavur]
Thalavenkati to Torgal	Venkatapa Naik to Nadi Alasi
Giriyeppa Naik to Tadpatri	Girikrishnaguru Veda to Chichalgala
Nagpadevar to Anegodi	Rayeppa Naik to Salaripattana
Yelaveduru to Bankapur	Gopal Naik to Madhra
Bisalapa Vedru to Krishnagad	

In short, this is an example of the genre of historical pastiche to which the *Rayavacakamu* also belongs. But it is better informed than other Marathi tradition in that the three rulers are not depicted in the entirely absurd light of household servants of Ramaraja. Its southern origins are also evident in that 'Akbar Jalaluddin Mughal emperor' was located at what was perhaps an important Mughal position in the early seventeenth century, the town of Jalna (central Maharashtra, near Aurangabad). Maratha traditions, even the most fantastic ones—invariably place the Mughals as ruling from Delhi. Finally, of course, if this narrative was indeed composed in Marathi, it is strange that almost none of the elements of the story are found in the Marathi traditions, which, as we saw, floated away entirely even from the limited geographical and historical knowledge found in this work. All this suggests that Chandorkar's text is a late translation into Marathi of a fragmentary Kannada manuscript—perhaps even a translation generated by his own search in the early twentieth century.

Nonetheless, such was the hunger for authentically indigenous accounts of Vijayanagara that several historians accepted Chandorkar's text as both authentic and contemporary to the battle. In 1952 Gramopadhye produced a small volume of selections from different *bakhars*, including this one.[47] It was probably intended for the use of university students of Marathi literature. In editing his selection, Gramopadhye largely omitted what he must have viewed as the 'non-historical' or perhaps 'fanciful' parts of the texts. This led to the omission of portions such as the lengthy descriptions of the emperor's visits to the palaces of his

---

[47] G. B. Gramopadhye ed., *Marathi Bakhar Gadya* (Pune: Mehta Publishing House, [1952] 1988). He titled it '*Rakshes Tagdicha Ranasamgrama*'—the Battle of Rakshes Tagdi, pp. 17–22; annotation pp. 170–1. This heavily edited text is briefly discussed in Rao, Shulman and Subrahmanyam *Textures of Time* (Delhi: Permanent Black, 2001), pp. 227–28.

three principal queens and the highly imaginative list of the fruits that he distributed. Perhaps for the sake of brevity, he also omitted the names of nobles who were killed and wounded on both sides and the list of nobles dispatched to different fortresses before the battle. The evidently embroidered list of military equipment is included as Gramopadhye evidently assumed it to be accurate. This presumption is reflected in his comment on the statement that there were oxen each carrying 28 projectiles (*bana*) so that there were about 80,000 such projectiles. As later allusions to their being lighted clearly indicate, these were obviously supposed to be the simple rockets widely used in South Indian warfare during the eighteenth century (but not recorded for the sixteenth). If so, then 28 per bullock would be a reasonable load. But Gramopadhye interprets *bana* as arrow and believes all these numbers to be factual. This is evident from his footnote 'Why would each ox carry only 28 *bana*? Each ox would easily carry one or two hundred *bana*'.[48]

Gramopadhye follows an earlier editorial tradition that, as Wagoner describes, mined texts 'for whatever veins of historical data it might contain embedded among more legendary and fanciful strata'. But, as Wagoner goes on to point out, such sifting (by the editors of the 1919 volume of *Sources* and the 1946 volumes *Further Sources* of Vijayanagara history) eliminated 'the very passages that would have provided the keys to understanding the *Rayavacakamu*'s unique vision of the past...' In his anxiety to find an authentic source from the Vijayanagara side, Gramopadhye also chose to ignore the various inconsistencies that simply make it unlikely that it dates from 1565. In his edition, he largely excised these elements of the narrative. He thereby also eliminated the internal clues that would have enabled an accurate dating of the work. Overall, these omitted portions would have enabled a proper understanding of the text as an account from a much later time, mediated through the sensibilities of its own setting.[49] Spiegel has called for the placing of texts in context and no context can be more important for historians than the chronological one.

Gramopadhye himself dates the text to 1613–14. This latter date is based on a statement in the concluding pages of the text that attributes the first copying to Venkaji Narayana Kulkarni in *Anandanama Samvatsara, Phalgun*, second day of the bright half. But this is merely

---

[48] Gramopadhye, 18 footnote.
[49] Wagoner, *Tidings of the King*, pp. 5–9.

the name of a year in the sixty-year astronomical cycle[50] and could, therefore, refer not only to 1613–14 but also to 1673–74, 1733–34, and so on. Gramopadhye's abbreviated text also omits the concluding scribe's notation that the copying was completed on 11th Jamadilakher Hijri year 1095 (or 26 May 1684).[51] It is, therefore, quite possible that the *Ananda samvatsara* of the copyist was, in fact 1673–74, a year of great importance in the Marathi- and Kannada-speaking world because preparations for the coronation of Shivaji were underway that year. It might have been seen as a fitting time to produce a text warning against reliance on the fealty of Muslim dependants and allies. In fact the later portions of the text essentially present Adilshaha as the successor to Vijayanagara. He is shown as deeply ambivalent about his part in the defeat of Rama Raya, and the latter refers to him as being like his son.

> The emperor Ramraj fell into the hands of Ali Yedalshah of the Kannadas, and said to him: 'You had called yourself my son. Then you suddenly seized me by treachery. Now what can I do? My whole army is slain.' He dressed himself in fresh clothes, a Portuguese *daiv* (?), placed a rose formed of gems and pearls in his cap and wrapped on a *mavishala* (?). Then having invoked his personal deity, he sent a message to Ali Yedalshaha saying: 'come alone and sword in hand; no one else is to lay a hand on me.' He made him promise this. Then Ali Yedalshaha came alone and cut off his head.

The effort is, therefore, clearly to present the Adilshahi regime as the least illegitimate successor to Vijayanagara. Could this reflect the role that Shahaji Bhosle, Shivaji's father had played in the southward extension of Adilshahi power and the fact that Shivaji's own home territory up to the 1650s was notionally an Adilshahi domain?

Gramopadhye was heir to an ambitious effort to connect Vijayanagara to the Marathi historical imagination made in the 1930s, as the sexcentenary of its foundation came up. This is why Chandorkar's *bakhar* was enthusiastically adopted as the authentic Marathi record of the great southern empire. The Commemoration committee contacted the Bharata Itihasa Samshodhaka Mandala and sought its cooperation in preparing a complete Marathi translation of the English volume being

[50] Every sixty years, the planets return to a particular configuration and the cycle resumes. Each year has a specific name–the first being *Prabhava* and the last *Akshaya*.

[51] Sovani ed., *Aitihasika Bakhari*, pp. 22–23.

prepared for that occasion.[52] The Mandala made a considerable effort and complied; in addition it commissioned several additional chapters and a chronological table that were added to the Marathi volume. Texts were also edited so as to be more accessible to the Marathi-reading public.[53] In a short preface titled 'The debt owed to Vijayanagara', delivered as an address on 26 December 1936 the noted historian T. S. Shejwalkar, began by arguing that while great civilizations like the Egyptian, Assyrian, Sumerian and Iranian had disappeared from the earth, Indian civilization still lived. In medieval times, it had been forced to take shelter in the South before being taken into the hands of the Marathas and brought further north. 'The protection of Vijayanagara gave this civilization its recent but crucial foothold, and it is the memory of this that we celebrate at this gathering today.' He paid Vijayanagara the highest compliment available to him by declaring that its founding six centuries earlier had the same historic significance as the birth of Shivaji three centuries later.[54] His full-length essay in the same volume made an explicit effort to connect the two arguing that Shivaji's object in his southern campaigns was to lay the foundation for a new empire like Vijayanagara, one that would be capable of confronting Aurangzeb. But he goes back to Shivaji's father, Shahaji. 'From one point of view Shahaji was grinding one Hindu empire into dust; from another point of view, he was laying the foundation of another Hindu empire'.[55]

But this effort was an artefact of the religious politics of the 1930s. The Maratha *Svaraj* (imperial domain) of the eighteenth century never constructed such a genealogy for itself. And so Vijayanagara, so important an origin in the southern half of the peninsula, was largely lost to Maratha historical memory until the new historical projects of the twentieth century brought it to mind once again. To return, then, to the issues raised at the beginning of this essay: for historians, narrative texts can only be understood in historical contexts and the context includes not merely what is remembered but—more crucially—what is forgotten. The historical approach to narratives of the past must historicize memory itself.

---

[52] On the political and cultural significance of the Mandala, see Prachi Deshpande, *Creative Pasts*, pp. 117–20.

[53] Karamarkar ed., *Vijayanagara Smaraka Grantha*, pp. 1–2.

[54] *Ibid.*, pp. 1–7.

[55] T. S. Shejwalkar, 'Vijayanagara Samrajyace Maratheshahivarila Parinama', in *Vijayanagara Smaraka Grantha*, pp. 64–65.

11

'Kiss My Foot,' Said the King:
Firearms, Diplomacy and the Battle for Raichur, 1520

RICHARD M. EATON*

• ✦ •

INTRODUCTION

Frontiers may be understood as spatial counterparts to revolutions: the one denotes a perceived break in continuous territory, the other a perceived rupture in time. In recent decades, historians have written of a worldwide military, or 'gunpowder' revolution that took place in the centuries following the fourteenth.[1] Such a notion has in turn prompted

* This essay draws upon a collaborative research project by the author and Phillip B. Wagoner, *Power, Memory, Architecture: Contested Sites on India's: Deccan Plateau, 1300–1600* (forthcoming). The essay is dedicated to the memory of two good friends and colleagues. One is my teacher, John F. Richards, who passed away on 23 August 2007. I count myself especially honoured to have been among John's students, and to have benefited from his expertise, his compassionate nurturing and his high standards of scholarship.

   The essay is also dedicated to the memory of Dr. Balasubramanya, with whom Phillip B. Wagoner and I had the good fortune to spend several memorable days at Hampi in June 2005, just four months before his untimely death robbed Karnataka archaeology of yet another of its brightest luminaries. Professor Wagoner and I are grateful to the Getty Foundation for a Collaborative Research Grant awarded for the period 2004–2006, which enabled us to carry out two seasons of exploratory field surveys in India. I also wish to thank Lois Kain for preparing the map of the Deccan plateau that accompanies this essay.

[1] See Michael Roberts, 'The Military Revolution, 1560–1660,' in his *Essays in Swedish History* (Minneapolis: University of Minnesota Press, 1967), pp. 195–225; Geoffrey Parker, *The Military Revolution: Military Innovations and the Rise of the West, 1500–1800* (Cambridge: Cambridge University

several lines of enquiry. Some have tried to locate the moment in time when this revolution occurred in particular regions.[2] Others have sought to identify and compare the various effects that the advent, spread and use of gunpowder had in different socio-political environments across the planet.[3]

The present essay explores a little-studied event in South Asian history, the Battle for Raichur (1520), with a view to evaluating that battle's relevance both to the idea of the frontier and to that of the military revolution. The city of Raichur occupies the heart of an exceptionally fertile tract in India's Deccan plateau—the so-called 'Raichur Doab'— which lies between the Tungabhadra and Krishna rivers (see Figure 1, Map). For several centuries before 1520, the Bahmani sultans to the north of the Doab and the kings of Vijayanagara to the south repeatedly fought over access to the Doab's economic resources.[4] Control of the fortified city of Raichur figured in all of these struggles. The battle in question was also a prelude to the more famous Battle of Talikota (1565), a conflict that permanently reconfigured the geopolitics of the Deccan plateau. One question, then, is temporal in nature: how did this battle stand out in the long-term struggle for control of the Doab, and how might it have figured in a 'military revolution' in India? The other question is spatial: in what ways did that battle define Raichur's frontier character?

Press, 1988); William H. McNeill, *The Age of Gunpowder Empires* (Washington DC: American Historical Association, 1989), pp. 27–40; Richard Hellie, 'Warfare, Changing Military Technology, and the Evolution of Muscovite Society,' in *Tools of War: Instruments, Ideas, and Institutions of Warfare, 1445–1871,* ed. John A. Lynn (Urbana: University of Illinois, 1990), pp. 74–99; David Eltis, *The Military Revolution in Sixteenth-century Europe* (London: Tauris Academic Studies, 1995); Bert S. Hall, *Weapons and Warfare in Renaissance Europe: Gunpowder, Technology and Tactics* (Baltimore: John Hopkins University Press, 1997), pp. 201–35; Jeremy Black, *War and the World: Military Power and the Fate of Continents, 1450–2000* (New Haven: Yale University Press, 1998).

[2] For India, see Iqtidar Alam Khan, *Gunpowder and Firearms: Warfare in Medieval India* (New Delhi: Oxford University Press, 2004), and Jos Gommans, *Mughal Warfare: Indian Frontiers and High Roads to Empire, 1500–1700* (New York: Routledge, 2002).

[3] See William H. McNeill, *The Pursuit of Power: Technology, Armed Force and Society since A.D. 1000* (Chicago: University of Chicago Press, 1982); Brian M. Downing, *The Military Revolution and Political Change: Origins of Democracy and Autocracy in Early Modern Europe* (Princeton: Princeton University Press, 1992); Kenneth Chase, *Firearms: A Global History to 1700* (Cambridge: Cambridge University Press, 2003); Gabor Agoston, *Guns for the Sultan: Military Power and the Weapons Industry in the Ottoman Empire* (Cambridge: Cambridge University Press, 2005). For a discussion of the theme as it relates to South Asia, see Sanjay Subrahmanyam, 'The Kagemusha effect: the Portuguese, Firearms and the State in Early Modern South India,' *Moyen Orient & Ocean Indien* 4 (1987), pp. 97–123.

[4] P. M. Joshi, 'The Raichur Doab in Deccan History—Re-interpretation of a Struggle,' *Journal of Indian History* 36 (1958), pp. 379–96.

Figure 1
Map of the Deccan

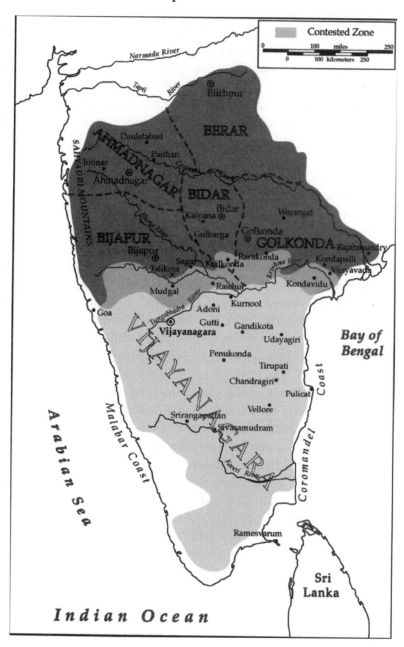

BACKGROUND

The Raichur Doab had been a contested region even before the Bahmani and Vijayanagara states came into being. In the twelfth and thirteenth centuries, the tract lay at the conjuncture of three regional powers—the Hoysala kings of Dwarasamudra, the Yadava kings of Devagiri and the Kakatiya kings of Warangal. In 1294 a subordinate of the last monarch of the Kakatiya dynasty seized the Raichur Doab from Yadava control and built the imposing complex of walls and gates that encircle Raichur's present core. With their massive slabs of finely dressed granite, these walls were, in their own day, considered an engineering marvel; even today, some local residents regard them as the work of gods, not men. They are certainly the most impressive of any Kakatiya fortifications still standing, apart from those in Warangal, the dynasty's capital.

Notwithstanding its strength, Raichur's fort got swept into the general chaos that engulfed the Deccan in the early fourteenth century following invasions by the armies of the Delhi Sultanate. After the collapse of the Kakatiya state in 1323, Sultan Muhammad bin Tughluq (r. 1325–51) systematically colonized much of the northern Deccan with settlers transplanted from north India. At the same time, he subcontracted the governance of much of the central and southern Deccan to local client-chiefs. Administration of the Raichur Doab appears to have been assigned to a chief who, appointed *amir* (commander) by the Delhi sultan in 1327, led an anti-Tughluq uprising nine years later. This rebel *amir* was likely Harihara Sangama, a Kannada chieftain known to have been in Tughluq imperial service in the 1330s.[5] By 1347, when Delhi lost control of all its Deccan possessions to anti-Tughluq rebels, Harihara and his brothers had carved out a new state centred on the city of Vijayanagara, located directly south of the Raichur Doab on the southern banks of the Tungabhadra river.

Raichur, however, did not long remain in southerners' hands. In the confusion surrounding the expulsion of imperial forces in 1347, the Doab apparently fell to the other power that simultaneously arose on the ashes of Tughluq imperialism in the Deccan, the Bahmani sultanate (1347–1538). Ruling from a series of capitals located to the north of the

---

[5] Ibn Battuta, *The Rehla of Ibn Battuta*, trans. Mahdi Husain (Baroda: Oriental Institute, 1953), p. 96; Zia al-Din Barani, *Tarikh-i Firuz Shahi*, in *The History of India as Told by its Own Historians*, ed. and trans. H. M. Elliot and John Dowson (Allahabad: Kitab Mahal, 1964), p. 3:245. 'Abd al-Malik 'Isami, *Futuhu's Salatin*, ed. and trans. Agha Mahdi Husain (London: Asia Publishing House, 1967), p. 3:902.

Raichur Doab—Daulatabad, Gulbarga and Bidar—the Bahmani sultans claimed the territory clear down to the Tungabhadra river, which included the Raichur Doab. Yet the fact that Vijayanagara's founders seem to have held the Doab *before* Vijayanagara's creation formed an important basis for the southern state's repeated claim to the tract. For the next century and a half, rulers of Vijayanagara and the Bahmani sultanate fought bitterly for the control of this agriculturally rich tract. For most of this period, however, the greater part of the Doab remained under Bahmani control, despite major invasions launched by Vijayanagara kings in 1362, 1378, 1398 and 1443.[6] From 1444, and possibly from as early as 1398, those kings were even forced to make annual tributary payments to the Bahmani treasury.[7]

In 1468 and 1469, capitalizing on new engineering technology imported from north India and the Middle East, Bahmani authorities built an entirely new wall around Raichur's old Kakatiya fortifications, complete with an outer moat, numerous bastions and imposing gates on the city's eastern and western ends.[8] Ironically, though, by this time the dynasty had begun experiencing crippling factional struggles within its ruling elite. On one side were 'Deccanis', or nobles descended from the original north Indian migrants who had settled in the upper Deccan in the 1320s. And on the other were the so-called 'Westerners' (*gharbian*), or immigrants freshly recruited from the Middle East, especially the Persian-speaking world of Iran and Central Asia.[9] Sectarian rivalries

---

[6] Vijayanagara's kings did achieve a few successes in the disputed region. In 1362, 1436 and 1443 their forces briefly seized Mudgal, which is located in the Doab some sixty miles west of Raichur city. On each occasion, however, the fort was soon recovered by Bahmani authorities. A. A. Kadiri, 'Bahmani Inscriptions from Raichur District,' *Epigraphia Indica, Arabic and Persian Supplement* (1962), pp. 54–55.

[7] Literary evidence suggests that during the second of his three campaigns against Vijayanagara, Sultan Firuz had forced Harihara II to make annual tributes to the Bahmanis. A 1444 Sanskrit inscription at Bidar confirms that one of Harihara's successors, Deva Raya II, was paying tribute to the Bahmani sultan, Ahmad Shah I. *Ibid.*, pp. 54–55.

[8] In the course of their Deccan campaigns, 'Ala al-Din Khalaji and Muhammad bin Tughluq had brought with them new siege technology, including extensive groundworks, earthen battlements (*pashib*), mines, wooden siege towers, mangonels and counterweight trebuchets. The Tughluqs, especially, were great fort builders. At sites like Tughluqabad, in Delhi, one sees their distinctive architectural features: massive projecting buttresses, merlons, turrets and crenellations. Such features quickly diffused to the Deccan, as at Daulatabad, where ramparts were replaced with a double line in lime-mortar masonry, round bastions and turrets. The Bahmani rulers continued these traditions in such major forts as Gulbarga, Firuzabad and Bidar. Gommans, *Mughal Warfare*, pp. 141–44.

[9] Some modern historians have referred to this group as *afaqi* or *'ajami*. Contemporary sources, however, call them *gharbian* ('Westerners'), or sometimes *ghariban* ('foreigners').

reinforced ethnic and linguistic differences between the two factions, as most Westerners were Shiʻi Muslims, and most Deccanis were Sunnis.

By the 1480s and ʼ90s Deccani–Westerner tensions had so intensified that the Bahmani sovereign, Sultan Mahmud (r. 1482–1518), could no longer command absolute loyalty among his most powerful nobles, some of whom began establishing *de facto* independent states within his domain. One of these was Yusuf ʻAdil Khan, a Westerner immigrant from Iran who, in 1490, carved out a new state of Bijapur from the Bahmani sultanate's western and southern districts, which included the Raichur Doab. Although Yusuf continued to pay formal homage to Sultan Mahmud, his audacious actions alarmed other independent nobles, one of whom sought to weaken Bijapur's position by inviting Vijayanagara's forces to invade Raichur. Accordingly, in 1492 the southern state invaded the Doab and momentarily seized Raichur city, although Yusuf ʻAdil Khan managed to retrieve the fort later the same year. Until as late as 1515, Sultan Mahmud's name continued to appear on Raichur's inscriptions as the region's legitimate sovereign, maintaining the fiction that Yusuf ʻAdil Khan and his successors in Bijapur were merely Bahmani ʻgovernors'. Nonetheless, Bijapur's rulers from Yusuf behaved as though they were independent sultans, as indeed later chroniclers styled them.[10]

Despite prolonged northern hegemony over the Raichur Doab, by the first decade of the sixteenth century the balance of power began to tilt towards the south for the first time since 1347. Already, by 1500, the integrity of the Bahmani state had become seriously compromised, and by the second decade of the sixteenth century, the kingdom had disintegrated into five *de facto* successor states. This meant that any invasion of Raichur from the south would now be met not by the full might of the old Bahmani sultanate, but by the ʻAdil Shahi rulers of Bijapur, who could field armies only a fraction the size of those of its parent state. What is more, Bijapur inherited the same Westerner-Deccani factionalism that had plagued the Bahmani sultanate, which compromised its socio-political cohesiveness.

---

[10] Two inscriptions of Raichur dated 1515, one on an unidentified mosque and the other on a bastion of the outer wall, record the names of both Sultan Mahmud Bahmani and Ismaʻil ʻAdil Khan, Bijapur's effective sultan. K. M. Ahmad, 'Inscriptions of Raichur in the Hyderabad Museum,' *Epigraphia Indo-Moslemica* (1939–40), pp. 14, 16. But it was not until 1538, after the last nominal Bahmani sovereign had sailed off on a pilgrimage to Mecca from which he never returned, that the fourth of Bijapur's rulers, Ibrahim, styled himself 'sultan'.

To the south of Raichur, meanwhile, a vigorous new dynasty of kings, the Tuluva, had arisen in the sprawling metropolis of Vijayanagara. In 1509 Vijayanagara's throne was occupied by the famous Krishna Raya (or 'Krishna Deva Raya', r. 1509–29), whose twenty years of rule are widely acclaimed as having seen the acme of Vijayanagara's power and glory. Between 1509 and 1520, while the Deccan north of the Raichur Doab fragmented into five mutually quarrelling states, Krishna Raya conquered and annexed the entire peninsula from the southern edge of the Raichur Doab nearly to Cape Comorin, thereby amassing immense manpower and capital resources available for any effort to regain from Bijapur the control of the Doab.

Another factor tipping the balance of power in Vijayanagara's favour at this time was the advent of the Portuguese *Estado da India*. A formidable coastal power since 1498, these European newcomers not only sought to monopolize control over the Arabian Sea commerce; arriving on the heels of Iberia's anti-Muslim *reconquista*, the Portuguese in India also sought to roll back Muslim states everywhere, and especially the newly emerged Sultanate of Bijapur, which had inherited from the Bahmanis control over a good deal of India's western seacoast in addition to the Raichur Doab. Such objectives naturally inclined the Portuguese to seek allies in Vijayanagara, that being the Deccan's principal non-Muslim power, and to exploit that kingdom's hostility towards Muslim states to its north.

A dramatic step in this direction was taken in 1510, when the Portuguese viceroy and master strategist Afonso de Albuquerque (1509–15), assisted by a coastal warlord loyal to Vijayanagara, seized the port of Goa from Bijapur's Yusuf 'Adil Khan. 'With this action in Goa', the viceroy wrote triumphantly to Portugal's King Manuel,

> . . . we can diminish the credit that is enjoyed by the Turks [i.e., Bijapur], and the fear in which they are held, and persuade them [Vijayanagara] that we are men who can do deeds as great on the land as on the sea.... [Let us] thus see if I can have them move their armies against the Turks in the Deccan, and desire our true friendship.[11]

The key to Albuquerque's newly acquired leverage over the states of the Deccan interior, both to the north and to the south of the Raichur

[11] R. A. de Bulhão Pato and H. Lopes de Mendonca eds, *Cartas de Affonso de Albuquerque eguidas e documetos que as elucidam* (Lisbon: Typ. da Academia real das sciencias de Lisboa, 1884), p. 1:28. Cited in Maria Augusta Lima Cruz, 'Notes on Portuguese Relations with Vijayanagara, 1500–1565,' *Santa Barbara Portuguese Studies* 2 (1995), p. 21.

Doab, lay in those states' dependency on warhorses imported by sea from the Middle East. Before 1510 Bijapur had imported most of its warhorses through its port of Goa, whereas Vijayanagara imported its horses through ports further down the coast, in particular Bhatkal. But after 1510, by negotiating separately with Yusuf 'Adil Khan and Krishna Raya, by seizing the port of Hormuz in the Persian Gulf (1515) and by deploying his sea power to pressure the merchants of Bhatkal, Albuquerque hoped to drive the entire traffic in warhorses to Goa, and thus through the hands of the *Estado*.[12]

The Portuguese also introduced new forms of gunpowder technology to the Deccan. The extent of their influence in this regard, however, depends on how one evaluates the state of Indian firearms before their arrival. Gunpowder had certainly been in use in India before the advent of the *Estado*. We know, for example, that in 1472 Bahmani engineers deployed explosive mines while besieging the fort of Belgaum, an ally of Vijayanagara.[13] But the move from exploding mines to firing cannon or matchlocks represents a major advance in military technology. Iqtidar Alam Khan has argued that Indians were using cannon cast in brass or bronze and handguns in the second half of the fifteenth century.[14] But the matter is complicated. The nomenclature of weapons changed over time; few Indian sources are contemporary with the battles they describe; and later sources often used terms anachronistically, projecting the terms of their own day backwards to earlier periods. In view of such considerations, Jos Gommans doubts Iqtidar Alam Khan's assertions respecting a fifteenth-century horizon for the earliest appearance of firearms in India.[15]

---

[12] As the viceroy cynically wrote to Yusuf 'Adil Khan's successor, Isma'il Khan of Bijapur, 'I shall be ever your friend, and I will assist you against the King of Deccan [Isma'il's nominal overlord, Sultan Mahmud Bahmani], and against your enemies; and I will cause all the horses that arrive here to be carried to your stations and your marts, in order that you may have possession of them.' Walter de Gray Birch trans., *Commentaries of the Great Afonso Dalboquerque* (1884; repr. New York: B. Franklin 1970), pp. 3:20–21. For further discussion, see Sanjay Subrahmanyam, *The Political Economy of Commerce: Southern India, 1500–1650* (Cambridge: Cambridge University Press, 1990), pp. 116–35. See also Jean Aubin, 'Un Voyage de Goa à Ormuz en 1520', *Modern Asian Studies* 22 (1988), pp. 417–32.

[13] John Briggs trans., *History of the Rise of the Mahomedan Power in India* (1829; repr. Calcutta: Editions Indian, 1966), 2:303. Firishta not only mentions the 'fire-workers' (*atish-bazan*) employed for the job, but states that until that time, peoples of the Deccan had never seen such battering devices or mines (*'bi sakhtan-i sarkub va naqb ki ta an zaman dar Dakan sha'i' nabud'*). Muhammad Qasim Firishta, *Tarikh-i Firishta* (Lucknow, 1864–65), p. 1: 352.

[14] Iqtidar Alam Khan, *Gunpowder*, pp. 42–44.

[15] Gommans, *Mughal Warfare*, p. 146, and footnote 52.

Notwithstanding Gommans' reservations, there is evidence that firearms were being used in western India before the establishment of Portuguese power in the region. Gaspar Correia records that in 1502 Portuguese naval squadrons were bombarded from the hilltop overlooking the port of Bhatkal.[16] According to the historian Firishta, gunners and rocketeers were among the 5,000 foot soldiers that Sultan Ahmad Nizam Shah of Ahmadnagar used on a 1504 military expedition into Khandesh.[17] About the same time, the Italian traveller Ludovico di Varthema recorded seeing artillery in the port of Chaul, then controlled by the same ruler.[18] In Bijapur, following the death of Yusuf 'Adil Khan in 1510, a palace struggle broke out between the royalists supporting the king's youthful son Isma'il and the latter's regent. Both sides in the conflict reportedly used firearms. Firishta speaks of 'matchlockmen' (*tufangi*), and of 'the fort's large cannon being brought up' in order to batter down the citadel's walls.[19] Albuquerque's son noted that when his father took Goa, also in 1510, Bijapuri defenders greeted the invaders with artillery fire.[20] Later that same year, after first losing and then reconquering the city, Albuquerque captured from Bijapur's defenders a hundred large guns (*bombardas*) and a 'large quantity' of smaller artillery.[21]

It appears, moreover, that many if not most of these weapons were locally manufactured, for when they seized Goa, the Portuguese found that the Bijapuris had already established their own munitions plant there.[22] In fact, Albuquerque was so impressed with Goa's gun-making

[16] Gaspar Correia, *Lendas da India*, pp. 1:289–90. Cited in Subrahmanyam, *Political Economy*, p. 124.

[17] 'Five thousand footsoldiers who were gunners, bowmen, and rocketeers, and five thousand mounted archers' ('*Panj hizar piada tup-chi va kamandar va ban-dar, va panj hizar sawar ki hama tir-andaz budand*'). Firishta, *Tarikh-i Firishta*, p. 2:98. Briggs translates *tup-chi* as 'matchlockmen.' Briggs, *History*, p. 3:124. The historian of Ahmadnagar's Nizam Shahi dynasty, 'Ali Tabataba, notes that on this occasion Sultan Ahmad Nizam Shah had with him a detachment of rocketeers and musketeers (*ban-kari va tufang-andazi*). 'Ali Tabataba, *Burhan-i ma'athir* (Delhi: Majlis-i Maktutat-i Farsiya Dihli, 1936), p. 223. T. W. Haig, 'The History of the Nizam Shahi Kings of Ahmadnagar,' *Indian Antiquary* 49 (1920), p. 126.

[18] John Winter Jones, trans. *The Travels of Ludovico di Varthema* (1863; repr. New York, n.d.), p. 114.

[19] '*Avardan-i tup-hayi kalan ki ham dar an qil'a budand.*' Firishta, *Tarikh-i Firishta*, p. 2:17. Briggs, *History*, p. 3:24.

[20] Birch, *Commentaries*, p. 2:89.

[21] *Ibid.*, p. 3:16.

[22] According to a document published by the sixteenth-century chronicler Gaspar Correia, at the time of the Portuguese conquest, there were in Goa 'large houses with storage space which the Turks [*os rumes*] had filled with all the materials necessary for shipbuilding [or, 'large houses

tradition that he sent to the king of Portugal samples of the heavy cannon used by the Muslims of that city, together with the moulds from which the guns had been cast.[23] On 1 December 1513, the Viceroy reported that the matchlocks manufactured by Goa's master gunsmiths were as good as those made in Bohemia; he even sent one of those gunsmiths to Lisbon to work for the Portuguese crown.[24] Several days later, Albuquerque reported to the king that the Muslim gunsmiths, who had formerly served the 'Adil Shahis but returned to Goa after the Portuguese conquest, were capable of turning out iron cannon and matchlocks of a higher quality than anything produced in Germany, then considered the source of Europe's finest guns.[25] From this point on, a tradition of German and Bohemian gun making that had been brought to India by the Portuguese seems to have merged with Turkish gun-making traditions already present in 'Adil Shahi Goa, producing what has been called an 'Indo-Portuguese' tradition of matchlocks. These weapons, evidently superior to anything produced elsewhere in India, would soon spread not only into the Deccan interior but, by the mid-sixteenth century, throughout Portuguese Asia as far as Japan.[26]

These important developments notwithstanding, before 1520 we hear of no major battles in which firearms were used in the Deccan, or indeed, anywhere else in the Indian interior. All this would change with the Battle of Raichur.

which the Turks used as armories'], and lots of iron and mortar artillery, large and small, and also two of our camel cannons and eight cradles and mortars which the Turks had brought from the defeat of Dom Lourenco at Chaul [in 1508], and other metal pieces in their fashion and a great number of metal guns, and a large quantity of gunpowder, saltpetre and utensils used in the making of these, and an enormous quantity of all kinds of weapons.' Gaspar Correia, *Lendas da India* (Lisbon: Typ. da Academia Real das Sciencias, 1860), p. 2:60. Translated in Rainer Daehnhardt, *The Bewitched Gun: the Introduction of the Firearm in the Far East by the Portuguese* (Lisbon: Texto Editora, 1994), p. 37. Further information on the identity of these Turks is furnished by the Portuguese historian Duarte Barbosa, who was in India from about 1500 to about 1516. He writes that 'Adil Shahi authorities in Goa had received Turkish escapees following the Portuguese defeat of an Ottoman navy at Diu in 1509. These men, writes Barbosa, were resettled in Goa with the help of Muslim merchants who financed the building of shipyards and plants for the manufacture of iron and copper ordnance. Mansel L. Dames, tr., *The Book of Duarte Barbosa* (1918, repr. Nendeln/Liechtenstein: Kraus Reprint, 1967), pp.1:175–77. It thus appears that Ottoman–Portuguese naval engagements off the Gujarat and Konkan coasts had led to the settlement of Turkish gunners and gunsmiths in Bijapuri territory after 1508.

[23] de Bulhão Pato and Mendonca, eds., *Cartas* p. 1:28. Cited in Daehnhardt, *Bewitched Gun*, p. 38.

[24] *Ibid.*, p. 1:174. *Ibid.*, p. 39.

[25] '...e asy se tornaram todolos oficiaees d artelharia, de bombardas e espimgardas, as quaees se fazem de ferro em goa milhores que has d alemanha.' *Ibid.*, p. 1:203. *Ibid.*, p. 38–39.

[26] *Ibid.*, p. 41.

THE BATTLE

Krishna Raya of Vijayanagara soundly defeated Isma'il 'Adil Khan in the 1520 contest for control of Raichur fort and the Doab.[27] Two original authorities can guide us in reconstructing the contours of the struggle. One is the above-mentioned Firishta, who lived in Bijapur and in 1611 dedicated his monumental *Tarikh-i Firishta* to Isma'il's great grandson, Sultan Ibrahim 'Adil Shah II (r. 1580–1627). The other is Fernão Nunes, who around 1531 wrote a chronicle of Vijayanagara kings based on local traditions and his own interactions with the Portuguese and Indians.[28] There is evidence that Nunes, a Portuguese horse trader who resided in metropolitan Vijayanagara for three years, had been living in coastal India since 1512, in which case he would have heard first-hand reports of the battle shortly after its conclusion.[29] Or, he might have recorded remembered traditions some eight years later, most likely from participants. It is even possible that he witnessed the battle himself.[30]

---

[27] It is sometimes claimed, based on Firishta's account, that Krishna Raya had invaded and occupied Raichur in 1512, and that Isma'il therefore moved an army there in 1520 to *reconquer* the city from Krishna Raya. See H. K. Sherwani and P. M. Joshi eds, *History of Medieval Deccan (1295–1724)* (Hyderabad: Government of Andhra Pradesh, 1973), p. 1:308. But such a possibility is refuted by epigraphic evidence confirming Isma'il's continued occupation of Raichur from his accession down to 1520. An inscription dated 1511–12 records the construction of the Hazara Baig mosque in the time of Isma'il 'Adil Khan and Sultan Mahmud Bahmani. An inscription dated 1513–14 records the construction of the Yak Minar mosque, mentioning the same two figures. In 1515–16 a third mosque was built in the city, with its inscription again mentioning Isma'il 'Adil Khan. And in the same year, a bastion was built onto the fort's outer wall, which mentions Isma'il 'Adil Khan. See Kadiri, 'Bahmani Inscriptions,' pp. 66 and 65; K. M. Ahmad, 'Inscriptions,' p. 14 and 16.

[28] Joan-Pau Rubiés, *Travel and Ethnology in the Renaissance: South India through European Eyes, 1250–1625* (Cambridge: Cambridge University Press, 2000), p. 270, fn. 49. For thoughtful discussions of Nunes as a chronicler of Vijayanagara, see *ibid.*, pp. 257–79, and Sanjay Subrahmanyam, *Penumbral Visions: Making Polities in Early Modern South India* (New Delhi, 2001), pp. 188–92.

[29] Rubiés writes that he can 'perhaps be identified with the Fernão Nunes who in 1512 was *escrivão de feitor* of Calicut, and who in 1526 appears as *escrivão de fazenda* in Cochin.' Rubiés, *Travel and Ethnology*, p. 204.

[30] Robert Sewell, who translated Nunes' account and also wrote the first modern history of Vijayanagara, notes that throughout Nunes's account of the battle, 'there is much that impels the belief that either himself or his informant was present at the Hindu camp while these events were taking place. The narrative of the campaign, in complete contrast to that of the remainder of the history, reads like the account of an eye-witness; especially in the passages describing the fortress of Raichur and the camp—where the supplies were so great that 'you could find everything that you wanted,' where 'you saw' the goldsmiths and artisans at work as if in a city, where 'you will find' all kinds of precious stones offered for sale. . . .' Robert Sewell, *A Forgotten Empire (Vijayanagara): a Contribution to the History of India* (1900, repr; New Delhi: Asian Educational Services, 1984), p. 153.

Firishta is the less trustworthy of the two sources, not only because he was writing about ninety years after the fact, but because he had the unenviable task of accounting for the crushing defeat of his patron's own forebear. In his version of events, Isma'il 'Adil Khan in 1520 took an army of 7,000 cavalry, all Westerners, down to the northern shore of the Krishna river in order to recover Raichur and Mudgal from Krishna Raya.[31] On learning of these manoeuvres, the Vijayanagara king brought up a much larger cavalry of 50,000 to the southern shores of the same river, seizing control of its ferries. Firishta here introduces the factor that doomed Isma'il's enterprise to failure. While the sultan was reposing in his tent soon after pitching camp, a Bijapuri courtier proposed a drinking bout. Isma'il responded enthusiastically and got so thoroughly inebriated that he decided to cross the river and attack Krishna Raya at once. Although his officers pleaded for more time to build sufficient boats and rafts for the operation, Isma'il ignored the advice and, mounting his elephant, rode straight to the river and plunged into the water, ordering his officers and soldiers to follow. On reaching the opposing side, however, the Bijapuris confronted a huge body of cavalry and also, so Firishta writes, cannon, matchlocks and rockets.[32] Isma'il now found himself trapped between two Krishnas: before him the king of Vijayanagara, and to his rear the swirling currents of the Krishna river. In panic and disorder, the Bijapuris retreated and tried to re-cross the river, in the process losing many men both to drowning and to the arrows and shot of Vijayanagara's pursuing forces. Isma'il, who himself barely survived the debacle, sank into deep remorse for his rashness and swore off wine for good.

Firishta thus framed his story as a morality play, the essential point being that the debacle had been the fault of the wine, or rather, Isma'il's weakness in succumbing to wine at a wholly inappropriate time. Only as an aside does he mention perhaps the most arresting feature of his account, namely, that while Isma'il's retreating men were attempting to re-cross the river, Vijayanagara's forces killed nearly half of Bijapur's army with cannon shot, matchlocks and rockets. We shall bear this in mind as we explore the contemporary, or near contemporary, account of Fernão Nunes.

---

[31] Firishta gives the date as 927 AH, which is not possible since that year began on 12 December 1520, and Sewell demonstrates that the battle took place earlier that year, in May and June. See Briggs, *History*, p. 3:29; Sewell, *Forgotten Empire*, pp. 140–47.

[32] The text reads '*zarb zadan-i tup va tufang va digar atish-bazi.*' *Tarikh-i Firishta*, pp. 2:19–20. Briggs, *History*, pp. 3:29–30.

Nunes' account is far more detailed, less tendentious and, above all, more contemporary with the battle than is that of Firishta. When he assumed the Vijayanagara throne in 1509, writes the Portuguese chronicler, Krishna Raya knew that his royal predecessor Narasimha Tuluva had regretted never having reduced three forts—Raichur, Mudgal and Udayagiri. His opportunity to invade the first two came about ten years into his reign, when he entrusted a Muslim merchant with the sum of 40,000 *pardaos* to purchase warhorses from Goa. Instead of proceeding to the Portuguese-held seaport, however, the merchant absconded with the money to Bijapur. When the king wrote Isma'il 'Adil Khan demanding the return of the merchant and the money, the sultan refused to oblige. He even gave the port of Dabhol to the merchant, which so enraged Krishna Raya that he resolved to invade that town. The king's advisors tried to dissuade him, noting that the sum given to the merchant—which would have purchased approximately 120 horses—was too trifling an amount over which to wage a war. But on seeing that the king could not be deterred from invading Bijapuri territory, his advisors counselled invading Raichur rather than Dabhol, since the former city had once belonged to Vijayanagara. Accepting this advice, Krishna Raya in early 1520 moved north with an immense force of 27,600 cavalry and 553,000 infantry. In all, writes Nunes, the army included archers, cavalry using a variety of weapons, matchlockmen (*espimgardeiros*), swordsmen with shields, war elephants and 'several cannon' (*allgūs tiros de fogo*).[33]

After crossing the Tungabhadra river, the Vijayanagara army camped in the town of Maliabad, an ancient Kakatiya fort situated some ten miles south of Raichur city, and from there it moved on Raichur itself. The city, writes Nunes, was defended with three lines of strong walls of heavy masonry made without lime-mortar and packed with earth inside. Built into the outer walls were bastions positioned so close to one another that men posted on them could hear the words spoken by those on neighbouring bastions. The defenders used matchlocks (*espimgardas*) and heavy cannon (*tiros de fogo grossos*), as well as bow and arrow. Along the walls were mounted thirty stone-hurling catapults (*trabucos*), 200 heavy cannon and many smaller cannon, all the artillery being positioned between the bastions. Garrisoned inside were 8,000 'Adil Shahi foot soldiers, 400 cavalry and 20 elephants.[34]

---

[33] 'Chronicle of Fernão Nuniz,' in Sewell, tr., *Forgotten Empire* pp. 316–28. David Lopes, ed., *Chronica dos Reis de Bisnaga* (Lisbon: Impr. Nac., 1897), p. 28.

[34] 'Chronicle of Fernão Nuniz,' p. 331.

While deploying his forces around the entire fort, Krishna Raya concentrated his main attack on the city's eastern side, probably near the present Kati Gate. Whereas the fort's defenders fired on Vijayanagara's forces with heavy cannon and matchlocks, together with arrows, the besiegers used no artillery against Raichur's walls. Instead, Vijayanagara's commanders offered their men monetary inducements to go directly to the walls and dismantle them with pickaxes, paying them in sums proportionate to the size of the stones dismantled. They were also paid for dragging off the bodies of comrades killed at the base of the walls. In this slow, dreary manner the siege dragged on for three months.[35]

In early May, while the siege was still in progress, Krishna Raya learned that Isma'il 'Adil Khan had marched down from Bijapur to relieve the embattled fort and was camped on the northern side of the Krishna river. With him were 18,000 cavalry, 120,000 infantry, 150 elephants, and considerable artillery. Suspending the siege of Raichur, the king moved his entire army up to the Krishna river to prevent the 'Adil Shahi forces from entering the Doab. The battle between the two armies began several hours after dawn on 19 May 1520 when the sultan, having moved his forces to the southern side of the river, fired all his artillery at once into Vijayanagara's massed front lines. When those lines broke and the 'Adil Shahi cavalry advanced, Krishna Raya became so desperate that he entrusted his ring to one of his pages, instructing him to show it to his queens as a sign of his death. The king then mounted his horse and moved forward with all of his remaining divisions, driving the Bijapuris back towards, and finally into, the Krishna river. Like Firishta, Nunes reports the horrific slaughter that then occurred by the river, in the midst of which Isma'il 'Adil Khan jumped on an elephant and barely escaped with his life.[36]

It is clear that Isma'il 'Adil Khan had brought a great deal of ordnance to the battlefield for, as Nunes reports, his retreating army was forced to abandon 400 heavy cannon and 900 gun carriages, in addition to 4,000

---

[35] *Ibid.*, pp. 330, 332.

[36] In Nunes' vivid account, 'The troops advanced thus, pursuing the foe, till the King reached the river, where, seeing the death of so many—for here you would see women and boys who had left the camp, there horses and men who through clinging one to another could not escape as there was so much water in the river—and the King's troops stood on the bank, so that whenever a man appeared he was killed, and the horses that tried to clamber up the bank of the river, unable to do so, fell back on the men, so that neither one nor the other escaped, and the elephants went into the stream, and those that they could seize were cruelly killed by them.' Sewell, *Forgotten Empire*, p. 339.

warhorses and 100 elephants.[37] In fact, writes Nunes, Isma'il boldly crossed the Krishna river not because he was drunk, as Firishta would later write, but because he was confident that the great strength of his artillery (*a gramde artelharya*) would give him a quick victory. Indeed, the sultan's opening barrage did give him temporary field advantage. But Nunes does not report that Krishna Raya used artillery in that battle, although Firishta, as we have seen, did make such a claim. Since Nunes wrote much closer in time to the event than did Firishta, it seems reasonable to conclude that if Krishna Raya used firearms at all on this occasion, they did not play a decisive, or even noticeable, role in the battle's outcome.

This inference is supported by Nunes' account of the siege of Raichur fort, an engagement that Firishta does not even mention, in which the Portuguese chronicler describes Krishna Raya's men clawing at the fort's walls with crowbars, rather than bombarding it with cannon. And in his description of Krishna Raya's immense army during its initial march to Raichur, the king is said to have brought along only 'several' cannon. All of this suggests that by 1520 cannon were being used in the field—extensively by Bijapur, at best minimally by Vijayanagara—but with only limited effect. Defensively, whereas cannon were mounted on Raichur's ramparts, they had not yet displaced stone-hurling catapults, which were also still present, fixed atop the fort's projecting bastions. In short, cannon appear to have made a noticeable appearance at Raichur, but they were not yet sufficiently effective as to play a decisive role in the outcomes of military engagements. After all, in Nunes' account, Isma'il possessed and used significant firepower in the battle by the Krishna river, yet he still lost that battle.

Having soundly defeated the Bijapuris on the battlefield, Vijayanagara's army returned to Raichur to resume its siege of the fort. At this point a new factor enters Nunes' narrative—the arrival of 20 Portuguese mercenaries who, led by one Cristovão de Figueiredo, had just joined Krishna Raya's forces at Raichur as matchlockmen (*espimgardeyros*). Noticing how fearlessly 'Adil Shahi defenders roamed about the fort's walls, fully exposed to the view of the besiegers, de Figueiredo and his men began picking them off with their guns. Nunes remarks, very significantly, that the defenders 'up to then had never seen men

---

[37] 'quoatro centos tiros grossos d artelharia, afora meuda, forão o numero das carretas d ellas nove-centas.. ..' Lopes, *Chronica*, p. 39. Sewell, tr, *Forgotten Empire*, p. 342.

killed with firearms nor with other such weapons'.[38] What is more, it seems that the fort's cannon proved ineffective against the besiegers, who continued to assault the fort's walls with crowbars and pickaxes as they had been doing before the battle by the Krishna river. The reason the fort's cannon were ineffective, Nunes explains, had to do with how they were mounted. Being placed high on the curtain walls, they could not fire down on those dismantling the walls at their base. And the defenders who tried to fire on them with arrows, matchlocks, or stones were themselves picked off by de Figueiredo's sharpshooters, allowing Krishna Raya's men to continue dismantling the walls relatively unhindered. This operation was so successful that the defenders were forced to abandon their first line of fortification and place their women and children in the city's hilltop citadel.

Several inferences may be drawn from this part of Nunes' narration. First, although the 'Adil Shahi defenders were using matchlocks to fend off the besiegers, those weapons must have been inferior to those of de Figueiredo and his men if, as Nunes reports, Bijapuri defenders at Raichur had never before been killed by firearms. This is quite possible, given that de Figueiredo would have had access to the superior firearms that were then being produced in the Goa arsenal, 'without doubt one of the largest arsenals of the world at that time'.[39] It was here that, during the early decades of the sixteenth century, the Portuguese and Muslim gunsmiths had been exchanging designs and developing the latest hybrid matchlocks.[40] Second, the inability of Raichur's cannon shot to reach besiegers at the base of the fort's walls indicates that while the defensive use of cannons on forts had certainly reached the Deccan interior by 1520, engineers had not yet learned how to manoeuvre them so as to screen the walls with flanking fire. Being fixed between the

---

[38] 'Chronicle of Fernão Nuniz,' p. 344. '. . .pellos mouros estarem tão descuydados e sem temor, como aquelles que atee ly numca lhe matarão homẽs com espimgardas, nem com outros tiros que lhe tirarão. ...' Lopes, ed., *Chronica*, p. 40.

[39] Daehnhardt, *Bewitched Gun*, p. 42.

[40] 'From the 16th century until the 19th century,' writes Daehnhardt, 'Portuguese and Goan gunsmiths worked side by side, harmoniously mixing technical influences and decorative capacities.' Daehnhardt, *Bewitched Gun*, p. 71. Portuguese anxieties that their gun-making techniques might migrate to their adversaries on the plateau is seen in an incident, cited by Sanjay Subrahmanyam, in which Goan authorities in the 1620s sent an assassin to Bijapur to eliminate a Portuguese cannon founder who had taken up service at the 'Adil Shahi court. The assassin first ingratiated himself with his victim and then, 'having eaten and drunk well, murdered him and buried him under the floor of his own house.' The killer was subsequently rewarded with a clerical position to the magistrate in Diu. Subrahmanyam, 'Kagemusha effect,' p. 111.

battlement's merlons and not mounted on swivels, the cannon would have been immobile and hence quite useless against besiegers beneath them.

A turning point in the siege was reached on June 14 when the governor of the city, seeking a better view of exactly where the Portuguese snipers were positioned, leaned out in front of one of the embrasures and was instantly killed by a matchlock shot that struck his forehead. This snapped the morale of Raichur's defenders, who promptly abandoned the wall. The next day the Bijapuris opened the city gate and filed out, begging for mercy. All that remained now was a formal ceremony of capitulation and a transfer of authority. That came the following day, when Krishna Raya, after performing his customary prayers, rode into the city accompanied by his highest-ranking officers. Along the way, the townspeople stood awaiting him—although, as Nunes remarks, they bore 'more cheerful countenances than their real feelings warranted'.[41] Speaking to a gathered crowd, the king generously assured the city's leaders that their property rights would be respected; he even gave them the option of leaving the city and taking their movable property with them.

Before returning to his capital, Krishna Raya lingered in Raichur for some days making arrangements for the city's new administration. Nunes reports that he also repaired the walls that had been damaged during the siege.[42] This is surely a reference to the new regime's programme of rebuilding the fort's northern walls.[43] Here they added a new gate, the Naurangi Darwaza, together with three bastions to the west of it, two of them round with projecting bracketed balconies, and one of them square with brackets only on the outer face. In the Naurangi Darwaza, they also built a large inner courtyard whose upper walls contain narrative sculptural panels depicting scenes from the *Mahabharata*, the *Ramayana*, the Krishna cycle, and Vaishnava *avataras*, as well as court scenes from metropolitan Vijayanagara. In all, this gateway complex and the new bastions to its west register a clear and deliberate attempt to stamp a distinctively Vijayanagara aesthetic onto this frontier site, which had for so long been a Bahmani and Bijapuri possession.

---

[41] 'Chronicle of Fernão Nuniz,' p. 347.

[42] *Ibid.*, p. 349.

[43] The radical renovations and additions made to the fort's northern side suggest that this was where the walls had been breached, and not the eastern side, where Nunes reports that Vijayanagara's forces had concentrated their attack.

POST-CONFLICT DIPLOMACY

Following Krishna Raya's return to Vijayanagara and the round of festivities that celebrated the king's victories at Raichur, an 'Adil Shahi ambassador arrived in the capital to negotiate a final settlement between the two adversaries. After keeping him waiting for a month, the king finally admitted the ambassador for a private audience. The latter conveyed an extraordinary request from Isma'il 'Adil Khan, namely, that should Krishna Raya restore to Bijapur the city of Raichur, together with the artillery, tents, horses and elephants that the 'Adil Shahis had lost in the battle, Isma'il would remain the king's enduring and loyal friend.

In response, Krishna Raya agreed to grant all these requests—and even to return Bijapur's highest-ranking officer, Salabat Khan, who had been captured in the debacle by the Krishna river[44]—on the sole condition that Isma'il first come down to Vijayanagara and kiss his foot. When this response was conveyed to Isma'il, the latter replied through his ambassador that, whereas he was 'of full mind joyfully to do that which the King wished', it was unfortunately not possible for him legally to enter another king's sovereign territory. On hearing this, Krishna Raya offered to accommodate the sultan's concerns by meeting him at their common border near the fort of Mudgal. There the sultan could kiss the king's foot. Without waiting for the sultan's response, Krishna Raya proceeded north to Mudgal, accompanied by a formidable army that was doubtless intended to focus the sultan's mind. But Isma'il, who had no intention of journeying to Mudgal or of ever enduring the humiliation of kissing the king's foot, stalled and prevaricated while his messengers notified the king that he was on the way and would reach Mudgal very soon.

However, when it became clear that Isma'il was not going to present himself at the border, Krishna Raya opted for an alternative course of action, namely, of bringing his foot to the sultan, so that the latter could kiss it in his own domain without having to travel anywhere. The king and his army then entered 'Adil Shahi territory, moving as far north as Isma'il's capital of Bijapur, which the sultan prudently vacated before the king's arrival. With Isma'il absent, Krishna Raya's men proceeded to damage several of the city's prominent houses, on the grounds that they needed firewood. When

---

[44] *Ibid.*, p. 342.

Isma'il, through envoys, protested this reckless behaviour, Krishna Raya replied that he had been unable to restrain his men from their destructive activities. Meanwhile the sultan, preferring to suffer the humiliation of his capital's desecration than to kiss Krishna Raya's foot, simply avoided his capital as long as the king was in the city. Eventually Krishna Raya, having made his point, returned to his own capital.

Two observations emerge from this discussion. First, Nunes' account of Krishna Raya's overbearing behaviour in the aftermath of the Raichur battle stands at odds with his image in modern scholarship, which tends to revere him as an ideal Indian monarch— heroic, virtuous, pious and just. Modern scholars have even dignified him with the name 'Krishna Deva Raya', even though contemporary sources generally refer to him simply as Krishna Raya. One twentieth-century scholar rejects outright the possibility that, notwithstanding Nunes' testimony, a man as 'noblehearted' as Krishna Raya could have demanded that an adversary kiss his foot.[45] But we need to evaluate the man by accounts of his own day. One might expect that court poets or chroniclers, who had a professional investment in glorifying the court they served, would celebrate, not suppress, the episodes in which their royal patron crushed or humiliated their enemies. But unfortunately, no contemporary poetry concerning Krishna Raya's Raichur campaign survives.[46] The sole evidence in the matter comes from an outsider, Fernão Nunes, who had spent three years in metropolitan Vijayanagara not as an ambassador, but as a horse trader who would have been in touch with the court's commercial agents. As such, he would not seem to have had any motive either to celebrate or to criticize the king. Besides, balancing the chronicler's matter-of-fact account respecting Krishna Raya's foot are his several references to the king's generosity, such as the latter's generous treatment of Raichur's defeated townspeople. In the final

---

[45] 'It is incredible,' wrote K. Raghavacharlu in the 1930s, 'to believe that the generous and noble-hearted Krishnaraya would behave in such a manner in respect to a fallen foe.' K. Raghavacharlu, 'Krishna Raya, the Man,' in *Vijayanagara: History and Legacy* ed., S. Krishnaswami Aiyangar (1936, repr; New Delhi: Aryan Books International, 2000), p. 183.

[46] The campaign is mentioned, but only in passing, by a fifth generation descendant of one of Krishna Raya's court poets. Kumara Dhurjati writes that the king 'marched against the frontier fortresses of Bijapur. The garrisons in many of these fortresses surrendered after defeat, and Krishna Raya spared the lives of their Governors. He then put fresh garrisons in the fortresses of Adavani (Adoni), Mudugallu (Mudgal) and Rachuru (Raichur) and directed his march towards Golkonda.' 'Krishna Raya Vijayam,' in *Sources of Vijayanagar History* ed., S. Krishnaswami Aiyangar (1919; repr. Delhi: Gian Pub. House, 1986), p. 131.

analysis, Nunes' account of the episode respecting Krishna Raya's foot serves to humanize the man, and as such can perhaps provide a much-needed corrective to the king's idealized, cardboard cut-out image found in most textbooks.[47]

Second, and far more serious, Krishna Raya's style of diplomacy in the wake of the Battle for Raichur arguably carried with it the seeds of his kingdom's demise. For the king, while waging his campaigns against Isma'il Adil Khan, had in his service a man who would subsequently display the same high-handed style of diplomacy, which in his case led to the destruction of metropolitan Vijayanagara. This was Rama Raya, an officer who had taken up service with Krishna Raya five years before the Battle for Raichur. The king was so impressed with the officer's abilities that he gave him his own daughter in marriage. After his patron's death in 1529, Rama Raya steadily rose in power, by 1542 becoming Vijayanagara's supreme autocrat, ruling the state through a nephew of Krishna Raya whom he had reduced to a mere puppet sovereign.

For several decades, Rama Raya cynically intervened in conflicts among the northern sultanates. But his manipulative and haughty behaviour finally induced those same sultanates, in 1565, to combine forces and crush him and his army at the Battle of Talikota. The immediate cause of that battle lay in an act that, in its brazen audacity, echoed that of Krishna Raya and his foot. In late 1561, Rama Raya demanded that if his current adversary, Sultan Husain Nizam Shah of Ahmadnagar, were to enjoy lasting peace with Vijayanagara, he must first come and eat *pan* (betel nut) from the autocrat's hand. Unlike Isma'il 'Adil Khan, who simply vacated his capital to avoid kissing Krishna Raya's foot, Sultan Husain succumbed to Rama Raya's humiliating demand. Determined to avenge this act, Husain took the lead in organizing a coalition of northern sultanates to wage the campaign in which Rama Raya was killed, his army destroyed, and metropolitan Vijayanagara demolished. Whereas no direct evidence proves the point, one suspects that Rama Raya's tactic of humbling his northern adversaries was something he could have learned by observing the overbearing diplomacy of his own father-in-law, Krishna Raya.

[47] Joan-Pau Rubiés speculates that 'the insight and perhaps also the bitterness bred of three years trying unsuccessfully to prosper by selling horses, leads [Nunes] towards an image in which the pretensions of ideal kingship, although not completely obliterated, are nevertheless reduced to human proportions.' Rubiés, *Travel and Ethnology*, p. 268.

CONCLUSION

The Battle for Raichur originated in a dispute between Vijayanagara and Bijapur over money intended for purchasing warhorses. It then saw the first notable instance of field and siege artillery used in the Indian interior. It effectively ended when the governor of Raichur was shot by a matchlock most likely made in Goa. In several respects, then, the 1520 battle represents a transitional phase in the military history of South Asia. It also played an important role in the diplomatic history of the Deccan.

From a military standpoint, the battle presents what might appear a paradox, namely, that the side that relied the more extensively on firearms not only lost, but lost decisively. In April 1526, just six years after the contest between Isma'il 'Adil Khan and Krishna Raya at Raichur, one of the most famous battles of Indian history was fought at Panipat, more than a thousand miles north of the Raichur Doab. In that battle, the Central Asian Turkish prince Babur deployed field cannon in defeating the last ruler of the Delhi Sultanate, which led directly to the establishment of the Mughal Empire. Given the significance of the battle's outcome, and the fact that the winning side used cannon, Panipat is sometimes seen as having inaugurated India's 'Gunpowder Age'.

On the other hand, states usually assimilate new technologies by a gradual process of trial-and-error, in respect to which failures can be as important as successes. It seems certain that a principal cause of Isma'il's crushing defeat by the banks of the Krishna river lay in his gunners' inability to quickly reload and fire successive rounds of shot before being overwhelmed by Vijayanagara's swift and powerful cavalry. Much had to be learned about the manufacture and deployment of field cannon, and considerable practice would be necessary, before this new technology could become truly lethal to opponents who had mastered the tactics and techniques of cavalry warfare. From this point of view, Isma'il 'Adil Khan's defeat represented a crucial and necessary step towards the full integration of field cannon into South Asian military traditions that theretofore had been dominated by the use of heavy cavalry. In the military history of India, then, the Battle for Raichur may be justly placed alongside Babur's far better known victory at Panipat, rather than omitted altogether.

If Isma'il was the first commander to use cannon in an important Indian battlefield engagement, he was also among the first to mount cannon on the battlements of forts in the Indian interior. But here, too, the technology's very novelty proved its users' undoing, for in 1520 Raichur's system of fortification was very much in a transitional phase of development. Before the city fell to Vijayanagara's army, its defenders were in the process of adopting, however imperfectly, a new technology that would ultimately improve and diffuse throughout the whole of India. Nunes reports that on the city's battlements, several hundred heavy and light cannon were positioned alongside thirty stone-hurling catapults, a device that had been used in Deccani siege warfare for several centuries before this engagement. However, owing to the arrangement of the fort's defences—with the catapults on the bastions and the cannons rigidly fixed in immobile positions between the merlons—Krishna Raya's men were able to dismantle a portion of the city's walls without suffering prohibitively high casualty rates. In effect, 'Adil Shahi engineers at Raichur deployed the new gunpowder technology in a manner that proved just as disastrous there as did Isma'il's deployment of field cannon by the Krishna river. Given his victories both by the river and at the fort, Krishna Raya could hardly be faulted for not seeing cannon warfare as the wave of the future.[48]

On the other hand, the Vijayanagara king was clearly impressed by the matchlocks used by Cristovão de Figueiredo and his fellow Portuguese mercenaries at Raichur. These men had in all likelihood been armed by the Goa arsenal, which was then producing 'Indo-Portuguese' weapons that appear to have been superior to anything then available in India. As Nunes noted, no Muslims at Raichur had ever been killed by such firearms until Krishna Raya's siege of the city. It was thus in the area of matchlock weapons, and not in that of field or fixed cannon, that new gunpowder technology contributed to the outcome of the Battle for Raichur.

The battle was also the first major conflict in the Indian interior in which European mercenaries are known to have participated. We know that European mercenaries and renegades had begun appearing in the

---

[48] The Battle for Riachur occurred towards the end of the period of Krishna Raya's major conquests in the Deccan and South India, which extended from 1509 to 1523. Unlike the sultans of Ahmadnagar and Bijapur during this period of time, Krishna Raya does not appear to have relied extensively on firearms in the course of these conquests.

service of Indian coastal powers as early as 1502, and that European gunpowder technology diffused into the Indian interior together with European matchlockmen, bombardiers, and cannon founders who sold their services to indigenous states in the interior.[49] But, as Maria Augusta Lima Cruz notes, in European accounts only those who served armies under Muslim control were understood as renegades.[50] Thus Cristovão de Figueiredo, otherwise a horse merchant, is described by Nunes as a proud Portuguese fidalgo who boasts to Krishna Raya that 'the whole business of the Portuguese was war' and that the greatest favour the king could grant would be to allow him to accompany the Vijayanagara army to Raichur.[51] Nunes never refers to de Figueiredo and his 20 fellow matchlockmen as renegades (*arrenegados*). He does use that term, however, in mentioning the fifty Portuguese who fought and died for Isma'il 'Adil Khan at the battle by the Krishna river.[52]

Finally, we must consider the battle's legacy in defining the Doab generally, and more particularly the city of Raichur, as a frontier zone. The city remained under Vijayanagara's control for only ten years, until 1530 when Isma'il 'Adil Khan re-conquered the fort following Krishna Raya's death. But during the decade 1520–30, Vijayanagara's governors, architects and engineers reshaped the city's physical appearance in ways that emphatically asserted the aesthetic vision of its new rulers. From epigraphic evidence we know that in July 1521, about a year after the city's transfer to Vijayanagara's authority, a patron named Kanthamaraju Singaraju dedicated a new temple in the city.[53] Unfortunately, that structure is not identifiable now. Very much visible today, however, are the structural additions or modifications that Vijayanagara's rulers made to the city's outer walls and gates, and it is in these features that one sees the victors' distinctive imprint. On the fort's northern side, especially, the exterior courses of several bastions are covered with sculptural reliefs

---

[49] Maria Augusta Lima Cruz, 'Exiles and Renegades in Early Sixteenth Century Portuguese India,' *Indian Economic and Social History Review* 23 (1986), p. 260.

[50] *Ibid.*, p. 258.

[51] 'Xpovão de Figueiredo lhe disse que o oficyo dos portuguezes não era outro senão ho da guerra.' Lopes, *Chronica*, p. 40; Sewell, *Forgotten Empier*, p. 343.

[52] Nunes nonetheless expressed full admiration for his fellow countrymen fighting under 'Adil Shahi command: 'the Portuguese did great deeds, and killed so many men that they left a broad road behind them which no one dared enter.' Sewell, *Forgotten Empire*, p. 342. Sewell mistakenly gives the number of these men as 500 instead of 50. Cf. Lopes, *Chronica*, p. 39.

[53] *South Indian Inscriptions* p. 4:789. Cited in Sherwani and Joshi, eds, *History of Medieval Deccan* p. 1:120.

bearing motifs identical to those of early sixteenth century metropolitan Vijayanagara. The most spectacular display of those motifs is found in the spacious courtyard that was built into the city's new, northern gateway complex, the Naurangi Darwaza, which combines large and small sculptural reliefs drawn directly from the tradition of metropolitan Vijayanagara.

However, because Vijayanagara's authorities in Raichur restricted their structural modifications to just several segments of an otherwise Bahmani (and 'Adil Shahi) fort, the overall result is a site in which two very different architectural and aesthetic traditions, the Bahmani and the Vijayanagara, are abruptly juxtaposed, one beside the other. It is, finally, this juxtaposition—a consequence of the 1520 battle—that most tellingly conveys the sense of a city teetering on the edge of two aesthetic worlds.

12

Frontiers of Family Life:

Early Modern Atlantic and Indian Ocean Worlds

Patrick Manning*

——— • ✦ • ———

I. Introduction

Not much analysis has yet been conducted on the global patterns and global interactions of family life. Anthropologists and sociologists have tended to analyse families as local, ethnically based organizations, whose rules and structures have been inherited from the ancestors and reproduced without much regard for the outside world. While the ethnic particularities of families are unmistakable, it would be strange if families were uniquely resistant to global influences in a world where economic, political and ideological trends are now thought to have circulated and interacted widely.

Migration opens an obvious avenue for thinking of family in transregional terms. One need only think of merchant families, stretched across the lengths of their trade routes, to recognize the significance of migration as a non-local factor influencing family life. Working from

* I wish to express thanks to Richard Eaton and Munis Faruqui for their guidance in making revisions to this study. I am also appreciative to Sanjay Subrahmanyam, whose line of questioning at the Duke conference put me on a path toward addressing a major complexity I had previously neglected: the accounting for both long-distance and intermediate-distance migration. Earlier versions of this study have been presented at the University of Kentucky (2002), the American Historical Association conference on Interactions, Washington, DC (2003); the University of California, Irvine (2003); and the World History Association annual meeting in Fairfax, Virginia (2004).

this insight, the present study considers migration and its influence on family structure. I argue that there exists a social nexus linking migration to family structure—that migration, though highly variable, is typical in family history. This interpretation focuses on modelling the dynamics of family structure, the dynamics of migration and the familial mixing resulting from their interaction. I present my interpretation of change and interaction in families by deploying and documenting several simplified models of family, migration and their interaction. If family structure can be shown through this analysis to have been influenced significantly by migration, the door is then opened to further studies of the influence of migration on the governance and ideology of family life.

The analysis centres on the Atlantic and Indian Ocean zones in the sixteenth and seventeenth centuries: an era recent enough for us to have substantial documentation on families and migration in those regions, and long enough ago that the phenomena of migration and social interaction were not as pervasive as they would later become.[1] In the sixteenth century, maritime contacts linked almost all regions of the world, and brought long-distance, sea-borne migration especially by Iberian voyagers, West African captives, and those who followed the sea lanes linking the South China Sea and the Indian Ocean. The seventeenth century brought a period of further migratory expansion, usually along the same paths: from Europe and Africa to the Americas, from Europe to Asia and among Asian regions distant from each other. Intermediate-distance migrations, mostly within continental zones and less fully documented, were likely of larger scale than oceanic migrations and surely interacted with them. As I will argue, the expanded terrestrial and maritime communication of the early-modern world led to the creation of new families and also brought the expansion, displacement, division and destruction of previously existing families. In not a few cases, the rules of family life underwent transformation.

These changes in family life, studied characteristically at familial and local levels, are susceptible to study at transregional and even global levels. I argue that migration created new families dominated by young people in areas of settlement; it transformed families and weakened some powers of family heads in regions of moderate in- or out-migration; and it made families smaller everywhere. Migration brought

---

[1] I believe that migration in previous periods was also influential in modifying family structure, though it will be more difficult to document the argument.

somewhat different changes to the Atlantic than to the Indian Ocean—the undermining of multigenerational families progressed more rapidly in the Atlantic, while the familial mixing of existing families was more prominent in the Indian Ocean.

The interplay of family and migration constituted a 'frontier' of families—a series of liminal zones where patterns of family life responded to the arrival and departure of migrants. This type of frontier could be thought of as a space, but was a space defined by changing family relationships. In these frontier spaces, people lived in close contact with—and shared family ties with—others whom they classified as different from themselves according to several criteria. These family-frontier zones were not just at the margin of conventional, ethnically homogeneous families, they were zones of additional complexity in family life.

For purposes of this overview, I offer definitions of family, migration and familial mixing that are intended to be appropriate to a world-historical level of analysis. *Families*, groups of related people, are defined everywhere by three overlapping criteria. *Formal families* are groups of people whose membership is defined through the legal limits of marriage, adoption and inheritance; this is usually the narrowest definition of family. *Biological families*, including all biological relationships, often extend well beyond the formally recognized membership—for instance, patrilineal families recognize descent only through the male line, and give no formal recognition to descent through the female line. *Informal families* can extend beyond formal limits to include fictive kin and co-resident persons.[2] Families thus defined, may be classified with qualitative variables (identifying family structures and the boundaries of familial and sub-familial groups) and with quantitative variables (identifying sex ratios, age ratios and total size of family groups). Of particular emphasis in the discussion below will be relative family size.

I define *migration* as the movement from one *habitat* to another, where a human habitat is taken to be a geographical zone in which ecology,

---

[2] In a related paper, I address the historiographical and conceptual aspects of the study of family at the world-historical level. There, I argue in general for the existence of global patterns of family development and interaction. I argue that historians are increasingly in a position to begin identifying and exploring such patterns, and that a world-historical standpoint leads to helpful clarification of the numerous and competing definitions of family. Patrick Manning, 'Family in Anthropology and World History: Definitions and Debates', unpublished paper.

language and culture exhibit commonality.[3] Thus, while there is a great deal of mobility from one household or one village to another, notably for purposes of marriage, this is labelled as *local mobility* within the habitat and not as migration, in that there are only minimal boundaries to cross.[4] I then divide migration into *intermediate-distance migration* and *long-distance migration*, where the difference between the two is as much a matter of familiarity as proximity. Long-distance migrants are seen, in the lands of their settlement, as culturally or physically different and also as unfamiliar. Intermediate-distance migrants are also seen as culturally or physically different, but they are familiar in that there is a history of interaction with them. For instance, along the Coromandel Coast, immigrants from the Deccan were different in language and culture, but had been known for centuries; immigrants from Europe were new and unfamiliar. The description of migration includes qualitative variables (social identity of migrants—e.g. slave, free and noble—and the character of their migration) and quantitative variables (on numbers of migrants, their age and sex distribution). In practice, for early-modern times, the difference between long-distance and intermediate-distance migration overlaps significantly with that between transoceanic and terrestrial migration. Long-distance migration of Europeans and those they transported (e.g. Africans) stands out because of the cultural distinctiveness of the migrants—in language, physical type, religion, social categorization, dress—and the accessible documentation we have of their movement and their lives. Intermediate-distance migration from one part to another of Africa, India or South America was almost certainly of greater volume than transoceanic migration. Further, intermediate-distance migration might have involved crossing social boundaries that were just as significant as those of transoceanic migration, although these movements are not marked so clearly in the historical record.

I define *familial mixing* as the formation of families by people from different backgrounds—the nature of sexual reproduction makes it necessary that all families are mixed according to numerous criteria. *Post-*

---

[3] For more detail on the definition of *habitat* and on the distinctive character of *local mobility*, see Patrick Manning, 'Cross-Community Migration: A Distinctive Human Pattern', *Social Evolution and History* 5 (2006).

[4] This definition does not account for the variations in status or class within a given habitat. For a lower-class person to join an upper-class family is to cross great social barriers, but rather lower barriers in language and culture.

migratory mixing is the formation of families by people from differing habitats or by the descendants of such people. Post-migratory mixing takes place through formal marriage and through informal unions. In practice, the mixing and its results are described through such terms as the race, ethnicity, colour, religion or occupation of the parents and the offspring of such unions. The mixing resulting from long-distance migration results in the creation of new identities in subsequent generations that are more obviously distinctive than the mixing resulting from intermediate-distance migration, because of the greater initial social distances.

Having defined terms, we now move on to characterize the data. Early-modern data are arguably sufficient to sustain an analysis of family and migration that reaches some specificity. Descriptions of *family size*, while scattered through the travel literature, are numerous, though they are commonly vague about whether they refer to the formal, informal or biological definitions of family. Descriptions of *family structure* are also dispersed through the travel literature—this is the variable emphasized, for instance, in the common generalizations that European families are small, nuclear families, while families elsewhere have been large and extended. Parish registers are for the Christian world only, and not all of it.[5] Yet other data on families include various types of censuses, genealogies for elite families, court records of family groupings and traveller reports on family structures and practices. Descriptions of decision-making in marriage and inheritance give insights into the governance of families. All in all, data of one form or another should permit cross-regional comparison of family structures. For quantities and composition of migratory movements, estimates of European and African migration have been the subject of substantial research; research on Indian Ocean migration is less developed but significant.[6] Overall, while the interpretation to follow relies as much on hypothesis as on documented reconstruction, I argue that four key variables—family size, family structure as seen through sex ratio, migration volumes and familial mixing as seen through ethnic and racial labels—are

[5] For an excellent compilation and analysis of parish records, see E. A. Wrigley and R. S. Schofield, *The Population History of England, 1541–1871: A Reconstruction* (Cambridge, MA: Harvard University Press, 1981).

[6] David Eltis ed., 'Voyages: The Trans Atlantic Slave Trade Database', http://www.slavevoyages. org/; Markus Vink, '"The World's Oldest Trade": Dutch Slavery and Slave Trade in the Indian Ocean in the Seventeenth Century', *Journal of World History* 14 (2003):131–77.

relatively well documented in the historical record of the sixteenth and seventeenth centuries.

DYNAMICS OF FAMILY STRUCTURE, MIGRATION AND FAMILY MIXING

To simplify the logic of family dynamics, one can begin by thinking of localized families, reproducing themselves over time within their own habitat. Steady familial reproduction creates multigenerational lineages, with widespread social ties and regulations for their behaviour. It is a situation of stable population in demographic terms and complexity in social terms. Various sorts of social systems develop among such multigenerational families: patrilineal descent systems tend to circulate women from family to family, while matrilineal systems tend to circulate both men and women; social systems for agricultural and pastoral peoples have developed further distinctions. Overall, however, populations with minimal migration elevate senior people, usually males, to family leadership, and these leaders set decisions on allocation of land or herds as well as residence and marriage of the younger generations. Such a system is often treated as the ideal type of family structure.

But families are always modified by migration, both in and out. Migration in human society is irregular, yet its irregularities conform to a few dependable dynamics.[7] Historically contingent mixtures of misfortune and opportunity lead to streams of migration, and these streams of migration rarely last for more than a generation without declining, though in some cases, migration rebounds after a time. Small streams of migration generally precede large ones, in effect establishing the most propitious paths for movement. Networks of migrants and non-migrants serve to facilitate the passage and settlement of migrants. Both in-migrants and out-migrants are generally young, often unattached, less constrained and less supported by family networks than those who stay at home.

Linking the dynamics of family and migration leads to further distinctions. In zones of settlement, migration usually brings mixing of immigrants with each other and with local families. An extreme case is that of migration to under-populated zones, where young people

---

[7] For a recent discussion of general patterns, see Patrick Manning, *Migration in World History* (London: Routledge, 2005).

arrive with no parents and no rules, so that anything can happen in the families they form. Few regions experience long-term stability in the level of migration, and for that reason, few regions experience long-term stability in their family structure. Rules for classification of families, which have generally been treated as stable descriptions and regulations, may better be seen as current statements of ideals that are periodically adjusted in response to migration and other factors. There are various other possibilities, including the end of immigration: when immigration declines for two or three generations, age and sex distributions become more like those of a stable population.[8]

To phrase the interaction in terms of population pyramids, the pyramid for a non-migrating population tends to have equal numbers of male and female populations of each age group, with smaller populations for cohorts of increasing age. Migration changes the size and shape of the pyramid.[9] In-migration usually brings additional young adults, especially males; out-migration reduces numbers of young adults, especially males. The rise and fall of adult female populations brings equivalent changes in the number of young children.

When migrants form relationships (marital or non-marital) with persons in their zone of settlement, demographic imbalance is likely to characterize the resulting families. For a male merchant marrying into an elite local family, the new family is very small on the husband's side and can be very large on the wife's side. For an immigrant female who becomes a concubine, her family is small on her side and can be very large on her master's side. For immigrant men and women forming relationships on island colonies, the families are small on both sides; imbalance would come where one was free and the other was enslaved.

In addition to demographic imbalance, familial mixing takes place as a result of migration. *Mixing* is a deceptive term, appearing simple when it is not. Biological mixing is inherent in the sexual reproduction of our species. Familial mixing is the labelling of family ties, such as the mixes of lineages required by rules of exogamy; it also includes mixes by ethnicity, physical type, religion, social stratum (caste, class, free or slave). In the first generation of familial mixes, the migrant family

---

[8] Historical studies of changing family structure tend to give minimal attention to migration. For one such study, see Wally Seccombe, *A Millennium of Family Change: Feudalism to Capitalism in Northwestern Europe* (London: Verso, 1992).

[9] Changes in birth rates and death rates can also change the size and shape of the population pyramid, but these are neglected here.

members tend to be treated as exceptions whose fate is governed within established rules. In the second generation of migration, the beginnings of new rules emerge with the labelling of categories of social mixes. In the third generation, a more complex set of mixes emerges, along with a revised set of rules setting identities in a hierarchy. That is, in the frontier zones of family life, the offspring of 'mixed' relationships come to be labelled through complex terminologies identifying generation, status, ancestry, birthplace and colour. Some of the mixed relationships are formalized by marriage, especially when property is held on both sides of the family. Others—as with the coupling of master and slave or across religious lines—tend to be left as informal liaisons, so that the boundaries of the biological family and the formal social family can be quite different.

REGIONAL VARIANTS

In this section, five types of regions are described empirically and analytically with regard to the character of their migration experience and the resulting changes in their family size and structure, including the character of their social mix. Exemplary regions of the Indian Ocean and the Atlantic Ocean—all coastal or within a week's walk from the coast—are paired, to demonstrate that each phenomenon showed up in both regions, though to different degrees.

Zones of Moderate In-migration: South India and Brazil

The Coromandel Coast of India, especially Tamil Nadu, received settlers from the Deccan to its north, notably in the fifteenth and sixteenth centuries. These intermediate-distance migrants found sparsely populated lands in the upper valleys of the region.[10] While sources do not give a breakdown, the usual pattern of migration suggests that the immigrants were mostly male, and that these men married local

---

[10] David Ludden, *Peasant History in South India* (Princeton, NJ: Princeton University Press, 1985); Sanjay Subrahmanyam, *The Political Economy of Commerce: Southern India 1500–1650* (Cambridge: Cambridge University Press, 1990). For other studies of migration and family in India, see Sumit Guha, 'Household Size and Household Structure in Western India c. 1700–1950: Beginning an Exploration', *Indian Economic and Social History Review* 35 (1998): 23–33; and Douglas Haynes and Tirthankar Roy, 'Conceiving Mobility: Weavers' Migrations in Pre-colonial and Colonial India', *Indian Economic and Social History Review* 36 (1999): 35–69.

women as well as women who accompanied them. The result was not so much a strict colonization, but formation of new societies relying significantly on pre-existing local traditions that were conveyed by local women. Somewhat later, the Malabar Coast towns of Goa and Calicut, as major commercial centres, attracted long-distance migrants, especially merchants, from all over the Indian Ocean and beyond.[11] By the seventeenth century, Portuguese, Dutch and English merchants and officials had settled in these and nearby towns. Some immigrant men of high status were able to marry into well-established local families. As a result the coastal Indian regions, now with sizeable minorities of in-migrants, developed new structures for linking multigenerational, local families to unaffiliated individuals from abroad. It was to the advantage of immigrant men to reside with their in-laws, to qualify for inheritance of family lands and goods; such families were large on the wife's side and small on the husband's side. Immigrant women, unless brought as spouses by immigrant men, came as women without power and entered into established families as subordinates, whether willingly or not, and had children in non-marital relationships.[12] These families were small on the wife's side and larger on the husband's side. In response to the expansion of these varying sorts of social mixes, local terms developed for the status, colour and occupation for these couples and their children.

On the northeast and southeast coasts of Brazil in the middle and late sixteenth century, Portuguese (and French) migrants similarly settled. The immigrant populations, dominantly male, initially married into local families (mostly of Tupi ethnicity), linking local to immigrant economic power.[13] By the seventeenth century, the Portuguese were able to establish political if not demographic dominance, gradually bringing enslaved Africans with them. Portuguese men became heads of family, displacing the men of the local families into which they had married. Thus, the new families of Brazil appeared at first to be like those formed on the Malabar Coast, with the local ethnicity dominating, but with time, the Brazilian families became more like those of the interior of Tamil Nadu, with the immigrant ethnicity dominating.

[11] M. N. Pearson, *Coastal Western India* (New Delhi: Concept Publishing Company, 1981).

[12] C. R. Boxer, *The Portuguese Seaborne Empire 1415–1825* (New York, NY: Knopf, 1969), pp. 69–78.

[13] Alida C. Metcalf, *Go-betweens and the Colonization of Brazil, 1500–1600* (Austin, TX: University of Texas Press, 2005); Filipe Eduardo Moreau, *Os Indios nas cartes de Nóbrega e Anchieta* (São Paulo: Annablume, 2003).

Zones with Little Migration: Mozambique and Bight of Biafra

Regions with little migration are easy to imagine, but difficult to document. Mozambique in the sixteenth and seventeenth century was a region of little migration. Localized families, with matrilineal organization, were able to maintain a multigenerational structure, and senior men were able to control the marriage and land use of their sisters' sons and those under their command. Some long-distance and intermediate-distance migration is known to have taken place. For the latter, the rise of the kingdom of Mwenemutapa and the later rise of the Malawi kingdom each led to out-migration from the new states and into the Zambezi Valley. Small numbers of Portuguese settlers came to the region as well.[14] In each of these cases, the immigrants were mainly male, and they formed families with local women. Aside from these movements, however, populations of the Zambezi Valley and the Mozambique coast were left with little migration.

The Bight of Biafra, including the eastern coast of modern Nigeria and the coast of Cameroon, was a region known to European voyagers, but rarely visited. The volcanic Mt Cameroon, over 4,000 metres at its peak, provided a well known and sometimes snowcapped landmark. Yet in the sixteenth and seventeenth centuries, there was little migration on this area of the continent, and even less overseas migration.[15] As a result, families remained multigenerational and linked to a given territory, and tended to be large on both male and female sides. In them, senior generations were able to control land, other resources and access of their offspring to marriage. Young people married with parental approval and married others from the same locality. They accepted and carried on the rules of their patrilineage and household. Mixing in this case consisted of normal biological mixing and perhaps also the local familial mixing of noble and commoner lineages or the occasional absorption of small families. Later on, as the slave trade peaked in the eighteenth century, the degree of migration became so high that the neighbouring Ijo peoples of the Niger Delta developed artificial lineages

---

[14] Allen Isaacman, *Mozambique: The Africanization of a European Institution. The Zambesi Prazos, 1750–1902* (Madison, WI: University of Wisconsin Press, 1972).

[15] Ralph A. Austen and Jonathan Derrick, *Middlemen of the Cameroons Rivers: The Duala and their Hinterland, c. 1600–c. 1960* (Cambridge: Cambridge University Press, 1999); Olfert Dapper, *Description de l'Afrique* (Amsterdam, 1686).

known as 'canoe houses', in which slave and free became combined into fictive kinship networks.[16]

Zones of Moderate Out-migration: Ethiopia and Bight of Benin

As early as the twelfth century, periodic warfare in the Horn of Africa, notably between Christians and Muslims, led to enslavement of captives and their dispatch to Arabia, Persia and India. This phenomenon expanded sharply in the sixteenth century with the rise of the sultanate of Ahmed Ibrahim al-Ghazi, who nearly destroyed the Ethiopian kingdom. A substantial stream of mostly male captives became long-distance migrants to the Deccan where, known as Habshis, they became the core of a slave army.[17] The result for Ethiopian regions was a relative shortage of young men. Young women in Ethiopia, whether of free or slave status, were as a result more likely to be drawn into polygynous relationships.

Later in the seventeenth century, warfare and slave trade erupted along the Bight of Benin (West Africa's Atlantic coast to the west of the Niger River). This became the largest slave-exporting region of Africa from the 1670s through the 1720s.[18] Since most out-migrants were male, the regional population became predominantly female in the young-adult years. The sexual imbalance enabled those men who remained to take additional wives or concubines. Enslaved women were thus required to enter into non-marital, residential, polygynous relationships: these families were small on the female side and large on the male side. Formal marriage remained under the control of established families. Large families were able to build their size by incorporating additional females, but the average regional family size declined because of the families that were broken up by enslavement. The familial mixes brought by slave exports included the circulation

---

[16] E. J. Alagoa, *Small Brave City-State: A History of Nembe-Brass in the Niger Delta* (Madison, WI: University of Wisconsin Press, 1964); G. I. Jones, *The Trading States of the Oil Rivers: A Study of Political Development in Eastern Nigeria* (Oxford: Oxford University Press, 1963).

[17] Richard M. Eaton, 'The Rise and Fall of Military Slavery in the Deccan, 1450–1650', in *Slavery and South Asian History*, eds Indrani Chatterjee and Richard M. Eaton (Bloomington, IN: Indiana University Press, 2006), pp. 115–135. Habshi generals were able to marry women from elite Deccan families; infantrymen formed relationships when possible with women of the Deccan or the small number of Habshi women who made the passage, or went with or without family ties.

[18] Willem Bosman, *A New and Accurate Description of the Coast of Guinea*, 4th ed. (New York, NY: Barnes and Noble, 1967); Robin Law, *The Slave Coast of West Africa 1550–1750* (Oxford: Oxford University Press, 1991); Patrick Manning, *Slavery Colonialism and Economic Growth in Dahomey, 1640–1960* (Cambridge: Cambridge University Press, 1982).

of enslaved women among ethnic groups and the rise of reproductive relations between free or noble men and slave women. One result was that the traditional pattern of marriage tended to be undermined by the increasing proportion of enslaved women.

An important contrast of these two cases was that the export of slaves from Ethiopia reached a peak in the mid-sixteenth century and then declined, while the export of slaves from the Bight of Benin continued at a substantial level until the mid-nineteenth century.

Zones of High In-migration: Mauritius and Barbados

The Mascarene Islands, unpopulated when the Dutch began relying on them as refreshment stops, provide an extreme case. Dutch officials and African slaves settled beginning in 1638: the numbers of migrants were small in absolute terms, but the proportion of in-migrants in the population remained very high. Young adult populations, very short on females, formed families, but the import of new captives kept the population pyramid biased heavily towards adult males for several decades.[19]

When English adventurers seized Barbados in 1627, the Amerindian population had already declined to a low level. In an initial wave of migrants, free and imprisoned English and Irish settlers came to the island. In a second wave of migrants, African slaves arrived from the 1650s.[20] Both waves created a range of family structures in which young people created their own families. Free people were able to choose their residence, while those in slavery were assigned their residence. Formally married couples had small families, but most relationships were non-marital. Because of the surplus of males, many males were unable to form families. Privileged males, in contrast, could form polygynous relationships: most of the privileged males were slave owners who had formal relationships with white women and informal relationships with women of African descent; in addition, a few black men formed polygynous relationships. Socially defined families included a large proportion of female heads of household.

---

[19] Markus Vink, "'The World's Oldest Trade": Dutch Slavery and Slave Trade in the Indian Ocean in the Seventeenth Century', *Journal of World History* 14 (2003): 131–77.

[20] Richard Dunn, *Sugar and Slaves: The Rise of a Planter Class in the English West Indies, 1624–1713* (Chapel Hill, NC: University of North Carolina Press, 1972); Peter H. Wood, *Black Majority* (New York, NY: Knopf, 1974).

New terms and categories of social differentiation (by birthplace, colour, status, etc.) developed especially in areas of high in-migration, where differences from the home societies were greatest. Families were small on the female side and on the male side. Males were in surplus; many were unable to marry, form households or have children; others chose to seek far for partners. Multigenerational families could rise to significance only after two generations (over half a century) from initial settlement, and then only if the rate of immigration declined; only then could multigenerational families become strong enough to control the marriage of young people.

Zones of Moderate Out-migration and In-migration: Gujarat and Netherlands

Gujarat in the sixteenth century was one of the busiest shipping zones of the Indian Ocean. Muslim merchants from Cambay and nearby ports dispatched large dhows especially to Aden and to Malacca. Many of the sailors also acted as traders in the distant ports, and many settled in distant entrepôts. The sultans of Gujarat invited merchants from other ports to settle and set up business, thus offsetting some of the outflow of men. In the 1530s, the Portuguese navy established hegemony over the region, and Portuguese settlers joined the others. As a result, Gujarat remained a region of net out-migration, especially of males, but this out-migration was partially offset by long-distance in-migration of high-status merchants by sea and presumably intermediate-distance in-migration of low-status workers from inland areas.[21]

The Netherlands, long a region with active migration, became even more involved in migration during the seventeenth century.[22] Men left the Netherlands as soldiers, sailors, merchants and settlers; women left in smaller numbers to settle in colonies of the Atlantic and the Indian Ocean. Since most out-migrants were male, the regional population became predominantly female in the young adult years. Males in-migrated, especially from neighbouring German states—some in

---

[21] M. N. Pearson, *Merchants and Rulers in Gujarat: The Response to the Portuguese in the Sixteenth Century* (Berkeley, CA: University of California Press, 1976); Satish C. Misra, *Muslim Communities in Gujarat: Preliminary Studies in their History and Social Organization* (New York, NY: Asia Publishing House, 1964).

[22] Jan De Vries, *The Dutch Rural Economy in the Golden Age* (New Haven, CT: Yale University Press, 1974).

response to opportunities left by departing males and others to join Dutch males as out-migrants. The surplus females either did not form families, or married immigrant men, thus departing from the system of families dominated by their fathers. (Few in this society took the option of non-marital relationships.) Most marriages remained under the control of established families and inheritance followed the male line. The familial mixes of Dutch society centred on mixes of ethnic groups, but also across status lines. Families of the immigrant males were small compared with the families of their locally born wives, though such couples were most likely on their own.

GLOBAL PATTERNS OF FAMILY AND MIGRATION

Comparing the two great regions in the seventeenth century, one observes readily that the Atlantic underwent greater impact of colonization and settlement than the Indian Ocean. The demographic collapse of the Americas in the sixteenth century gave more demographic and social influence to surviving migrants. Zones of moderate in-migration, such as South India and Brazil, stand out in early modern history as centres of prosperous exchange; productive regions in which both local populations and immigrants could take part in the productivity. Zones of little migration, such as Mozambique and the Bight of Biafra, appear to have been independent and self- sufficient societies, though they were not isolated. Certain zones of moderate out-migration, such as Ethiopia and the Bight of Benin, were undergoing hardship and accompanying conflict. Zones of high in-migration were limited to islands and to mainland areas (almost all in the Americas) that had been vacated by declining or displaced populations. Zones of moderate out-migration accompanied by in-migration, such as Gujarat and the Netherlands, tended to be prosperous regions that were benefiting from trade with other regions. Similarly, Portugal and Spain were regions of moderate out-migration in the same era, in response to promises (real or illusory) of advance for the migrants.

In the overall regional pattern of migration, the total number of migrants in the Indian Ocean zone during the seventeenth and eighteenth centuries very likely exceeded the equivalent number for the Atlantic, both for long-distance and intermediate-distance migrants. A net flow of migrants left the Atlantic and entered the Indian Ocean basin. Further, migration from Europe into the Indian Ocean equalled or exceeded European migration to Atlantic destinations. In particular, more Portuguese migrants went to Asia than to the combination of the Americas and Africa, but they were a smaller portion of regional population in the Indian Ocean than in the Atlantic.[23] Long-distance Indian Ocean migration (yet to be quantified) may have equalled European in-migration. Intermediate-distance migration may have been greater in the Indian Ocean than long-distance migration. For the Americas, long-distance migration from Europe and Africa was proportionately large, but so was intermediate-distance migration of Amerindian populations, and the shifts in local European and African populations accompanying out-migration.

In the overall temporal pattern of migration, the experience of the two ocean basins diverged in a different fashion. For the Atlantic, the sixteenth and seventeenth centuries established unprecedented migratory movements.[24] For the Indian Ocean, migrations of the sixteenth and seventeenth centuries modified earlier patterns, but there were precedents for virtually every sort of early-modern migration. One can easily extend these observations to a longer time frame. Before the sixteenth century, Atlantic migrations were tiny in comparison to those of the Indian Ocean. For most of the sixteenth and seventeenth centuries, migrations in Atlantic and Indian Ocean basins were of comparable size. By the end of the seventeenth century, however, long-distance migration from Africa to the Americas exceeded all other long-distance movements. In the eighteenth century, Atlantic migrations expanded and exceeded Indian Ocean migrations; then in the nineteenth and twentieth centuries, migrations in both basins grew greatly, and those of the Indian Ocean virtually caught up to those of the Atlantic. Family structures in all the regions of each basin changed in response to the changing patterns of migration.

Based on this comparison of two great world regions, one may venture some worldwide assertions about the impact of migration on family. First, the global patterns of out-migration and in-migration created a mosaic of regions, each characterized by resultant patterns of family life. These patterns did not then become inherent for each locality,

---

[23] Nicholas Canny, ed., *Europeans on the Move: Studies on European Migration, 1500–1800* (Oxford: Clarendon Press, 1994).

[24] Language distributions of the Americas, however, demonstrate that intermediate-distance migrations had been a regular characteristic of pre-Columbian Amerindian societies.

but continued to change along with changing patterns of migration. Second, families became smaller. That is, to the degree that migration in general increased during the sixteenth and seventeenth centuries, one consequence of expanded migration was that it made families smaller in regions of both out-migration and in-migration, to the degree that migrants left their original families.[25] Third, migration decentralized families. It reduced the ability of senior family members to control creation of new family units and increased the ability of young people to decide on starting their own families—especially in regions of heavy in-migration, and elsewhere to a lesser degree. (By the same token, migration reduced the ability of young people to call on relatives for support.) Development of these new systems arguably laid groundwork for the marital and non-marital forms of families in more recent times, in which young people have increasingly migrated away from parental homes and have started families by their own choice.

Fourth, increased migration expanded the mix of families, especially in regions of in-migration. Practices of marriage and affiliation changed, either when prestigious immigrants married into leading local families or when immigrant men took slave women as concubines in plantation colonies. Migration probably increased the proportion of non-marital relationships.[26] Even in regions of out-migration, the patterns of affiliation changed, as the shortage of young-adult men led to new arrangements for unmarried women. High levels of migration brought increased attention to birthplace. In American colonies of high settlement, for instance, people came to be categorized by birthplace and generation. The distinction of *criollo* (American-born) and *peninsulare* (Spanish-born) among whites in Spanish America is well known; blacks, in turn, were known in some parts of Spanish America as *criollo* (American-born) or *bozal* (African-born). Categorization by race or colour overlaid the categorization by birthplace and generation.

---

[25] Further, it made families smaller in biological, residential and social terms.

[26] One can get a sense of the range of marriage practices by asking any pair of biological parents whether they are formally married, whether the relationship is monogamous or polygamous (that is, if either party is in another relationship), whether the parents reside together, and whether the children are recognized by both parents. Of the 16 logically possible combinations of these four factors, roughly half were actually utilized with some frequency in the seventeenth-century world as described here. For instance, there were few marriages which were formalized, monogamous and co-resident in which the parents denied recognition to their children. But there were informal, polygynous, non-coresident relationships in which the male parent denied recognition to his children.

Figure 1

Migrating men change the ethnicity of a zone of settlement

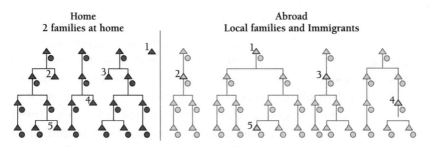

Note: Numbers indicate men who migrated abroad.

To use the categorization of eighteenth-century French Louisiana, three ancestral communities were identified as 'blanc' (white), 'noir' (black), and 'sauvage' (Amerindian). Initial mixes among these were known as 'mulatto' (white and black), 'métis' (white and Amerindian) and 'grif' (black and Amerindian). With the passage of time, more complex mixtures were observed and a more complex terminology developed. Legal status distinguished those who were free and slave, those who were indentured or ex-slaves and occupational labels.[27] In addition, colonial regions commonly had different legal or court systems for people distinguished by nationality, religion or birthplace.

Fifth, migration occasionally led beyond influencing the character of families to transform ethnic identities through intermarriage. Figure 1 provides an heuristic example of the changes in identity that can be brought by a campaign of migration. The home population (shown in black) reproduces itself over time, with occasional migration of males—those numbered both at home and abroad where they settle. As prestigious emigrants, these men form families with local women (shown in white). In a patriarchal system, they pass their immigrant identity on to their children, especially the males (shown in gray). Regardless of whether the women are of local or 'mixed' ancestry, the combination of 'mixed' second- and third-generation male immigrants with the continuing stream of new male immigrants means that, as of the fourth generation, this population has gained, overwhelmingly, an

---

[27] Janet Ewald, 'Crossers of the Sea: Slaves, Freedman, and Other Migrants in the Northwestern Indian Ocean, c. 1750–1 914', *American Historical Review* 105 (2000) : 69–90.

immigrant identity—even though in biological terms, the great majority of its ancestry is local rather than immigrant. Such a story might well apply to parts of Brazil.

Sixth, migration and familial mixing brought new criteria for hierarchy and new devices for social order. In societies with little migration, generational seniority in large families—supplemented by status ranking—provided the support for hierarchy and mobilization. People knew their place in society through their lineage. In contrast, for societies with more migration and more variegated family ties, families among people recently displaced became too weak and fragmented to provide for much social order. In these complex and mixed migratory societies, other distinctions came to function as the markers of hierarchy and mobilization: ethnicity, birthplace, legal status and racial or colour categorization. In sum, the full range of identifiers for a child included his or her biological parentage (when acknowledged), birthplace (and that of parents), racial or colour designation (and that of parents), status (noble, free, slave or alien, along with the status of parents) and relationship (including residence) of parents. All of these social distinctions arose in large measure from migration and became current wherever migration was significant. The model suggests that certain social patterns recurred widely: for instance, a male spouse on the small side of a family was likely to be of high status, while a female spouse on the small side of a family was likely to be of low status. The latter instance is of particular interest: the expansion of migration and the resulting familial mixes in the seventeenth century suggests that a growth in extra-marital relationships may have brought new sorts of oppression and inequality to family life.

To recapitulate, this exploratory study makes the case for a world-historical approach to family, to supplement the advances in family history at more localized levels.[28] It argues that early modern family tructures were not simply an accumulation of ethnic traditions, but were restructured through of the demographic, economic and social conditions of what A. J. R. Russell-Wood has called a 'world on the

---

[28] If these basic considerations on the interplay of migration and family structure can be confirmed, further analysis could address in more detail the various types of migration and family structure. In later times, the degree of migration and familial interaction increased, and the amount of documentation increases substantially, but the magnitude and the complexity of the processes makes the analysis more difficult. Patrick Manning, *Navigating World History: Historians Create a Global Past* (New York: Palgrave Macmillan, 2003), pp. 315–16.

move'.[29] These changes were proportionately greater in the Atlantic than in the Indian Ocean, but the varying types of changes were to be found in every region. The mosaic of family structures brought by migration brought with it a web of familial frontiers, marking the differences in the rules and the reality of family across each social boundary. Approaching family history with this framework has yielded hypotheses on changes in family size and structure in response to migration. Further exploration of these cases might suggest feedback effects, in which changing family structures may in turn have expanded or limited the rates of migration. In addition to identifying these interactions among regions, this approach also permits summing up the regional results, yielding global hypotheses that families worldwide became smaller in response to expanded migration and that the heads of large families became relatively less dominant. Further, while this study has focused on simple measures of family size and structure, the context of the discussion provides reminders that families are institutions not only for social reproduction, but also for the exercise of power, for the family as a whole or individuals within it.[30]

---

[29] A. J. R. Russell-Wood, *World on the Move: The Portuguese in Africa, Asia, and America, 1415–1808* (New York: St. Martin's Press, 1993).

[30] Monica Chojnacka, 'Power, Family, and Household in Early Modern Italy', *Journal of Family History* 22 (1997), pp.491–95.

13

Chinese Revenue Farms
and Borders in Southeast Asia

CARL A. TROCKI

———— • ✦ • ————

INTRODUCTION

This essay examines the role of Chinese revenue farmers in defining the
borders of the various colonial territories and the states of Southeast
Asia during the nineteenth century. The role of these individuals has
largely been neglected in the current writing on the formation of state
boundaries. Nicholas Tarling, in his *Southeast Asia: A Modern History*,
notes, 'Between the late eighteenth and the early twentieth almost all
southeast Asia was divided into colonies or protectorates held by the
Western powers, and new boundaries were drawn with the object of
avoiding conflict among them'.[1] His view is typical of most who have
studied the period.

While his comment acknowledges the role of the Western powers in
surveying the boundaries, drafting treaties and map making, it really
says nothing about how those divisions were actually policed and
made real on the ground. This aspect of 'border making' was left to the
independent Chinese monopolists who worked on behalf of the colonial
regimes. This essay examines their role during the middle years of the
nineteenth century and attempts to give an account of their significance

---

[1] Nicholas Tarling, *Southeast Asia: A Modern History* (Oxford and New York: Oxford University
Press, 2001), p. 44.

in the organization of colonial governance and in giving substance to the formalistic pronouncements of remote diplomats and statesmen.

BORDERS AND POPULATIONS

Southeast Asia presents a unique case historically because despite the fact that the major states have long-standing historical traditions, until the nineteenth century, most lacked clearly defined borders. It can be considered to have been a region without borders or clearly defined frontiers between major political units.

This situation seems to have been the result of a number of environmental factors. On the one hand, the region is almost uniformly tropical and thus was originally covered by dense tropical rainforest. This forest, to a great extent, remained uncut and uncleared until the second half of the twentieth century. Likewise, the coasts and great river valleys of the region were covered by large tracts of swampy lowlands, which required considerable inputs of manpower before being available for cultivation. Coastlines in many areas were marked by vast expanses of mangrove swamp, and even inland, by swamp forest.

These conditions and the warm, moist temperatures of the equatorial and subequatorial areas militated against the settlement and growth of large concentrations of human beings. Even where it may have been possible to bring large numbers of people together at any one time, continued residence in one spot would ultimately create considerable sanitation problems which would lead to the proliferation of parasites and the outbreak of epidemics. As a result, population densities throughout the region tended to be historically low.

Historically, throughout most of Southeast Asia, land by itself has not been a scarce resource. The most valuable productive resource before the nineteenth century was manpower. Manpower was necessary to man armies, to build monuments and to produce exportable commodities and especially to produce more food to produce more manpower. The natural accumulation of manpower, however, was a long, slow and irregular process. Anthony Reid estimates that the population of the region in 1600 was just over 22 million. Vietnam, the largest, had only about 4.7 million, concentrated in the north and the centre. Java (4 M), Burma (3.1 M), Sumatra, (2.4 M) and Siam (2.2) followed. None of these represented a single political unit. By 1800, the entire region had increased by a little under 50 per cent,[2] but compared with Europe, China, India and even the Middle East, this was still an area marked by 'demographic immaturity'. Reid comments:

> Its overall density of population of about 5.5 persons per square kilometer contrasted with densities for South Asia of about 32 and for China (excluding Tibet) of about 37 (after McEvedy and Jones 1978). Further away Europe had roughly double the Southeast Asian population density.

Reid argues that the main reasons for the extraordinarily low populations were warfare and religion.[3]

Even though there were areas of extremely fertile soils, such as the volcanic islands of Java and Bali, and many fertile alluvial areas, land clearance and intensive agriculture required inputs of labour and this key factor of production was always in short supply. As a result, where powerful political units did develop, they often did so by the means of 'capturing' a population and subjugating it to labour in the service of the king.

One area where populations tended to grow was near the seacoasts where smaller river valleys and coastal lowlands, such as those along the coasts of the Malay Peninsula and the Gulf of Siam existed. These were more manageable than the larger river deltas such as those of the Irrawaddy/Salween, the Chao Phraya and the Mekong. With such areas under rice cultivation, and the nearby sea and rivers as sources of protein, pockets of population could flourish. It was necessary, however, to be able to defend themselves from enemies that might arrive by the sea.

It is well known that Southeast Asian waters were periodically dominated by 'pirates' from the earliest recorded times. The phenomenon of piracy in this area needs to be understood in relation to the demographic situation. One of the main targets of sea-borne raiders was the people themselves. James Warren's discussion of the activities of the Illanun raiders during the late eighteenth and early nineteenth centuries in the Philippines and around the coasts of Borneo and the Malay Peninsula shows the political and economic utility of such activity. Captives could be sold, and they could also be brought back to the home base and

---

[2]   A. Reid, *Southeast Asia in the Age of Commerce 1450–1680: The Lands below the Winds* (New Haven and London: Yale University Press, 1988), p. 15.

[3]   *Ibid.*, p. 16.

employed in the business of producing export commodities to trade with Chinese and other foreign traders who visited the Sulu Sultanate.[4]

It is probable that the first major Indianized state of the region, Funan, located near the mouths of the Mekong River managed to establish itself by means of such raids on nearby populations. Likewise, the chronicles of Ayutthaya constantly refer to the practice of 'sweeping up' populations by armies moving between the Siamese heartland and the Cambodian population centres around Angkor in the fifteenth and sixteenth centuries. Later, during the nineteenth century, we see the same sort of activity along the eastern shore of the Gulf of Siam between the mouth of the Chao Phraya and the Bassac. Warfare in eastern and central Java in the sixteenth century reduced populations in that area, as did warfare in central Sumatra during the eighteenth and nineteenth centuries.[5] The goal of every political leader or leadership group was to draw population, whether by transport, intimidation or by enticement.

Reid points out that lives were not necessarily lost in warfare, rather he points to the 'instability created by constant low-level warfare'.[6]

> The larger states mobilized a substantial proportion of their male population into vast, ill-organized armies, without providing adequate supplies either for the soldiers or for their families left behind. Thousands of captives were marched back home by the victorious armies of Burma and Siam, or shipped home by Aceh and Makassar, with incalculable losses on the voyage. Perhaps an even more important factor demographically was the need to be constantly ready for flight in troubled times. This probably meant avoiding births at least until the older children were able to run by themselves.[7]

The resulting demographic situation was that not only did overall population densities remain quite low, but that populations were generally concentrated in pockets of intensive wet-rice agriculture or else in maritime trading cities that, according to Reid, were 'surprisingly large in relation to the overall population'.[8] Such groupings provided safety in numbers, since large population concentrations were better able to

---

[4] J. F. Warren, *The Sulu Zone, 1768–1898: The Dynamics of External Trade, Slavery, and Ethnicity in the Transformation of a Southeast Asian Maritime State* (Singapore: Singapore University Press, 1981).

[5] Reid, *Southeast Asia in the Age of Commerce*, p.15.

[6] *Ibid.*, p. 17.

[7] *Ibid.*, p. 17.

[8] *Ibid.*, p. 18.

defend themselves. As such, these groupings also served the ends of the rulers as well, since it placed their key resource within easy reach.

I argue here that one of the results of this demographic situation has been a particular style of political and geographical imagination that was characteristic of ruling groups in the region. Benedict Anderson's pioneering article on the idea of power in Java speaks to the demographic and historical reality of most of Southeast Asia.[9] Anderson argued that power was seen as something to be concentrated and accumulated around the person of the ruler. This is the way in which Southeast Asian rulers handled their subject populations. They brought them close to the capital and worked to prevent the growth of the outlying accumulations, which might challenge their own centrality.

MANDALAS AND MAPS

This principle applied even to provincial towns, which were regularly cut down to size, often as staging areas for wars, or as outlying buffers that could be sacrificed to defend the capital. In fact, provincial towns, far from the centre could just as easily either fall into enemy hands, or, even worse, change sides and join forces with an enemy. The Burmese invasions of Siam in the 1760 were certainly facilitated by the defection of these outlying centres such as Chiang Mai. This led to a policy of centralization, which is explained in Pornpun Futrakul's thesis on Siamese provincial towns before the twentieth century.[10]

As a result, borders or frontiers between countries, such as those between Siam and Burma, or Siam and Cambodia, were generally nothing more than extensive tracts of wasteland or forest. They were largely uninhabited except for the few hunter-gatherers who dwelt in the deep interior well away from marauding armies and slave catchers. In the Malay world, the key geographic limit of a 'country' a *negri* was normally a river valley. To be technical, the border was the watershed, but in practice the border was an extensive area of *ulu*, or simply the 'up-river' area, which was empty of people.

The centripetal state structure that emerged from these conditions is expressed in the 'mandala' theory of interstate relations, a concept

---

[9] B. Anderson, 'The Idea of Power in Javanese Culture', in *Language and Power: Exploring Political Cultures in Indonesia* (Ithaca and London: Cornell University Press, 1990), pp. 17–77.

[10] P. Futrakul, *The Environmental History of Pre-modern Provincial Towns in Siam to 1910* (Ithaca, NY: Cornell University, 1989), pp. xv, 424.

elaborated both by Anderson and by O. W. Wolters.[11] Anderson points out that the mandala presupposes that one's immediate neighbour is one's enemy, because power is not distributed equally in the kingdom, but is concentrated at the centre and is weakest at the edges, on the border. This is just where, as Anderson says, a ruler's...

. . . sphere of Power merges into the perimeter of his neighbour's. Thus, if his control is not to be diminished and weakened by the pull of his neighbour's Power, he must first exert his own Power against the neighbour. We may recall how the idea that the total quantity of Power in the universe is constant implies that any increase of Power in one place means an equivalent diminution elsewhere. Since Power is also fluid and unstable, always ready for dispersal and diffusion, interstate aggression necessarily becomes a basic assumption about interstate relations.[12]

A border, as we understand it today, was never a site of negotiation or regulation between congenial neighbours, rather it was either a site of conflict or else, a wasteland.

Along with this political principle, Wolters also argues that a ruler's mandala was not necessarily territorial. Rather, the mandala could easily be somewhat interrupted. Political power did not need to be contiguous over a piece of territory. What mattered were networks of relationships and bonds of loyalty. This was particularly true of island Southeast Asia where the port-polities of the Malay world could maintain far-flung alliances with other quite distant political units.[13] This model applied to states as diverse as eighth-century Srivijaya, fifteenth-century Melaka, seventeenth-century Banten and nineteenth-century Sulu. Even seventeenth- and eighteenth-century Ayutthaya seems to fit their model.

If we look at Stanley Tambiah's mapping of pre-modern Siam's 'galactic polity' as it may have existed in the seventeenth century, we get an idea of the manner in which Southeast Asian kingdoms were organized[14] (Figure 1). The state was really composed of the capital area and its immediate dependencies, smaller principalities and towns that were under the direct

---

[11] O. W. Wolters, *History, Culture and Region in Southeast Asian Perspectives*, Southeast Asia Program Publications, Cornell University in cooperation with the Institute for Southeast Asian Studies, Ithaca, NY and Singapore, 1999.

[12] Anderson, *Language and Power*, p. 44.

[13] J. Kathirithamby-Wells and J. Villiers eds, *The Southeast Asian Port and Polity: Rise and Demise* (Singapore: Singapore University Press, 1990).

[14] S. J. Tambiah, *World Conqueror and World Renouncer: A Study of Buddhism and Polity in Thailand Against a Historical Background* (Cambridge: Cambridge University Press, 1976), pp. 134–37.

Figure 1
Tambiah's galactic polity of Ayutthaya c. 1700

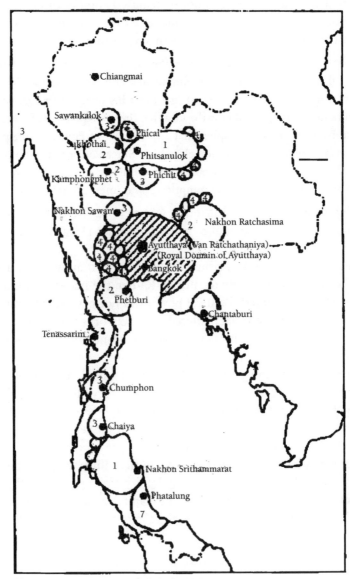

Note: ▬ ▪ ▬ ▪ Present borders of Thailand (1975).
▨▨▨ Van Rachathani: royal domain of Ayutthaya
1. First class provinces
2. Second class provinces
3. Third class provinces
4. Fourth class provinces

control of either the royal family or powerful groups within the court. Beyond them, both in distance and levels of central control were the first-, second- and third-class provinces. The first- and second-class provinces were principalities that were nearly autonomous tributary kingdoms in their own right, some of which had their own dependencies, such as Phitsanulok, Nakorn Rachasima (Khorat) or Nakorn Srithammarat (Ligor). Beyond these were even more autonomous political units such as Cambodia, the Malay states of Patani, Kedah, Kelantan, etc. and Chiang Mai. These latter ones were only occasionally under the control of Ayutthaya and merely sent the gold and silver flowers as tokens of their subsidiary status. In times of war, they might be called upon to provide troops, but they could just as easily be won over by alien powers in the next circle such as Vietnam, Burma and Aceh or Johor.

Although based on a reading of Siamese chronicles discussed in terms of Siamese ideas of statecraft, Tambiah's maps are his own creation and represent a construct that is informed by the late twentieth century concepts of geographical space. Thongchai Winichakul, on the other hand, has tried to explain what he sees as the contemporary Siamese concepts of space. His study, *Siam Mapped* looks at a number of early 'maps' of the kingdom.[15] The earliest ones appear to be more concerned with a cosmic vision (that is, the Traiphum, or the Buddhist cosmology) rather than any kind of realistic representation of a portion of the earth's surface. One of the early maps does, however, seem to offer some degree of representation, that is what he calls the Coastal map[16] which dates from the time of Taksin (1767–82), but it appears to come from an earlier period since it is an Ayutthaya-centred map and does not show Bangkok or Thonburi. This is Thongchai's description:

> There is another fascinating map in the Thonburi version of the Traiphum pictorial manuscript: a coastal map from Korea to Arabia which was incorporated into the description of the human world in the Traiphum scheme... In this map, all the coasts are lined up along the bottom part of the map and all the seas are in the upper part. It begins with Korea and Japan situated in the sea, followed by the Chinese coast opposite Taiwan rightward to Canton. The Vietnamese coast appears like a peninsula jutting into the sea with the mouth of the Mekong River at its peak and

---

[15] T. Winichakul, *Siam Mapped: A History of the Geo-Body of a Nation* (Honolulu: University of Hawaii Press, 1994).

[16] *Ibid.*, Figure 4.

the coast along the Gulf of Siam in a trough (panel 2). At the bottom of panel (3), Ayudhya appears as the biggest city in the gulf.[17]

Figure 2
Coastal map from Vietnam to the Malay Peninsula

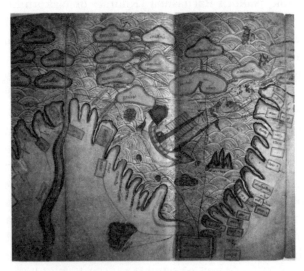

Source: E. Klemp, A. Wightman, and A. Wightman, *Asien auf Karten von der Antike bis zur Mitte des 19 Jahrhunderts = Asia in Maps from Ancient Times to the mid–19th century, herausgegeben underl autert von EgonKlemp; [translated from the German by Alison and Alistair Wightman],* (VCH (Acta Humaniora), Weinheim, Germany, 1989), Map 42.

It is of interest too, that the map, even though a Siamese map, does not really show Siam as a kingdom or as any kind of a unitary entity, rather it simply shows Ayutthaya as a bigger and slightly more elaborate square than all of the other polities shown there. Also, while the various polities around the Gulf of Siam appear to be in the more-or-less correct location, in terms of their north-south orientation along the shore, there is no scale of distance (although the distances between towns are given in notations) nor is there any attempt to represent landforms as anything other than blobs. The Gulf is a large 'trough' with Ayutthaya at its base. The Malay Peninsula, to the west of Ayutthaya is simply a wide wedge of land similar to the Indochinese Peninsula to the east. The various principalities along the coast are represented by rectangles with

[17] *Ibid.,* p. 29.

the name written inside. Schematic indentations along the coastline show river mouths (Figure 2).

In other words, Southeast Asian kingdoms, or states, or polities, or whatever we want to call them, were not seen to exist, either substantively or figuratively as contiguous blocks of territory surrounded by sharply defined borders. Rather they were towns surrounded by undefined territory. Borders, or frontiers, were broad zones of emptiness, and to some extent were systematically kept that way.

What counted were the towns and areas where population was concentrated. On the maps, all we really see are the towns.

In a very real sense, this sort of geographical thinking was quite appropriate. The blank spaces in between the kingdoms were, to the contemporary peoples, simply spaces of undifferentiated forest and wasteland, inhabited only by forest savages or wild beasts. There would be no real reason to change their thinking about frontiers until such time as there were people to fill them up. There would, of course, be even more pressing reasons to demarcate clear borders when Europeans began to seize territories in the region and draw the borders themselves. This is perhaps the most well-recognized reason for the institution of borders in the region.

This line of causation is the one adopted by Thongchai. He sees the 'mapping' of Siam as an enterprise that grew out of pressures on the Siamese state by both the British and the French. British activities on the Malay Peninsula and Burma led to the demarcation of a border between Siamese and British territories there. French interest in Cambodia called for a line in the east. As late as the 1880s, Siam still had no border and had not been mapped in such a way as to show the actual shape of the kingdom with a clear line drawn around it. Lines had only been drawn to mark out the borders of Siam with Kedah and Kelantan in the south, and another line between Battambang and Siem Reap cutting through the Great Lake. The north-eastern borders with Cambodia and the borders with Laos and Burma in the east, north and west did not yet exist.

I would like, however, to look beyond these well-documented colonial actions and to dwell on another, perhaps subsidiary factor that supported the border-making process in Southeast Asia. There is no doubt that European expansionism was one of the key factors driving the creation of maps and the demarcation of frontiers in the region. Another aspect of the frontier issue in Southeast Asia that needs attention is the role of the Chinese. I would argue that Chinese were important in a number of ways that have been largely overlooked.

The first role played by Chinese was as pioneers. Their role has generally been ignored in the mainstream discourse of growth and economic development in the region. In my own work over the past few years, I have begun to develop an argument that would shift the focus, at least partially, to the activities of the Chinese. If we go back to the eighteenth century, to a time and place when European activities within Southeast Asia were rather limited, it is clear that a new era of Chinese settlement in the region was already underway. A glance at the map of the region as of about 1780 shows that twenty or so settlements, a number of them exclusively Chinese, had been established in the region since the beginning of the century. This included places like Hatien, Trat, Chantabun, Songkla, Trengganu, Sambas, Pontianak, Riau, Phuket and Bangka. These settlements can be seen as a part of what we have come to call the 'water frontier' (Figure 3).[18]

Southeast Siam, particularly the towns of Bang Plasoi (now Chonburi), Rayong, Chantaburi and Trat—all ranged along the coast of the Gulf of Siam, between the eastern coast of the Bight of Bangkok and the Cambodian border—was a key area of the water frontier. Together with Hatien, founded around the 1680s or 1690s, they seem to have been among the first settlements of Chinese labourers in Southeast Asia. By the mid-eighteenth century, we hear of tin-mining settlements appearing at a number of places in the Malay Peninsula: Chumphon, Nakron Srithammarat and Songkhla in southern Siam; Kelantan and Trengganu in the Malay states on the east coast. On the west coast, there were Chinese tin miners in Perak and Phuket (Junk Ceylon). There were pepper and gambier planters on Bentan Island in the Riau Archipelago, gold miners in Pontianak, Sambas, Mempawa and other sites on the Kapuas river in western Borneo; pepper planters in Brunei; and tin miners in Bangka. All of these were established during the eighteenth century, and all were characteristically commercial establishments. In general, they had little or nothing to do with European trade or colonialism and were purely a part of the expansion of the mainland Chinese economy at the height of the Qing boom during the reign of the Qianlong emperor.

There were earlier Chinese settlements in Southeast Asia, but these were almost exclusively in important European colonial capitals (e.g.,

---

[18] N. Cooke and T. Li eds, *Water Frontier: Commerce and the Chinese in the Lower Mekong Region 1750–1880* (Singapore: Rowan and Littlefield and Singapore University Press, 2004).

Figure 3

Indian Ocean and South China Sea showing major sites of Chinese settlement in the eighteenth century

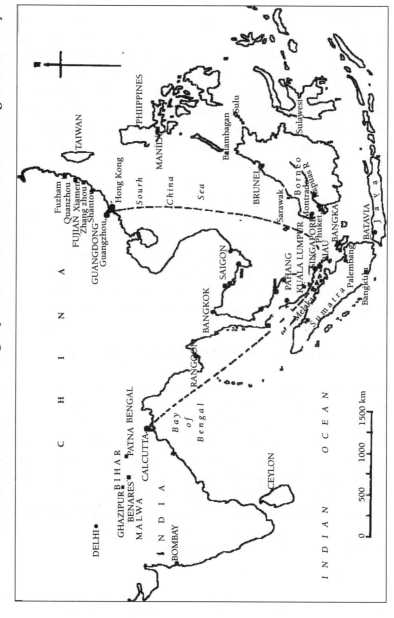

Melaka, Batavia, Manila, etc.) or else in Southeast Asian state capitals such as Ayutthaya, Hue, Kedah, Palembang, Tanjong Pinang and other significant port-polities in the region. Except for limited Chinese populations of craftsmen, mariners and some urban labourers, these were primarily merchant settlements. The new development in the eighteenth century was marked by the establishment of colonies of Chinese labourers. These settlements were 'economic' in nature in that they were rooted in commercial production for export. They produced commodities that were saleable in China. The key commodities in question at the outset, in the eighteenth century, were pepper, sugar, gambier, tin and gold.

How did these settlements spur the demarcation of borders? First of all, it is worth noting that the places chosen for settlement were in areas that were not heavily settled. Mineral deposits, in particular, are almost always found in sparsely populated hinterland areas, and in the mountains or foothills. Agricultural settlements, while often close to earlier Southeast Asian settlements, were not always near the largest ones. In many respects, the new Chinese settlers were moving into those blank spaces on the map that had previously been uninhabited. Moreover, these new settlers were now making them economically significant regions, providing taxable commodities produced by taxable subjects.

CHINESE SETTLERS ON THE SIAMESE BORDER

One area that has drawn my interest is the Siam–Cambodian border region along the Gulf of Siam. In the towns of Chantaburi (formerly Chantabun) and Trat (formerly Tung Yai), we can see the process of border formation in action. Before the eighteenth century, Chantabun, the largest and oldest town in the area, was one of those border principalities that typically got overrun and reduced by marauding armies from both the east and the west. The earliest mentions of the town are in the Chronicles of Ayutthaya where it is claimed as one of the dependent kingdoms of Ayutthaya in 1351, during the reign of King Ramathibodi, the first king of Ayutthaya.[19]

---

[19] See R. Cushman, *The Royal Chronicles of Ayutthaya* (Bangkok: The Siam Society, 1996), pp. 10–11. The other dependencies mentioned at the time included Melaka, Chawa (Java), Nakorn Srithammarat, Tenassarim, Martaban, Moulmein, Songkhla, Phitsanulok, Sukhothai, Phichai, Sawankalok, Phicit, Kamphaeng Phet and Nakhorn Sawan.

However, during his reign, the city was sacked by a Cambodian army and depopulated. The population was restored some years later by King Ramasuen (1388–95) who, after defeating Chiang Mai, deported its population to Chantabun and other cities on the Malay Peninsula.[20] The chronicle mentions a second depopulation of Chantabun at the end of the sixteenth century during the reign of King Thammaracha (1569–90). In fact, the Cambodians 'swept up' the population of the entire coastline.

> At that time the King of Lawaek [Cambodia] repeatedly organized troops to scout about, both by land and by boat, and the inhabitants of Chanthaburi, the inhabitants of Rayong, the inhabitants of Chachoengsao and farmers were speedily lost to the Lawaek enemy in great numbers.[21]

These are the only two mentions in the Chronicle of the systematic relocations of population that happened on the Thai–Cambodian border during the Ayutthaya period. No doubt there were more. There are other reports that tell of a major Thai invasion of Cambodia in about 1720. While Chantaburi is not mentioned in the accounts, one might be safe in assuming that the city's male population was targeted for conscription into the military, if nothing else. The invasion was described as a failure, and so it is probable that not many of them came home. British country trader Alexander Hamilton visited Siam and other countries in the region around the beginning of the eighteenth century reported:

> In 1717 the King of Siam made war against Cambodia & sent an army of 50,000 by land and 20,000 by sea and committed care of his Armies to his *Barkalong* [Prah Klang] a *Chinese*, altogether unacquainted with War. The *China* man accepted of the Charge with much Reluctancy, but the King would not be denied. The War proved unsuccessful... .[22]

At the time, Hamilton remarked on the desolation of the Siamese–Cambodian coastline: '...for 50 Leagues and more along the Sea-shore, there are no Sea-ports, the Country being almost a Desert'.[23]

---

[20] *Ibid.*, pp. 12–13.

[21] *Ibid.*, p. 77.

[22] A. Hamilton, *A New Account of the East-Indies Being the Observations and Remarks of Capt. Alexander Hamilton who Resided in those Parts From the Year 1688 to 23 Trading and Treveling by Sea and Land, to most of the Countries and Islands of Commerce and Navigation, between the Cape of Good-Hope and the Island of Japan* (London: A. Bettesworth and C. Hitch, 1739), p. 97.

[23] *Ibid.*, p. 104.

Fifty years later, however, conditions had undergone a major trans-formation. The towns of Chonburi (Bang Plasoi) Rayong, Chantaburi and Trat (Tung Yai) were all thriving settlements, populated by a highly variegated mix of peoples that included Siamese, Chinese, Vietnamese, Malays, Cambodians and other indigenous groups. Where had these people come from and what were they doing there?

It is clear that one important group which had settled there was a community of Chinese pepper planters. Indications are that these were mostly Teochew agriculturalists that probably had some links to the Teochew pirates who were said to roam the coasts of south-eastern Siam. Other reports also suggest that there was a similar settlement of pepper planters further east at Tung Yai.

There was also a community of Cochinchinese Christians who had fled from persecutions in Dang Throng. They were under the leadership of the French missionaries of the *Missions Étrangéres de Paris* (MEP) who had established missions in various parts of Vietnam, Siam and Burma. They do not appear, however, to have been the first Vietnamese to arrive in Chantaburi. There were also many non-Christian Vietnamese in the town.

The presence of Malays, Bugis, Orang Laut, Chams and other Southeast Asian seafarers would have been a common thing in the region for many centuries before. French and Dutch reports from the early eighteenth century indicate that a large proportion of the population of Ayutthaya were Malays. It seems clear that Malay seafarers were active throughout the Gulf of Siam before the nineteenth century. The Natuna and Anambas islands were important rendezvous sites for the Orang Laut of the Johor–Singapore straits and the Bugis.[24]

This portion of the water frontier was anchored by the port of Hatien, also known as Cancao and Puntaimas. Founded by the Chinese seafarer, and perhaps pirate, Mac Cuu in about 1690, the settlement had grown into a flourishing entrepot by the middle of the eighteenth century. Although the town was listed as a tributary by the courts of Vietnam, Cambodia and Siam, it was largely autonomous during the eighteenth

---

[24] See R. Ali Haji ibn Ahmad, *The Precious Gift (Tuhfat al-Nafis)* (Kuala Lumpur: Oxford University Press, 1982).The *Tufhat al-Nafis* begins with the voyage of the five Bugis brothers to Cambodia. While there, Daing Marewa's wife was left at Tambelan where she gave birth to a son who was later named Daing Kemboja in honor of his father's winning a cockfight in Cambodia.

century. It too had a mixed population of Siamese, Cambodians, Chinese, Vietnamese, Malays, etc.[25]

It was sacked by the Siamese in the 1720s, but the port recovered and continued to be important in the newly emerging economy of the Gulf of Siam and the mouth of the Bassac. Records from Macau indicate that Hatien shipped considerable quantities of rice, timber, tin and pepper to China. Since none of these goods were produced in Hatien, one assumes they must have been drawn there through a shipping network that linked it to the Gulf, the Straits of Melaka and even Java. Mantienne notes that it had a prosperous trade and welcomed Chinese junks from Batavia, China, Melaka, Siam and Cochinchina. During the 1760s and 1770s, while Siam, Cambodia and Vietnam were disrupted by civil war and invasion, Hatien was a place of refuge. It was here that the French priests of the MEP moved their base as did the Franciscans who had been active in Vietnam. The missionaries and their flocks were welcomed by Mac Thien Tu who had succeeded his father as the ruler of Hatien.[26]

Although the populations in towns such as Chantabun were mixed, one must assume that it was the Chinese who were largely responsible for the increase. The large numbers of labourers were producing new wealth and thus a spurt in economic activity that created a general wave of prosperity. In fact, Paul Van Dyke, working on the Canton trading system has actually been able to trace the money. He shows a pattern of European company merchants in Canton and Macau (British, Danish, German, etc.) advancing money or participating in joint ventures with the Hong and other Canton merchants. This cash not only helped work the tea trade, but also financed the Chinese merchants' trade to the Nanyang, much of which was in search of commodities that were accessories to the tea trade (e.g., rattan, tin, lead, rice, etc.).[27]

As the Chinese filled up the blank spaces on the map, the regions drew the interest of nearby Southeast Asian rulers and colonial powers. Chantabun, by way of example, with a thriving population of Chinese planters and others became an important site in the 1760s. Particularly, in 1767, after the Burmese had sacked Ayutthaya, the region of southeast

---

[25] F. Mantienne, *Les relations politiques et commerciales entre la France et la péninsule Indochinoise (XVIIIe siècle)* (Paris: Les Indes Savantes, 2003), p. 45.

[26] *Ibid.*, pp. 41–48.

[27] P. A. Van Dyke, *The Canton Trade: Life and Enterprise on the China Coast, 1700–1815* (Hong Kong: Hong Kong University Press, 2005).

Siam along the eastern shore of the Gulf was one of the few areas that had been spared the ravages of war. It was thus to Chantabun that Phrya Taksin retreated. He was a Sino-Thai trader and tax farmer who had helped to defend the capital. He fled to Chantabun in June of 1767 with a force of about 500 men. He left from there six months later with an army of 5,000 men and 100 ships (some of which he built and others he confiscated from Chinese traders/pirates in Trat). With this force, he returned to the Chao Phraya and defeated the Burmese at Bangkok and established his new capital across the river at Thonburi.

The Chinese of Chantabun and Trat were vital resources in restoring the kingdom. Not only did he recruit much of his new army from the region but also, for much of Taksin's reign, the Chinese merchants and mariners whom he had recruited there played key roles in building up his treasury and reconstructing the Siamese state. These were mostly Teochews and Taksin's patronage gave them key positions in the Thai state even after he was deposed.[28] Even though the most prominent Chinese during the Ayutthaya period were Hokkiens, the power of numbers and influence shifted to the Teochews from then on until the present time.

The earlier connection between the southeast coast and Hatien was, from the very beginning, a major issue for Taksin. As it turned out, a major competitor for the kingship of Siam was Mac Tien Tu, the ruler of Hatien. The latter was actually named as the ruler of Chantaburi in one Thai source.[29] This was probably an error, but it indicates the level of power in the region that Hatien had come to exercise by the end of the Ayutthaya period.

There was, however, a greater threat from Hatien. Mac Tien Tu had given refuge to two princes from the Ayutthaya court who, according to Chinese ideas of legitimacy, should have been the legal successors to the Siamese throne. Chen Ching Ho has written at length on the issue and has shown sources that tell us Mac Tien Tu wrote to the Chinese court challenging Taksin's right to succeed. Indeed, it was not until the very end of his reign that Taksin's control of Siam was recognized by the Qing court.

---

[28] N. Aeusrivongse, *Thai Politics in the Reign of King Taksin* (in Thai, *Kanmuang thai samai phrachao krung thonburi*) (Bangkok: Sinlapawatthanatham Publishing, 1986), pp. 135–38.

[29] S. Chaowatratanawong, 'The Role of the Chinese in Thailand from the Lae Ayutthaya Period to the Reign of King Rama III, 1629-1851', *History* (Bangkok: Chulalongkorn University, 1997), p. 111.

In the immediate wake of Taksin's conquest of the Burmese garrison at Bangkok, Mac launched an attack on Siam's southeast coast and took both Chantabun and Trat. The following year, in 1769, Taksin retaliated, retaking Chantabun and Trat and then going on and sacking Hatien. These struggles between Taksin and Mac Tien Tu have been interpreted in a number of ways. Yumio Sakurai has seen it as a struggle between Teochews and Cantonese.[30] Chen Ching Ho has seen it as a struggle between two Chinese warlords[31] and Puangthong Rungsawadisab has called it a struggle for control of the Gulf of Siam and the Trans-Mekong trade.[32] Whatever the case, certainly an underlying factor in the continuing struggle in this area would be the real lack of a recognized border between the Siamese, Vietnamese and Cambodian realms, together with the possibility that Chinese adventurers like Mac Cuu, his son and Taksin could all hope to carve out a kingdom of their own in the region.

It would be more than another century before the border dispute in this region would be decided. Taksin and Mac Tien Tu fought again in the 1770s when Taksin captured Tien Tu and brought him back to Thonburi to die in prison. In the 1780s, the Tayson rebels moved into the region and further reduced the power of Hatien. The town was henceforth a part of the battleground where Gia Long, in his extended struggle, defeated the Tayson brothers in the 1780s and 1790s. In the 1830s, a new war erupted between Rama III and the Vietnamese Minh Mang emperor, which would lead to further devastation in the region. On the other hand, Bangkok strengthened its command of the south-eastern shore of the Gulf throughout the period from 1820 to the 1860s. Crawfurd reports that taxation of Chantaburi's pepper crop had increased significantly in the Bangkok period over what it had been before 1767. The real border, however, would not be finally drawn until

---

[30] Y. Sakurai, 'Eighteenth Century Chinese Pioneers on the Water Frontier of Indo-China', in N. Cooke and L. Tana eds, *Water Frontier. Commerce and the Chinese in the Lower Mekong Region, c. 1750–1880* (Singapore: Rowman & Littlefield Publishers Inc. and Singapore University Press, 2004) pp. 35–52.

[31] C. H. Chen, 'Mac Thien Tu and Phraya Taksin: A Survey on Their Political Stand, Conflicts and Background', in *Seventh International Association of Historians of Asia Conference*, Vol. 2, (Bangkok: Chulalongkorn University Press, 1977) pp. 1534–75.

[32] P. Rungswasdisab, 'Siam and the Contest for Control of the Trans-Mekong Trading Networks from the Late Eighteenth to the Mid-Nineteenth Centries', in N. Cooke and T. Li eds, *Water Frontier: Commerce and the Chinese in the Lower Mehong Region, 1750–1880* (Singapore: Singapore University Press and Rowman and Littlefield Publishers, 2004), pp. 101–18.

the early twentieth century. Chantaburi and Trat were seized by the French in 1893 in their final imperial push in the region to expand the frontiers of Cambodia and Laos at Siamese expense. The territories were not returned to Siam until the treaty of 1907, which forced Siam to give up all of the eastern Cambodian provinces (Siem Reap, Sisiphon, Battambang and the western end of the Tonle Sap) that it had held since the 1840s.[33]

BORDERS AND *KANGCHUS*

Clearly, the borders were finally hammered out as the result of political power plays by both, the French and the Siamese, but it was the presence of Chinese settlers who made this border a contested area in the first place. If we turn our attention to the Malay world, we see similar border-drawing activities inspired by the Chinese presence. During the nineteenth century, the state of Johor came to be populated by Chinese pepper and gambier planters moving there from Singapore. Here it is somewhat difficult to distangle Chinese systems of boundary drawing from those of the Malays.

The first Chinese settlements in the region had been made at Riau in the mid-eighteenth century. While the evidence is not entirely clear, it appears that territories on Bentan Island were parcelled out to Chinese headmen known as *kangchus* (Lord of the port). About the time Raffles signed the treaty with Temenggong Abdul Rahman and took possession of Singapore, Chinese pepper planters were already establishing themselves there. By the 1840s, the cultivation was exhausting the available land in Singapore and began to move across the strait to the Peninsula. I have argued in my earlier work that this was simply the same system of cultivation moving from one place to another.[34]

In Johor each *kangchu* was given a small river valley and allowed to bring in labourers to develop the land within his watershed. He was also charged with managing the revenue farms, that is, the tax concessions. He was given the right to sell or provide smokeable opium (chandu), spirits, gambling, prostitution, betel nut and even theatrical performances.

---

[33] P. Tuck, *The French Wolf and the Siamese Lamb: The French Threat to Siamese Independence, 1858–1907* (Bangkok: White Lotus, 1995).

[34] C. A. Trocki, *Prince of Pirates: The Temenggongs and the Development of Johor and Singapore, 1784–1885* (Singapore: Singapore University Press, 1979).

It seems natural that the Malay rulers would have divided their territories up according to river valleys and watersheds. The river was the established focus of the Malay *negri*, and under the Malay political system, these riverine states were divided by subsidiary tributaries, each one under a *pengulu*, literally, the headman of the *ulu*, or upriver area. The unique thing about the *kangchu* system was that all of the nomenclature was Chinese, rather than Malay. The Chinese headman was a *kangchu*, and his place of residence was the *chukang*, and the place was usually named with the surname of the headman. Thus the *kangchu's* settlement on the Tebrau river in Johor was Tan Chukang, named after Tan Kye Soon, who founded it. The names of the old pepper and gambier settlements on Singapore island are still in use: Lim Chukang, Yio Chukang, Chua Chukang, etc.

This use of Chinese names suggests that the system actually owed more to the Chinese settlers than to the Malay rulers. In Singapore, it seems that the system was entirely of Chinese creation and management, since the Malays were not in possession of the island when the Chinese planters occupied those portions of it. It is difficult to say how much the system may have owed to Malay/Bugis management when it began in Riau. By the time the Chinese reached Johor, (in the 1840s) the system seems to have become fixed and under the Malay ruler was more formally systematized with the issuance of written documents to the kangchus and overall management of the system by Malay bureaucrats.[35]

There are two issues that concern us here. One is that the system of land division and border marking seems to have owed something, if not everything to Chinese initiative. Beyond that, it owed a great deal to Chinese management. The second thing is that in addition to being a division of territory for settlement and exploitation, it was also a division of territory for the taxation regime: the revenue farms. In fact, the question of control of the revenue seems to have been one, if not the key matter of concern in the issuance of the *surat sungai*, or 'river document' which the Sultan issued to the *kangchu*. The fact that the *kangchu* controlled the revenue concession on his river was mentioned in every single *surat sungai* in the collection of these documents in the Johor archives. If we look at the map of the *kangchu* settlements as of

---

[35] *Ibid.*

Figure 4
Johor *Kangchus* as of 1860

the mid 1860s, we get some idea of the areas under settlement and the regions controlled by Chinese tax farmers (Figure 4).[36]

In another example from Johor, a few decades later we find a Malay explication of how land was divided. In this case, after a number of disputes among Chinese tin miners in the territory of Bukit Mor, the Sultan had sent his brother, Ungku Abdul Rahman along with the Dato Bentara Dalam, Ibrahim bin Munshi Abdullah. In his memoir, Ibrahim explained the principle of territorial division according to watersheds.

> What I have described as rivers are not like most rivers, big and deep and flowing into the sea, but are merely creeks or rivulets. Every stream invariably flows to low ground or a swamp (kuala), and always runs between two hills, and rises on a hill. Whenever a stream flows down from a hill, passes between hills and reaches a swamp, it ceases to flow and empties itself there. This point is called its mouth, and outlets of this sort always have hills to the left and right of them. It has been decided that the limits of a river-mouth are where the hills on either side come to an end. It has also been decided where the boundaries of the rivers are, and that each river shall be owned by one towkay. Each river shall extend from the farthest point upstream to the mouth, excluding the hill in which it rises. The width shall be 300 feet from the river-bank to the left and right, and no more. If there is another river or stream nearby, then the boundary must be half-way between the two. The boundaries of a swamp must not go beyond the foot of the hills on either side of it nor must its length exceed 1,800 feet square.[37]

For nineteenth century Malays, hilltops and watersheds were the keys of land division. On the whole, these were not lines on a map, but tended to be rather remote and thinly populated zones, where travel was slow and difficult, and the rule of the raja was rarely exercised with much effect. However, when it was clear that those using the land would be occupying the entire territory, these principles could be refined to actual lines on a map as they were later in Borneo.

SINGAPORE'S OPIUM FARMERS

If we look at the revenue farming systems that operated in Singapore, we see the much larger superstructure of which the Johor chukangs were

---

[36] *Ibid.*

[37] M. Ibrahim, *The Voyages of Mohamed Ibrahim Munshi* (Kuala Lumpur: Oxford University Press, 1975), p. 23.

merely a component. The opium and spirit farms for Singapore island, during the nineteenth century were the largest and most lucrative tax regimes in British Malaya. They were managed by the wealthiest and the most powerful Chinese businessmen in the colony and, in Singapore, regularly constituted between 40 per cent and 60 per cent of the entire revenue. The entire colonial enterprise in Southeast Asia was financed by revenue farms. Every colony, every state farmed out the bulk of its revenues to Chinese tax farmers.

We cannot understand the nature of European colonialism in Southeast Asia without acknowledging the role of opium. In virtually every colony, the revenue collected from the sale of *chandu*, or smokeable opium, was one of the mainstays of the colonial revenue. If Singapore was, perhaps, an extreme case, this was only because of its commitment to free trade and to its lack of taxable exports. Other colonies drew revenues from taxing the export of tin, pepper, rubber, rice, etc. or from head taxes on Chinese or other Asian immigrants. Even in them, however, opium revenues rarely constituted less than 30 per cent of the gross state income.[38]

For the purpose of this study, the important issue is that the tax farms were territorially based. That is, each tax concession was issued after competitive bidding, to a specific individual (usually to his company or syndicate) for a limited period of time (usually three years) over a specific piece of territory. This left to the Chinese businessman who collected the revenue, the task of maintaining the boundary of that territory and of preventing the smuggling of opium, or spirits, or whatever commodity was being controlled across that boundary. Europeans may have drawn and surveyed the borders, but it was the Chinese businessmen who policed them and gave them reality on the ground.

If we look at the Dutch and French settlements in the region, the story is very much the same. It may be that the Chinese who ended up controlling the opium farms of French Indochina controlled some of the same territories before the French arrived. Whether they did or not is immaterial, the fact is that as soon as the French began to define their boundaries, they began to employ Chinese farmers to patrol them and give them substantial meaning.

If we return to the territories of the old Water Frontier during the 1860s, we find that after a disastrous attempt to allow the farms

---

[38] C. A. Trocki, *Opium, Empire and the Global Political Economy: A Study of the Asian Opium Trade, 1750–1950* (New York and London: Routledge, 1999).

of Cochinchina to be managed by Europeans, the French had given the revenue farming contract to a syndicate of Cantonese led by a merchant known as Wangtai (his trade name), but his syndicate only held it for the year of 1864. The following year it was taken over by a group of Singapore Chinese led by one Banhap (also a trade name). He and his partners, the three Tan brothers, (Tan Keng Ho, Tan Keng Hoon and Tan Keng Seng) held the Cochinchinese farms for nearly two decades, from 1865 to 1882.[39] It was these Chinese businessmen and their employees who policed the new boundaries of Cochinchina and divided it from Cambodia on the west and from 'Annam' on the north and east. French sources report that the rivalry between the transplanted Singapore Hokkiens and the Cantonese shifted off and on into the 1870s. Sometimes the Cantonese came into a partnership with Banhap, other times, they were rivals. In 1871, another Cantonese, Watseng, was able to take control of the Cambodian farms. Apparently, both syndicates launched smuggling operations against each other and, to a certain extent, patrolled the newly drawn border between French Cochinchina and the protectorate of Cambodia. A French official in Cambodia wrote warning of the threat of armed clashes between the forces of the two farmers.[40]

The key point of interest here is that the major smugglers were usually other opium farmers, very often the rival competitors for the same farm. The best means of retaliating after being defeated in the bidding for a particular farm was to obtain the concession for a neighbouring farm. Even if the neighbouring territory was not really a very lucrative opportunity as such, it offered the possibility for the losing syndicate to both stay in business and to get revenge on their rivals.

This was a common strategy and it provided the occasion for opium farmers to both define and violate the newly created colonial borders. In Singapore, it was always necessary for opium farmers to go to pains to obtain the similar farms for the Dutch islands of Riau, and those of the Malay state of Johor. In Penang, the farmer had to be sure to obtain the farms for Kedah. In Hong Kong, the strategic offshore territory was Macau. Beyond that, Hong Kong itself was a prime smuggling location

[39] J. Dumarest, 'Les Monopoles de L'Opium et du Sel en Indochine', In *La Faculté deDroit* (Lyon: L'Université de Lyon, 1938), pp. 44–45.

[40] J. Moura, 'Letter from Jean Moura to Governor of Cochinchina', 6 April 1871, Centre des Archives d'Outre-Mer, Phnom Penh, Dossier 10763.

for the China market. Almost every major colonial city had an adjacent 'suburb' of sorts that lay in another jurisdiction and thus lent itself to smuggling. It was in these areas that the Chinese businessmen who managed the revenue farms showed their mettle by both defining and violating the border.

This phenomenon of cut-throat competition between revenue farmers was a paradoxical thing. While it was often seen as a 'problem' by colonial governments, it was actually an integral part of the system. In order to obtain the highest possible price for the farm, the government relied on a process of competitive bidding. But, that always left a loser. Moreover, it left a loser who, if he was a serious competitor, already possessed wealth, power, influence and the necessary infrastructure to run the farms. That infrastructure was expensive to maintain, and so smuggling was not just an opportunity for revenge. It was a necessity for survival.

James Rush has told the story of the revenue farms of Java, and he too has called attention to the propensity of rival farming syndicates to smuggle against one another there.[41] In my earlier work, I have shown that these smuggling contests could be the cause of considerable social unrest. Normally, the various revenue farmers had alliances with one or another secret society, and once they were armed the propensity for serious violence was very high. In Singapore, individuals such as Tan Seng Poh and Cheang Hong Lim had shown they could provoke significant disruptions in their struggles through the 1860s.[42] Similar violence periodically erupted in French Cochinchina, in Penang, southern Siam and in Java.

If these conflicts were seen as a problem for the colonial governments, there was one thing that was worse. That was collaboration. In Singapore, Penang, Cochinchina and even Hong Kong, the syndicates ultimately came to terms with one another. They decided to create joint farms, amalgamate the adjoining territories (despite political boundaries) and split the profits. This led to the situation of the same syndicates policing both sides of the various borders. While this created social peace, it also meant that the farmers could present the government with an offer that

---

[41] J. R. Rush, *Opium to Java: Revenue Farming and Chinese Enterprise in Colonial Indonesia, 1800–1910*, (Ithaca, NY: Cornell University Press, 1990).

[42] C. A. Trocki, *Opium and Empire: Chinese Society in Colonial Singapore 1800–1910* (Ithaca, New York: Cornell University Press, 1990).

it could not easily refuse: an offer that was usually far below the real value of the farms.

The loss of revenues led to further internationalization of the revenue farms. The first steps had already been taken by the farmers in amalgamating adjacent territories under the same farming syndicate. The farming syndicates were thus not just states within states, but states that transcended states. In 1879, the governor of Hong Kong John Pope Hennessey (a man who had formerly served in the Straits), invited the Singapore revenue farmers to bid for the Hong Kong farms. He was dissatisfied with the low bids being offered by the local Cantonese joint farm and decided to force their hand. The result was something far more sweeping than he had expected.

One of the Singapore farmers formed a combine with the above-mentioned Straits-born farmers of French Indochina and took over the Hong Kong farms. In 1879, Banhap joined his Saigon partner, Tan Keng Seng,[43] the Singapore opium farmer, Cheang Hong Lim and a few other Hong Kong Cantonese. Apparently, the aim here was to create a truly global opium monopoly. By this time, small groups of Straits-born Chinese had come to control both the Singapore and Saigon opium farms. It appears that they also dominated the traffic in coolies from Fujian and the Chaochou region of Guangdong to Singapore and much of western Southeast Asia. The two rival opium groups in Hong Kong also controlled the traffic in Cantonese coolies to the United States, Australia and the other parts of the Pacific Rim. Together with the coolie traffic, they also controlled the flow of prepared opium to those settlements. Had Banhap and his partners succeeded in keeping their company and their concessions together, they would have been in a position to dominate the entire world market in opium and Chinese coolies.

Although it seems ironic, the Straits-born Chinese of Singapore had moved beyond the mere business of maintaining colonial borders and were attempting to create networks and alliances that not only spanned those borders, but also violated them. It was an attempt to create an

---

[43] The Hong Kong sources report that Tan Keng Seng was the Singapore opium farmer (C. A. Trocki, 'The Internationalization of Chinese Revenue Farming Network', 2004), but there are no Singapore records to confirm this. At the time, Cheang Hong Lim, Tan Seng Poh and Tan Hiok Nee were listed as the Singapore farmers C. A. Trocki, 'The Collapse of Singapore's Great Syndicate', in J. B. H. Dick eds, *The Rise and Fall of Revenue Farming: Business Elites and the Emergence of the Modern State in Southeast Asia* (New York and London: St. Martin's Press, 1993), pp. 166–81, and Tan Keng Seng was located in Saigon with his two brothers.

empire within an empire. Like many over-ambitious enterprises, the vast Banhap syndicate collapsed almost as soon as it was born. It was attacked from virtually every angle. The ousted Hong Kong company adopted the usual strategy of securing the Macau farm and began to smuggle into the markets that Banhap had hoped to dominate.[44] Moreover, their business to the California and Australian coolies was in prepared opium (chandu) rather than raw opium and opium farming. What commanded the market was brand recognition. In this case, the rival Cantonese syndicate still owned the brand names that were favoured in those markets. They also attacked the combine from the inside by having some members join and then file lawsuits when financial difficulties arose.

Europeans also moved to destroy the business of this combine, although it is probable that they had other aims in mind. Opium shipments and the coolie trade to California and Australia were both discouraged by restrictions on Chinese immigration, newly enacted in those countries—another aspect of border maintenance. In Saigon, the French finally decided to take the farms away from Banhap and create a state-run monopoly, and in Singapore, Cheang Hong Lim's company lost the farms to an outsider from Penang. So, by 1881, the entire venture had collapsed.

It was inevitable, perhaps, that the colonial governments would tire of these games, and from the 1880s onwards, as they gained resources and as attitudes against revenue farming hardened, governments created their own monopolies. In 1882, the French were the first. They took the farms from Banhap and company and created the first *régie*.[45] In the 1890s, after a series of smuggling squabbles and excessive bidding by potential farmers, the Dutch in Java followed the French and created a monopoly.[46] Finally, in 1910, after a spectacular financial debacle in which the Singapore farms collapsed and the farmer went bankrupt, the British too, decided to take the opium business into their own hands.[47]

The creation of government monopolies marked the end of an era in Southeast Asia. Throughout the nineteenth century, opium farms and

---

[44] 'Consul de France, a. Hong Kong to Gouvernor de Cochinchine,' 28 Sept. 1879, *achive Outre-Mer, Gov. Gem. Indo-Chine*, 14.058.

[45] C. Descours-Gatin, *Quand L'Opium Financait La Colonisation en Indochine: L'élaboration de la régie générale de l'opium (1860– 1914)*, Editions L'Hartmann (Ouvrage publié avec le concours du Centre National des Lettres), Paris, 1992.

[46] Rush, *Opium to Java*.

[47] Trocki, *Opium and Empire*.

opium farmers had been the key instruments of border maintenance for the colonial states. With the system of monopolies, the colonial governments not only undertook the business of manufacturing and retailing prepared opium to their populations, they also undertook the police functions of protecting their monopolies, which included the whole business of border maintenance. It is no accident that Eric Tagliacozzo[48] focuses his study of smuggling and smuggling prevention on the period between 1870 and 1910, for these are the years in which we see the internationalization of opium farms and the first moves by colonial powers to take direct control of their borders.

CONCLUSION

This has been a wandering excursion on the ins and outs of Southeast Asian mapping and border making, along with a discussion of Chinese settlement and opium farming. The aim here is to bring together all these disparate threads.

The overall point is that Chinese migration and business development have been an important part of the 'bordering' of Southeast Asia. It might be possible to argue that in the beginning, even though there were states, there were no borders. This was largely because there was an insufficient population. While indigenous Southeast Asian populations were probably beginning to increase by the beginning of the eighteenth century, it is clear that major increases came from Chinese migration. It is also important to note that a significant portion of this Chinese migration was exactly to the border areas that had previously been empty. This process of migration to Southeast Asia continued throughout the nineteenth and into the twentieth century, not slowing until the 1930s.

From the 1830s, Southeast Asia entered a period when the newly established colonial governments came to rely largely on Chinese opium farmers to aid them in the management of their new states. The middle years of the nineteenth century up to the 1880s, is generally recognized as a period of laissez-faire colonial rule in the region. Even in directly ruled territories such as the Straits settlements, Hong Kong and Cochin china, much power and many functions of government were delegated

---

[48] F. Tagliacozzo, *Secret Trades, Porous Borders: Smuggling and States along a Southeast Asian Frontier, 1865–1915*, (Cambridge, Mass: Yale University Press, 2007).

to private actors. To the revenue farmers fell much of the task of border maintenance and tax collection. In fact, it was during these years that most of the borders were actually defined, if not precisely surveyed and mapped.

The years after 1880 saw the progressive rationalization of the colonial states throughout the region. Colonial bureaucracies were professionalized and the functions of government, particularly tax collection, policing and border control were gradually taken fully into the hands of the state. Professional surveyors, on both sides of the notional borders precisely defined the lines. Police forces and coast guards were deployed to man the borders and to regulate the movement of goods and people across the newly established frontiers. By 1910–15, much of this process was complete, and the need for Chinese business people to carry out the functions of the colonial state was no longer as necessary as it had once seemed.

Finally, it is necessary to draw attention to the fact that these new borders have, for the most part, defined the current nation-states of Southeast Asia. Within the 'histories' of these nations, the role of the Chinese and of the revenue farmers is generally ignored. National history should be made by national actors, and the Chinese do not generally qualify for that role.

Publications

JOHN FOLSOM RICHARDS

———— • ✦ • ————

PUBLICATIONS

A. Works in Print Books:

Mughal Administration in Golconda (Oxford: Clarendon Press, 1975).

(Ed.), *Kingship and Authority in South Asia* (Madison: Center for South Asian Studies, University of Wisconsin, 1978. Reprinted, Delhi: Oxford University Press, 1998).

(Ed.), *Precious Metals in the Later Medieval and Early Modern World* (Durham: Carolina Academic Press, 1983).

(Ed.), with Richard Tucker, *Global Deforestation and the Nineteenth Century World Economy* (Durham: Duke Press Policy Studies, 1983).

Document Forms for Official Orders of Appointment in the Mughal Empire: Translation, Notes, and Text (London: E. J. W. Gibb Memorial Series, Gibb Memorial Trust, 1986).

(Ed.), *The Imperial Monetary System of Mughal India* (New Delhi :Oxford University Press, 1987. Reprinted in paperback, 1999).

(Ed.), with Richard Tucker, *World Deforestation in the Twentieth Century* (Durham: Duke University Press, 1988).

(Ed.), with B. L. Turner, W. C. Clark, R. W. Kates, J. T. Mathews and W. B. Meyer, *The Earth As Transformed by Human Action* (Cambridge: Cambridge University Press, 1991).

The Mughal Empire, The New Cambridge History of India, I: 5 (Cambridge: Cambridge University Press, 1993).

Power, Administration and Finance in Mughal India (Ashgate: Variorum Collected Studies Series CS419, London, 1993).

(Ed.), *Land Property and the Environment* (Oakland, CA: Institute of Contemporary Studies Press, 2002).

The Unending Frontier: Environmental History of the Early Modern World (Berkeley and Los Angeles: University of California Press, 2003).

Articles

'The Economic History of the Lodi Period: 1451–1526,' *Journal of the Economic and Social History of the Orient* 8 (1965), pp. 48–67.

'The Islamic Frontier in the East: Expansion into South Asia,' *South Asia* 4 (1974), pp. 91–109.

'European City-States on the Coromandel Coast,' in *Studies in the Foreign Relations of India,* Professor H.K. Sherwani Felicitation Volume, ed. P. M. Joshi (Hyderabad: State Archives, Government of Andhra Pradesh, 1975).

'The Hyderabad Karnatik, 1687–1724,' *Modem Asian Studies* 9 (1975) pp. 241–60.

'The Seventeenth Century Concentration of State Power at Hyderabad,' *Journal of the Pakistan Historical Society* 23 (1975), pp. 1–35.

'The Imperial Crisis in the Deccan,' *The Journal of Asian Studies* 35 (1976), pp. 236–56.

With Ralph W. Nicholas, 'Symposium: The Contributions of Louis Dumont,' *Journal of Asian Studies* 35 (1976), pp. 579–650. Published as a separate reprint by the Association for Asian Studies.

'Mughal Retreat From Coastal Andhra,' *Journal of the Royal Asiatic Society* (1978), pp. 39–50.

'The Formulation of Imperial Authority Under Akbar and Jahangir,' in *Kingship and Authority in South Asia,* ed. J. F. Richards (Madison: Center for South Asian Studies, University of Wisconsin, 1978), pp. 252–85. Reprinted in *The Mughal State 1526–1750,* eds Muzaffar Alam and Sanjay Subrahmanyam (Delhi: Oxford University Press, 1998).

With Velchuru Narayana Rao, 'Banditry in Mughal India: Historical and Folk Perceptions,' *Indian Economic and Social History Review* 17 (1980), pp. 95–120.

'The Indian Empire and Peasant Production of Opium,' *Modern Asian Studies* 15 (1981), pp. 59–82.

'Mughal State Finance and the Pre-Modem World Economy,' *Comparative Studies in Society and History* 23 (1981), pp. 285–308.

'Outflows of Precious Metals From Early Islamic India,' in *Precious Metals in the Later Medieval and Early Modern World*, ed. J. F. Richards (Durham: Carolina Press, 1983), pp. 183–205.

With Michelle McAlpin, 'Cotton Cultivating and Land Clearing in the Bombay Deccan and Karnatak, 1818–1920,' in *Global Deforestation and the Nineteenth Century World Economy*, eds Richard Tucker and J. F. Richards (Durham: Duke University Press Policy Studies, 1983), pp. 68–94.

'Norms of Comportment Among Imperial Mughal Officers,' in *Moral Conduct and Authority*, ed. Barbara Metcalf (Berkeley: University of California Press, 1984), pp. 255–89.

'Documenting Environmental History and Global Patterns of Land Conversions,' *Environment* 26, 9 (1984) 7–13, 34–38.

With Richard Tucker, 'The Global Economy and Forest Clearance in the Nineteenth Century,' in *Environmental History: Critical Issues in Comparative Perspective*, ed. Kendall E. Bailes (Lanham: University Press of America and American Society for Environmental History, 1984), pp. 577–85.

With James R. Hagen and Edward S. Haynes, 'Changing Land Use in Bihar, Punjab and Haryana, 1850–1970,' *Modern Asian Studies* 19, (1985), pp. 699–732.

With James R. Hagen and Edward S. Haynes, 'Changes in the Land and Human Productivity in Northern India, 1870–1970,' *Agricultural History* 59 (1985), pp. 523–48.

With Stewart Gordon 'Kinship and Pargana in Eighteenth Century Khandesh,' *The Indian Economic and Social History Review* 22 (1985), pp. 371–97.

'World Environmental History and Economic Development,' in *Sustainable Development of the Biosphere*, eds W. C. Clark and R. E. Munn (Cambridge: Cambridge University Press, 1986), pp. 53–71.

'Official Revenues and Money Flows in a Mughal Province,' in *The Imperial Monetary System of Mughal India*, ed. J. F. Richards (Delhi: Oxford University Press, 1987), pp. 193–231.

'The Imperial Capital,' in *Fatehpur Sikri*, eds M. Brand and G. D. Lowry (Bombay: Marg Publications, 1987), pp. 65–82.

With J. Hagen, 'A Century of Rural Expansion in Assam, 1870–1970', *Itinerario*, II (1987), pp. 193–208.

'Environmental Changes in Dehra Dun Valley, India: 1880–1980,' *Mountain Research and Development* 7 (1987), pp. 299–304.

'Rice Paddies for Mangroves: Domesticated Wetlands in South and Southeast Asia', in *Tropical Wetlands: A Threatened Landscape*, ed. Michael Williams (London: Basil Blackwell, 1990), pp. 217–33.

'The Seventeenth Century Crisis in South Asia', *Modern Asian Studies* 24 (1990), pp. 625–38.

With Elizabeth Flint, 'Long-Term Transformations in the Sundarbans Wetlands Forests of Bengal', *Agriculture and Human Values* 7 (1990), pp. 17–33.

With Elizabeth P. Flint, 'Historical Analysis of Changes in Land Use and Carbon Stock of Vegetation in South and Southeast Asia', *Canadian Journal of Forest Research* 21 (1991), pp. 91–110.

'Land Transformation' in *The Earth as Transformed by Human Action*, eds B. L. Turner et al. (Cambridge: Cambridge University Press, 1991), pp. 163–78.

With Elizabeth P. Flint, 'Contrasting Patterns of *Shorea* Exploitation in India and Malaysia in the 19th and 20th Centuries', in *Changing Pacific Forests: Historical Perspectives on the Forest Economy of the Pacific Basin*, eds John Dargavel and Richard Tucker (Durham, NC: Forest History Society, 1992), pp. 89–104.

With Elizabeth P. Flint, 'A Century of Land Use Change in South and Southeast Asia', in *Effects of Land Use Change on Atmospheric Concentrations: Southeast Asia as a Case Study*, ed. V. H. Date (New York: Springer-Verlag, 1994), pp. 15–66.

With Elizabeth P. Flint, 'Trends in Carbon Content of Vegetation in South and Southeast Asia Associated with Changes in Land Use', in *Effects of Land Use Change on Atmospheric Concentrations: Southeast Asia as a Case Study*, ed. V. H. Dale (New York: Springer-Verlag, 1994), pp. 201–99.

'Historiography of Mughal Gardens', in *Mughal Gardens: Source, Places, Representations, and Prospects*, eds, James L. Wescoat, Jr. and Joachim Wolshke-Bulmahn (Washington, D.C: Dumbarton Oaks, 1996), pp. 259–66.

'Early Modern India and World History', *Journal of World History* 8 (1997), pp. 197–209.

'Only a World Perspective is Significant: Settlement Frontiers and Property Rights in Early Modem World History', in *Earth, Air, Fire, Water*, eds Jill Ker Conway, Kenneth Keniston and Leo Marx (Cambridge, MA: MIT Press, 1999), pp. 102–18.

'The Mughal Empire,' in *The Magnificent Mughals*, ed. Zeenut Ziad (Karachi: Oxford University Press, 2001), pp. 3–23.

'Toward a Global System of Property Rights in Land,' in *Land, Property and the Environment*, ed. J. F. Richards (Oakland, CA: Institute for Contemporary Studies Press, 2002), pp. 13–37.

With Meena Bhargava, 'Defining Property Rights in Land in Colonial India: Gorakhpur Region in the Indo-Gangetic Plain,' in *Land, Property and the Environment*, ed. J. F. Richards (Oakland: Institute for Contemporary Studies Press, 2002), pp. 235–62.

'The Royal Commission on Opium of 1895', *Modern Asian Studies* 36 (2002), pp. 375–420.

'The Opium Industry in British India', *Indian Economic and Social History Review*, Dharma Kumar Special Issue, (2002), pp. 149–80.

'Opium's Moral Economy in Colonial India' in *Drugs and Empires: Essays in Modern Imperialism and Intoxication 1500–1930*, eds James Mills and Patricia Barton (London: Palgrave, 2007).

Index